THE OTHER FACES OF THE EMPIRE

ORDINARY LIVES AGAINST SOCIAL ORDER AND HIERARCHY

T0385599

Koç University Press: 275   HISTORY I OTTOMAN STUDIES

The Other Faces of the Empire: Ordinary Lives Against Social Order and Hierarchy
Editor: Fırat Yaşa

Translator: Esra Taşdelen
Copyeditor: Aron Aji
Proofreader: Anthony Howson
Book design: Eylem Zor, Hatice Çavdar
Cover design: Emre Çıkınoğlu
Cover image: The horse body made up of people (Murakk. Behz.d, TSMK, Hazine 20, No:2165,vr.36)

İmparatorluğun Öteki Yüzleri: Toplumsal Hiyerarşi ve Düzen Karşısında Sıradan Hayatlar
Originally published in Turkish by Koç University Press, 2020.

Print: 12.Matbaa   Certificate no: 46618
İbrahim Karaoğlanoğlu Cad. No:35 Kat:1 Kağıthane/İstanbul   +90 212 281 25 80

Koç University Press   Certificate no: 51577
Rumelifeneri Yolu 34450 Sarıyer/İstanbul   +90 212 338 1000
kup@ku.edu.tr • www.kocuniversitypress.com • www.kocuniversitesiyayinlari.com

Koç University Suna Kıraç Library Cataloging-in-Publication Data

The other faces of the Empire : ordinary lives against social order and hierarchy = İmparatorluğun öteki yüzleri : toplumsal hiyerarşi ve düzen karşısında sıradan hayatlar /|ceditor Fırat Yaşa. İstanbul : Koç Üniversitesi Yayınları, 2022.

328 pages ; 16,5 x 24 cm. -- Koç Üniversitesi Yayınları ; 275. Tarih

ISBN 978-605-7685-68-1

1. Turkey—History--Ottoman Empire, 1288-1918. 2. Turkey--History--Ottoman Empire, 1288-1918--Social conditions. 3. Turkey--Social life and customs. 4. Turkey--Social conditions. I. Yaşa, Fırat. II. Title.

DR432.I47313 2022

The Other Faces Of The Empire

Ordinary Lives Against Social Order and Hierarchy

EDITOR: FIRAT YAŞA

KUP

If everyone looks like each other in a place, this means there is no one there.

—Michel Foucault

Contents

Foreword

This book project departs from the historiographical approach that we are relatively familiar with in Ottoman historiography. It strives instead to understand the various dimensions of the lives of individuals mostly drawn from various archival documents, mainly court registers. It therefore inclines towards a micro-history. To understand a marginal story and give it meaning, it is necessary to consider several factors such as the wars, the victories, the economic circumstances, natural disasters, technological advances and epidemics that occurred during the historical period under study. Failing to do so will make it difficult to contextualize the stories of individuals.

The primary objective of this book is to touch on the "ordinary" lives of "common" people who produce, pay taxes, and make up the majority of the population. As will be seen throughout the text, some of the unexpectedly extraordinary profiles are even at times marginal as well. Naturally it is much more difficult to expose the small worlds (microcosmos), the everyday lives, fears, individual deeds, crimes, expectations, and mindsets of ordinary people in Ottoman society when compared with European societies which transitioned to written culture much earlier. The Ottoman society had low literacy rates and largely preserved an oral culture; the sources (such as memoirs, journals, travelogues and correspondence) that we can use to learn about the lives of common people are limited in number and mostly generated by the state. Therefore, it is extremely difficult to follow information and data on groups or individuals in a sustained manner. It becomes necessary to adopt a multidisciplinary approach that involves collaboration with disciplines other than history such as law, psychology, sociology, anthropology and ethnology, and research of sources from these disciplines.

Our study is not free from limitations and challenges either. For this reason, we recognize that our book, aiming to understand the world of ordinary people, may receive criticism for over-relying on fiction and imagination at times, for overusing storytelling, or for being too literary. Nevertheless, we hope to have made a contribution to the efforts of understanding the small worlds of small people—who in reality comprise the base and majority of the social pyramid—by observing them at their level.

The book in your hands may seem a departure from current historical studies in terms of not just its method and content, but also its preferred style. For example, the fictionalizing approach to describe the events surrounding a person tracked down from records has only recently gained currency in Ottoman historiography. The majority of the essays in this volume emerged while weaving on our proverbial loom the stories of common people that fell in the "exceptionally normal" category, people we came across in court registers and archives of the various cities of Anatolia.

Almost in all the essays, we preferred using "Thick Description" as our method; instead of making general observations by piling together numerous documents. We sought to understand historical facts by approaching them from multiplicity of angles and, at times, by constructing diverse narratives about them. In other words, by positioning individuals in the center of their relationships and tracking the events that affected them directly or indirectly, we were able to emphasize their networks of relations, identities, their frameworks of meaning, and their individual outlook.

Each author who started off with this conviction and contributed in meaningful ways to this book has aimed to widen a bit further the gateway to the lives of ordinary people who have been left "off stage" in Ottoman historical literature.

Every book carries traces of the mind that produced it and hints at stories. This book too has its story. Anyone interested in court registers will, intentionally or not, witness interesting stories about the lives of common people. The desire to transmit what we discover is inevitable for most historians. I too had come across dramatic stories of common people while researching court registers and had shared these stories with Zeynep Dörtok Abacı whom I periodically visited in 2016, in her office at Bursa Uludağ University. In the course of these meetings, I became aware of the existence of other historians who, like me, wished to understand and interpret the lives of common people--a subject that, by then, had obtained great importance for me. After that, the rings of the proverbial chain gradually multiplied, and we arrived at the current group of authors. I especially thank Cemal Çetin and Özlem Başarır who did not spare any help throughout the project and, at its completion, were as excited as I was.

Finally, I am indebted to Suraiya Faroqhi who encouraged me, guided me with her advice, and after reading all the contributions carefully and meticulously, composed a superb introduction to our volume. I am grateful to her for believing in me and devoting her valuable time to this work, thereby enriching both this book and my life.

The drive towards perfection and flawlessness that all researchers feel in preparing such a work might have confused me, and from time to time I might have gotten a bit lost in the complicated mazes of knowledge. Nevertheless, when readers provide feedback in the form of critique as well as interest and appreciation, I will have achieved the goals I set out for myself as an editor.

Fırat Yaşa

Bursa 2021

INTRODUCTION

Ordinary Subjects of the Sultan, Confronted with the Social and Political Elites: Can We Extricate Their Stories?

Suraiya Faroqhi

In the Ottoman context, writing about ordinary people is a recent innovation, and we hope this book will encourage historians to further proceed along this path. Given the sources at hand, the authors focus on situations in which townspeople and villagers confronted the bureaucratic apparatus put in place by sultans and viziers. There must have been decisive events in people's lives in which *qadis*, military commanders and scribes took no part, but we know very little about them.

In terms of topics covered, we can divide the fourteen articles making up this volume into two groups, with a perhaps unclassifiable case attached at the end. The first section deals with people whose activities have entered the record because rightly or wrongly, their neighbors and fellow townspeople/or villagers had accused them of crimes. We encounter the theft of a horse, murder and mayhem in Anatolian villages, prostitution and once again murder, but this time in a medium-sized city, criminal families operating in Bursa, a Roma woman accused of immoral behavior, and a nineteenth-century slave dealer who badly mistreated his slaves.

A second group consists of cases in which the functioning or malfunctioning of Ottoman officialdom is crucial. Thus, sixteenth-century bureaucratic rules concerning appointments determined the fate of a young scholar, who after imprisonment in the 'lands of the unbelievers' tried to resume his interrupted career as an Ottoman scholar-bureaucrat. With the consent of the local *qadi*, Chios villagers elected representatives, who were to collect their taxes and negotiate with the authorities on their behalf. As for a local notable of early nineteenth-century Diyarbekir, he apparently did not realize that if he went on a collision course with the representatives of the central power, he was unlikely to win. In the Hamidian period, ordinary subjects of the sultan had trouble making their voices heard as well. In legal terms, they might well be in the right, but the reluctance of the bureaucracy to enforce the existing rules unless influential people complained, and the tendency of officials in Istanbul to not question the actions of their representatives on site, made it very difficult for even well-placed complainants to obtain redress.[1]

Whatever criteria we use, somebody or something will always defy categorization. Thus, we will end this book with the story of Nicolò Algarotti, a Venetian subject of the early 1600s. By the criteria applied when putting together the present volume, the Algarotti case is unique: for only in this chapter do we deal with a dispute involving two polities, namely the Ottoman Empire and Venice. Algarotti's adventures and probable misdeeds thus remind us that Istanbul, Egypt and Western Anatolia certainly were part of the Ottoman Empire, but they belonged to a wider, Mediterranean world as well.

The present Introduction begins with a discussion of the primary sources covering the lives of the sultans' ordinary, unprivileged subjects: firstly we survey the texts in Ottoman Turkish, and as a second step, source materials written in Armenian, Greek and Arabic.[2] While non-elite women appear whenever they become visible in these sources, the recent surge of studies related to slavery makes it appropriate to devote a special section to this topic. A brief summary of recent methodological discussions concerning the use of the *qadi* registers, and especially the gaps that characterize these records, leads the reader to the summaries of the papers proper. As noted, a discussion of people confronted with the workings of the Ottoman bureaucracy follows a first and sizeable selection of crime stories. Denizens of the empire are the main focus, but occasionally outsiders appear as well.

'Ordinary People' in Ottoman Historiography: Source Texts in Ottoman Turkish

In all patriarchal societies including the Ottoman variety, information on women is scarce because the sources relegate people who are not adult males to the background of the historical scene — if they appear at all. On the other hand, in modern-style Ottoman historiography, female members of the urban subject population and ordinary people 'in general' have emerged as academically credible subjects at about the same time. With respect to young males, the path-breaking studies

---

1   For the attempts of Ottoman subjects to solve their problems on a political level, see Antonios Anastasopoulos (ed.), *Political Initiatives 'From the Bottom Up' in the Ottoman Empire: Halcyon Days in Crete VII, A Symposium Held in Rethymno 9-11 January 2009* (Rethymno/Greece: University of Crete Publications, 2012).

2   Doubtless due to my linguistic limits, I have not been able to find ego-documents written by Jews living in the early modern Ottoman Empire.

are by Mustafa Akdağ. In his book on the Celali uprisings originally published in 1963, he has linked the rebellions of former peasants turned mercenaries or madrasa students to the population increases of the sixteenth century and the difficulty of establishing new farmsteads in presumably overcrowded villages.[3]

As for women, in 1975 Ronald Jennings first demonstrated that the *qadi* registers of certain Anatolian towns, including Kayseri, contained significant stores of information on female property-holding and the attempts of women to end unwanted marriages.[4] At a later stage, the work of Madeline Zilfi on female-initiated divorces in eighteenth-century Istanbul and that of Leslie Peirce on women appearing before the mid-sixteenth century *qadi*'s court of Ayntab, today's Gaziantep, showed how by means of judicial decisions, women tried to solve their problems. The latter included constant marital conflicts, but being unmarried and pregnant was an issue as well.[5] In addition, Peirce demonstrated that despite the limited access of females to the written word, there were women attempting to teach other women, a risky enterprise when the teacher aroused suspicions that she might not be a mainstream Sunni.[6]

Admittedly, most of the available sources concern townspeople; apart from the last fifty years of the empire's duration, our knowledge of peasants and nomads, the vast majority of the Ottoman population, is very limited indeed. As for town dwellers, even if illiterate, these men and women had friends and neighbors to turn to for help in composing a petition, so that they might express their wishes and complaints in a form acceptable to the Ottoman authorities. Or else, townspeople with basic literacy might find experts to help them in the composition of simple texts, intended for readers of varying educational levels, perhaps fellow townsmen. In families where boys trained as future religious scholars, women might receive some education too; and Cemal Kafadar has authored a memorable study on the letters written by a female mystic resident in the town of Üsküp/Skopje, who wrote to her sheikh because as a

---

3   Mustafa Akdağ, *Celâlî İsyanları 1550-1603* (Ankara: A.Ü. Dil ve Tarih-Coğrafya Fakültesi, 1963); idem, "Medreseli İsyanları," *İstanbul Üniversitesi İktisat Fakültesi Mecmuası*, 11, 1-4 (1949-50), 361-87.

4   Ronald Jennings, "Women in early 17th century Ottoman Judicial Records: The sharia court of Anatolian Kayseri," *Journal of the Economic and Social History of the Orient* (from now on: *JESHO*), XVIII, 1 (1975), 53-114.

5   Madeline Zilfi, "We Don't Get Along," in *Women in the Ottoman Empire: Middle Eastern Women in the Early Modern Era*, edited by Madeline Zilfi (Leiden: Brill, 1997), pp. 264-96; Leslie Peirce, *Morality Tales: Law and Gender in the Ottoman Court of Aintab* (Los Angeles, Berkeley, and London: The University of California Press, 2003).

6   Peirce, *Morality Tales*, pp. 251-75.

woman, she could not easily visit him in person.[7] As for urban males, Kafadar has written a pioneering study as well, which concerns the seventeenth-century diary of an anonymous dervish, who Kafadar has shown to be Seyyid Hasan, in later life, sheikh of a Celvetiyye lodge in Istanbul. This diary is especially memorable because the author wrote about matters that in this period, most people did not consider worth recording, such as eating good-quality fruit and fine cheese, drinking coffee with relatives, visiting with friends and attending funerals — including the interment of one of the author's wives, probably a victim of the plague.[8]

Even so, the most remarkable 'ego document' of the Ottoman seventeenth century is the travelogue of Evliya Çelebi (1611-sometime after 1683), who has included a significant quantity of biographical information in his multi-volume work. For a twenty-first century reader, it may come as a surprise that he does not name his mother, but perhaps he wished to observe the socially approved reticence with respect to female relations — on the other hand, he did tell many tales about Princess Kaya Sultan, apparently a relative by marriage.[9] Nor does Evliya record whether he ever married or had children. As his work did not attract much attention before the mid-nineteenth century, Evliya Çelebi's name does not appear in biographical dictionaries of the 1600s and 1700s, and as no gravestone has survived, we do not know for sure when and where he died.

When it comes to documenting ordinary people, Evliya's work is so valuable because, despite being a somewhat eccentric member of the elite, he was willing to flout the conventions of Ottoman prose, discussing matters to which most authors of the time paid little attention. As the spectrum of his acquaintances was far wider than the circle of friends and relatives gravitating around Seyyid Hasan, Evliya offered a broad panorama of human interactions, recording for instance his

---

7   Cemal Kafadar, "Mütereddit bir Mutasavvıf: Üsküp'lü Asiye Hatun'un Rüya Defteri 1641-43," *Topkapı Sarayı Müzesi, Yıllık* V (1992), 168-222.

8   Cemal Kafadar, "Self and Others: The Diary of a Dervish in Seventeenth Century Istanbul and First-person Ottoman Literature," *Studia Islamica*, 69 (1989), 121–50. At Sabancı University, Istanbul, Tunahan Durmaz has recently defended an MA thesis, which carries Kafadar's study several steps further: Tunahan Durmaz, "Family, Companions, and Death: Seyyid Hasan Nûrî Efendi's Microcosm (1661-1665)" accessed through https://www.academia.edu/38297349/_Family_Companions_and_Death_Seyyid_Hasan_N%C3%BBr%C3%AE_Efendis_Microcosm_1661-1665_M.A._Thesis_Sabanc%C4%B1_University_04.01.2019_ (accessed on 10 July 2019).

9   Compare the index of Evliya Çelebi, *Evliya Çelebi Seyahatnâmesi, Topkapı Sarayı Bağdat 304 Yazmasının Transkripsyonu –Dizini*, vol. 1, edited by Robert Dankoff, Seyit Ali Kahraman and Yücel Dağlı (Istanbul: Yapı Kredi Yayınları, 2006).

discussions with Shiite gentlemen in Tabriz, who he visited when traveling in Iran. Thus, Evliya's work allows us to at least furtively glimpse the manner in which educated inhabitants of the Ottoman and Safavid realms communicated with one another, politely 'agreeing to disagree' whenever necessary.[10]

In the eighteenth century, diaries and narratives written for a limited, domestic audience became more frequent. Admittedly, we do not understand the reason very well, but probably the increasing number of schools established by local dignitaries, even in a medium-sized Anatolian town such as Sivas, made it easier for people to gain some literacy and knowledge of literary models.[11] Whatever the background may have been, the diaries and memoirs that have surfaced to date were often — but not always — the works of religious scholars. Selim Karahasanoğlu has studied the text written by a *qadi*, who lived in the early to mid-eighteenth century and — as was customary — periodically returned to Istanbul when his provincial appointments had come to an end; for he needed to solicit the army judges (*kadıaskers*) for new positions.[12] Karahasanoğlu's 'hero' was thus familiar with the Ottoman capital, where he went sightseeing when the fountain of Ahmed III, inaugurated in 1729, was a novelty. From the very early 1800s, we possess the diary of Hafız Mehmed Efendi, who was the imam of Istanbul's Soğan Ağa mosque and recorded family events including the religious education of his sons, as well as the political vicissitudes that marked the troubled reign of Sultan Selim III (r. 1789-1807).[13]

A text from the eighteenth-century Balkans, written in Ottoman Turkish but by a native speaker of the Bosnian language follows a similar format; for the author combines an account of his life with the narration of local events, as in a chronicle. However, Molla Mustafa Bašeskija of Sarajevo (about 1730-1809), an imam like Hafız Mehmed Efendi and in addition, a public scribe who wrote letters for the families of soldiers

---

10   For recent biographies compare: Robert Dankoff, *An Ottoman Mentality: The World of Evliya Celebi* (Leiden: Brill, 2006); Bekir Karlığa et al., *Evliya Çelebi Atlası* (Istanbul: MEDAM, 2012); Nuran Tezcan, Semih Tezcan and Robert Dankoff eds., *Evliya Çelebi — Studies and Essays Commemorating the 400th Anniversary of his Birth* (Ankara: Republic of Turkey, Ministry of Culture, 2012).

11   Ömer Demirel, *Osmanlı Vakıf Şehir İlişkisine Bir Örnek: Sivas Şehir Hayatında Vakıfların Rolü* (Ankara: Türk Tarih Kurumu, 2000). I have excluded the memoirs of Feyzullah Efendi (b. 1703) because he was a member of the highest ranks of the Ottoman elite and in no way an ordinary person.

12   Selim Karahasanoğlu, *Kadı ve Günlüğü : Sadreddinzade Telhisî Mustafa Efendi Günlüğü (1711-1735) üstüne bir İnceleme* (Istanbul: Türkiye İş Bankası Kültür Yayınları, 2013).

13   Kemal Beydilli, *Osmanlı Döneminde İmamlar ve bir İmamın Günlüğü* (Istanbul: Tarih ve Tabiat Vakfı, 2001).

fighting against the Russians and/or the Austrians, has produced a much longer work. He seems to have hoped that it would circulate among a broad public in his hometown. Baseskija's chronicle has interested historians of the twentieth and twenty-first centuries as well, who have made ample use of his descriptions of plague epidemics, guild festivals, victory celebrations and very prominently, the miseries of war.[14] In addition, Molla Mustafa's text allows the reader to evaluate the intellectual life of an important Ottoman provincial town: What books did people study, and what skills did a person need to possess if he wanted his fellow citizens to consider him a learned man?

Concerning a slightly later period, Gülçin Tunalı Koç has studied the diary of a mid-nineteenth century Ankara astrologer and occasional substitute judge (*naib*) named Sadullah Efendi (d. 1855), who tried to derive humanly comprehensible messages from the configurations of the stars, in his attempt to make sense, of among other issues, the catastrophic Ankara drought of 1845.[15] While Sadullah Efendi does not seem to have gone hungry, he certainly suffered and was well aware of the consequences for people less well placed than he was; this 'bourgeois' perspective contrasts with the abject misery of small peasants and agricultural laborers during those same years.

Later in the nineteenth century, the Mevlevi candidate member (*muhibb*) Aşçı Dede İbrahim Efendi, in the diaries that he kept from 1828 to the beginning twentieth century, wrote about both mystical experience and bureaucratic sociability.[16] In the study of Carter Findley, Aşçı Dede appears as the representative of a significant section of the nineteenth-century Ottoman administration, namely of people without any interest in the novelties of the Tanzimat, who nonetheless enjoyed successful bureaucratic careers. Visibly, the relationships which Aşçı Dede built with his fellow mystics helped him find suitable employments, while at the same time his sincere religious commitment consoled him during the vicissitudes of life.[17] Many more Ottoman subjects, both Muslims and non-Muslims, wrote diaries and memoirs in the nineteenth century than had been the case in earlier

---

14 Kerima Filan, "Life in Sarajevo in the 18th Century (According to Molla Mustafa's *mecmua*)" in *Living in the Ottoman Ecumenical Community: Essays in Honour of Suraiya Faroqhi*, edited by Vera Constantini and Markus Koller (Leiden, Boston: Brill, 2008), pp. 317-45.

15 Gülçin Tunalı Koç, "An Ottoman Astrologer at Work: Sadullah el-Ankarâvi and the Everyday Practice of *İlm-i Nücûm*," in *Les ottomans et le temps*, edited by François Georgeon and Frédéric Hitzel (Leiden: Brill, 2012), pp. 39-60.

16 Aşçı Dede, *Aşçı Dedenin Hatıraları*, 4 vols., edited by Mustafa Koç and Eyyüp Tanrıverdi (Istanbul: Kitabevi, 2017).

17 Carter Findley, *Ottoman Civil Officialdom: A Social History* (Princeton: Princeton University Press, 1989), pp. 174-382.

times; but regrettably we cannot introduce them all, and Aşçı Dede will have to serve as the sole representative of an entire genre.[18]

Furthermore, in the eighteenth and early nineteenth centuries, literacy and 'first person narratives' were no longer a privilege of people with a religious education. Jan Schmidt and at a later stage Tolga U. Esmer dwelt on the stories of an 'Ottoman irregular' known as Deli Mustafa, who wrote or perhaps dictated a chronicle covering the period from 1801-02 to 1832-33, in which his own adventures featured prominently.[19] In this sense, he followed the format used by Molla Mustafa and Hafız Mehmed Efendi. By origin, Deli Mustafa was a villager from the region of Tokat in North Central Anatolia, who became a mercenary because his father, also a professional soldier, had inducted him into the military. Because the author presented himself not as a simple soldier but as a man who knew all the tricks of his trade, Esmer has chosen to focus on the public to which this discourse might appeal. Put differently, in Esmer's perspective, the public that Deli Mustafa hoped to reach is at least as important as the author himself. A man who had spent most of his life on campaigns and battlefields, Deli Mustafa had few qualms about telling stories of blood and gore. We can only hope that at least some of them were the product of his imagination. Whatever the truth of the matter may have been, his blood-curdling stories probably did not offend his listeners. Thus, there must have been an emotional and cognitive bond between narrator and audience, and for this connection, the term 'interpretive community' (*yorumlayıcı çevre*) has recently become popular. It is Esmer's main concern to make this connection between narrator and audience visible and intelligible.

'Ordinary People' in Ottoman Historiography: Sources in Greek, Armenian, Bulgarian, and Arabic

Not all Ottoman subjects who highlighted their own persons and experiences in their writings necessarily wrote in Ottoman Turkish. To readers unfamiliar with Armenian, Greek or Arabic translations and secondary studies, they permit at least a general impression. After all, the period, in which most historians comfort-

---

18   For research on this topic, compare the project of the Orient Institut der Deutschen Forschungsgemeinschaft (DFG) Cihangir/Istanbul on late Ottoman ego-documents, coordinated by Richard Wittmann, beginning in 2010: https://www.oiist.org/selbstzeugnisse-als-quellen-zur-geschichte-des-spaten-osmanischen-reichs/ (accessed on 27 July 2019).

19   Tolga U. Esmer, "The Confessions of an Ottoman Irregular: Self-Representation and Ottoman Interpretive Communities in the Nineteenth Century," *Osmanlı Araştırmaları/ The Journal of Ottoman Studies 44, Living Empire: Ottoman Identities in Transition 1700-1850* (2014), 313-40.

ably equated Ottoman history with the history of present-day Turkey has by now receded into the past.

A short text by the Armenian priest Grigor, from the Eastern Anatolian town of Kemah is an early example of first-person accounts from a non-Muslim milieu.[20] Grigor of Kemah refers to two attempts to send the refugees from Eastern Anatolia, who had fled the Celali rebellions and settled in Istanbul and Tekirdağ, back to their home towns and villages. The first campaign of this kind took place in 1609, in the reign of the still very young Sultan Ahmed I (r. 1603-17). The second attempt, poorly documented because the manuscript used by the translator is fragmentary, bears the date of 1635. Apparently in both cases, Grigor of Kemah played a significant role in negotiating with the authorities and organizing the relevant caravans.

Grigor's account is so impressive because on the one hand, he focuses on the miseries of people, both Muslims and non-Muslims, some of whom had been born in Istanbul and were terrified of leaving. In this context, Grigor described the often harrowing circumstances under which the moves took place, stressing that when under pressure, people were ready to denounce their neighbors, sometimes merely because of envy or vengeance. On the other hand, the author has recorded that within the Ottoman elite, some people heartily disapproved of this project. Intriguingly, the most prominent critic was Bayram Paşa, the grand vizier of Murad IV (r. 1623-40), who seems to have done his best to limit the number of people actually sent off to Eastern Anatolia. Disagreements of this kind do not usually feature in archival documents.

An early seventeenth-century chronicle written in Greek, is the work of Papa Synadinos (1600-about 1670), who was an Orthodox priest and local notable in Serres/Serrai, today in northern Greece. This text is comparable to some of the Ottoman works discussed above; for this author too has combined the format of town chronicle with a first-person narrative.[21] Moreover, some seventeenth-century Ottoman chroniclers writing about and working for the central government have included the biographies of prominent statesmen and/or scholars.[22] Often, they

---

20   Hrand D. Andreasyan, "Celâlilerden Kaçan Anadolu Halkının Geri Gönderilmesi," in *Ord. Prof. İsmail Hakkı Uzunçarşılı'ya Armağan*, no editor, introduced by Uluğ İğdemir (Ankara: Türk Tarih Kurumu, 1976), pp. 45-53.

21   [Papa Synadinos of Serres], *Conseils et mémoires de Synadinos prêtre de Serrès en Macédoine (XVIIᵉ siècle)*, edited, translated and commented by Paolo Odorico, with S. Asdrachas, T. Karanastassis, K. Kostis and S. Petmézas (Paris: Association Pierre Belon, 1996).

22   In medieval Arab literature, this custom went in and out of fashion: Dana Sajdi, *The Barber of Damascus: Nouveau Literacy in the Eighteenth-century Ottoman Levant* (Stanford:

have appended this information, which may have enhanced the usefulness and popularity of their work, to the individual chapters covering the reigns of this or that sultan. In the same mode, Papa Synadinos has included biographies, but in his case, of people enjoying purely local prominence. His tale sometimes contains juicy gossip, to say nothing of the maledictions that the author has affixed to the names of recent converts to Islam.

Remarkably, the author has expressed a very positive opinion of Murad IV, for the simple reason that this ruler seems to have terrified 'the Turks', who for Papa Synadinos were simply the local Muslims. Furthermore, this chronicle shows how prominent Orthodox people in Serrai managed to adorn their churches, although any permission to renovate after, for instance, a major fire, explicitly excluded the beautification of the buildings.

While Papa Synadinos reflects on how one might survive as an Orthodox subject of the sultan, the life story of Stoyko Vladislavov or 'Sinful Sofroni' (1739-1813) as the bishop of the Bulgarian town of Vratsa liked to call himself in later life, focuses on the author's misadventures. As for the political troubles of the time, they appear in so far as they impinge on his life.[23] In Bulgaria, this text is popular, being one of the very first non-religious texts in Bulgarian, which became a written language at around this time. Sofroni has produced some memorable paragraphs on how as a young boy, he visited Istanbul together with his relatives, who as *celep* were businessmen supplying sheep to Istanbul. Being an inexperienced provincial, the boy fell into the hands of kidnappers; and if neighbors had not reacted to his cries for help, he might well have ended up as a slave. At a later stage of his story, Sofroni reflected on his feelings of guilt when he abandoned his bishopric and sought refuge in Wallachia. However, as marauders had robbed most of his property, he no longer had the money to forward the taxes, which a bishop of the period needed to collect and send on to Istanbul. Sofroni's story dramatically shows that when the sultan was no longer able to protect his subjects from local exploiters, the previously very solid legitimacy of Ottoman rule in the Balkans rapidly crumbled: in his later years, Sinful Sofroni became a partisan of the Russian tsar.

A large number of texts concerning 'ordinary' Ottoman subjects have originated in the Arab provinces; but among historians of the central lands, these texts have not attracted the attention that they clearly deserve. While the language

---

Stanford University Press, 2013), pp. 115-28.

23 Vraca'lı Sofroni, *Osmanlı'da Bir Papaz, Günahkâr Sofroni'nin Çileli Hayat Hikâyesi 1739-1813*, tr. by Aziz Nazmi Şakir-Taş (Istanbul: Kitap Yayınevi, 2003).

barrier is a major reason for rendering the relevant primary sources difficult of access to historians working on the Turkish-speaking parts of the empire, the lack of interest in the history of the early modern Arab world, on the part of scholars and the Turkish reading public, is surely an inhibiting factor as well. After all, in present-day Turkey, the history of the Arab world is either the province of people working on Islam as a religious/cultural project, or else of persons whose main interest is in the conflicts of the present world. For researchers and readers concerned with these topics, the history of Syria and Egypt in the 1600s and 1700s, by contrast, seems to be quite marginal. The 'wall' separating the historiographies on ordinary people in the Arab provinces from the work done on Istanbul, Bursa or Ankara becomes even higher because a significant part of the secondary literature, which otherwise would provide at least a modicum of access, is in Arabic, French or German. Perhaps the present volume will encourage historians of social life in Istanbul or Anatolia to take a closer look at Aleppo, Damascus, Tunis, or Cairo.

In the limited space available here, we focus on two groups of texts. As a first step, we briefly visit the work of four Arab religious scholars who in the sixteenth and seventeenth centuries traveled to Istanbul in search of patronage. Not that they wanted to become *qadi*s of Damascus or Aleppo, for the Ottoman central government reserved these positions for people who had studied in Bursa, Edirne and Istanbul. Close proximity to Ottoman power-holders allowed some religious scholars-in-training to build relations of mutual trust with viziers and high-ranking scholar officials; this was an important concern, as Mamluk rule in Damascus and Cairo had ended only in 1516-17. Moreover, at the same time, Sultans Selim I (r. 1512-20) and Süleyman (r. 1520-66) were at war with the Safavid rulers, who, at the same time, were sheikhs of a dervish order that Sunni religious scholars deemed heretical. Despite these tensions, possibilities of employment in the judicial and teaching sectors were open to scholars from Syria or Egypt. In the major Arab cities, a large part of the population did not adhere to the Hanefi law school favored by the Ottoman elite, and the sultans appointed subordinate judges (*naib*s) to deal with their cases. Typically, these men were from the Arab provinces. In addition, there were positions as madrasa teachers and administrators available in large and small towns; and for all these appointments, it was essential to obtain recommendations from influential figures in Istanbul.

We can access the descriptions of travels to Istanbul by Badr al-Dīn al-Ghazzī, Muhibb al-Dīn al-Ḥamawī, Ḥāfiẓ al-Dīn Qudsī and Muḥammad Kibrīt through the study of Ralf Elger, who has focused on these reports not so much as depictions of 'reality' but as literary works.[24] Discovering intertextual relationships is thus a major focus of his work; and Elger has unearthed for instance, that the so-called description of an Istanbul hospital of the Süleymanic period by Badr al-Dīn al-Ghazzī is mostly a calque of a description penned by a fourteenth-century Moroccan traveler, who had written about a hospital in Cairo.[25] In other cases, intertextual connections between authors writing in Arabic are likely but not proven; it is intriguing that we do not hear much about intellectual exchanges with scholars from the Ottoman center, who quite often wrote Arabic texts as well. Why did visitors from the Arab lands mostly ignore them? Moreover, Elger has pointed out that the journeys of scholars and literati, while obviously dealing with the promotion of their careers, could serve the authors as a means of expressing general sentiments about the setting in which they lived. At least Muḥammad Kibrīt used his travelogue to express his radical skepticism towards the ways of the world in general.[26]

Thus Elger's work encourages Ottoman historians to read the four Arabic travelogues in a manner that may resemble the approach of educated denizens of the Ottoman sixteenth century. Put differently, readers need to focus on the intellectual/emotional content of these texts, and consider their merits as compositions, rather than viewing them as descriptions of the places visited by the travelers at issue. Admittedly, appreciating the beauty of the language is impossible for a person knowing little or no Arabic. Even so, Elger's observations are a timely lesson for people, who like the present author, used to read travelogues largely for their informational value and who, after learning what can happen to historians disregarding the role of literary topoi, have timidly begun to think about the formats, in which authors of the sixteenth or seventeenth centuries may have expressed their thoughts.

While the four scholars discussed by Elger were not part of the central elite, the very fact that they had received advanced training in religious studies and in poetry, shows that they were not commoners either. It would make sense to describe them as members of provincial elites, of a type that had existed in Syria and North Africa ever since the Middle Ages. However, in the eighteenth century, people of lower social status began to write as well, and they often favored chronicles. We are fortunate to possess the work of a Damascene barber named Ibn Budayr, who

---

24 Ralf Elger, *Glaube, Skepsis, Poesie: Arabische Istanbul-Reisende im 16. und 17. Jahrhundert* (Beirut and Würzburg/Germany: Ergon Verlag, 2011).

25 Elger, *Glaube, Skepsis, Poesie*, p. 54. I do not dare to imagine how many literary topoi in Evliya Çelebi's work still remain undiscovered.

26 Elger, *Glaube, Skepsis, Poesie*, pp. 174-82.

worked during the first half of the eighteenth century. Though from a poor family, this artisan succeeded in setting up shop in the center of the city where he became acquainted with some fairly influential personages.[27] Similar to Papa Synadinos and Molla Mustafa, Ibn Budayr wrote about historical events as they affected his home city, occasionally inserting personal observations into his text. Most remarkably, he was not alone. In the area between Aleppo in the north and Jerusalem in the south, during the 1700s people from a variety of non-elite backgrounds wrote comparable texts, including Shiite farmers, Sunni soldiers, a Greek Orthodox priest, and even a scribe from the tiny Samaritan community. All these men wrote chronicles, a genre hitherto reserved for religious scholars and the sultan's officials.[28]

Dana Sajdi has studied the manner in which these people made a place for themselves in the world of written culture, a place, which at least in the case of Ibn Budayr, later became an object of controversy. After all, a late nineteenth-century Damascene scholar and editor of Ibn Budayr's work, known as al-Qāsimī, profoundly disapproved of the self-confident 'plebeian stance' of the earlier author. While according to al-Qāsimī, in a pinch, a non-elite figure might write about current events, such a man did not have the right to insert himself into the story, use a style more appropriate for popular epics than for scholarly history-writing, or highlight his contacts with people 'above his station'.[29] We are left with the question why provincial figures of the Ottoman central lands so rarely appropriated this genre.

The Sultan's Under-Underprivileged Subjects: Male and Female Slaves

Ibn Budayr and his fellow chroniclers were not part of the elite, but neither were they at the bottom of the social pyramid. It is well known that the Ottoman Empire, like many polities of the past and present, contained subjects or citizens, who might be of the 'first' or 'second' class. If we attempt a very rough categorization, Muslim adult males were first-class subjects, while non-Muslims — and non-elite Muslim women and children as well — were clearly subjects with fewer rights and limited prestige. However, slaves were clearly in an even lower category, and as a novelty of the last few decades, historians have discovered that the Ottoman archives, and in particular the *qadi* registers, contain quantities of documents that allow us to contextualize the reports of the few ex-slaves who made it back to their European

---

27 Sajdi, *The Barber of Damascus*.

28 Sajdi, *The Barber of Damascus*, p. 7.

29 Sajdi, *The Barber of Damascus*, p. 203.

homelands. In this field, contextualization is essential, as the authors of captivity accounts needed to conform to the demands of patrons back home, who alone could ensure that a given report made it into print.[30] Needless to say, such former slaves returned to their homes with their own opinions and biases as well.

Given Ottoman archival sources, we can now, at least to some extent, differentiate between certain — more or less clearly demarcated — categories of slaves on the one hand and non-slave dependents on the other; the latter sometimes had very little occasion for agency.[31] While Islamic religious law only distinguishes between slaves and free persons, recent historians of slavery have concluded that it is more realistic to imagine a spectrum of dependencies.[32] Among the enslaved, the most powerful were the 'elite slaves' or *kul* of the sultan, put differently the Ottoman viziers and other top-level administrators that were not religious scholars. Admittedly, in their relations with the ruler these men suffered from significant disabilities, such as the risk of execution without trial. Even so, with respect to non-elite people, the sultan's *kul* were very powerful, to the point that seventeenth-century mercenaries rebelled in order to force the central administration to accept them into the army of the *kul*.[33] Prominent women of the sultans' harem were another category of people who were legally slaves but often influential in practice. At the other end of the spectrum, we find the menials, such as the men rowing the sultans' galleys and performing hard labor in the naval arsenal.[34] As for the mass of enslaved women, they were household drudges, serving as maids of all work in the palace and in wealthy Istanbul homes, with limited prospects even after manumission.[35]

---

30 For an instructive example see Michael Heberer von Bretten, *Osmanlıda bir Köle, Brettenli Michael Heberer'in Anıları 1585-1588* translated by Türkis Noyan (Istanbul: Kitap Yayınevi, 2003).

31 The foundational article is: Halil Sahillioğlu, "Slaves in the Social and Economic Life of Bursa in the late 15th and early 16th Centuries," *Turcica*, XVII (1985), 43-112.

32 Ehud Toledano, "The Concept of Slavery in Ottoman and Other Muslim Societies: Dichotomy or Continuum?" in *Slave Elites in the Middle East and Africa: A Comparative Study*, edited by Miura Toru and John Edward Philips (London and NY: Kegan Paul International, 2000), pp. 159-76.

33 Halil İnalcık, "Military and Fiscal Transformation in the Ottoman Empire 1600-1700," in idem, *Studies in Ottoman Social and Economic History* (London. Variorum Reprints, 1985), no. V, at p. 297-99.

34 Nida Nebahat Nalçacı, *Sultanın Kulları : Erken Modern Dönem İstanbul'unda Savaş Esirleri ve Zorunlu İstihdam* (Istanbul: Verita Kitap, 2015).

35 Suraiya Faroqhi, "Manumission in seventeenth-century suburban Istanbul," in *Mediterranean Slavery Revisited (500–1800) – Neue Perspektiven auf mediterrane Sklaverei (500–*

As scholarship on *qadi* registers expands, a few historians have begun to focus on the activities of slave traders. Among them, we find Zübeyde Güneş Yağcı, who has contributed a study on this topic to the present volume. In part, the behavior of the slave traders was a corollary of their business interests; in other cases, however, 'power trips' and even sadism were at issue. Thus, the work of Fırat Yaşa on slave suicides has highlighted the role of slave dealers in making people despair of life; and in a still unpublished study, Maryna Kravets has touched upon this issue as well.[36]

Military slavery has been another fulcrum of slavery studies, of particular importance since in different versions it existed among the Ottomans and in Safavid Iran and Southern India as well. In the fifteenth century, it was common enough to include prisoners of war into the Ottoman armies. After all, the supply of captives controlled by the monarch was plentiful, because the latter could claim one fifth of all war booty. When dealing with this early period, we may therefore regard the janissaries as soldier-slaves of the sultans. Even so, the 'slavery' aspect lost most of its importance in the course of the sixteenth century, particularly when the sons of janissaries entered the corps in sizeable numbers and formed close links to the artisans and shopkeepers in the empire's larger cities.

A different kind of military slavery existed in Egypt. After the Ottoman conquest, the sultans had discontinued the practice of administering Syria through Mamluk dignitaries, customary in the now defunct Mamluk sultanate. Instead, the Ottoman sultans introduced a system of government resembling the practices current in the central provinces. In Egypt however, the governor continued to administer the province together with dignitaries who originally had entered Egypt as military slaves, although they were not very important in the first century of Ottoman domination. Even afterwards, these men no longer acted as a major fighting force, as had been true before 1517, but focused on the collection of taxes. The sultans intended to balance these Egyptian Mamluks by soldiers recruited by the central government, the so-called *ocak*. However, in the course of the 1700s, the Mamluks established control over the *ocak* of Egypt and became so powerful that in the last quarter of the eighteenth century, before Napoleon's invasion of 1798, the most prominent Mamluk *beys* were aiming at quasi-independence from the

---

1800), edited by Stefan Hanß and Juliane Schiel, with assistance from Claudia Schmid (Zurich: Chronos Verlag, 2014), pp. 381-401.

36 Fırat Yaşa, "Desperation, Hopelessness, and Suicide: An Initial Consideration of Self-Murder by Slaves in Seventeenth-Century Crimean Society," *Turkish Historical Review*, 9, 2 (2018), 198 – 211 DOI: 10.1163/18775462-00902003 (accessed in 2018).

Ottoman center.[37] Infighting among the *beys* of the late 1700s, resulting in high and arbitrary taxation, was a major reason for the economic crisis that the city of Cairo suffered in this period.

We know less about the non-elite slaves that must have made up a large share of the servile population working in the households of well-to-do subjects of the sultans. In the sixteenth century, after major campaigns, slaves might become so cheap that even prosperous villagers might acquire them. In Bursa during the 1400s and earlier 1500s, slaves served merchants and master weavers; in quite a few cases, the owners released their slaves after they had served for about ten years.[38] However, for other Ottoman cities, there is little evidence of slave artisans, and even in Bursa, poor but free people replaced slaves once the population increase of the 1500s had made a sufficiently large workforce available. It appears that in the seventeenth and eighteenth centuries, slaves, and especially male slaves, were becoming less accessible to provincial householders. Thus, few slaves were on record in the estate inventories of late seventeenth- and early eighteenth-century Damascus, which Colette Establet and Jean Paul Pasqual have studied with great care.[39] In seventeenth-century Istanbul, by contrast, female slaves, usually of Ukrainian background remained quite numerous, not only in Muslim households but sometimes in Christian and Jewish families as well.[40]

Apart from slaves originating in South Eastern Europe, Ukraine or Georgia, who had arrived in the Ottoman central provinces after often grueling journeys, and passed through the slave markets of Bursa or Istanbul, recent studies have focused on the sultans' subjects that fell into the hands of Christian pirates or corsairs, or else entered the world of Latin Christianity as prisoners of war. If their families could afford to ransom them, or if they managed to escape, these men sometimes returned home. In the present volume, Yasemin Beyazit has studied the life story of such a returnee, who even succeeded in reinserting himself into the line of applicants for judicial and/or teaching positions. However, most prisoners of war must have

---

37 André Raymond, *Grandes villes arabes à l'époque ottomane* (Paris: Sindbad/La Bibliothèque Arabe, 1985), pp. 74-76, and 143.

38 Sahillioğlu, "Slaves," p. 116 states that most masters required a period of service ranging between three and seven years; however presumably in many cases, the master and slave only entered the relevant contract after the slave had been in service for some time.

39 Colette Establet and Jean Paul Pasqual, *La gent d'état dans la société ottomane damascène* (Damascus : Ifpo, 2011).

40 Yaron Ben-Naeh, "Blond, Tall, with Honey-Colored Eyes: Jewish Ownership of Slaves in the Ottoman Empire," *Jewish History*, 20 (2006), 73-90.

remained in the 'lands of the infidels', and if there was no chance of return, some of them accepted baptism. In the archives of the German city of Leipzig, Manja Quakatz has unearthed the story of Wolff Christoph Lustig, who was a convert from 'Turkey' and around 1720 became a master tailor. Previously, Lustig had been a 'senior journeyman' (*Altgeselle*), whose role it was to represent his colleagues in disputes with their masters.[41] Lustig's insertion into the notoriously unwelcoming guild milieu must have been spectacularly successful.

Some Methodological Considerations:
Why It is Essential to Carefully Study Qadi Registers...

How do we access the sources that cover the ordinary subjects of the Ottoman sultans introduced here, people who rarely escaped their subordinate status but might, if especially fortunate, end up as small-town teachers and judges? In other words, as marginal members of the governing elite? These people occur in the petitions they presented to the central administration, or in registers listing their obligations as taxpayers. However, the most likely venue are the court cases on record in the registers of the nearest Islamic judge or *qadi* (*sicil, sicillât*). It is therefore not surprising that quite a few contributors to the present volume use documents from this source. While these authors interpret Ottoman court records in a fashion that differs significantly from what historians have previously attempted, they still belong into a field of '*sicillât* studies' that during the last fifty years or so has become an established part of Ottoman historiography.[42] Despite its innovative character, it thus makes sense to situate this historiography with respect to its predecessors.

---

41 Manja Quakatz, "Gebürtig aus der Türckey: Zur Konversion und Zwangstaufe osmanischer Muslime im Alten Reich um 1700," in *Europa und die Türkei im 18. Jahrhundert / Europe and Turkey in the 18th Century*, edited by Barbara Schmidt-Haberkamp (Göttingen: V & R unipress, 2011), pp. 417-32.

42 While space limitations do not allow a comprehensive bibliography, here are a few examples from the early stages of *qadi sicilleri* studies: Ronald Jennings, "Loans and Credit in Early 17th Century Ottoman Judicial Records: The Sharia Court of Anatolian Kayseri," *JESHO*, 16, No. 2/3 (1973), 168-216; idem, "Women in early 17th century Ottoman Judicial Records"; Özer Ergenç, "1600-1615 Yılları Arasında Ankara İktisadi Tarihine Ait Araştırmalar" in *Türkiye İktisat Tarihi Semineri, Metinler-Tartışmalar...*, ed. Osman Okyar and Ünal Nalbantoğlu (Ankara: Hacettepe Üniversitesi, 1975), pp. 145-68; Murat Çizakça, "Price History and the Bursa Silk Industry: A Study in Ottoman Industrial Decline, 1550-1650," *The Journal of Economic History*, XL, 3 (1980), 533-50. Akif Erdoğru and Ali Efdal Özkul have edited another *sicillât*-based work by Ronald Jennings, deceased in 1994: *Village Life in Cyprus at the Time of the Ottoman Conquest* (Istanbul: The Isis Press, 2009).

For a long time, Ottoman historians tended to believe that summarizing archival documents and if possible, connecting the information available in a variety of records, was the only method open to the historian. Thus, it was inevitable that officials and their doings took center stage; for by definition, archival records result from the business conducted by the institution that later on, takes responsibility for preserving and perhaps sharing them. Taken by itself, this state of affairs might not have been too problematic; but as noted, the Ottoman historian has to cope with the fact that very few non-state documents have survived. It is, therefore, difficult to check the claims made in archival documents, although people with some worldly experience know that at all times, a certain number of errors and 'non-truths' find their way into archival records.

Therefore, it was most exciting that in the late 1970s, Ahmet Yaşar Ocak found and published the archives of a small Anatolian dervish lodge, known as Emirci Sultan: for while documents issued by the sultans' administration played a role in this collection, the initiative to preserve the records at issue was that of provincial dervish sheikhs and their adherents, who had only very limited connections to the sultans' administration.[43]

To the historian's misfortune, the archives of the lodge of Emirci Sultan remained an exception, although the central lodge of the Mevlevi dervish order in Konya possessed an archive as well.[44] In the ordinary course of affairs, even if two subjects of the sultan produced documents recording for instance the sale of a house or a slave, the *sicillât* of the Islamic judges, in which evidence of the transaction has come down to us, were the products of scribes employed by these judges. If they served the 'general public' as well, this was a secondary concern. Furthermore, the fees that a *qadi* and his scribes might demand were significant considerations for townspeople with limited budgets. Financial considerations might thus determine whether sellers and purchasers had their sales recorded, or preferred to rely on the testimonies of witnesses, as the sharia permitted — and indeed encouraged — them to do.[45]

An even more significant gap is due to the accessibility or otherwise of the law courts. In a settlement of some size, the inhabitants of urban wards located at the margins of the built-up area might not be very familiar with the town center

43   Ahmet Yaşar Ocak, "Emirci Sultan ve Zaviyesi", *Tarih Enstitüsü Dergisi*, 9 (1978), 129-208.

44   Abdülbaki Gölpınarlı, "Konya'da Mevlâna Dergâhının Arşivi." *İstanbul Üniversitesi İktisat Fakültesi Mecmuası* 17: 1-4 (1955-1956), 156-78.

45   Boğaç Ergene, "Costs of Court Usage in the Seventeenth- and Eighteenth-Century Ottoman Anatolia: Court Fees as Recorded in Estate Inventories," *Journal of Economic and Social History of the Orient*, 45:1 (2002), 20- 39.

and have inhibitions about applying to the office of the *qadi*, who after all was a member of the elite. Especially women, with few opportunities to leave their own neighborhoods, might have trouble accessing the law court. Furthermore, peasants, semi-nomads and nomads often lived far away from the *qadi*'s seat, even if the latter sent out representatives (*naibs*) to deal with rural cases in his stead. Thus, the *qadi* registers, while very rich in content, deal only with a small minority of the Ottoman population and concentrate on the even smaller minority of urban adult males.

...Yet Avoid Staying Glued to Them

Given these constraints, it is understandable that authors who first used the *sicillât* as sources for monographs covering Ottoman towns, much in vogue between the 1960s and 1980s, allotted a great deal of space to public buildings and to the officials, military men and other administrators, who dominated these venues and ran the town in question, together with the surrounding province. Pious foundations (*vakıf, evkaf*) were a favored topic too, and continue to be so, because their establishment and operation generated much paperwork, preserved at least in part. In addition, historians paid special attention to temporary officeholders such as tax farmers and market inspectors. In urban studies constructed according to this particular model, ordinary shopkeepers and artisans often remained in the background.

Until the millennium, few Ottoman historians objected to this situation, probably at least in part because few people in Turkey questioned the paramount position of the state; to the real or alleged advantage of the latter, it seemed acceptable to sacrifice the needs and life chances of individuals. Though much decried, the spread of capitalism and market relations during the last seventy years has probably helped to make ordinary people more visible: If the powers-that-be expected them not only to work but to consume as well, it became necessary to focus on their needs and preferences at least to some extent.[46] Ever since the 1950s, the rise to power of people, whose newly prominent families had not been part of the late Ottoman and early Republican elites must have further encouraged historians to think about non-elite figures in the early modern Ottoman world. How do we describe the economic and social capital that provincials might accumulate, and which during the past fifty years allowed their sons, and to a more limited extent their daughters as well, to obtain professional qualifications and perhaps enter politics?

---

46 On the role of consumption in present-day Turkey compare Şevket Pamuk, *Uneven Centuries. Economic Development in Turkey since 1820* (Princeton: Princeton University Press, 2018), pp. 282-83.

During the first stage of research involving the *qadi* registers, historians con-centrated on the collection and evaluation of 'raw' data.[47] This procedure included the identification of cases that were widespread as opposed to others that were exceptional; for example, in late sixteenth-century Ankara, the sales, purchases and debts of mohair traders were often on record, while if a (possible) wholesaler of shoes emerged, this was an exceptional case.[48] As a result of this spadework, from the mid-1970s onwards, we have accumulated a sizeable number of studies on loan and credit arrangements, the economic activities of women, the role of small-scale urban power-holders and the sale of houses, to name but a few. Among other matters, these *sicil* studies have thrown some light on the manner in which Ottoman practice conformed — or did not conform — to sharia prescriptions. Thus, Eleni Gara has shown that in seventeenth-century Ottoman Macedonia, Muslim rural dignitaries lent money to Orthodox villagers; and the *qadi*s did not make sure that the borrowers paid their debts whenever a lender or borrower died, as they should have done according to the sharia.[49] On the contrary, villag-ers inherited the debts of their fathers, and entire rural communities remained indebted over the generations.

Intriguing Gaps: Problems of Coverage and Compilation

However, by the 1990s and 2000s, several historians had begun to warn that in order to understand what the documents in the *qadi* registers tell us, we must know much more about how the *qadi* ran his court and how his scribes did their work. Boğaç Ergene has pointed out a troubling phenomenon, namely that in the ample documentation covering at least a few privileged court cases, there is no reference to the use of the *qadis*' registers as evidence.[50] Does this mean that these enormous

---

47   For a pioneering work, see Fahri Dalsar, *Türk Sanayi ve Ticaret Tarihinde Bursa'da İpekçilik* (Istanbul: İstanbul Üniversitesi İktisat Fakültesi, 1960).

48   On mohair traders, compare Özer Ergenç, *Osmanlı Klasik Dönemi Kent Tarihçiliğine Katkı, XVI. Yüzyılda Ankara ve Konya* (Ankara: Ankara Enstitüsü Vakfı, 1995). On an Ankara shoe trader, see Suraiya Faroqhi, *Towns and Townsmen of Ottoman Anatolia, Trade, Crafts, and Food Production in an Urban Setting 1520-1650* (Cambridge: Cambridge University Press, 1984), p. 165.

49   Eleni Gara, "Lending and Borrowing Money in an Ottoman Province Town," in *Acta Viennensia Ottomanica: Akten des 13. CIÉPO Symposiums (Comité International d'Études Pré-ottomanes et Ottomanes)* edited by M. Köhbach, G. Prohazka Eisl and Claudia Römer (Vienna: Institut für Orientalistik, 1999), pp. 113-19.

50   Boğaç Ergene, *Local Court, Provincial Society and Justice in the Ottoman Empire: Legal Practice and Dispute Resolution in Çankırı and Kastamonu (1652-1744)* (Boston and Leiden: Brill, 2003), pp. 125-41.

collections of documents had no legal status? Ergene has suggested that the registers may have served as an aide-mémoire for the incoming *qadi*s who otherwise would not have known what had transpired under their predecessors. In another study, the same author has suggested that written documents might help the *qadi* determine whether the plaintiff or the defendant should bear the burden of proof. Given the functioning of the courts that Ergene has studied, receiving the judge's permission to prove one's case was not a burden but a significant advantage. In this context, the *qadi* registers might assume a more significant function than serving as a mere aide-mémoire.[51]

From a different perspective, we need to remember that in the 1600s and 1700s, criminals for various reasons targeted the building in which the *qadi* officiated (*mahkeme*), in most cases probably a sizeable house with two courtyards where the *qadi* resided with his family, and which had enough space for the operation of the court and the storage of its paperwork.[52] At least in some instances, the intruders might add a fake document 'proving' their claims. Thus, the Register of Important Affairs (Mühimme Defteri) of 1617-18 begins with the story of a complaint lodged by Mâryem bt Muhammad, heir of a tax farmer (İstanbul mukâtaacısı). For reasons unspecified, this woman claimed 500,000 *akçe* from Menes, who must have been a significant Jewish businessman.[53] Mâryem had no witnesses, but when the court examined the *qadi* register on which she based her claim, it turned out that the relevant page was a later fraudulent addition, as apparent from the difference in size and handwriting. In addition, the judge of the relevant court testified that he had not ordered any such entry. On this combination of oral witness and written document, the two army judges decisively rejected Mâryem's claim. As for a case discussed in the present volume, the remarkably powerful courtesan Mâryem of Konya, whose case Cemal Çetin has analyzed, has certainly left 'traces' in the *qadi* registers that in later years, she or her associates might have wished to get rid of. Even so, other motives including robbery were probably frequent as well, as the *qadi*s, even those not belonging to the high elite, were often much richer than local peasants and nomads, who might live in great poverty. When a *qadi* had overseen

---

51 Boğaç Ergene, "Document Use in Ottoman Courts of Law: Observations from the Sicils of Çankırı and Kastamonu," *Turcica*, 37 (2005), 83-112.

52 Suraiya Faroqhi, "Räuber, Rebellen und Obrigkeit im osmanischen Anatolien," *Periplus*, 3 (1993), 31-46.

53 *82 Numaralı Mühimme Defteri (1026-1027/1617-1618) Özet -Transkripsiyon -İndeks ve Tıpkıbasım*, eds. Yusuf Sarınay et al. (Ankara: T.C. Başbakanlık Devlet Arşivleri Genel Müdürlüğü, 2000), No. 1, pp. 3-4.

the execution of a highway robber leaving sons or friends, revenge was a likely motive as well.[54] However, although we can assume that the *sicils* were not the only item in a *qadi*'s residence that might attract attackers and/or manipulators, it is likely that they had a role to play.

At the same time, the most important argument in favor of some type of practical use for the registers is the expense of compiling them, and the time and dedication needed to induce perhaps recalcitrant ex-*qadis* to turn in their registers. At a later stage, protecting the documents from humidity, fire and bookworms cost efforts and money as well. Despite these difficulties, in quite a few cities, Ottoman *qadi* registers survive in their hundreds, and it is hard to imagine officials ensuring their preservation if the registers were not of significant value in the operation of the court. In the early seventeenth century, the central administration commonly demanded a copy taken from the *qadi* registers (*suret-i sicil*), when a provincial court had established the facts of a major case and bureaucrats in Istanbul wanted to make the final decisions.[55] It is even harder to imagine Ottoman townspeople of limited resources paying the scribes to enter their cases into the *qadi* registers, if these records had not brought them any benefits. Perhaps the bias of the sharia in favor of oral testimony caused Ottoman judges, plaintiffs and defendants to be reticent about their use of written records: clearly, these matters require further study.[56]

Another problem that historians have pointed out — without necessarily solving it — is the use of 'legal tricks', which exist all over the world and presumably, were current in certain Ottoman court cases as well. Thus, historians dealing with the problems of women in court have pointed out that we have great difficulty in evaluating so-called *hul'* divorces, which are on record as due to the initiative of the wife. In such cases, the woman appears to have 'purchased' the permission of her husband by giving up her rights to the 'deferred dowry' (*mehr-i müeccel*) and to the support payments over three months, which her ex-spouse would have had to pay if he unilaterally divorced her. In some cases, a woman of some property and/or with family support may have indeed terminated an unhappy marriage

---

54   *82 Numaralı Mühimme*, No. 167, p. 112.

55   *82 Numaralı Mühimme*, No. 42, pp. 28-29; No. 85, pp. 57-58; No. 104, p. 68, No. 115, p.76; No. 139, pp. 93-94.

56   For important methodological considerations see Iris Agmon, "Women's History and Ottoman Sharia Court Records: Shifting Perspectives in Social History," *Hawwa* 2, 2 (2004): 172–209. doi:10.1163/1569208041514680 (accessed on 1 December 2018).

in this fashion.[57] On the other hand, in other cases a man may have put pressure on his wife that was serious enough for her to consent to a *hul'* divorce. By this maneuver, he avoided paying the *mehr-i müeccel* and the three-month support. In the overwhelming majority of cases, we are unable to decide whether this or some other trick was at issue. Even so, it is good to keep an open mind.

Similarly, the *qadi* registers show that high-ranking persons, both male and female often avoided attending court in person and sent representatives (*vekil*) instead. However, if the male relatives of a woman represented her in court, they may have used this occasion to make deals at her expense, especially in inheritance cases, where only men of integrity would have been willing to sacrifice their own material interests in favor of a mother or a sister.[58]

Another serious problem confronting the historian trying to write social history with the help of *qadi* registers is the absence of detailed coverage of any given case, a matter, which Ergene has already pointed out some fifteen years ago.[59] Normally, the registers document any particular case only by a single record, so that we often learn how a complainant initiated a court case but not what happened at a later stage. Among the authors represented in this collection, Cemal Çetin has been fortunate enough to locate several documents dealing with the same issue, and this advantage clearly shows in his narration. However, one of the largest collections of documents from the *qadi* registers concerning a single case has come down to us in the one and only surviving *sicil* of sixteenth century Çorum.[60] These texts deal with the robberies committed by a group of men who may have been deserters from the Ottoman armies marching towards the Iranian frontier. We learn about the circumstances surrounding the arrest of the robbers, the complaints detailing the crimes of which the inhabitants of the region had been the victims, and, with a certain wealth of detail, the robbers' attack against the residence of a local *qadi*.

---

57 Zilfi, "We Don't Get Along," p. 284; Fırat Yaşa, "Kanuni Dönemi Bursa Mahkemesinde Bir Hülle Vakası ve Düşündürdükleri," in *Kanuni Sultan Süleyman Dönemi ve Bursa*, edited by Burcu Kurt (Bursa: Gaye Kitabevi, 2019), pp. 477-88.

58 Sometimes, a scribe of the court might visit a high-ranking woman in her home, perhaps to spare her an appearance in public, but alternatively, because the woman had expressed doubts about the probity of her male relatives.

59 Ergene, "Document Use," pp. 89-90.

60 Suraiya Faroqhi, "The Life and Death of Outlaws in Çorum," in eadem, *Coping with the State: Political Conflict and Crime in the Ottoman Empire, 1550-1720* (Istanbul: The Isis Press, 1995), pp. 145-62. The documents have appeared in an appendix 61 covering the period from 1938 to 1943, to the journal *Çorumlu*, published by the local Halkevi between 1938 and 1946.

The culprits claimed to be soldiers, a claim rejected by the administration, and after imprisonment in the fortress of Çorum, the men finally were executed. As the goods they left behind were of such minimal value, it is hard to romanticize the life of a robber in sixteenth-century Anatolia: evidently, it was nasty, brutish and short.[61]

The Papers, Section 1: Accessing People Through Their Crimes

Knowledgeable about the gaps in the *qadi* registers as outlined here, Nurcan Abacı and Zeynep Dörtok Abacı have suggested ways of escaping from the narrow horizons, in which the limitations of these document collections seem to confine the historian. Nurcan Abacı focuses on an issue treated mostly by sociologists and social psychologists, namely the wish to make a name for oneself within the micro-society of which one is a part. To show how Ottoman subjects before the motor age tried to distinguish themselves, Abacı focuses on the possession of a horse, which was expensive to buy and maintain; moreover in some places, such as Egypt, only soldiers had the privilege of horse-riding. Thus, the fortunate owner of a horse might arouse envy in his neighbors. To demonstrate the everlasting competitiveness of the search for prestige, Abacı points to the behavior of present-day young men, who in certain large Turkish cities, drive around in their noisy cars for no other purpose than making their peers feel envious.

Being a historian rather than a sociologist, Abacı has focused his discussion on a seventeenth-century case from the Bursa *qadi* registers, in which a man had his horse stolen. He traced the whereabouts of the animal, probably with considerable effort, and finally retrieved it with the help of the Bursa court. To further support his point about horses being 'objects of desire', the author might have pointed out that in the late 1700s and early 1800s, rural notables in Western Anatolia kept records of the horses gifted to them by relatives and retainers, carefully noting which horses had been born in their own stables. Abacı's point becomes even more convincing if we remember that in the Hamidian period, owning a horse and carriage was a status symbol among Ottoman gentlemen; however, as prices increased in the early 1900s, a middle-level bureaucrat might not be able to retain this symbol of prosperity.[62] A study of how those Ottomans who could afford horses related to their animals is definitely a desideratum.

---

61 Faroqhi, "The Life and Death of Outlaws," pp. 156-57.

62 Suraiya Faroqhi, "Means of transportation and sources of pride and joy: horses in the hands of Ottoman officials and notables," in *Animals and People in the Ottoman Empire*, edited by Suraiya Faroqhi (Istanbul: Eren, 2010), pp. 293-311; Paul Dumont and Fran-

Zeynep Dörtok Abacı has focused on another and more disturbing social phenomenon, namely aggression and the manner in which a suicidal person may direct aggressiveness against him/herself. The starting point is once again a court case, this time from the year 1700, which involved a certain Deli Şaban from the settlement of Miranos (sometimes: Minaros, today: Orhaniye) near Ankara. This man had quarreled with his fellow villagers, who accused him of contacting local administrators in order to proffer false accusations against his neighbors. In his frustration, the accused had twice attempted to commit suicide, apparently with the secondary intention of putting the villagers in a difficult position. Perhaps the latter might have had to pay blood money if the dead body turned up without any evidence of the killer; and finding the body of a fellow villager near the local mosque or in a well probably used by the community, must have been distressing too. The court decided on imprisonment in a fortress until the authorities considered that the accused had reformed. The Ottoman administration of the 1700s often used this type of punishment against Muslims, while non-Muslims accused of similar misdeeds were more likely to wind up as forced laborers in the sultans' arsenal.[63] Once the authorities released Deli Şaban, they would forbid him to return to Miranos.

In contradistinction to what we find in other chapters highlighting people of bad reputation, Dörtok Abacı is not interested in the punishment of the culprit, but in Deli Şaban's motivation. As a model, she suggests a set of phenomena that social psychologists call the 'dark triad' of narcissism, Machiavellianism and psychopathy. If the personality of the accused did in fact fit this model, Deli Şaban would have been excessively proud of his own achievements, willing to lie and deceive in order to get what he wanted, and unable to empathize with the pain of others. Certainly, any 'diagnosis' is hypothetical for, as Dörtok Abacı stresses, we cannot possibly submit a historical person to psychological tests. If the villagers' complaints about Deli Şaban's disruptive behavior were indeed accurate, he might have fit into the pattern outlined by present-day social psychologists. However, we have no way of knowing the truth of the matter. Possibly, the accused for one reason or another had made enemies among his fellow villagers, and these people had driven him to the brink of suicide. Possibly, those with a more balanced view of the situation had been too scared to intervene. At the same time, Dörtok Abacı

çois Georgeon, "Un bourgeois d'Istanbul au début du XX⁰ siècle", *Turcica*, XVII, 1985, 127-82, at pp. 168-70.

63 *Neşe Erim*, "Osmanlı İmparatorluğunda *Kalebentlik* Cezası ve Suçların Sınıflandırılması Üzerine bir Deneme", *Osmanlı Araştırmaları*, 4 (1984), 79-88.

has good reasons for interpreting the case in a manner that she does not hesitate to describe as speculative: For only by thinking about the possible implications of an outwardly straightforward record can we begin to imagine the alternatives available to an ordinary villager of the sixteenth or eighteenth century. Or else, we can imagine that in his frustration, Deli Şaban saw no alternative at all and therefore attempted suicide.

Fırat Yaşa's chapter deals with another aggressive misfit, named Hamza, an armed follower of an unnamed *timar*-holder. Hamza had managed to assemble a few like-minded men. Together with this gang, he committed a number of small-scale robberies, at a time when all over Anatolia, mercenaries were rebelling and plundering with increasing frequency. In the autumn of 1580 Hamza entered the record, because he had made himself a nuisance in his native village of Evciler, located in the district of Bursa near the water course known as the Nilüfer Çayı. As more and more complaints reached the Bursa court, the local judge wanted to call him to account; but for some time, it was impossible to find him. As Yaşa has emphasized, the distance of Evciler from the judge's seat in Bursa partly accounted for the long-lasting impunity of this dangerous robber. Among Hamza's misdeeds, there was an attack on the local mosque during night prayers in the month of Ramadan. In this case Hamza was pursuing a fellow villager, whose fate remains unknown; likely, it was unfortunate. In addition, Hamza had entered the house of a villager, presumably for the purpose of rape. In this case, the problem was that the local males had not seen the attack; and for an unknown reason, the judge did not ask the nearly-raped woman to swear that Hamza had been the attacker. In addition, this bandit had appropriated some real property and attacked another villager and his wife, as the couple worked in their garden or vineyard. Once again, he had unsuccessfully tried to rape the woman. Despite his aggressiveness towards females, Hamza apparently had contracted an irregular union with a woman, who had probably been divorced, forming a cohabitation which he seems to have regarded as a legal marriage.

Hamza's misdeeds resemble those of Deli Şaban in that they were crimes of violence, although Hamza, armed and acting together with his fellows was likely a more serious danger to the villagers than Şaban in his isolation could ever have been. Given the many crimes of which the locals accused their tormentor, Yaşa has focused on the possible punishments that the judge could have inflicted; for as so often, the judicial decision has not entered the *qadi* registers and thus remains unknown. Using contemporaneous fatwas and sultanic commands, Yaşa suggests that the judge may have sentenced Hamza to the galleys, while he probably banished the 'wife' of the accused from the village.[64] Hamza's punishment should have been more serious than that of Deli Şaban, but there is no way of being sure...

Evidently, ordinary Ottoman subjects were most likely to enter the records if they had committed major crimes, and Cemal Çetin's story of the misdeeds of the prostitute Mâryam and her followers in 1730s Konya is no exception. If Mâryam's claim was believable — but it soon turned out to be a tissue of lies and half-truths — two men had murdered her husband Artin, who seems to have been quite prosperous, being the headman of the local furriers' guild. Either Mâryam or the two murderers had buried the dead body within the house where the couple had lived, and where the governor's men ultimately tracked it down. It is unclear whether the woman was responsible for the murder of an earlier husband as well; for we do not know whether the 'Artin' and the 'Yasef' mentioned in the documents were two different people, or whether the locals including the *qadi*'s scribes called the same person by both names. It is just as unclear whether Mâryam took an active part in the murder(s) of her husband(s), or whether she had merely encouraged the two miscreants, by promises of gain and/or seduction. In any event, while she was in prison awaiting trial, the inhabitants of the town quarter where Mâryem had lived and the local Armenian community as well, wanted to get rid of her as soon as possible.

However, Mâryam had unsuspected resources; for by arguments that we cannot retrieve, she persuaded some wealthy local Armenians to lend her a very large amount of money. After paying over this sum, in part as the penalty fine known as *cürm ü cinayet*, she emerged from prison, but tried to renege on paying back part of the money that she had borrowed. Alternatively, the lenders may have overcharged her. In the end, the court banished Mâryam from the city, and she disappeared from the records.

Apart from telling a fascinating crime story, with ramifications documented in far more detail than is customary in other Ottoman court cases, Cemal Çetin's analysis has focused on the relationship of the sultan's administration, represented by the *qadi* and the provincial governor, to the 'ordinary people' whose taxes kept the empire going. For Çetin, it is obvious that even in a town such as Konya, located on major pilgrimage and military routes and thus accessible to the forces of order, lawless behavior was sometimes quite blatant. After all, Mâryam managed to run a disorderly house and despite her poor reputation, borrow a large sum of

---

64   Elyse Semerdjian, *Off the Straight Path: Illicit Sex, Law and Community in Ottoman Aleppo* (Syracuse NY: Syracuse University Press, 2008), pp. 82-84.

money from the Armenian community, to say nothing of the sizeable amounts that the governor collected from her, far more than was customary in such cases. In the end, no document in the *qadi*'s registers detailed who had collected how many silver coins (*guruş*) for what ostensible purpose; and we can only speculate about the background story.

As all readers of Mafia stories know, some criminals operate as families. Young people may learn the 'trade' of thieving or robbery from their parents, or else, as in the case discussed here, husbands and wives may associate in theft. In any event, it would have been difficult for a woman who discovered after her marriage that her husband was a thief, to disassociate herself from his activities.

In Saadet Maydaer's study of two late sixteenth-century Bursa families known for their thievery, the emphasis is on the close interest that the inhabitants of any urban ward took in the activities of their neighbors, and their readiness to come to the aid of a crime victim that shouted for help. While this willingness to assist the victims was doubtless a deterrent to thieves, Maydaer has realistically admitted that in this culture of mutual observation, some people might falsely accuse their neighbors of theft or other crimes. Sometimes, the accusers wanted to get the accused into trouble with the authorities right away, but perhaps even more importantly, they might wish to ensure that if the accused had ever to appear in court again, he/she would be on record as a 'suspicious' character.

With much ingenuity, Maydaer has disentangled the story of two men, one with one wife and the other with two spouses. In addition to these five people, there were two male associates, so that the thefts were the work of seven people, a situation that would have acquired a degree of organization and coordination. By close analysis of the documents, the author has moreover determined that one man and one woman were clearly the leaders; these people, both married to a less prominent member of the gang, had aroused so much suspicion among their neighbors that it became possible to bring witnesses into their houses in order to conduct a search, invading the otherwise sacrosanct privacy of an Ottoman subject. In the long list of retrieved goods, textiles were especially prominent, as the latter were expensive when compared to foodstuffs or even modest homes. The thieves had been lucky in so far as nobody had ever caught them in the act; and as usual, the available documents say nothing about penalties. Therefore, similar to Fırat Yaşa, Maydaer has studied the sources that inform us about sixteenth-century punishments. She has concluded that the thieves may well have saved their skins, and only suffered banishment.

The chapter contributed by Emine Dingeç concerns a group of probably young men from the township of Bor, where the *qadi* registers go back to the 1520s. In 1529 these four men confessed to having had sexual relationships with a Roma woman known as Gülpaşa, with the scribes recording that no violence or coercion was at issue when the court extracted these confessions. However, in this case even more that in others, caution is of the essence. Dingeç has assembled quite a few documents showing that Ottoman bureaucrats were much inclined to view Roma women as engaging in irregular sexual relationships; and these a priori assumptions set the tone of official documents. Alternative scenarios are therefore possible; perhaps, the four men had been guilty of gang rape.

However, as a member of a community of despised outsiders, Gülpaşa may have been unable to defend herself; and historians will do well to take Dingeç's warning to heart: As historians of the twenty-first century, we must avoid accepting the prejudices of sixteenth- or seventeenth-century bureaucrats without prior critique. As Islamic religious law emphasizes the responsibility of the individual, scholars of today should do likewise and examine each case on its own merits.

The last chapter in this section, by Zübeyde Güneş Yağcı, concerns the misfortunes of a mid-nineteenth-century slave of African background named Selim, who was the property of a slave trader named Mehmed, based in Manisa. In the local court, this slave, who must have known enough Turkish to make his complaint understood, showed the rather serious wounds that the slave dealer had inflicted upon him, after Selim had unsuccessfully tried to escape. Apart from the attempted flight, Mehmed accused Selim of disobedience and of the even more serious misdeed of having endangered the master's life and property. After all, if the slave entered the owner's harem to commit aggression of this kind, some judges considered that the owner was guiltless if he killed the culprit. Perhaps to add some spice to the story, Mehmed claimed, in addition, that Selim had taken a woman with him when he fled to the forested mountains near Manisa. However, the slave presented numerous witnesses to the physical aggression that he had suffered; thereupon, the court ordered the imprisonment of Mehmed for mistreatment of his slave. After all, in this period, Ottoman lawgivers had adopted the confinement of people in prison as a form of punishment.[65]

Güneş Yağcı has discussed this case in the context of Islamic legal opinion, which differently from Christian and Jewish laws, emphatically orders slave own-

---

65   Kent Schull, *Prisons in the Late Ottoman Empire: Microcosms of Modernity* (Edinburgh: Edinburgh University Press, 2014).

ers to treat their slaves kindly and see to their needs. However, some unanswered questions remain; for it is troubling to see that complaints by slaves against mistreatment from their owners are more frequent in the 1800s than they had been in the sixteenth or seventeenth century, at least if the *qadi* registers are reliable guides to what happened in Ottoman courtrooms. As the mistreatment of slaves surely occurred in earlier periods too, why did this issue occupy the courts mostly during the final decades of the empire's existence?

The Papers, Section 2: Helpful to Ordinary People— or Rather not: The Workings of the Ottoman Bureaucracy

From judicial operations and the *qadis'* courts, the focus moves to the efforts and expense required when a subject of the sultan confronted the Ottoman administration. Such a person might need official intervention when building a career, trying to enter local councils, and struggling for power on the provincial level. Perhaps most importantly, petitioners, candidates for office and even schoolboys might experience the difference between what rules and regulations prescribed and what actually happened 'on the ground'.

To begin with the tribulations of career building: Yasemin Beyazit has focused on a man named Alaeddin from the Macedonian town of Üsküp/Skopje. This person appears in a register (*ruznamçe*) from the 1570s, concerning the appointment of young scholars to candidacies (*mülazemet*) in the legal and religious establishment. For madrasa teachers and judges when beginning their careers, it was crucial to obtain the patronage of an established scholar, following his lessons and serving him when required. At certain stages of the senior scholar's career, as well as after his death, a certain number of his students might advance to a candidacy, which in turn was the precondition for appointment to a teaching position in an esteemed madrasa. As for those young men who —even after several attempts— failed to acquire a candidacy, they might teach in small madrasas that were 'dead ends' for career purposes, administer pious foundations, or teach on the elementary level.

Alaeddin was very unlucky: for when he traveled in the service of his patron, who had become the *qadi* of Baghdad, pirates/corsairs captured him and he spent several years in captivity among the 'unbelievers'. While Alaeddin ultimately returned home, his teacher had retired and could not do much for the career of his former student. Only when the ex-*qadi* of Baghdad finally died, did Alaeddin become a *mülazim*. Unfortunately, the register says nothing about his further career; and Beyazit has therefore 'fleshed out' her story with a discussion of other educated Ottoman subjects, who at some stage of their careers, fell into 'the hands of the infidels'.

Remarkably, the author has found another student who was in the same position as Alaeddin: after a long imprisonment in a land that the document did not name, this man returned home and was fortunate enough to find his teacher in a position to procure him a candidacy. In this case, the returnee did in fact become a *qadi*, albeit in a small place. Obviously, then as now, a student at the beginning of his career was subject to the caprices of fate, whether in the form of scholarly patrons or grant-giving agencies. Sophisticated network-construction, which this chapter makes visible in fine detail, was certainly helpful, but only up to a point.

To a volume that focuses on the lives and maneuverings of individuals, Filiz Yaşar has contributed a study that focuses more on the functioning of town or village councils (*dimogerontia*) as a social practice, rather than on any particular individual. Even so, the author has selected a 'hero' for her story, namely a person known as Papaz Nikola. Together with other villagers, in 1696 this priest became a *dimogerontas* of Kalamoti on the island of Chios. As the author points out, it is still too early to decide whether the *dimogerontia* was an institution or else a social and cultural formation — in this matter, she agrees with Eleni Gara, who has worked on village affairs in the north of continental Greece.[66] However defined, the job of the *dimogerontas* involved representing the villagers before the Ottoman authorities; most importantly, he needed to collect their taxes. While the local notary recorded the results of the election in his register, the crucial factor was the assent of the *qadi*, without whose document of appointment (*hüccet*) the *dimogerontas* could not function. These village officials thus resembled the *kocabaşıs* of the mainland, who needed official endorsements as well.

In Yaşar's perspective, the control of the Ottoman bureaucratic apparatus over a non-Muslim community is the decisive factor; however, we need to know more about the social relations that induced the villagers to select Papaz Nikola rather than some other personage. Yaşar has suggested that as a priest, Nikola would have been literate; while this skill was an advantage, perhaps other considerations, such as the patronage of an Ottoman official, played a role as well. On a different level, one does wonder who the voters may have been; did every villager, rich and poor, have a voice in the election?

Yaşar's villagers lived in the late seventeenth century, while the following chapter, by Özlem Başarır, focuses on local notables of the early 1800s, who inhabited

---

66 Eleni Gara, "In Search of Communities in Seventeenth Century Ottoman Sources: The Case of the Kara Ferye District," *Turcica* 30 (1998), 135-61.

Diyarbekir, which was/is a city of importance. This was a difficult period in the history of the empire, with Mahmud II (r. 1808-39) trying to reassert the control of the central government. A set of measures culminating in the abolition of the janissaries (1826) began a season of repression in which many people lost their lives. Others died of cholera, a sickness that in the 1830s spread all over the Middle East and to Europe as well. While these disasters were obvious to everybody, for the notables of the city, the overall 'drift' of Ottoman politics would have remained invisible. Thus, these men would not have known that over time, Mahmud II would eliminate the most important magnates of the region, often linked to nomadic or semi-nomadic groups. On the other hand, the disappearance of these power-holders would allow the sheikhs of dervish communities to reach a temporary prominence as mediators in local disputes.[67] Nor would most of Diyarbekir's prominent men have known very much about the growing power of Mehmed Ali Paşa, who governed Egypt from 1805 to 1848 and in 1832, sent an army into Anatolia that defeated the Ottoman forces several times and advanced all the way to Kütahya.[68]

By contrast, for a person such as Mehmed Bey from the Şeyhzâde family (d. 1849), the main aim was to play a significant role in the running of Diyarbekir province, and thus retain the prominent position of his family, which had produced powerful magnates for several generations. However, as Başarır has expressed it, Mehmed Bey's attempts to expand his influence led to a series of conflicts with Diyarbekir governors, which included local uprisings.[69] Despite their generally very short tenures of office, governors mandated by the sultans had Mehmed Bey banished for many decades: short-term confrontations, fought out at great cost without long-term gain. During those years, struggles of this type took place in other parts of Anatolia as well; as one example among many, we may mention an uprising in early nineteenth-century Sivas, of which İlhan Ege has produced a remarkable analysis.

Another struggle for local power is at issue in a study by Faruk Yaslıçimen. Once again, the 'locals' lost out, in this case against the bureaucracy of Sultan Abdülhamid II (r. 1876-1909). In the 1890s, the sultan and his servitors regarded the provinces of Iraq as a sensitive area, for a significant part of the population was Shiite. As in

---

67   Martin M. van Bruinessen, *Agha, Shaikh and State: The Social and Political Structures of Kurdistan* (London: Zed Books, 1992).

68   Muhammet Hanefi Kutluoğlu, "Kavalalı Mehmed Ali Paşa (ö. 1849)," https://cdn.islamansiklopedisi.org.tr/dosya/25/C25008102.pdf (accessed on 24 July 2019).

69   İlhan Ege, "Sivas'ta gizli kalmış bir İsyan," in *Prof. Dr. Necmi Ülker Armağanı*, edited by Nilgün Nurhan Kara, Latif Daşdemir, and Özer Küpeli (Izmir: Meta Basım Matbaacılık, 2008), pp. 455-71.

the British perspective, Iraq lay on the way to India, any disputes among Sunni and Shiite inhabitants in the opinion of Sultan Abdülhamid might lead to British intervention, in a place where Ottoman control was not very strong. After all, in Yemen, where he had reason to fear British intervention too, the sultan engaged in a long and costly war to re-attach the country to the Ottoman Empire. As for the religious aspect, the monarch proceeded in a manner familiar to Christian mission-aries, namely by founding schools and having preachers exhort the population to convert, in this instance, to the Sunni variety of Islam. Surely, the ruler's religious convictions had a role to play, but political concerns must have occupied center stage.

As for the victims of this provincial crisis, they were Shiites, two brothers named Nureddin and İsmail. Admittedly, these men did not show any inclination to participate in sectarian conflicts; rather, as Yaslıçimen has demonstrated, they were prosperous tax farmers who to their misfortune, had entered a conflict with Hasan Paşa, the powerful governor of the province of Baghdad. The latter had the brothers banished from their hometown of Hılle to the unfamiliar and uncongenial environment of Mosul. By pointing out that Nureddin and İsmail 'were known from the past to have fomented rebellion', the governor was able to maintain the two brothers in their place of banishment, despite the decision of the Council of State (Şûrâ-yı Devlet) that declared the punishment of Nureddin as devoid of any justification. Even when the file of documents studied by Yaslıçimen ended, it was still not clear whether the two brothers would ever be able to return to Hılle. As the author has shown, the brothers continued to hope for the intervention of the central government, which, as many provincials liked to believe, would behave more equitably than the sultan's men on the spot.

If the late Ottoman bureaucracy had functioned according to clear and uni-versally obeyed rules, Hasan Paşa would not have been able to keep Nureddin and İsmail in banishment after the Council of State had declared that there was no valid reason for doing so. A comparable issue, namely the lack of regular controls over the activities of the late Ottoman bureaucrats, is at issue in the chapter contributed by İsmail Yaşayanlar, which deals with the conflicts between higher- and lower-level officials employed in the state educational establishment of Bursa. The trouble started with four students absconding from the local high school, or Mekteb-i İdâdî-i Mülkî to cite its official name. Certainly, these teenagers did not have the passports for domestic travel (*mürûr tezkeresi*), which they would have needed to use public transportation or spend the night in a khan. The authorities recaptured the boys quickly. When questioned the schoolboys indicated that relations between the Maarif Müdürü or overseer of state schools and the assistant school principal were so bad that student morale suffered. As an investigating committee soon found out, the Maarif Müdürü had held an examination under irregular conditions, perhaps to help students who needed to go to Istanbul to apply to a college-level institution, the well-known Mekteb-i Mülkiye-i Şâhâne — or perhaps for other less laudable motives. In addition, there was evidence of other dubious transactions. While the authorities finally dismissed the errant Maarif Müdürü, he soon was back in position, albeit in another town.

In this context, Yaşayanlar points out that Ottoman officialdom was in the habit of not intervening unless there was a complaint. Otherwise, it was common practice to let matters take their course. While inspectors with known responsibilities existed, they did not on their own initiative try to ensure compliance with official policies. These observations match the conclusions of Faruk Yaslıçimen in the present volume; and in his last published article, the late Donald Quataert has used investigative reports (istintaknâme) to arrive at similar results.[70]

The Papers, Section 3: Out of Line, Out of Category: The Adventures of a Dubious Broker

Our last chapter once again contains a crime story; however, in this case, inter-empire complications are at issue. Focusing on a Venetian broker named Nicolò Algarotti, Buket Kalaycı has studied Ottoman documents preserved in the archives of the Venetian bailo.[71] A number of merchants resident in Venice had entrusted Algarotti and his Venetian associate with the typical products of late sixteenth and early seventeenth century Venetian industry, namely woolens, paper and glassware, which they wanted their brokers to sell in Egypt. As a return cargo, Algarotti was to purchase spices, and for this enterprise, the merchants at issue remitted some extra cash. However, Algarotti, who had contracted major debts, seems to have passed off the goods entrusted to him as his own property. As for the rightful owners of the woolens, paper and glassware, they mobilized the Venetian government, asking for the retrieval of these items. For this reason, the bailo in Istanbul turned to the Ottoman authorities referring to the ancient privileges known as ahidnâme,

---

70   Donald Quataert with David Gutman, "Coal Mines, the Palace, and Struggles over Power, Capital, and Justice in the Late Ottoman Empire," *International Journal of Middle East Studies*, 44,2 (2012), 215-35.

71   Serap Mumcu, *Venedik Baylosu'nun Defterleri/The Venetian Bailo's Registers (1589-1684)* (Venice: Edizioni Cà Foscari Digital Publishing, 2014). https://www.academia.edu/9454342/Venedik_Baylosu_nun_Defterleri_The_Venetian_Baylo_s_Registers_1589-1684_ (accessed on 26 July 2019).

and received a command from Sultan Ahmed I (r. 1603-17). However, we do not know whether the Venetian traders ever saw their goods or their money again, as Algarotti converted to Islam and died shortly afterwards.

It was always risky to entrust goods and money to people traveling to places where the investors had little control, and astute wanderers between the Muslim world and the territories of Latinate Christianity might use (sometimes multiple) changes of religion for thorough worldly ends.[72] Even so, it is worth remembering that we do not know Algarotti's point of view. Not all the statements of his accusers were necessarily true; and a broker might find that buyer and seller agreed that he, the middleman, was responsible for their troubles...[73]

Bibliography

Primary Sources

Andreasyan, Hrand D. "Celâlilerden Kaçan Anadolu Halkının Geri Gönderilmesi." in *Ord. Prof. İsmail Hakkı Uzunçarşılı'ya Armağan*, 45-53. Ankara: Türk Tarih Kurumu, 1976.

Aşçı Dede. *Aşçı Dedenin Hatıraları*. 4 vols., eds. Mustafa Koç and Eyyüp Tanrıverdi. İstanbul: Kitabevi, 2017.

Beydilli, Kemal. *Osmanlı Döneminde İmamlar ve Bir İmamın Günlüğü*. İstanbul: Tarih ve Tabiat Vakfı, 2001.

Evliya Çelebi. *Evliya Çelebi Seyahatnâmesi, Topkapı Sarayı Bağdat 304 Yazmasının Transkripsyonu–Dizini*. vol 1., eds. Robert Dankoff, Seyit Ali Kahraman and Yücel Dağlı. İstanbul: Yapı Kredi Yayınları, 2006.

Heberer von Bretten, Michael. *Osmanlıda Bir Köle, Brettenli Michael Heberer'in Anıları 1585-1588*. Translated by Türkis Noyan. İstanbul: Kitap Yayınevi, 2003.

Ocak, Ahmet Yaşar. "Emirci Sultan ve Zaviyesi." *Tarih Enstitüsü Dergisi* 9 (1978): 129-208.

---

72 Florence Buttay, *Histoire véridique de l'imposteur Giorgio del Giglio, qui renia la foi chrétienne et prétendit servir Soliman le Magnifique* (Paris: Payot, 2018); Ariel Salzmann, "A Travelogue Manqué? The Accidental Itinerary of a Maltese Priest in the Seventeenth-Century Mediterranean," in *A Faithful Sea: The Religious Culture of the Mediterranean, 1200-1700*, edited by Adnan A. Husain and Katherine E. Fleming (Oxford: Oneworld Publications, 2007) pp. 149-72.

73 For the rare voice of an aggrieved broker, see Suraiya Faroqhi, "Honour and Hurt Feelings: Complaints Addressed to an Ottoman Merchant Trading in Venice" in *Merchants in the Ottoman Empire*, edited by Suraiya Faroqhi and Gilles Veinstein (Leuven: Peeters, 2008), pp. 63-78.

Sarınay, Yusuf and others (eds.). *82 Numaralı Mühimme Defteri (1026-1027/1617-1618) Özet-Transkripsiyon-İndeks ve Tıpkıbasım*. Ankara: T.C. Başbakanlık Devlet Arşivleri Genel Müdürlüğü, 2000.

[Serresli Papa Synadinos]. *Conseils et mémoires de Synadinos prêtre de Serrès en Macédoine (XVIIᵉ siècle)*. Edited, translated and commented by Paolo Odorico with S. Asdrachas, T. Karanastassis, K. Kostis and S. Petmezas. Paris: Association "Pierre Belon", 1996.

Vracalı Sofroni. *Osmanlı'da Bir Papaz, Günahkâr Sofroni'nin Çileli Hayat Hikâyesi 1739-1813*. Translated by Aziz Nazmi Şakir-Taş. İstanbul: Kitap Yayınevi, 2003.

Secondary Sources

Agmon, Iris. "Women's History and Ottoman Sharia Court Records: Shifting Perspectives in Social History." *Hawwa* 2, no. 2 (2004): 172-209. Accessed on: 1 December 2018. DOI:10.1163/1569208041514680.

Akdağ, Mustafa. "Medreseli İsyanları." *İstanbul Üniversitesi İktisat Fakültesi Mecmuası* 11, no. 1-4 (1949-50): 361-87.

———. *Celâlî İsyanları 1550-1603*. Ankara: A.Ü. Dil ve Tarih-Coğrafya Fakültesi, 1963.

Ben-Naeh, Yaron. "Blond, Tall, with Honey-Colored Eyes: Jewish Ownership of Slaves in the Ottoman Empire." *Jewish History* 20 (2006): 73-90.

Buttay, Florence, *Histoire véridique de l'imposteur Giorgio del Giglio, qui renia la foi chrétienne et prétendit servir Soliman le Magnifique*. Paris: Payot, 2018.

Çizakça, Murat. "Price History and the Bursa Silk Industry: A Study in Ottoman Industrial Decline, 1550-1650." *The Journal of Economic History* XL, no. 3 (1980): 533-50.

Dalsar, Fahri. *Türk Sanayi ve Ticaret Tarihinde Bursa'da İpekçilik*. İstanbul: İstanbul Üniversitesi İktisat Fakültesi, 1960.

Dankoff, Robert. *An Ottoman Mentality: The World of Evliya Celebi*. Leiden: Brill, 2006.

Demirel, Ömer. *Osmanlı Vakıf Şehir İlişkisine Bir Örnek: Sivas Şehir Hayatında Vakıfların Rolü*. Ankara: Türk Tarih Kurumu, 2000.

Dumont, Paul and François Georgeon. "Un bourgeois d'Istanbul au début du XXᵉ siècle." *Turcica* XVII (1985): 127-82.

Durmaz, Tunahan. "Family, Companions, and Death: Seyyid Hasan Nûrî Efendi's Microcosm (1661-1665)" Accessed on: 10 July 2019. https://www.academia.edu/38297349/_Family_Companions_and_Death_Seyyid_Hasan_N%C3%BBr%C3%AE_Efendis_Microcosm_1661-1665_M.A._Thesis_Sabanc%C4%B1_University_04.01.2019_

Ege, İlhan. "Sivas'ta Gizli Kalmış Bir İsyan." in *Prof. Dr. Necmi Ülker Armağanı*, eds. Nilgün Nurhan Kara, Latif Daşdemir and Özer Küpeli, 455-71. İzmir: Meta Basım Matbaacılık, 2008.

Elger, Ralf. *Glaube, Skepsis, Poesie: Arabische Istanbul-Reisende im 16. und 17. Jahrhundert*. Beirut and Würzburg/Germany: Ergon Verlag, 2011.

Ergenç, Özer. "1600-1615 Yılları Arasında Ankara İktisadi Tarihine Ait Araştırmalar." in *Türkiye İktisat Tarihi Semineri, Metinler-Tartışmalar...*, eds. Osman Okyar and Ünal Nalbantoğlu, 145-68. Ankara: Hacettepe Üniversitesi, 1975.

———. *Osmanlı Klasik Dönemi Kent Tarihçiliğine Katkı, XVI. Yüzyılda Ankara ve Konya*. Ankara: Ankara Enstitüsü Vakfı, 1995.

Ergene, Boğaç. "Costs of Court Usage in the Seventeenth- and Eighteenth-Century Ottoman Anatolia: Court Fees as Recorded in Estate Inventories." *Journal of Economic and Social History of the Orient* 45, no. 1 (2002): 20-39.

———. "Document Use in Ottoman Courts of Law: Observations from the Sicils of Çankırı and Kastamonu." *Turcica* 37 (2005): 83-112.

———. *Local Court, Provincial Society and Justice in the Ottoman Empire: Legal Practice and Dispute Resolution in Çankırı and Kastamonu (1652-1744)*. Boston and Leiden: Brill, 2003.

Erim, Neşe. "Osmanlı İmparatorluğunda Kalebentlik Cezası ve Suçların Sınıflandırılması Üzerine Bir Deneme." *Osmanlı Araştırmaları* 4 (1984): 79-88.

Erler, Mehmet Yavuz. "Animals during Disasters." in *Animals and People in the Ottoman Empire*, ed. Suraiya Faroqhi, 333-52. İstanbul: Eren, 2010.

Esmer, Tolga U. "The Confessions of an Ottoman Irregular: Self-Representation and Ottoman Interpretive Communities in the Nineteenth Century." *Osmanlı Araştırmaları/The Journal of Ottoman Studies, Living Empire: Ottoman Identities in Transition 1700-1850* 44 (2014): 313-40.

Establet, Colette and Jean Paul Pasqual. *La gent d'état dans la société ottomane damascène*. Damascus: Ifpo, 2011.

Faroqhi, Suraiya. "Honour and Hurt Feelings: Complaints Addressed to an Ottoman Merchant Trading in Venice." in *Merchants in the Ottoman Empire*, eds. Suraiya Faroqhi and Gilles Veinstein, 63-78. Leuven: Peeters, 2008.

———. "Manumission in Seventeenth-Century Suburban Istanbul." in *Mediterranean Slavery Revisited (500-1800) – Neue Perspektiven auf mediterrane Sklaverei (500-1800)* , eds. Stefan Hanß and Juliane Schiel, with assistance from Claudia Schmid, 381-401. Zurich: Chronos Verlag, 2014.

———. "Means of Transportation and Sources of Pride and Joy: Horses in the Hands of Ottoman Officials and Notables." in *Animals and People in the Ottoman Empire*, ed. Suraiya Faroqhi, 293-311. İstanbul: Eren, 2010.

———. "The Life and Death of Outlaws in Çorum." in *Coping with the State: Political Conflict and Crime in the Ottoman Empire, 1550-1720*, 145-62. İstanbul: The Isis Press, 1995.

———. "Räuber, Rebellen und Obrigkeit im osmanischen Anatolien." *Periplus* 3 (1993): 31-46.

———. *Towns and Townsmen of Ottoman Anatolia, Trade, Crafts, and Food Production in an Urban Setting 1520-1650*. Cambridge: Cambridge University Press, 1984.

Filan, Kerim. "Life in Sarajevo in the 18th Century (According to Molla Mustafa's *mecmua*)." in *Living in the Ottoman Ecumenical Community: Essays in Honour of Suraiya Faroqhi*, ed. Vera Constantini and Markus Koller, 317-45. Leiden, Boston: Brill, 2008.

Findley, Carter. *Ottoman Civil Officialdom: A Social History*. Princeton: Princeton University Press, 1989.

Gara, Eleni. "In Search of Communities in Seventeenth Century Ottoman Sources: The Case of the Kara Ferye District." *Turcica* 30 (1998): 135-61.

————. "Lending and Borrowing Money in an Ottoman Province Town." in *Acta Viennensia Ottomanica: Akten des 13. CIÉPO Symposiums (Comité International d'Études Préottomanes et Ottomanes)*, ed. M. Köhbach, G. Prohazka Eisl and Claudia Römer, 113-19. Vienna: Institut für Orientalistik, 1999.

Gölpınarlı, Abdülbaki. "Konya'da Mevlâna Dergâhının Arşivi." *İstanbul Üniversitesi İktisat Fakültesi Mecmuası* 17, no. 1-4 (1955-1956): 156-78.

İnalcık, Halil, "Military and Fiscal Transformation in the Ottoman Empire 1600-1700," in *Studies in Ottoman Social and Economic History*, No. V. London: Variorum Reprints, 1985.

Jennings, Ronald, "Women in early 17th century Ottoman Judicial Records: The sharia court of Anatolian Kayseri," *Journal of the Economic and Social History of the Orient*, XVIII, 1 (1975): 53-114.

Jennings, Ronald. "Loans and Credit in Early 17th Century Ottoman Judicial Records: The Sharia Court of Anatolian Kayseri." *Journal of the Economic and Social History of the Orient* 16, no. 2/3 (1973): 168-216.

————. *Village Life in Cyprus at the Time of the Ottoman Conquest*, eds. Akif Erdoğru and Ali Efdal Özkul. İstanbul: The Isis Press, 2009.

Kafadar, Cemal. "Mütereddit Bir Mutasavvıf: Üsküp'lü Asiye Hatun'un Rüya Defteri 1641-43." *Topkapı Sarayı Müzesi, Yıllık* V (1992): 168-222.

————. "Self and Others: The Diary of a Dervish in Seventeenth Century Istanbul and First-person Ottoman Literature." *Studia Islamica* 69 (1989): 121-50.

Karahasanoğlu, Selim. *Kadı ve Günlüğü: Sadreddinzade Telhisî Mustafa Efendi Günlüğü (1711-1735) Üstüne Bir İnceleme*. İstanbul: Türkiye İş Bankası Kültür Yayınları, 2013.

Karlığa, Bekir et al. *Evliya Çelebi Atlası*. İstanbul: MEDAM, 2012.

Kutluoğlu, Muhammet Hanefi. "Kavalalı Mehmed Ali Paşa (ö. 1849)." Accessed on: 24 July 2019. https://cdn.islamansiklopedisi.org.tr/dosya/25/C25008102.pdf

Maksudyan, Nazan. *Orphans and Destitute Children in the Late Ottoman Empire*. Syracuse NY: Syracuse University Press, 2014.

Mumcu, Serap. *Venedik Baylos'nun Defterleri/The Venetian Bailo's Registers (1589-1684)*. Venice: Edizioni Cà Foscari Digital Publishing, 2014. Accessed on: 26 July 2019. https://www.academia.edu/9454342/Venedik_Baylosu_nun_Defterleri_The_Venetian_Baylo_s_Registers_1589-1684_

Nalçacı, Nida Nebahat. *Sultanın Kulları: Erken Modern Dönem İstanbul'unda Savaş Esirleri ve Zorunlu İstihdam*. İstanbul: Verita Kitap, 2015.

Pamuk, Şevket. *Uneven Centuries. Economic Development in Turkey since 1820*. Princeton: Princeton University Press, 2018.

Peirce, Leslie. *Morality Tales: Law and Gender in the Ottoman Court of Aintab*. Los Angeles, Berkeley and London: The University of California Press, 2003.

Quakatz, Manja. "Gebürtig aus der Türckey: Zur Konversion und Zwangstaufe osmanischer Muslime im Alten Reich um 1700." in *Europa und die Türkei im 18. Jahrhundert / Europe and Turkey in the 18th Century*, ed. Barbara Schmidt-Haberkamp, 417-32. Göttingen: V&R Bonn University Press, 2011.

Quataert, Donald and David Gutman. "Coal Mines, the Palace, and Struggles over Power, Capital, and Justice in the Late Ottoman Empire." *International Journal of Middle East Studies* 44, no. 2 (2012): 215-35.

Raymond, André. *Grandes villes arabes à l'époque ottomane*. Paris: Sindbad/La Bibliothèque Arabe, 1985.

Sahillioğlu, Halil. "Slaves in the Social and Economic Life of Bursa in the Late 15th and Early 16th Centuries." *Turcica* XVII (1985): 43-112.

Sajdi, Dana. *The Barber of Damascus: Nouveau Literacy in the Eighteenth-century Ottoman Levant*. Stanford: Stanford University Press, 2013.

Salzmann, Ariel. "A Travelogue Manqué? The Accidental Itinerary of a Maltese Priest in the Seventeenth-Century Mediterranean." in *A Faithful Sea: The Religious Culture of the Mediterranean, 1200-1700*, eds. Adnan A. Husain and Katherine E. Fleming, 149-72. Oxford: Oneworld Publications, 2007.

Schull, Kent. *Prisons in the Late Ottoman Empire: Microcosms of Modernity*. Edinburgh: Edinburgh University Press, 2014.

Semerdjian, Elyse. *Off the Straight Path: Illicit Sex, Law and Community in Ottoman Aleppo*. Syracuse NY: Syracuse University Press, 2008.

Tezcan, Nuran, Semih Tezcan and Robert Dankoff, eds. *Evliya Çelebi-Studies and Essays Commemorating the 400th Anniversary of His Birth*. Ankara: Republic of Turkey Ministry of Culture, 2012.

Toledano, Ehud. "The Concept of Slavery in Ottoman and Other Muslim Societies: Dichotomy or Continuum?" in *Slave Elites in the Middle East and Africa: A Comparative Study*, eds. Miura Toru and John Edward Philips, 159-76. London and NY: Kegan Paul International, 2000.

Tunalı Koç, Gülçin. "An Ottoman Astrologer at Work: Sadullah el-Ankaravî and the Everyday Practice of *İlm-i Nücûm*." in *Les ottomans et le temps*, eds. François Georgeon and Frédéric Hitzel, 39-60. Leiden: Brill, 2012.

Van Bruinessen, Martin M. *Agha, Shaikh and State: The Social and Political Structures of Kurdistan*. London: Zed Books, 1992.

Wittmann, Richard. Geç Osmanlı Ego-Belgeleri Üstüne, Orient Institut der Deutschen Forschungsgemeinschaft (DFG). Accessed on: 27 July 2019. https://www.oiist.org/selbstzeugnisse-als-quellen-zur-geschichte-des-spaten-osmanischen-reichs/

Yaşa, Fırat. "Desperation, Hopelessness, and Suicide: An Initial Consideration of Self-Murder by Slaves in Seventeenth-Century Crimean Society." *Turkish Historical Review* 9, no. 2 (2018): 198-211. Accessed on: 2018. DOI: 10.1163/18775462-00902003

———. "Kanuni Dönemi Bursa Mahkemesinde Bir Hülle Vakası ve Düşündürdükleri." in *Kanuni Sultan Süleyman Dönemi ve Bursa*, ed. Burcu Kurt, 477-88. Bursa: Gaye Kitabevi, 2019.

Zilfi, Madeline. "We Don't Get Along." in *Women in the Ottoman Empire: Middle Eastern Women in the Early Modern Era*, ed. Madeline Zilfi, 264-96. Leiden: Brill, 1997.

SECTION ONE

Accessing People Through Their Crimes

CHAPTER ONE

Sitting in a Stable while Singing Palace Songs: On Horse Ownership as Self-Display*

Nurcan Abacı

"Out of a thousand centuries they drew the ancient admiration of the foot-man for the horseman. They knew instinctively that a man on a horse is spiritually as well as physically bigger than a man on foot."

—John Steinbeck[1]

Introduction

In stop motion animation, the objects used in the scene are manually moved and recorded, but when we watch it, we don't notice this. I think Turkish historiography resembles this technique. Even though we know that documents and records are part of a narrative, fictionalizing the entirety of the narrative is still in its infancy. In this article, I will try to contribute to the historical narrative, by shedding light on the meaning of horse ownership, a sign of prestige among the lower classes aspiring to emulate the ruling class.

Actually, Fırat Yaşa, the editor of this volume, had requested an article narrating "the story of one individual." When I accepted his request, I knew that my contribution would have something to do with horses. This creature that is invisible on the margins of contemporary society was, in the early modern world—my research period— clearly at the center, both in terms of its function and its representation. I want to describe both in relation to a person.

However, as I worked, the subject matter evolved into something else, and my essay, leaving humans in the background, began to read more like an introductory

---

*   Bursa, 1670

1   John Steinbeck, *The Red Pony*, (USA: Penguin Books, 1994), 12

text that I hoped would provoke questions and uncover the meanings assigned to horses at least in one historical period.

I intended this essay for two groups of people. For the reader of traditional history, I want my narrative to act as a catalyst. For the majority of those in this group, the text can at first seem like a chain of meaningless and unfounded claims. However, I hope that after reading this essay, they will be wondering why they cannot hear the sounds of hooves in those other text that they read on horses.

The second group of readers, also my ideal audience, may not even exist: an imagined group that I wish existed just for the purpose of reading this text. These readers would be familiar with contemporary approaches and methods concerning world history and other social sciences. If they were to join the field as commentators and even authors, I am certain that our practice of historiography would change rapidly. In my opinion, what historiography needs are not answers but questions, as it is abundantly clear that the current practice is unlikely to produce transformative ideas.

The Desire to Be Emulated: Enviers Perish!

'Your twenty-somethings will be here any minute.' Clearly, to understand the meaning of this remark at the cashier in the gas station, I needed to keep listening. After a bit of eavesdropping, I understood: It was Sunday and the 'twenty-somethings' that the gas station employee mentioned were the youth that drove around the neighborhoods in their "bird series" cars on their day off. The number referred to how much gas they bought for their cars, and not necessarily to their age group. This transaction had become so customary that it now had a name.

The noisy, gasoline-boosted drive that attention-seeking youth embark on is the expression of a need. As I will elaborate below, we all have to construct our identity and our outer appearance. Our happiness and peace of mind depends, to a large extent, on the outcome of this mostly unconscious urge. The flaunting that I talk about in this article, namely, horse ownership, is among the methods our ancestors chose for self-actualization, and I will try to tell the story of this phenomenon.[2]

---

2   Even though it is not directly about the behavior I mentioned, the following article might be eye opening: L.J. Morrell, J. Lindström and G.D. Ruxton, "Why Are Small Males Aggressive?" *Proceedings of the Royal Society B: Biological Sciences* 272, no. 1569 (2005): 1235-41. The people who drive the domestic brand cars that I gave as an example, despite having common characteristics, do not have class-consciousness. Another group similar to this one and living in the ghettoes of large cities seems to be developing a consciousness, as it were. I am informed of this area that is outside of my knowledge

All of us look for ways that will make us feel better. Like every person whose basic physical needs are met and who wants to self-actualize, I, too, try to seek attention: After laboring over each word in an article, the publication makes me happy when a few of my students tell me, 'We read it and it was amazing as always.' The extent to which their statements reflect reality is not that important. I am comfortable because I have built my acquaintance network with people who most probably will not shake the foundations of my worldview. Every now and then others invade this personal space and imply the falsehood of my reality, and I label their words as jealousy. These people can only be enviers who cannot stand

FIGURE 1.1 A horse figure, the body made up of humans (Murakkâ Behzâd, TSMK, Hazine 20, No: 2165, vr. 36).

my ideas that will surely come to be appreciated in time, right? In the end, as mortals with fragile egos, none of us can bear to constantly face reality.[3]

As readers, you can do likewise by using some of what you read as social capital, thereby attracting attention. Three basic principles govern the psychological mechanism at work here: attracting attention/being valued, taking revenge, and underscoring success. In different periods of our lives, we feel these either separately or all at once, and practice them either consciously or subconsciously. If you are

---

through the change in the lyrics of the rap songs that my students listen to. They increasingly point to other social classes as the reason for their pain. I hope that sociologists take a break from their research dominated by translation while leaning on the founding fathers and become more involved with the streets in which the 'Tauruses with full tanks" roam, and that they show us if the change in the song lyrics corresponds to social change or not.

3 We can interpret the comments by followers on posts shared in social media in this way. Just so the spell is not broken, everyone talks of the beauty of the emperor's clothes and expects the same treatment for himself. Those who do not abide by this unwritten rule are either silenced or removed from the list.

not a nihilist or have not spent half of your life in social isolation, it is not possible for you to exist independently of this mechanism.[4]

On our own, we cannot decide if we have reached our goal or not. As difficult it is to accept, in most cases our social circles determine if we have a good life or not. When we look at the issue from this angle, how others perceive us is more important than we think. The perception of those around you can manifest as either emulation or envy, and in both cases this is hierarchical.[5] Either they want to emulate you, or they envy you, and both are signs that you are ahead of them. Consequently, you feel successful and happy. In short, we need feedback from those around us.[6]

The emotions you evoke in a person depend on the other person as much as you. The desire for emulation that you spark in those around you does not harm anyone and often motivates them to do better. Envy is very different. Those who envy either harm themselves or look for ways to hurt the object of their envy.[7] Sometimes both can happen at the same time.[8] Regardless, being emulated or envied is the formula for happiness.[9] In essence, the way your actions are evaluated by those around you determines your happiness. Without any feedback, it is not possible for you to decide if you are happy or not. "What will other people say" is a prevalent worry and not unfounded. It is likely that members of the early modern Ottoman society also experienced this anxiety. For them it was quite inconceivable that they would be buried in a cemetery other than the one where their ancestors were laid to rest.[10]

There is considerable literature on the psychological situation that I summarized, and this behavior is not learned; on the contrary, it is intrinsic to being human. Even if it changes its modes of expression according to the period one lives in, it endures. I will try to describe in this essay how, through horses, the people who lived in the period I study satisfied their need to inspire emulation and protected

---

4   In reality, even in social isolation you would be operating by these principles.

5   There might be no one who cares about you; however, since this is not acceptable, your mind will perceive this act of ignoring as either jealousy or envy.

6   For this reason, Tanpınar describes this act of ignoring as a 'assassination by silence'.

7   You might be curious about the barn fires that erupt in villages in the harvest season.

8   Niels van de Ven, Zeelenberg Marcel and Pieters Rik, "Leveling Up and Down: The Experiences of Benign and Malicious Envy," *Emotion* 9, no. 3 (2009): 419-29.

9   Were evil eyes who were jealous of you not the cause of your sudden headache upon your return from the wedding where you looked very nice?

10   In the early modern period where there was a responsibility of solidarity, the concerns about other people's opinions had other and more important functions, yet due to the subject, I did not mention this.

themselves from feeling envy. For this, unfortunately I need to use a more didactic style than I would like.

First, I must discuss the *bon vivant* (Ehl-i Keyif) that the lower class used as a point of reference to designate its own position. I will then consider mostly illiterate folk who were exempt from taxes, and elaborate on the limits of their worldview. After pointing to the connotations that the horse carried as a sign of privilege, I will complete my essay by discussing how the sound and the image of the horse were used in displays.

The Ehl-i Keyif Class

The study of horses in Ottoman history is, like in many other fields, aimed at mostly quantifying rather than understanding. If you are curious about distances across networks of communication or about horses used in warfare, you can get some information - albeit limited - on the number of horses and their cost/value. However, if, like me, you come up with a question like: "What meaning does the horse have in the world of those who pay taxes?" you find next to nothing, as it happens with most of the attempts at qualitative inquiry.

For this reason, to describe the issue well, we need to leave out the traditional scholarly literature on Ottoman history. According to the theory that Veblen developed for another cultural circle and time-period, the upper class follows a consumption pattern that will manifest its status. The main motivation behind consumption choices is, more than the benefit received from the product bought, the fact that it will be perceived by others as a sign of status. To maintain respectability, power needs to be displayed. Both the consumption of goods and how time is spent are reflective of the status of this class, and they are not necessarily rational; on the contrary, they are aimed at vanity.[11] I build this essay on the assumption that Veblen's approach is key for understanding the early modern Ottomans.

In the period we are interested in, this type of behavior is specific to dignitaries: the group that sets the norm, collects the tax income, and spends it. The rest of society is constantly striving to be included directly in this group or trying to get a hold of its symbols of privilege. The lower class that wants to emulate the upper class—to get on the proverbial bandwagon—imitates it and wants to blend into it.

---

11   Thorstein Bunde Veblen, *The Theory of the Leisure Class*, (B.W. Huebsch, 1912). I do not agree with the translators on whether the '*Leisure Class*' should be translated as the '*aylak sınıfı*' (idling class). It would have been a more correct choice to translate it as the '*Ehl-i keyif*' (bon vivant).

When the symbols of privilege start being used by the lower class, the upper class moves away from these and turn toward novelties.

Even though the upper classes, i.e., the ones who spend the tax income, try to protect their symbols of privilege, the demands from the lower class make it difficult to impose any such measures.[12] At this very juncture, the horse remained as a symbol of privilege that the upper classes could not abandon, and was also used by the lower classes due to the circumstances of the early modern period.

What I have so far discussed about the *bon vivant* also shows the limits of my essay. In line with the Central Asian nomadic tradition, our relationship with the horse concerns both genders; however, I deliberately left women outside of the scope of this study, as men follow a simpler and more predictable pattern of behavior in their self-displays when in pursuit of happiness. In a previous article I addressed the ways in which Ottoman women display themselves.[13] No doubt, women are inevitably included in the audience of men. Because I am primarily concerned here with introducing new concepts and approaches into the scholarly literature, my focus on the world of men has been inspired by their predictability, rather than their importance.

How the Illiterate See and Know

Nowadays, our relationship with animals has been reduced almost solely to entertainment and consumption. The species that have been a vital part of our lives until recently do not concern us much anymore unless they are wearing a collar or packed in a cooler at the grocery store. Within this framework, the horse for us is a creature without a function, the meaning of which is not even worth wondering about. Today, only field experts could come up with such observations as those that were once so naturally uttered by Halil from Kütahya or any ordinary subject of the Ottoman state.

In order to understand how much space the horse occupied in the minds of the early modern Ottomans, we need to talk about the elements that shaped their *Weltanschauung*. As you will see, all these elements were considered to be limitations.

---

12 From a cultural standpoint, the Ottoman example is a peculiar case, the lower classes being omnivores, and the upper classes being univores. The literature tells us the opposite. See: Danielle Kane, "Distinction Worldwide?: Bourdieu's Theory of Taste in International Context," *Poetics* 3 (2003): 403-21.

13 Nurcan Abacı, "Koca Olsun Bu Gece Olsun: Kırk İki Günde Üç Kez Âdet Gören Bursalı Fatma'nın Hikâyesini Kurgulamak (17. Yüzyıl)," in *Âb-ı Hayât'ı Aramak, Gönül Tekin'e Armağan,* eds. Ozan Kolbaş and Orçun Üçer (Istanbul: Yeditepe Yayınevi, 2018), 689-99.

To begin with, we know that they were not literate in the true sense of the word. Very few people could read, and this could be shown in a line graph that slopes down as we move from the center to the rural areas. Even fewer people could both read and write. They inevitably learned in visual and aural ways.

Furthermore, they had significantly shorter lifespans than our contemporaries. For the majority of the population, the world was limited to what they could experience, and the borders of that world extended no further than the shadow of the *minaret* of the mosque where they usually prayed.[14] Beyond this was the rest of the world. They were informed of this unseen place verbally, and their knowledge was limited to the place where they made a living.

It was necessity that wholly determined who knew what. Let me try to illustrate this point with a small trick: "I tied my *Equus ferus caballus* to a *Quercus*." I daresay that the popular folk song that starts with "I tied my horse to an oak" has, in this strange form, possibly alienated you. If you are not into taxonomy, this sentence will probably sound quite meaningless to you at first. Yet, if you are interested in the subject, you will immediately realize that the oak part is incomplete. This little trick stems from the difference between scientific taxonomy and folk taxonomy. In scientific taxonomy, oak is the name of a genus. It is technically impossible to tie our horses to an oak. We absolutely need to specify the species. "I tied my *Equus ferus caballus* to a *Quercus robur*" (English oak) would be a much more complete statement.

Halil from Kütahya could tie his horse with a black mole to an oak anytime he wanted or needed to, and he did not even need to know the species of the tree. If he was a casket-maker, he would immediately know the species of the tree and whether he could use it or not. If he was a shepherd, he had to know which oak species had the leaves most loved by his herd, because his sustainment depended on this knowledge. This personal body of knowledge, determined by necessity, shrunk the tangible world in size, particularly in settlements with small populations that could not foster a division of labor. To continue with the oak example, in a settlement where there were no carpenters, oak would be perceived as only a fare for animals and fuel for humans, yet in a place where people practiced carpentry, the word 'oak' could have additional meanings.[15]

---

14   A note for early modern Ottomanists: I am aware that this is anachronistic. The word *minare* has been used figuratively.

15   To give an example for what kinds of qualities people acquire by necessity, we can point to a primitive tribe able to see the lights of Venus with the naked eye, a quality that we don't possess in our present day and age. See Claude Lévi-Strauss, *Myth and Meaning*, Schocken; Reprint edition (March 14, 1995), 49.

For many generations, in a region where all sounds rang familiar for those who lived by rendering the unfamiliar world into finite set of concepts, the horse was one things that people commonly knew and ascribed the same meaning to. With the direct benefits it provided, the horse was a status symbol, having the attributes of both financial capital and social capital. Due to the nature of life in a centralized empire, it symbolized power and might everywhere. Halil from Kütahya and his contemporaries possessed a body of experiential knowledge that enabled them to figure out a horse's age from its teeth, and its character from its trot, even when observed from a distance.[16] If the social media posts that contemporary men share on various platforms are examples of genetic inheritance, one of the most important conversation topics among men in the early modern world must have been the horse.

A Horse is Never Just A Horse[17]

Thousands of cases of lost and stolen horses in court records can at first glance be perceived as ordinary ownership disputes. Ultimately, the property in question was not real estate and could move either on its own or with the help of others. However, what was lost and being pursued was not a horse but a meaning, albeit changing according to the time and place. Therefore, when Halil from Kütahya found his horse with a black mole on his neck that he lost two years ago in Iznik and retrieved it with a court decision, he was happy on account of two reasons: One that he himself was aware of, the other he did not know of, since it had not been named yet in that period.[18]

---

16   Depending on the lifestyle, this skill still exists in some circumstances. In a tweet by Yüksek, who shared the video that Halil Öz recorded, a little girl can keep the tally of goats in a herd and say their names one by one, showing that she knows each one of them individually. See: Özcan Yüksek, Tweet, February 28, 2018, 8:34, https://twitter.com/ozcanyuksek/status/968721003340877824. It is certain that in areas of limited botany, they were more informed than the present day.

17   I am not so sure about the pipe.

18   "Medîne-i Kütahya'da Sultânbağı Mahallesi sükkânından Halîl bin Nasûh nâm kimesne mahfil-i kazâda Mehmed bin Alî nâm kimesne mahzarında üzerine da'vâ ve takrîr-i kelâm idüp târîh-i kitâbdan iki sene mukaddem işbu meclisde mevcûd ve müşârün ileyhe olan alnı sakar ve boynu tarafında siyâh beni olan bir re's al aygır atımı Kasaba-i İznik Hânı'nda zâyi' itmişidim hâlâ mezbûr Mehmed'in yedinde buldum su'âl olunup takrîri tahrîr ve zikri sebk iden at bana teslîm olunmasın taleb iderim didükde gıb- be's-su'âl mezbûr Mehmed cevâbında zikri mürûr iden atı târîh-i kitâbdan iki ay mukaddem Mahrûsa-i Bursa'da Mehmed Beğ oğlı Hasan nâm kimesneden yirmi beş gurûşa iştirâ eyledim mârru'z-zikr at vech-i muharrer üzre müdde'î-i mezbûr Halîl'in mülkü olup mülkün- den zâyi' olduğı ma'lûmum değildir deyü inkâr idicek müdde'î-i mezbûrdan da'vâsına mutâbık beyyine taleb olundukda udûl-i müslimînden olup Kasaba-i Karahisâr'a tâbi' Beğ nâm karye

Until recently, in the once- Ottoman frontier region including Bosnia Herzegovina, there were Guslari, storytellers with ancient origin who narrated myths. These oral performers, narrating heroic tales with musical accompaniment in various gatherings, had become experts at improvising and changing their stories according to the expectations of their audiences, captivating their attention, whether they were Christian or Muslim. A perennial motif in their stories was the horse and its beauty.[19] Guslari depended on the audience's appreciation of the stories they told and therefore pointed to a form of happiness that everyone would most likely agree on.

As a means to satisfy the desire to emulate, the horse has no equal. This is due to both its features and the meanings attributed to it. Its predisposition to being trained and its ability to bond with its owner are some of its main characteristics that make it special. If it has a good relationship with its rider, the horse can become an extension of the rider's physical body. Thus, as you will agree, the horse that becomes one with the person riding looks more impressive in its trot, canter and gallop than a horse without a rider.[20] There are no distinct terms to describe the desired effect, i.e., a rider able to move together with the horse, which has become almost a part of his body.[21]

sükkânından Hâcî Emîr İbn Mahmûd ve Bektaş bin Ma'den ve İbrâhim bin Halîl li-ecli'ş-şehâde meclis-i şer'e hâzırûn olup eserü'l-istişhâd fi'l-vâki' işbu mec- lisde mevcûd olan alnı sakar ve boynu tarafında siyâh beni olan al aygır at müdde'î-i mezbûrûn mülkü olup târîh-i kitâbdan iki sene mukaddem mülkünden zâyi' olduğı bizim ma'lûmumuzdır biz bu husûsa şâhidleriz şehâdet dahi ideriz deyü her biri edâ-i şehâdet-i şer'iyye eylediklerinde ba'de ri'âyeti şerâyiti'l-kabûl oldukdan sonra müdde'î-i mezbûr Halîl'e zikri sebk iden atı âhara bey' ve hibe itmeyüp taraf-ı şer'iyyeden bir tarîk ile mülkünden ihrâc itmedüğine yemîn teklîf olundukda ol dahi 'alâ vefkı'l-mes'ûl yemîn bi'llâhi'l-aliyyi'l-a'lâ itmeğin zikri sebk iden atı müdde'î-i mezbûr Halîl'e teslîme mezbûr Mehmed'e tenbîh..." See: Nurcan Abacı, *The Ottoman Judges and Their Registers, the Bursa Court Register B-90/295 (Dated Ah 1081/Ad 1670-71, Introduction and Text (Entries 1-600). Vol. I,* Sources of Oriental Languages and Literatures 79 (Cambridge: Harvard University, The Department of Near Eastern Languages and Civilizations, 2007), 49.

19   See: Albert B. Lord, *The Singer of Tales* (Cambridge: Harvard University Press, 1960). A book that we must read both to understand the method he used to analyze the process of formation of Homer's narratives, and to be exposed to ideas on the formation and transmission of sagas in the rest of the Ottoman territories.

20   However, today, science still has not shown us how the bond between horses and their riders is formed. See: Martine Hausberger et al., "A Review of the Human–Horse Relationship," *Applied Animal Behaviour Science* 109 (2008): 1-24.

21   The functioning of the system depends on how much the method people choose for asserting themselves overlaps with acceptable norms because what lies at the heart of interpersonal communication is building consensus. If your behavior has a meaning for your audience, it will reach your goal. Non-consensus building behavior will be defined as

To understand this point, we need to talk briefly about the body. According to the approach I am using, we in fact have two bodies: Our body with physical and material needs, and our social body. Whereas the first one perishes when its needs are not met, if the demands of the second body are not satisfied, the principal outcome will be unhappiness. The needs of the first body are universal on account of it being a living organism, whereas the needs of the second body have to do with culture. Furthermore, the two are constantly interacting with each other.[22] What makes the horse much more than a mere beast of burden in early modern Ottoman society is related precisely to this perspective.

The animal we nowadays call by its species name—due to its diminished usefulness—held a much more special place in the early modern world. Whether the horse is male or female, its age, personality, and trot are characteristics that both its owners and those who look at it either knew or were curious about. A horse is rather pricy and difficult to keep when compared to its equals, the mule and the donkey. The most important reason why the horse was owned by those who depended neither on its speed nor on its role in combat was because it could serve as an instrument of self-display.[23] In the early modern world where literacy was very limited, the mechanism at work had to do with processes of seeing and knowing.

Hear me: Hoof beats as Personal Insignia

Although our ears are the same as those of the early modern Ottomans, what we hear and how we interpret it is different. In the present day, especially in cities, we are exposed to environmental noise whether we want it or not, and if there is no specific reason for us to focus, we constantly ignore this irritation. However, in the time period we are examining, the sounds around people almost always pointed to a live activity. They knew both how to discern a sound, and to interpret it in a

---

flaunting: Just like the youth driving around with their domestic brand cars. I think that all of us who remain outside of their audience are in agreement.

22 Mary Douglas, *Natural Symbols, Explorations in Cosmology* (London: Routledge, 1996), 69.

23 Calculations show that in the same period, the cost of horse care in Europe was three to seven times more than that of oxen. Even if we take local differences into account, there is no doubt that this was also valid for the Ottoman case. See: Clive Ponting, *Dünyanın Yeşil Tarihi*, (*A Green History of the World: The Environment and the Collapse of Great Civilizations*, Penguin, 1991), translated from the English by Ayşe Başcı-Sander (İstanbul: Sabancı Üniversitesi, 2000), 239.

cultural context.[24] In any case, they were not exposed to jarring noises that they had to ignore.

In early modern Ottoman society, people could, without hesitation, distinguish between animal sounds they heard from near or far. More than being an indicator of skills, this was a natural ability. A shepherd who lost his herd could follow the sound of bells and find the lost animals on the plateau where tens of flocks wandered and sounds of bells kept ringing. This memory of sound and skill that today only very experienced shepherds and some animal owners possess was commonplace in the early modern world.

There is no doubt that in such a time period, the emotions the horses' hoof beats evoked in those who heard them were different from those of today. What determines this is who hears the Hoof beats and when they are heard. For those inside a house, a group of riders galloping into a neighborhood in the dead of night would indicate a problem, whereas the sound of a horse approaching with an amble around sunset could bring the good news to a child of a father's return, after being out of town for business. Or, when a young girl walked to the water fountain, the clops of a horse suddenly going from an amble to a trot might have been the display of a known or secret suitor. All these sounds and their likes are sounds that we have forgotten, having no longer a need for them. However, they are sounds that our ancestors could *read*.[25]

As a result, it is not difficult to surmise that people used these sounds, and especially the sound of hooves, for their own purposes, and often consciously. Given that the horse is different from the donkey and the mule in obeying commands, you can use the horse as an extension of your body and practice self-display with the sounds of hooves. In this way, you can transcend especially borders of privacy that prevent oral communication. Even if the person you address is not interested in you or your message, they will not be able to avoid being exposed to it since they are endowed with the skill to read sound. As good readers of history, you know that I am limiting my narrative to cities, as the sounds of hooves are much more effective on stone pavements than on bare earth. For this reason, I did not feel the need for an additional explanation. The big picture and the interpretations are of course not limited to cities.

---

24 For a general summary and a literature review, see: David Garrioch, "Sounds of the City: The Soundscape of Early Modern European Towns," *Urban History* 30, no. 1 (2003): 5-25.

25 Nowadays I can say that the "youth going on gas" that I mentioned in the introduction have a similar skill. Between them, they can distinguish the sounds of their favorite brands of cars from a distance, even when the vehicle is not in sight.

See me: The State Always Arrived on a Horse

And it arrived in both of the commonly understood senses of the word. Because it is portable, the horse carries your standing with you anywhere you go, unlike, say, real estate which, as a sign of wealth, will only be seen and appreciated in a limited circle, in the region where you live. Moreover, in the early modern Ottoman society, real estate investments were not economically advantageous, as they were directly or indirectly taxed. Besides, a large house displaying your status could be a target for those who wanted to steal what you stored inside. For this reason, a horse that would carry one's reputation further was a more functional source of happiness.

A chief reason for the horse's privileged status was its function as a mark of social standing, as Guslari also mentioned in the stories they narrated. In the early modern period, the state exercised its authority through its officials and the privileges given to them, especially in rural areas. With the horse, this group would carry the ruler's authority to the farthest reaches. It is not possible to say that people liked these individuals who conveyed the requests of the rulers to the regions they travelled to – partially due to the abuse of power that increased in direct proportion to the distance from the center. However, this did not affect the horse's aspired status as an indicator of power. Both for those who wish to show off and for the audience, the horse was, beyond question, an object of desire and power.

Horse Ownership as a Status Symbol and the Pecking Order

We know that social structure is by nature multifarious. One person can be a part of different groups, or in time, can move upward or downward in social class. Within this context, no matter how idealized the typology is or how cautiously we need to approach it, we cannot deny the role of the political center in establishing social layers in Ottoman society. From the perspective of the Ottoman rulers, the stability of the social order necessitated that the ruling class and the subjects remained separate, with minimal mobility between them. Indeed, 17th century reformist intellectuals, while critiquing the poor condition of the state and its affairs, offered the following: "...In short, the *timar* holders have come to function as laborers"

"If the subjects get used to riding horses and wielding swords, they will grow accustomed and cannot go back to being mere subjects".[26] This is a rhetoric that both legitimizes the privileges of the ruling class at the top of the hierarchy and

---

26 Zuhuri Danışman, *Koçi Bey Risalesi* (İstanbul: Milli Eğitim Bakanlığı Basımevi, 1993), 7. Also see: Mehmet Öz, *Osmanlı'da "Çözülme" ve Gelenekçi Yorumcuları* (İstanbul: Dergâh Yayınları, 1997). Ahmet Kolbaşı, "Koçi Bey Risalesi'ne Göre XVII. Yüzyılda Osmanlı

explains why the rest of the public should stay socially immobile. When we think in terms of the Ottoman social structure, the center determines where the one stands in the hierarchy, and unless the center approves, it is very difficult to change one's standing through individual effort.

Let me bring up at this point the concept of the 'pecking order', a concept that I have not come across in Turkish publications, and one that I think is highly suitable for understanding and describing the Ottoman social structure. When zoologists were curious about the order in which chicks lined up, they discovered a hierarchy (that historians could also use). In every flock, the chick in front of the line could peck the ones behind it, and the chick at the end of the line could be pecked by all the others. The rest lined up between these two, according to various characteristics.[27]

The pecking order is intrinsic to winged animals, and it can only be altered by force and over time. In the Ottoman social hierarchy, the main arbiter was the state, and those who at birth were at the front of the line maintained this status all their lives. As for the rest of the subjects, if you want to be at the front of the pecking order, you have to follow one of two paths. The first is demonstrating that you deserve to be at the front. The second one is easier and more frequently used: Replacing the one in front of you by proving either directly or indirectly that they do not deserve to be there in the first place, and thereby moving up at least one level. The most effective way to achieve this is through gossip. The negative connotations of the word in Turkish notwithstanding, gossiping is an important information management system. All of us, in the framework of our self-interest, either hold on to what we have learned about others or spread it. This situation provides an advantage to us in accessing resources against our rivals. For example, according to evolutional psychology, the curiosity about the sex lives of others, a widespread trait in our society, either has to do with competition or because of partnership or kinship ties that make us interested.

When information on others obtained from various sources starts to spread, the truth of the information is less important than how it may advantage the gossip in

---

İmparatorluğu'nda Devlet-Halk Münasebetlerini Etkileyen Faktörler," *Sosyal Bilimler Araştırma Dergisi (SBArD)* VI/12, (2008): 125.

27   Edward T. Hall, *The Silent Language*, (New York: Doubleday, 1959), p. 63. Instead of widely used terms such as 'social structure'...etc., I think we should use a term like this. The original expression is "pecking order" and it can be translated literally as 'the order/hierarchy of pecking'. If we try to relay the meaning, we need to find a counterpart such as 'an order of seniority'. Bearing its catchiness in mind, I preferred the phrase "pecking order".

the social struggle. Thus, we harm our rivals or mask our weaknesses.[28] Exactly in the same manner, the horse obtains significance: due to the competition for positions among those in the back row of the pecking order. Because horse ownership itself is at the same time a marker of social status, the horse has to meet the beauty standards of the period Next, it is imperative that the harness and tack are selected with care so that they create the desired effect. All of the elements in question, from the criteria required to ride it to the stirrup, should have features that represent the status of the owner.

The care of the horse should also be done accordingly. So that the audience can fully recognize the status of the rider, all aspects of riding, from mounting to dismounting, need to be in line with an individual's position in the pecking order. Certainly, these were known by means of experiences passed from generation to generation, where gestures and expressions were learned through imitation. Since each of these aspects and accoutrements were obtained at a cost, it was the privileged who could afford to distinguish themselves from the lower classes.

For the rider who wants to display himself physically as well as aurally, the audience of this act is more important than the time at which he rides the horse. This is because he might as well not have ridden the horse if no one saw him. As the social body is constructed by the society, it needs an audience. This must have inevitably determined the time of horse riding, for the status is perceived only when its signs are displayed.

Instead of a Conclusion: Don't be a Showoff

Considering the rules of research, the most interesting part of the story of Halil from Kütahya, who lost his horse and found it two years later, ought to be how he found his horse and retrieved it. No historian who confines himself to the scholarly literature in Turkish will try to infer what I have discussed so far of early modern Ottoman forms of self-display based on the documents that I have transcribed in the footnotes. For we can find neither a sound nor the purpose of the horse-rider in conventional histories that have been recorded to fulfill a need. For this reason, we historians, owing to our conceptual shortcomings concerning the stories of stolen/lost horses (hundreds of which can be found in court records) always search for an external reality and cannot access the inner reality.

---

28 Additionally, we can assess the value of our lives by way of gossip. J.H. Barkow (1995), "Beneath New Culture Is Old Psychology: Gossip and Social Stratification," J.H. Barkow, L. Cosmides ve J. Tooby (eds.), *The Adapted Mind: Evolutionary Psychology and the Generation of Culture* (New York, NY: Oxford University Press, 1992), 628-9.

That is to say, the image that we come up with is the forest, and it saves us from having to count the species of trees one by one. As historians, nearly all the documents we cite are about singular trees and plants, from the cedar to the crabapple, that is to say, singular facts. So long as the documents neither mention the word "forest" nor foreground the forest as a concept, historians will continue to enumerate tree names one by one, as if they are suffering from visual, aural and spatial agnosia.

For many centuries, the ancestors of those who nowadays fill the streets with the smell of gasoline and burnt tires late at night, tried to display themselves with their horses in densely populated surroundings where the act of flaunting rounded off the edges of their characters. If we can describe the meaning of this self-display as a concept and demonstrate how it changes according to time and place in the literature, it will be a bit easier to understand both the past and the present. Horses are the embodiment of one soul in more than one body, and listening for the hoof beats, the sounds of the past, and asking the right questions by using the signs in the documents, will enable us to understand the importance horses held in our lives in the past.

Bibliography

Abacı, Nurcan. "Koca Olsun Bu Gece Olsun: Kırk İki Günde Üç Kez Âdet Gören Bursalı Fatma'nın Hikâyesini Kurgulamak (17. Yüzyıl)." in *Âb-ı Hayât'ı Aramak, Gönül Tekin'e Armağan*, eds. Ozan Kolbaş and Orçun Üçer, 689-699. İstanbul: Yeditepe Yayınevi, 2018.

———. *The Ottoman Judges and Their Registers, the Bursa Court Register B-90/295 (Dated Ah 1081/Ad 1670-71, Introduction and Text (Entries 1-600). Vol. I*, Sources of Oriental Languages and Literatures 79. Cambridge: Harvard University, The Department of Near Eastern Languages and Civilizations, 2007.

Danışman, Zuhuri. *Koçi Bey Risalesi*. İstanbul: Milli Eğitim Bakanlığı Basımevi, 1993.

Douglas, Mary. *Natural Symbols, Explorations in Cosmology*. London: Routledge, 1996.

Garrioch, David, "Sounds of the City: The Soundscape of Early Modern European Towns." *Urban History* 30, no. 1 (2003): 5-25.

Hausberger, Martine et al. "A Review of the Human–Horse Relationship." *Applied Animal Behaviour Science* 109 (2008): 1-24.

Kane, Danielle "Distinction Worldwide?: Bourdieu's Theory of Taste in International Context." *Poetics* 3 (2003): 403-21.

Kolbaşı, Ahmet. "Koçi Bey Risalesi'ne Göre XVII. Yüzyılda Osmanlı İmparatorluğu'nda Devlet-Halk Münasebetlerini Etkileyen Faktörler." *Sosyal Bilimler Araştırma Dergisi (SBArD)* 6, no. 12 (2008): 119-29.

Lévi-Strauss, Claude. *Mit ve Anlam*, translated by Gökhan Yavuz Demir. İstanbul: İthaki Yayınları, 2013.

Lord, Albert B. *The Singer of Tales*. Cambridge: Harvard University Press, 1960.

Morrell, L.J., Lindström, J., and G.D. Ruxton. "Why Are Small Males Aggressive?" *Proceedings of the Royal Society B: Biological Sciences* 272, no. 1569 (2005): 1235-41.

Yüksek, Özcan, Twitter message. 28 February 2018, 8:34, https://twitter.com/ozcanyuksek/status/968721003340877824.

Öz, Mehmet. *Osmanlı'da "Çözülme" ve Gelenekçi Yorumcuları*. İstanbul: Dergâh Yayınları, 1997.

Ponting, Clive. *Dünyanın Yeşil Tarihi*, translated by Ayşe Başcı-Sander. İstanbul: Sabancı Üniversitesi, 2000.

Veblen, Thorstein Bunde. *Aylak Sınıfın Teorisi*, translated by Eren Kırmızıaltın and Hüsnü Bilir. Ankara: Heretik Yayıncılık, 2015.

Ven, Niels, van de Zeelenberg, and Pieters Rik Marcel. "Leveling Up and Down: The Experiences of Benign and Malicious Envy." *Emotion* 9, no. 3 (2009): 419-29.

An Ill-Behaved, Illegitimate Son and a Tattling, Restless Soul: The Suicide Attempts of Deli Şaban[*]

Zeynep Dörtok Abacı

My soul, do not seek eternal life, but exhaust the realm of the possible.

—Pindar

Introduction

Man lives in the shadow of death and is destined to perish. Like all other beings, beyond reproduction and pleasure, survival is the most indispensable and powerful basic instinct. Trying to evade death and seeking the idea of immortality have existed since the beginning of human history.[1] For centuries, humans, striving to rule over their bodies and the environment produced various tools such as science and technology, and thereby tried to survive and thrive. On the one hand, the fear of death has rendered the struggle for survival affirmative and valuable. Vast constructions such as culture, ideology and the state have come to exist as a result of the complicated efforts of what is thought to be individual or collective heroic acts. So much so that without mortality there might be no culture and humanity.[2] However the human being, besides

---

[*]   Ankara, 1700

[1]   Freud even interprets religious designs that are narratives of the helplessness of humans when faced with an invincible nature and fate as coping mechanisms as an area of escape from the idea of mortality. See: *Uygarlığın Huzursuzluğu* (*Das Unbehagen in der Kultur*) 5. edition, translated from the German by Haluk Barışcan (İstanbul: Metis Yayınları, 2014), 17. For example, Malinowski, studying primitive communities in Melanesia and Australia, states that the idea of immortality has always been exciting, and for this reason humans have found a solution in leaning towards the perception of death as a door that opens to the afterlife. Bronislaw Malinowski, *Büyü, Bilim ve Din*, (*Magic, Science and Religion and Other Essays*. Glencoe, Illinois: The Free Press (Reissued Long Grove, IL: Waveland Press, 1992), translated by Saadet Özkal (Istanbul: Kabalcı Yayınları, 2000), 43.

[2]   Zygmunt Bauman, *Ölümlülük, Ölümsüzlük ve Diğer Hayat Stratejileri* (*Mortality, Immortality and Other Life Strategies*. Cambridge, 1992), translated from the English by Nurgül Demirdöven (İstanbul: Ayrıntı Yayınları, 2012), 17.

his ability to kill within its species as well as animals, is also aware of his ability to kill himself, even if this act is contrary to his nature and often prohibited by rules of faith and ethics. In this respect, we cannot claim that any historical period has been free of suicides.[3] Suicide is both a social phenomenon and a largely individual act: 'the worm is in man's heart. That is where it must be sought. One must follow and understand this fatal game that leads from lucidity in the face of existence to flight from light.'[4] For survival and persistence are sometimes subject to the judgment of the body and instincts, more than the judgment of the mind. As for suicide, it is a willful choice between life and death. Suicide as a social phenomenon is both simple and complicated.

There is an extensive literature of abstractions, theories, specific experiences, religio-ethical stances on and scientific approaches towards suicide that almost justify Albert Camus' quote: "There is but one truly serious philosophical problem, and that is suicide. Judging whether life is or is not worth living amounts to answering the fundamental question of philosophy".[5] In this framework, suicide is an act that, despite being within the scope of several disciplines such as psychology, philosophy, theology and sociology, no single discipline can exhaust studying it by itself, an act that is complicated to explain and explicate, and one that potentially can contribute to works on the history of consciousness and emotions. However, when it comes to the history of suicide, sources on especially pre-modern societies suddenly fall silent, despite the fact that it is not a completely modern question. In pre-modern societies where members of the community are not isolated from each other, and where interdependence and control prevail, is it possible to understand and analyze

---

3   In the saga of Dede Korkut this subject has not been glossed over, and there is a mention of sin and the suicidal desires of Cyclops (Tepegöz), the carrier of sin. It's as if the Cyclops, before death, confesses to Basat and reclaims its sins: "I made white bearded old men cry. The curse of the white beard must have done me in. I made white haired old women cry. Their tears must have done me in…" If we look at this statement, it looks like the Cyclops is aware of his sin and has an unfulfilled wish in terms of punishing himself. The Cyclops had tried to kill himself many times before coming to Basat. "I said I would stay in my place. I said I would break my promise to the senior Oğuz beys. I said I would break the newborn. I said for once let me take my fill of human flesh. I said let the senior Oğuz beys crowd to me. I said let me escape into the Salahana rock. I said let me throw heavy rocks with a catapult. I said let me go down and die with a rock falling on my head." The suicide wish of the Cyclops is really the aesthetic and logical end of this character. Kamal Abdulla, *Mitten Yazıya veya Gizli Dede Korkut* (From Myth to Writing or the Secret Dede Korkut), adapted to modern Turkish by Ali Duymaz, 2nd Edition (İstanbul: Ötüken Neşriyat 2015), 321-2.

4   Albert Camus, Albert Camus, *Sisifos Söyleni* (*Le Mythe de Sisyphe*, 1942), translated from the French by Tahsin Yücel, 15th Edition (Istanbul: Can Yayınları, 2010), 16.

5   Ibid, 15.

such an act that has been forbidden in the three monotheistic religions, one that has been characterized as rebellion to God that condemns the perpetrator to eternal pain?

In current times, no act or behavior specific to humans is alien to researchers. The focus of this current volume itself is Ottoman social history from the perspective of ordinary people. However, on the question of understanding the inner worlds, fears and expectations of ordinary people who work, produce and pay taxes, it would not be wrong to claim that we are still at the beginning of our journey due to both the quality of primary sources and the choices

FIGURE 2.1 - The hanged man and mourners (Acâibü'l-Mahlûkât, Fârisî Musavver, Ta'lîk 17, TSMK, Hazine 20, No: 404, vr. 88).

of subject matter by historians. The volume of studies on the history of suicide is relatively large in the West. Regarding Ottoman social history, however, suicide has been the subject of very few studies, focused mostly on the capital and in the 19th century.[6] These studies have inevitably utilized as sources newspapers, novels and documents of the Justice Ministry and the Directorate of Public Safety in the Ottoman archives. Through sample cases, as required by the nature of the issue, researchers have analyzed society's approach towards suicide, its causes and methods.

In this study, I will first analyze the failed suicide attempts of Deli Şaban b. Mehmed who was defined as 'an ill-behaved and illegitimate son', from the village of Miranos of the township of Murtazaabad, and *Sanjak* of Ankara in the 18th century, a time synonymous with crisis, depression and decline in Ottoman history. Following a multidisciplinary outlook, I will trace the effects of the dissolution or stretching of norms holding society together on incidents of suicide. Certainly, suicide has numerous causes that concern both the individual and the society. For this reason, in this study I will focus on one striking example but also include other suicide cases compiled

---

6   For historical studies on the late Ottoman and early Republican periods, see: *İntiharın Tarihi: Geç Osmanlı ve Erken Cumhuriyette İstemli Ölüm Halleri* (İstanbul: Kitap Yayınları, 2018); Rüya Kılıç, "Gerçeklik ve Kurgu Olarak Osmanlı'dan Cumhuriyet'e İstanbul'da İntihar," *Modern Türklük Araştırmaları Dergisi* 10, no. 4 (2013): 44-70. Nurullah Şenol, "Suicidal Tendencies: Culture of Self-destruction in Ottoman Society," M.A. thesis, Boğaziçi Üniversitesi, 2003; Nurullah Şenol, "Arşiv Belgeleri Işığında Osmanlı Toplumunda İntihar," *Toplumsal Tarih* 110 (2003): 52-5. Aslı Güller, "XIX. Yüzyıl Arşiv Belgelerine Göre Osmanlı Toplumunda İntiharlar," M.A. thesis, Ordu Üniversitesi, 2015.

from court records and will try to comprehend the motives behind acts of suicide as well as injuring and harming others in pre-modern Ottoman society.

The Ones Who Give Up Early

Certainly, anyone who commits suicide or attempts to has valid reasons if you ask them. However, in traditional structures that are characterized as a congregation, for the perpetrator's community, that is to say, those who are left behind, suicide is an act of betrayal, a crime committed against both God and the society. Those who commit suicide are ones who, instead of giving thanks to God, defy him, who, instead of working for the benefit of society, run away, give up. The attitudes of Christian (especially Catholic) and Muslim societies towards voluntary death are mostly similar: as set by religious and ethical rules, suicide is strictly forbidden.[7] During the first centuries of Christianity, there was a relatively indecisive approach towards suicide. The voluntary deaths of the Disciples were lauded;[8] the Christian moralists, while condemning suicide in and of itself, allowed one to kill oneself to escape from an unbearable fate in exceptional situations such as falling captive or being a victim of rape. However, after the Council of Carthage in 381, it became the norm to view those who kill themselves, except the lunatics, as hell-bound, regardless of the reason. With St Augustine's description of killing oneself as the biggest sin and his argument that those who committed suicide did not deserve to attain a better life after death, the perception of suicide as a major sin grew even stronger.[9] Until the 17th century, especially in Catholic countries, practices such as dragging the body of the person who committed suicide on the streets for humiliation, hanging the body and leaving it to rot, denying it a religious ceremony, and confiscating their property by

---

7   In principle, Judaism does not approve of suicide either. Even though in the Old Testament there is no clear statement on suicide being lawful or unlawful, within the context of the principle of preserving life, rabbis saw self-destruction as a wicked and detestable sin. Therefore, the ban on suicide entered the Jewish Halakha as well.

8   For example, the suicide of one of the Apostles of Christ, Judas Iscariot, is mentioned in the gospels: "When Judas, who had betrayed him, saw that Jesus was condemned, he was seized with remorse and returned the thirty pieces of silver to the chief priests and the elders. "I have sinned," he said, "for I have betrayed innocent blood." "What is that to us?" they replied. "That's your responsibility." So Judas threw the money into the temple and left. Then he went away and hanged himself." (Matthew 27:1-37, New International Version)

9   Georges Minois, *İntiharın Tarihi: İstemli Ölüm Karşısında Batı Toplumu* (*History of Suicide*), translated from the English by Nermin Acar (Ankara: Dost Kitabevi, 2008), 32. In the Christian faith, suicide is the equivalent of murder and the rejection of life, which is a gift from God; therefore, it is considered a sin.

the judiciary authority regardless of their will, were continued.[10] For this reason, the families of those who committed suicide insisted on alleging in court that they killed themselves due to a frenzy or insanity. In sum, the person attempting suicide had to risk being remembered as a sinning criminal if they were not successful in killing themselves, or a frenzied lunatic, if they were.[11] In Islamic faith, since the person does not have a right to destroy his own soul, entrusted to him by Allah, it is vital that the self, that is to say, life, is preserved. The prohibition of the act of suicide, or killing oneself (*qatala nafsuhu*) according to Islam, has first been supported by some *ayah*s: "Whoever kills a soul, not in retaliation for a soul or corruption on the land, is like one who has killed the whole of mankind; and whoever saves a life is like one who saves the lives of all mankind."[12] In this *ayah*, killing someone else is perceived to be the equivalent of ending one's own life. There are expressions indicating that suicide is a major sin in other *ayah*s of the Qur'an as well.[13]

The strongest evidence for the Islamic faith's perception of suicide as a fully prohibited act and a major sin is in *al-Nisa* 4/29: "O believers, do not consume your wealth illegally, unless there be trading by mutual agreement among you; and do not kill yourselves. Allah is indeed Merciful to you!"[14] In this *ayah* too, humans are advised to avoid behavior that will endanger their lives and lead to death.

Suicide is prohibited in the *hadith* as well. The emphasis is on the fact that the punishment for committing suicide will match the suicide method, and for all eternity: "Whoever throws himself down from a hill and kills himself will roll around in hell for all eternity. Whoever drinks a poison and kills himself will be

---

10   Michael MacDonald, Terence R. Murphy, *Sleepless Souls: Suicide in Early Modern England* (Oxford: Clarendon Press, 1993), pp 2-3.

11   Alfred Alvarez, *İntihar Kan Dökücü Tanrı*, 2nd edition, translated from the English by Zuhal Çil Sarıkaya (Ankara: Öteki Yayınevi, 1994), 51.

12   Surah Al-Ma'idah, 5/32.

13   As examples of ayahs that prohibit suicide: "Do not kill the soul which Allah has forbidden except for a just cause..." (Isra 17/33). "...and do not cast yourselves with your own hands into destruction" (Al-Baqarah 2/195). "And he who kills a believer intentionally will, as punishment, be thrown into hell, dwelling in it forever; and Allah will be angry with him, curse him and prepare for him a dreadful punishment." (An-Nisa 4/93). "And those who do not call upon any other god than Allah, and do not kill the soul which Allah forbade, except justly; and they do not commit adultery. He who does that shall meet with retribution." (Furqan 25/68). In these verses there is an emphasis on respecting human life as an essential duty and principle.

14   An-Nisa 4/29. However, as this ayah is on trade in general, we should keep in mind that there are scholars who indicate that it is controversial in terms of meaning and interpretation.

holding his poison in his hands for all eternity and he will drink from it in hell. Whoever kills himself with a metal instrument will stab himself in the belly with it in hell, repeatedly, for all eternity.'[15]

In Islamic faith, according to both religion and ethics, suicide of all kinds has been forbidden and defined as an evil act. The right to take back the life and the soul belongs solely to the one who grants them in the first place. However, while suicide is viewed as a major sin, it is not possible for the perpetrator to be ostracized from the faith or from the religious community. For this reason, the body of the person who committed suicide is washed, the funeral prayers are performed, and they can be interred in a Muslim cemetery. If the person who attempted suicide is not successful and remains alive, a corporal punishment is recommended.[16]

Regardless of faith, each society has a collective conscious and social tendencies that it reproduces by means of its own organizations and members. This structure is also embodied in suicidal tendencies. In traditional societies, as religious identity and consequently social integration are relatively stronger, suicide rates are lower.[17] The tendency to congregate was very strong in Ottoman social organization where a largely collectivist, social cohesion[18] had been ensured with religious, ethical, cultural values and norms as well as institutions such as the family, the neighborhood, the religious order and the guild. This was valid for not only the Muslims but also the non-Muslim subjects (*reaya*). For which reasons and under which conditions

---

15   Ebu Abdillah M.B. İsmail Buhari (ed.), *Sahih-i Buhari Muhtasarı Tecrid-i Sarih*, translated from the Arabic by Abdullah Fevzi Kocaer, II (Konya: Hüner Yayınevi, 2004), 718.

16   Hayati Hökelekli, "İntihar," *DİA* 22, (2005): 352.

17   Upon hearing the word 'suicide', almost all social scientists are reminded of Durkheim's work suicide, published in 1897 towards the end of the nineteenth century when industrialization accelerated, individualism was on the rise, and the negative effects of modern lifestyles were beginning to be prevalent. The studies in this field gained momentum after this groundbreaking work that paved the way to the perception of suicide as a social phenomenon. This phenomenon originated in the collapse of the relationship between the individual and the society. Durkheim states that as Catholicism, when compared with Protestantism, offers a system of wide dogmas and duties to individual members of its community. It therefore ensures strong ties between the faith communities, and because the possibility of losing this connection is much lower, in Catholic societies suicide rates are lower in comparison to Protestant societies. Emile Durkheim, *İntihar: Bir Toplum İncelemesi (Le Suicide: Etude de Sociologie*, 1897), translated from the French by Z. Zühre İlkgelen (Istanbul: Pozitif Yayınları, 2013), 395.

18   Nurcan Abacı, "Osmanlı Kentlerinde Sosyal Kontrol: Araçlar ve İşleyiş," in *Şinasi Tekin'in Anısına Uygurlardan Osmanlıya*, Günay Kut, Fatma Büyükkarcı Yılmaz, ed.s, (İstanbul: Simurg Yayıncılık, 2005), 101-11.

in Ottoman society does suicide occur, even if it is considered a major sin in the Islamic faith and therefore never endorsed in any way from the standpoint of ethical and cultural values?

Nowadays, suicide is linked to several psychological, religious, sociological and economic reasons such as mental illness, personality disorders, heredity, climate conditions, alcohol and drug addiction, culture shock, alienation, infatuation/love, bankruptcy, desperation and hopelessness. Suicide is the act of expressing how life has become overwhelming, and something no longer worth to struggle for. Despite how easy it is to define suicide as a concept, the situation becomes extremely difficult when the exact reasons are investigated. So much so that in approaching self-killing, psychodynamic theory centers on subconscious anger, cognitive theory on a negative outlook towards oneself, the world and the future, sociology on the social structure, and biology on genetic and biochemical diversity.[19] However, it is important to bear in mind that despite all approaches and theories, each suicide attempt has attributes specific to the person. In that respect, in this study I will first focus on the two unsuccessful suicide attempts of Deli Şaban. When the person is able to go through with killing himself, we can study the reason for his suicide through the statements and thoughts of the ones who are left behind. Whereas when the act is not seen through to the end, we can get information in a more direct way on the emotional state of the person attempting to commit suicide.

A Soul Captive to the 'Dark Triad': Deli Şaban

On March 13, 1700, a day in late winter that was passing to make way for warm and sunny spring days, Ibrahim Efendi b. al-Haj from the village of Miranos, of the township of Murtazaabad, and *Sanjak* of Ankara, filed charges at the court against Deli Şaban b. Mehmed from the same village. According to his claim, Deli Şaban was ill-behaved and an illegitimate son, and had along with his friend Kuşçu Mehmed (missing at that time) wrongfully and repeatedly reported the village community to the *ehl-i örf* (*subaşı* and *timar* holders), forcing them pay charges. Deli Şaban, five days prior to coming to court, had, with bad intentions, stopped by the village, and fought with the youth there. As was his custom, Deli Şaban set out to report the villagers to the *ehl-i örf* when the townsfolk caught him on the road to Kütahya, brought him to the village to be detained, so he could be tried by a court. While detained at the mosque, however, Deli Şaban somehow escaped,

---

19 Kasım Tatlılıoğlu, "Sosyal Bir Gerçeklik Olarak İntihar Olgusu: Sosyal Psikolojik Bir Değerlendirme," *AİBÜ Sosyal Bilimler Enstitüsü Dergisi* 12, no. 2 (2012): 136.

climbed the *minaret* and had been caught just as he was about to throw himself down, presumably to harm the townsfolk. The villagers later brought him to the house of Müderriszade Abdurrahman Efendi who would be present at the court.

At dawn, Deli Şaban jumped in the water well with the intention of killing himself once again, and when the townsfolk became aware of the situation, they pulled him out of the well. Consequently, the townsfolk present at the court—Hatip Mustafa Halife, Abdullah bin Mehmed, Seyyid Abdülkerim bin Kasım, Himmet Beg bin Abdülkadir, Receb bin Abdülkerim, Ramazan bin Satılmış and Mehmed bin Yunus—requested Receb bin Bayram and Ahmed bin Mehmed to be questioned about the status of Deli Şaban and Kuşçu Mehmed (missing). The Receb and Ahmet confirmed that the events occurred as told and affirmed Deli Şaban's 'misbehavior.' Furthermore, Deli Şaban admitted to having twice tried to kill himself. The court decided that Deli Şaban was to be kept prisoner until he corrected his behavior, and afterwards, would be banished from the village.[20] Based on a cursory analysis, we could say that Deli Şaban's hostility was either due to his inability to get along with the townsfolk or his ill will towards them, and that he tried to end his life twice due to a fear of punishment, a bout of rage or a feeling of being trapped. However, we will choose the more difficult way and, reading the situation more deeply, opt for an interpretation that will take into account more factors and possibilities.

Time and Place

Let us start off with the date of the incident: The record for the proceedings shows March 13, 1700. As for the suicide attempts of Deli Şaban, they would have occurred five days prior, that is, around March 9-10. Contrary to popular belief, suicides grow in frequency not in the gloomy and dark winter months, but in the spring and summer when serum cholesterol (lipid) levels tied to suicidal behavior such as violence, impulsiveness and aggression fluctuate. I can almost hear the reader asking: 'How correct would it be to claim this based on one document?' However, I want to point out that most (but certainly not all) of the other suicide events that we were able to glean from the documents happened in the months of March, April and July as well.[21] If the reader is still not convinced, then, since the issue has to

---

20 *Ankara Court Registers (ACR)*, 79/55.

21 For example, the suicide of Aliye bint-i Ahmed from the Akçakavak village of Bolu township, March 6, 1688. *Bolu Court Registers*, 836/31. As for Ayşe bint-i Veli from the Yenice Neighborhood of the district of Ankara, she hung herself on July 13, 1660. *Ankara Court Registers,* 46/149. Mezid bin Ali from the neighborhood of Arab Mescidi in the city of Karahisar-ı Sâhib ended his own life by cutting his throat on April 28, 1667. *Afyon*

do with our biological cycle, I would suggest that they review a few of the studies conducted on this subject by researchers from different disciplines, from psychology to medicine and sociology, supported by statistical data and empirical methods.[22]

Guided as we are by the historian's reflexes it would be fitting for us to look next at the setting. According to the document, the plaintiff, the defendant and the witnesses were from the Miranos (Orhaniye) village of the Murtazaabad Township of the *Sanjak* of Ankara. At the end of the 17th century, the *Sanjak* of Ankara had been divided into six *timar* regions and nine judicial sections. Murtazaabad, along with the townships of Şorba, Çukurcak, Bacı and Yörük, had an itinerant *qadi* system, rather than a settled one. The *qadi*s, instead of residing in one place, offici-ated while roaming with the *ehl-i örf* from place to place.[23] Miranos was one of the villages linked to the Ankara Kızıl Bey Medresesi Foundation. From the number of complaints related to property taxes, we can see that the village previously had a certain percentage of non-Muslim population.[24]

When we analyze the time and place together, we can state that the suicide at-tempts of Deli Şaban happened at the beginning of spring, in a period when after lengthy wars, the first territorial losses of the Ottoman State took place, in a region where *ehl-i örf* officials were trying to ensure public safety, and in a small village that was *waqf* land at the same time.

Interpretations for Me, Speculations for Others

The "Efendi" title in the name of Ibrahim Efendi bin el-Hac Hüseyin who appealed to the court as claimant and plaintiff, and the fact that his father was called 'el-

---

Court Registers, 509/50. Hüssamzade Osman Ağa bin Ahmed Ağa from the Debbağhane neighborhood of Trabzon stabbed himself while intoxicated on November 27. *Trabzon Court Registers*, 1865/6. Kefeli Receb bin el-Hâc Hüseyin from the Çukur neighborhood of the city of Ayıntâb attempted to end his life by stabbing himself on July 8, 1650. *Ayıntâb Court Registers*, 21/100.

22　For the breakdown of suicides taking place in Denmark, Belgium, France, Saxonia Ba-varia, Austria and Prussia between the years 1858 and 1872, see: Durkheim, *Intihar* (*Le Suicide*), 81, 82. For the connection between suicide attempts and serum lipid levels, see: Heon- Jeong Lee and Yong-Ku Kim, "Serum Lipid Levels and Suicide Attempts," *Acta Psychiatrica Scandinavica* 108 (2003): 215/221. Sandeep Verma et al., "Serum Lipid Pro-file in Suicide Attempters," *Indian Journal of Psychiatry* 41, no. 4 (1999): 300-6. Özgür Erdem et al., "Suisid Girişiminde Bulunma ile Serum Lipid Düzeyi Arasındaki İlişkinin İncelenmesi," *Düzce Tıp Dergisi* 15, no. 1 (2013): 41-5.

23　Hülya Taş, *XVII. Yüzyılda Ankara* (Ankara: Türk Tarih Kurumu Yayınları, 2014), 40.

24　Jülide Akyüz Orat, "Avârız Vergisi Üzerine Bir Çalışma: 18. Yüzyıl Başlarında Ankara Uygulamaları," *Uluslararası Sosyal Araştırmalar Dergisi* 5, no. 22 (2012): 229-30.

Hac', allow us to get a general impression of his status. While it is difficult for us to analyze conclusively the social status of titles such as *Çelebi, Efendi, El-Hac, Beg* and *Ağa*,[25] it is probably safe to state that Ibrahim Efendi was one of the prominent residents of the village. As for Deli Şaban, the defendant, he was a free male from the same village. If he were a slave, this would have been specified in the records, since it would have changed his legal status. We do not know his marital status or his age. However, given that he fought with the village youth and was able to harass the villagers with his actions, we can say that he was at an age of adequate physical strength and skill. The *Deli* (Mad) nickname before his name reflects his character as well as the impressions the village folk had of his mood. (In Anatolia, nowadays there are still nicknames that emphasize the distinctive physical traits of people such as "bald", "beardless", "hunchback", "lame", "cripple", "walrus mustached", "red-head", "the old man", "weasel", "rooster", "dwarf", "high-pitched", "jinn", "dull"...etc.)[26] Considering his acts, the nickname does not seem like an unfair attribution.

We see that Deli Şaban had on multiple occasions been defined in the documents, and not just by Ibrahim Efendi, as ill mannered, illegitimate, and a tattler. In addition, the report of his 'bad manners'[27] in the court by several people also reveals clearly how he did not have a good reputation and was not held in high esteem. Deli Şaban exhibited a personality profile that social values and norms could not condone, one that was far from the desired, idealized type of person (for men, performing the daily prayers, living a simple life, and inspiring approval and gratitude in the people they interacted with...etc.)[28] Additionally, along with his friend Kuşçu[29] Mehmed, he had for some time now gotten into the habit of

---

25 Güçlü Tülüveli, "Mikro-Tarihçilik ve Kaynak Kullanımı Problemi: Trabzon Kadı Sicilleri Örneği," *Tarih Yazımında Yeni Yaklaşımlar* (Istanbul: Tarih Vakfı Yayınları, 2000), 271.

26 Şeref Boyraz, "Lakaplar Konusunda Bazı Dikkatler ve Bir Yöre Örneği," *Türklük Bilgisi Araştırmaları* 7 (1998): 107-38. For the titles of Ottoman statesmen, also see: Erol Çağlar, *Osmanlı Lakapları* (Istanbul: Tuti Kitap, 2016), 19-179.

27 Ibrahim Etem Çakır, "XVI. Yüzyılda Ayntab'da Toplumsal Kontrol Aracı Olarak Mahalle Halkının Rolü," *Bilig* 63 (2012): 33-34.

28 Hülya Taş, "Osmanlı Şehrinde 'Mahalleli'nin Ortak Sorumluluğu Nasıl Değerlendirilebilir?," *XVI. Türk Tarih Kongresi Bildirileri* 4, no. 1 (Ankara: Türk Tarih Kurumu Yayınları, 2010), 535-7.

29 The Kuşçu (Birder) nickname, when used for ordinary people, indicates those who feed birds and pigeons, and who place bets as they force them to do tricks and make money. As we know of the existence of such people even today, the term does not have very good connotations.

attacking, fighting, as well as financially harming the village residents by making members of the *ehl-i örf* pay fines with false statements.

Now we face a complicated question: How can we explain the tendencies of both Deli Şaban and people in general who are in the habit of harming others knowingly and willingly, and who engage in evil deeds? Certainly, we can settle this question once and for all by choosing the answer that persisted from the Ancient Greeks to modern times in European thought: 'Man is evil by nature.' However, if a social scientist recognizes that this notion that some humans are unable to curb their animal instincts owing to their evil nature is in and of itself a cultural construct, he will turn away from this oft-repeated explanation.[30]

Then why does Deli Şaban constantly want to engage in evil deeds and harm others? First, we need to mention how he was not the only example, or an exceptional one. Every researcher who has dabbled in court records has come across these tattling and ill-mannered types.[31] Research in clinical and social psychology

---

30 For a well-organized source on the 'man is by nature evil' discussion, see Marshall Sahlins, *The Western Illusion of Human Nature* (Chicago: Prickly Paradigm Press, 2008). Sahlins in his work argues strongly that we cannot speak of man's nature as separate from culture.

31 If we still need to give a few examples: "Bi'l-fi'il Karahisar-ı Sâhib hamâ-ha Allahu te'âlâ 'ani'l-musaib mütesellimi olan kıdvetü'l-emâsil ve'l-akrân İbrâhim Ağa hazretlerinin taraf-ı şerîflerinden husûs-ı atiyü'z-zikre mübâşir tayin olunan Ali Bey Sincanlı kazâsına tabi Köni nâm karye sâkinlerinden Ramazan bin Söndek nâm kimesne Mahfel-i Şer'-i hatîr-i lâzımü't-tevkîrde yine karye-i mezbûre sükkânından el-hâc Ali bin el-hâc Mehmet nâm kimesneyi ihzâr ve mahzârında da'vâ ve takrîr-i kelâm edip mezbûr Hacı Ali salyâne husûsunda kadı ve bey ve subaşı benim deyip iki elimi akdedip asayla beni darb eyledi suâl olunub takrîri tahrîr ve terkîm olunması matlûbumdur dedikte gıbbe's-suâl ve akibi'l-inkâr müddeî-i mezbûrun sıdk-ı makalini beyyin mebniyye taleb olundukta 'udûl-i ricalden Sefer Bey bin Hıdır nâm kimesneler li-ecli'ş-şehâde Meclîs-i Şer'e hâzırân olup fi'l-hakîka mezbûr Hacı Ali karye-i mezbûre salyâne husûsunda merkûm Ramazan'ın iki ellerini akdedip kadı ve bey ve subaşı benim deyip asayla darb eyledi biz bu husûsa şahidleriz ve şehâdet dâhi ederiz deyi her birleri edâ-i şehâdet-i şer'iyye eylediklerinden sonra mübâşir-i mûmâ-ileyhe mezbûr Hacı Ali'nin kayfiyeti hâlî işbu hâzır-ı bi'l-meclîs olan karye-i mezbûre ahâlilerinden istihbâr olunsun dedikte İvaz bin Veli ve Es-seyyid Mehemmed bin budak ve Şeyh Muslu bin Amrullah Efendi ve Mehmet bin İsmail ve Hüssam bin İsa ve Durmuş bin Ahmed ve Musa bin Halil ve Hıdır bin Armağan ve sairleri cevaplarında fi'l-vâki' mezbûr Hacı Ali'nin beylerbeyi ve subaşı yanına varıp dilediğini gammâz edip hilaf-ı şer' mallarını ahz ettirir ve daima kâr-ı rüşvet alıp ba'zı kimesnelerin hakk-ı da'vâlarını iptal ve hedm ettirdiğinden ma'ada bu diyarda kadı ve bey ve subaşı benim deyi müslimûnu darb ve ta'cizden hâlî değildir ve kandi halinde olmayıp sa'y-ı bi'l-fesad-ı fi'l-'arzdır deyicek gafir ve cemaat-i kesir mezbûr Hacı Ali'nin su-i halini haber verdiklerinde mâ-vâki'a' hafaza li'l-makal ketb ü terkîm olundu cerâ zâlike hurrire fi'l-yevmü's-sabi' aşere min Zi'l-kadeti'ş-şerîfe sene sittûn ve seb'îne ve elf."

has shown that the tendency to engage in evil deeds and to harm others for one's own benefit is linked to certain character traits. Paulus and Williams propose an approach they call the 'Dark Triad,' and identify the darker character traits of narcissism, Machiavellianism and psychopathy as the likely sources of selfish behavior, superficial human relations, focus on self-interest and benefit, search for power and attention, social incompatibility, and being manipulative and goal oriented.[32]

Those who have darker character traits are narcissists. They aggrandize their own qualities and try to establish authority by disparaging others; as they cannot satisfy their basic psychological need to feel valued, and to compensate for this shortcoming, they seek power. Since they are intent on reaching their personal goals, they are prone to lying. These tendencies merge with the qualities of Machiavellianism and become more prominent. Machiavellianism, the strategies, tactics and points of view emphasized in Niccolo Machiavelli's 'The Prince', can be summarized as lying, cheating and deceit if need be, manipulating people and situations for one's own benefit, and engaging in selfish, utilitarian and cynical behavior. Psychopathy, the final link in the Dark Triad, is characterized by conduct such as unethical behavior, the lack of a pang of conscience, failure to build connections and show loyalty in human relations, incompatibility, difficulty in getting along with others, aggression and impulsivity. In people who tend to harm others and do evil, all or

---

Hacer Demirbağ, "509 Numaralı Afyon Şer'iyye Sicili'nin Transkripsiyonu ve Değerlendirilmesi," M.A thesis, Gazi Üniversitesi, 2007, document no. 5/12, 74-5. Another example is "Bozkır Kazâsı'na tâbi' Akkilisa nâm karye sipâhisi fahrü'l-akrân 'Abdullah Ağa'nın subaşısı ve vekîli olan Receb Beg meclis-i şer'-i hatîr-ı lâzımü't-tevkîrde karye-i merkûme sâkinlerinden râfi'ü'l-kitâb Enbiyâ bin Satı mahzarında takrîr-i kelâm idüp mezbûr Enbiyâ karye-i merkûmede sâkin Süleymân nâm kimesnenin 'avratı Hadîce'nin evine hıyânet kasdıyla gâyib-i 'ani'l-meclis olan 'Osmân nâm kimesne dâhil olmuş deyu bana gammâz eyledi su'âl olunub takrîri tahrîr olunması matlûbumdur didikde gıbbe's-su'âl ve 'akîbe'l-inkâr ve ba'de'l-'acz 'ani'l-beyyine istihlâf itmeğin mezbûr Süleymân'ın 'avratı Hadîce'nin evine hıyânet kasdıyla mezkûr 'Osmân dâhil olmuş deyu mezbûr Receb Beg'e gammâz eylemediğine merkûm Enbiyâ'ya yemîn teklîf olundukda ol dahî 'alâ vefki'l- mes'ûl yemîn-i billahi'l-'azîm itmeğin mâ-vaka'a bi't-taleb ketb olundu fî'l-yevmi's-sâlis min şehr-i Ramazâni'l-mübârek li- sene selâse ve semânîn ve elf." Ayşe Yürekli Tutar, "16 Numaralı Konya Şer'iye Sicili (1083-1083/ 1672-1673) Değerlendirme ve Transkripsiyon," M.A. Thesis, Selçuk Üniversitesi, 2018, document no. 103/3, 255.

32 Delroy L. Paulhus, Kevin M. Williams, "The Dark Triad of Personality: Narcisisism, Machiavellianism, and Psychopathy," *Journal of Research in Personality* 36 (2002): 556- 63. As an example of psychohistory in this framework of Ottoman historiography, see: R.A. Abou- El-Haj, "The Narcissism of Mustafa II (1695-1703): A Psychohistorical Study," *Studia Islamica* 40 (1974): 115-31.

some of these character traits exist in different ratios.[33] Anyone who reads this description may think they exhibit similar tendencies from time to time.[34] However, what is meant here is cases where the dark character traits (personality, disposition) dominate in a person and go beyond being mere thoughts, putting this triad into practice through acts and deeds.[35] For this reason, we distinguish between normal people and those with dark character traits by considering additional factors and indicators, such as open-mindedness and ability to accept criticism, extroversion, level of neuroticism, reconciliation and conscientious sensibility.[36] The science of history being what it is, we do not have the opportunity to perform personality tests on Deli Şaban to determine whether he carried dark character traits or not. However, the information in the documents affords us an inventory of his behavior—i.e., lying, not refraining from cheating and deceit, incompatibility with society, immorality, failure in building connections and showing loyalty to others, failure in getting along with others, manipulating others, aggression and impulsivity (impetuousness). And assessing this behavior based on the Dark Triad (a theory introduced in modern, even recent times), would not, I suppose, be called anachronism, as it aims at explaining a certain psychological case. However, borrowing this approach from the discipline of psychology can bring us historians one step closer to understanding and explicating historical events, beyond merely describing and narrating them.

Why did Deli Şaban attempt suicide twice? From the viewpoint of sociology, when a person's ties to faith, political class and family weaken, they feel alone, and their life can lose its meaning. Due to alienation, they feel on the margins of society, and thus isolate themselves from the collective consciousness and may

---

33 John F. Rauthmann, Gerald P. Kolar, "How 'Dark' Are the Dark Triad Traits? Examining the Perceived Darkness of Narcissism, Machiavellianism, and Psychopathy," *Personality and Individual Differences* 53 (2012): 888.

34 This situation is related to a behavior that is defined as the 'Barnum effect' or the 'Forer effect' in psychology. In 1848, the psychologist Bertram R. Forer, after administering a personality test made up of broad and ambiguous statements and features to his students, revealed that people, without realizing it, are inclined to perceive and accept even such broad and ambiguous qualities as unique or specific to them. For this reason, the Barnum effect or Forer effect brings fortunetelling and astrology to mind. Richard E. Nisbett, *Düşüncenin Coğrafyası* (*The Geography of Thought*, Free Press, 2003), translated from the English by Gül Çağalı Güven (Istanbul: Varlık Yayınları, 2005), 142-3.

35 Sharon Jakowitz, Vincent Egan, "The Dark Triad and Normal Personality," *Personality and Individual Differences* 40 (2006): 335.

36 Philip A. Vernon et al., "A Behavioral Genetic Investigation of the Dark Triad and the Big 5," *Personality and Individual Differences* 44 (2008): 448.

commit suicide.[37] Deli Şaban may have persistently attempted suicide due to social alienation, and the weakening of his ties to social and ethical norms.

It is also possible that he attempted suicide twice due to his fits of rage, despair, feelings of being backed into a corner and the fear of punishment. Some people may attempt suicide to show other people the difficulty of the situation they are in.[38] Maybe the suicide attempts of Deli Şaban were a cry for help. In the document, there are repeated mentions of his acts being intended to harm the village folk. Once more, we should not overlook the possibility that his goal was to arouse feelings of grief, sorrow or pangs of consciousness in those whom he wanted to accuse or punish.

Finally, in the context to Islamic law concerning *tazir* crimes[39] it was decided, albeit with the ambiguous stipulation, 'until improvement', that Deli Şaban would be punished with confinement, and due to his illegitimacy and tattling, he would be expelled from the village.

It would be useful to remind ourselves of the gap or difference between legal rules and their application: when the *şeyhülislam* and *müftü*s gave *fatwa*s and the *qadi*s made decisions, they used their own judgment; and all these aforementioned law officials belonged to the same cultural circles. In this respect we also need to answer this question: What kind of presuppositions inform the *fatwa*s issued in the cases of those who committed suicide or attempted it? For example, when we are dealing with the *fatwa*s of Şeyhülislam Ebussuud Efendi, the following lines on those who commit suicide stand out:

"The problem: Is it permissible to not wash the body (*ghusl*) of the person who murders himself, as a martyr?

The answer: He is not a martyr, as he killed himself, his body is not to be washed (*ghusl*)"[40] According to the Islamic faith, the survivors have certain duties and responsibilities towards the deceased. The rituals of washing the body (*gasl-ı*

---

37   Durkheim, in his categorization, defines this situation as selfish (egoistic) suicide. He also states that being single and childless makes the decision of killing oneself easier. Durkheim, *Intihar* (*Le Suicide*), pp 159-211.

38   Ernest Hilgard, Richard C.Atkinson, Rita L. Atkinson, *Psikolojiye Giriş* (*Introduction to Psychology*) translated from the English by Yavuz Alogan (Istanbul: Arkadaş Yayınları, 1999), 541.

39   Esra Yakut, "Tanzimat Dönemi'ne Kadar Osmanlı Hukuku'nda Taziri Gerektiren Suçlar ve Cezaları," *Türk Hukuk Tarihi Araştırmaları* 2 (2006): 26-9.

40   M. Ertuğrul Düzdağ, *Şeyhülislâm Ebusuûd Efendi Fetvaları Işığında 16. Asır Türk Hayatı*, 2nd edition, (Istanbul: Enderun Kitabevi, 1983), fatwa 858.

meyyit: each body that has fallen as a martyr in the battlefield needs to be washed), performing the funeral prayer, carrying the body to the grave and burying it are all *fard kifaya*.[41] Therefore, Ebussuud's decision concerning the body of the person who killed himself (even though we don't know to what extent this *fatwa* was observed in reality), means that one of the religious duties to the deceased would not be fulfilled, and merits analysis since it demonstrates society's negative attitude towards those who commit suicide.

There is a striking similarity between Ebussuud's approach and the prohibition of religious ceremonies and rituals for those who have murdered themselves, especially in Catholic countries in Europe until the 17th century.

What Can Other Cases of Suicide Tell Us?

Although suicide was considered a great sin in Islam and in no way condoned by ethical or cultural values, there were doubtlessly others in the Ottoman society besides Deli Şaban who were able to carry through the act of suicide to its end. In this respect, it is necessary to review other cases to discover the causes of suicide, its methods, and society's perceptions of it.

First, let us look at cases of women who committed suicide. Ömer Ağa bin Abdülkadir and Mustafa Halife bin Hüseyin from the Akçakavak village of the Bolu township, having found out on Wednesday night that their niece, Aliye bint-i Ahmed, had hung herself in the storage room of the house she lived in, requested the court to investigate case. The scribe Mustafa Efendi was sent for the investigation.

After the body was examined, it was confirmed that Aliye had indeed hung herself. Ömer Ağa bin Abdülkadir and Mustafa Halife bin Hüseyin had testified that they did not have any claims regarding blood money from anyone among the village folk.[42] In this example, there is no information regarding the reasons behind Aliye's suicide. The absence of a reference to a spouse in the document makes us think that she was probably single. It is hard to guess whether Aliye committed suicide or was a victim of an honor killing.[43] In any case, the goal of those who came to the court for the investigation, and of the village folk was, more than explaining Aliye's death or her suicide, to ensure that the event was not registered as

---

41   Salim Söğüt, "Ölü," *DİA* 34 (2007), 31.

42   *Bolu Court Registers*, 836/31.

43   For the status of women from the context of gender, see: Leslie Pierce, *Morality Tales: Law and Gender in the Ottoman Court of Aintab*, (University of California Press, 2003).

a murder, since their main aim was to guarantee an exemption from liability and the obligation to pay blood money.[44]We observe opacity with regard to deaths of women in various ways. For example, El-Hac Mehmed Ağa, bailiff of the governor of the Karaman province es-Seyyid Ahmed Paşa, called in to the court es-Seyyid Abdülcelil ibn es-Seyyid Ahmed, a resident of the Hacıeymir neighborhood of Konya, to ask him about the death of his daughter Alime. According to rumor, Alime had expressed a desire to go to a wedding without the permission of her father and es-Seyyid Abdülcelil had reportedly locked her home. She ingested poison and after three days, passed away. When the bailiff consulted the statements of the neighborhood residents on this issue, Molla Yakub ibn Hasan, es-Seyyid el-Hâc Ali ibn el-Hâc Mehmed, es-Seyyid Esad Efendi ibn es-Seyyid Mehmed Efendi, el-Hâc Mehmed bin Ahmed and others testified that no neighborhood weddings had taken place in the past fifteen days, that es-Seyyid Abdülcelil did not lock her daughter away, that the rumors of Alime poisoning herself were baseless, and that she had passed away three days after having contracted measles. Es-Seyyid Abdülcelil also corroborated this statement and indicated that there was no one involved with the incident (May 14, 1716).[45]It would be useful to touch upon a few suspicious details concerning Alime's death. First, a sudden death within three days of contracting a contagious disease such as measles is curious. Naturally we are not informed of Alime's general state of health. Maybe her immune system was weak, and she was feeble. However, even so, we know that after a person contracts the disease, the incubation period goes on for at least five to seven days. On the seventh through fourteenth days after contracting the measles virus, respiratory complaints, fever, and most importantly, red patches and a rash on the skin appear.[46] Besides, suspicious deaths and even cases of battery, wounding or illness warranted court investigation for the sake of people who reside in the same neighborhood or village, in order to protect them from litigation.[47] The investigation would record in detail the totality of the wounds and marks from beatings on the body of the person—whether dead, dying or wounded. Yet in Alime's case, neither her father

---

44 In the context of approaches to women's suicides, it is possible to come across other examples as well. See: *Konya Qadi registers 47 (1128-1129/1716-1717)*, İzzet Sak (Konya: Konya Büyükşehir Belediyesi Yayını, 2014): 454. I am indebted and thankful to my colleague Cemal Çetin who generously shared with me records on incidents of suicide that he came across while researching this subject.

45 *Konya Qadi Registers, 47*, 34-35.

46 Nevin Hatipoğlu et al., "Kızamık," *JOPP Derg* 5 (2013): 105-113.

47 Özen Tok, "Kayseri Kadı Sicillerindeki Yaralanma ve Ölüm Vakalarıyla İlgili Keşif Raporları (1650-1160)," *Erciyes Üniversitesi Sosyal Bilimler Enstitüsü Dergisi* 22 (2007): 331.

nor the neighborhood residents—at least according to the records we have—had requested an investigation. If the investigation had taken place and discovered measles symptoms on the girl's body, it would be possible to speak more clearly on the cause of her death.

Another noteworthy detail in this incident is who whispered into the bailiff's ear the story of Alime killing herself with poison after being locked up by her father. Was it the people who knew the "real" cause of death and could not carry this burden of conscience anymore, or ill-intentioned people who were the enemies of es-Seyyid Abdülcelil and wanted to harm him? Or did the bailiff El-Hâc Mehmed Ağa feel the need for such an investigation as part of his own meddling? We may never learn the answers to these questions.

Even in cases when the victim of suicide is female and so are the ones who provoke it, and those who want answers, the focus and scope of the investigation do not vary significantly. For example, Ayşe bint-i Veli, resident of the Yenice neighborhood of the Ankara District committed suicide by hanging herself. The mother of the victim, Şehriban bint-i Hızır and her sister Cennet appeared in the presence of Mehmed Çelebi bin Ahmed, Seyyid Receb Çelebi, Seyyid Bayram Çelebi bin Mehmed Dede, Mehmed Çelebi bin Mehmed Efendi, etc., and declared that they did not claim any blood money from the neighborhood residents. However, when testifying before the *qadi*, Şehriban and Cennet stated that the unlucky Ayşe had taken her own life due to the threats and bullying of some women, and that their plea had to do with these women (July 13, 1660).[48] How could the women whom the grieving mother and daughter saw as the cause for Ayşe's death have threatened and frightened her? Here the documents unfortunately fall silent once again. When we think about the circumstances of the period, the reason why the women around Ayşe were able to frighten her, so much so that she would end up taking her own life, probably had something to do with honor.

In a traditional society such as the Ottoman one, the psychological harm and stress that a tainted reputation, dignity and honor caused in women were naturally experienced much more significantly than today. As we see in this and in similar examples, the smokescreen over the deaths and suicides of women covered the truths and blurred them, in a way urging later historians to approach this subject with greater caution.

Regardless of gender, a common cause of suicide in Ottoman society was physical and mental illness. Those who are terminally ill might choose the path

---

48 *Ankara Court Registers* 46/149.

of suicide because they have no more expectations in life, or due to the pain they feel. Current clinical studies show that people suffering from ailments such as cancer, epilepsy or dementia appear 20 to 25 per cent more inclined to commit suicide than healthy people.[49] Consistent with these findings, historical court records include incidents of suicide due to epilepsy and madness (insanity) as well. For example, Mezid bin Ali, a resident of the Arap Mescidi neighborhood of Karahisar-ı Sâhib (Afyon), committed suicide by cutting his own throat due to epilepsy. His wife Ayşe, his son Receb, and his daughter Hatice reported that their father, while sitting in the house of their uncle Ebubekir in the Burmalı neighborhood, suddenly started having a seizure in mid-afternoon and cut his own throat with a knife. They requested an investigation from the court. Mevlana Seyyid Mehmed Efendi and Ömer Ağa, sent by the court to the location of the incident, entered the house, examined the body and confirmed the incident. Ayşe, Receb and Hatice remarked that they would not sue their uncle Ebubekir or anyone in the neighborhood. (April 28, 1667).[50]

In 50% of people suffering from epilepsy, the frequency of seizures and the course of the disease cause mental illnesses such as major depression, melancholia, and bipolar disorder. During the epileptic seizures, even though the symptoms may vary, there can be twitching of the muscles and the eyes, memory loss, foaming at the mouth due to muscles tensing and relaxing, urinary incontinence, and loss of consciousness.[51] We do not know the extent of Mezid bin Ali's illness; however, it looks probable that he committed suicide due to epilepsy or an accompanying mental disorder.

Suicidal ideation and acts are closely related to mental disorders. Schizophrenia, bipolar disorders, unipolar depression, borderline and antisocial disorders and anxiety are the major mental disorders as they relate to the tendency to commit suicide.[52] Clearly, we cannot expect to identify and categorize the aforementioned mental disorders in early modern Ottoman society. The documents cite as 'due to insanity' the cause of suicides because of any mental disorders. For example, Ayşe bint-i Osman, a resident of Konya Kerimdede neighborhood, finding the house empty, had committed suicide by hanging herself from the wooden beam behind

---

49 Marco Mulo, "Epilepsi ve Depresyon: Klinik Problemler ve Terapötik Yaklaşımlar," *Epilepsi* 18, (2012): 4-5.

50 *Afyon Court Registers* 509/50.

51 See Nevzat Yüksel, "İntiharın Nörobiyolojisi," *Klinik Psikiyatri* 2 (2001): 5-15.

52 Meltem Atay, D. Gündoğar, "İntihar Davranışında Risk Faktörleri: Bir Gözden Geçirme," *Kriz Dergisi* 12/3 (2005): 41.

the front entrance while her spouse was at work. Thereupon Mevlana Mustafa Efendi bin Hasan Efendi and the bailiff Mehmed Ağa from the court were sent to the location of the incident for an investigation. Other than the ligature marks on Ayşe's neck, no other wounds or signs of battery were found in any of her limbs. When deposed, her spouse Ismail, her brother Mehmed and her sister Eşe all indicated that Ayşe was 'mecnune' (mad or insane). Also, they added that they did not have any claims for blood money from the neighborhood residents (October 19, 1726)[53] As we can see, taking the conditions of the period into consideration, the mental disorder that paved the way to the suicide of an individual was usually marked as '...insanity.'

Substance abuse and excessive use of alcohol are other factors that increase the risk of suicide. When the person reaches a chronic level in alcohol abuse, nearly all the family, work and social relations break down. In this situation, the person who is deprived of social ties and support sinks increasingly into feelings of despair, inadequacy, detachment and loneliness. As it is, alcohol itself increases suicidal urges.[54]

Certainly, alcohol is forbidden for Muslims and has been banned by the religion, but this does not mean that there were no transgressors. In the documents we scanned, we have come across two examples of suicide due to alcohol abuse and intoxication. El-Hâc Ahmed bin Davud from the Hisayunlu neighborhood of Kayseri requested an investigation from the court after reporting that his son-in-law Seyyid Hamid bin Seyyid Ahmed had gotten drunk and hung himself in his room at night. Court official Mevlana Musli Efendi, bailiff Ismail Beg from the *sanjak* governor's party and other Muslims went to the room where Seyyid Hamid lived. Upon inspecting the body, they noted that Seyyid Hamid had blood on his throat, yet had no other wounds in other parts of his body.[55]

---

53 *Konya Court Registers, 47, 454.*

54 Bahadır Bakım et al., "Alkol ve Diğer Madde Kullanım Bozukluklarında İntihar Girişimleri ve Tamamlanmış İntihar," *Bağımlılık Dergisi* 8, no. 2 (2007): 91.

55 *Kayseri Court Registers*, 91/217. We can follow the post-trial developments through the records. Approximately 10 days after the incident, the heirs of the victim, Seyyid Hamin bin Seyyid Ahmed, his wife Havva bint-i el-Hâc Ahmed, and his cousin Seyyid Osman Efendi bin Seyyid Bayram Çelebi were once more present at the court. Despite the fact that the murderer of Seyyid Hamid, who ended his life by hanging himself, was unknown, Seyyid Osman Efendi accused El-Hac Ahmed bin Davud and his daughter Havva by saying 'You caused his death'. However, as he did not have any evidence to prove his claim, he offered an oath to the other party. In the end, with the arbitration of intermediaries, they arrived at a compromise for the price of 50 *esedi guruş* (piasters) and a purple baize fur. *Kayseri Court Registers*, 91/220.

In the second example, Hüssamzade Mahmud Ağa and Mehmed Ağa bin Ahmed Ağa from the Debbağhane neighborhood of Trabzon appealed to the court and requested an investigation after stating that their brother Osman Ağa had arrived in the house where they shared a yard in an intoxicated state, and wounded himself on his right thigh, his corpse now resting inside the front door. Mevlana Ahmed Efendi from the court went to the house with Ömer Beşe bin Abdullah and other Muslims. They saw a wound on the right thigh of Osman Ağa's body and a bloody knife with a white handle by his side.

When asked about the situation once more, Mahmud Ağa, Mehmed Ağa and their tutor Murtaza bin Abdullah testified that on the night of the incident, Osman Ağa, while facing the house, shouted threats and stabbed himself, and when they brought the wounded body to the yard, he died, and that they did not have any claims of blood money from the neighborhood residents. The mother of the suicide victim, Şükriye and his sisters Emine and Belkıs stated that Osman Ağa had a habit of harming and hitting himself while intoxicated, and on that night had killed himself with a knife.[56] In the first of the aforementioned examples, we see a *seyyid* committing suicide while intoxicated, and in the second one, someone from a relatively more renowned, upper class urban family doing the same. Certainly, we do not know the extent of their alcohol abuse and if they had other discernable mental disorders. However, especially in the second document, the statements of Osman Ağa's siblings, tutor, and in particular his mother and his sisters regarding his habit of harming himself while intoxicated lead us to think that sooner or later, they were expecting this outcome.

Instead of a Conclusion

In analyzing the examples of Deli Şaban and others, I attempted at psychohistory by presenting the psychological bases of the tendency of harming others and engaging in evil acts, and the reasons behind the drive to take one's own life. I offer my findings up for the opinions and critique of the readers.

Perhaps one of the most important traits of the discipline of history is the multiplicity of interpretations. Taking this trait as my point of departure, I tried to present the issue by utilizing a single document while every so often taking into consideration different elements, possibilities and viewpoints. In the cases I analyzed, suicide and suicide attempts (even though not expressed openly) were due to such reasons as honor, damaged reputation, physical and mental illnesses, alcohol abuse,

---

56 *Trabzon Court Registers* 1865/6.

and fits of rage and despair. It is known that women, as part of their constitution, resort much less frequently to methods of suicide that require physical strength, and especially refrain from those acts that damage the integrity of the face or body such as cutting themselves with a knife or jumping from a high place. The suicides of the women that I analyzed mainly involved hanging.

In the periods when poison was expensive to buy and not everyone owned firearms, hanging oneself was the easiest, cheapest and most accessible suicide method. For this reason, it is perceived more as a preference specific to the lower classes. Likewise, cutting implements such as knives, being widely available, were among the most convenient tools used for suicide.

In European Catholic countries, suicide victims were denied religious ceremonies and therefore were absent from church records. In the Ottoman context, because of the public oath, *kasame,* in the application of the Islamic/Ottoman penal code, people would be inclined to request investigations from the court for incidents of suicide, to free themselves of incrimination. In that regard, we are lucky. However, as research on the court records is done piecemeal, and not all records have yet been read, the issue of suicide remains a complicated one. Besides, it is obvious that we need to be meticulous in determining which of the cases of death presented to the court as self-destruction or taking one's own life were actually suicides and which were murders. Simply put, it is almost required that we approach the sources in a hypothetical way. Otherwise, it seems impossible to go beyond interpreting each suicide case as a single and unique experience.

Bibliography

Archival Sources
Ankara Şer'iyye Sicili, 79/55.
Ankara Şer'iyye Sicili, 46/149.
Afyon Şer'iyye Sicili, 509/50.
Ayıntâb Şer'iyye Sicili, 21/100.
Bolu Şer'iyye Sicili, 836/31.
Kayseri Şer'iyye Sicili, 91/217-220.
Trabzon Şer'iyye Sicili 1865/6.

Secondary Sources

Abacı, Nurcan. "Osmanlı Kentlerinde Sosyal Kontrol: Araçlar ve İşleyiş." in *Şinasi Tekin'in Anısına Uygurlardan Osmanlıya*, eds. Günay Kut, Fatma Büyükkarcı Yılmaz, 101-11. İstanbul: Simurg Yayıncılık, 2005.

Abdulla, Kamal. *Mitten Yazıya veya Gizli Dede Korkut*, edition, translated to modern Turkish by Ali Duymaz. İstanbul: Ötüken Neşriyat, 2015.

Abou-El-Haj, A. Rıfat. "The Narcissism of Mustafa II (1695-1703): A Psychohistorical Study." *Studia Islamica* 40 (1974): 115-31.

Alvarez, Alfred. *İntihar Kan Dökücü Tanrı*, 2. edition, translated from the English by Zuhal Çil Sarıkaya. Ankara: Öteki Yayınevi, 1994.

Atay, Meltem and D. Gündoğar. "İntihar Davranışında Risk Faktörleri: Bir Gözden Geçirme." *Kriz Dergisi* 12, no. 3 (2005): 39-52.

Atkinson, L. Rita. *Psikolojiye Giriş*. translated from the English by Yavuz Alogan. İstanbul: Arkadaş Yayınları, 1999.

Bakım, Bahadır et al. "Alkol ve Diğer Madde Kullanım Bozukluklarında İntihar Girişimleri ve Tamamlanmış İntihar." *Bağımlılık Dergisi* 8, no. 2 (2007): 91-96.

Bauman, Zygmunt. *Ölümlülük, Ölümsüzlük ve Diğer Hayat Stratejileri*, translated from the English by Nurgül Demirdöven. İstanbul: Ayrıntı Yayınları, 2012.

Boyraz, Şeref. "Lakaplar Konusunda Bazı Dikkatler ve Bir Yöre Örneği." *Türklük Bilgisi Araştırmaları* 7 (1998): 107-38.

Buharî. Ebu Abdillah M.B. İsmail (ed.), *Sahih-i Buhari Muhtasarı Tecrid-i Sarih*, translated by Abdullan Fevzi Kocaer, II. Konya: Hüner Yayınevi, 2004.

Camus, Albert. *Sisifos Söyleni*, translated from the French by Tahsin Yücel, 15. edition. İstanbul: Can Yayınları, 2010.

Çağlar, Erol. *Osmanlı Lakapları*. İstanbul: Tuti Kitap, 2016.

Çakır, İbrahim, Etem. "XVI.Yüzyılda Ayntab'da Toplumsal Konrol Aracı Olarak Mahalle Halkının Rolü." *Bilig* 6 (2012): 31-54.

Demirbağ, Hacer. "509 Numaralı Afyon Şer'iyye Sicili'nin Transkripsiyonu ve Değerlendirilmesi." M.A. Thesis, Gazi Üniversitesi, 2007.

Durkheim, Emile. *İntihar: Bir Toplum İncelemesi*, translated from the English by Z. Zühre İlkgelen. İstanbul: Pozitif Yayınları, 2013.

Düzdağ M. Ertuğrul. *Şeyhülislâm Ebusuûd Efendi Fetvaları Işığında 16. Asır Türk Hayatı*, 2. edition. İstanbul: Enderun Kitabevi, 1983.

Erdem, Özgür et al. "Suisid Girişiminde Bulunma ile Serum Lipid Düzeyi Arasındaki İlişkinin İncelenmesi." *Düzce Tıp Dergisi* 15, no. 1 (2013): 41-5.

Freud, Sigmund. *Uygarlığın Huzursuzluğu*, 5. edition, translated from the German by Haluk Barışcan. İstanbul: Metis Yayınları, 2014.

Güller, Aslı. "XIX. Yüzyıl Arşiv Belgelerine Göre Osmanlı Toplumunda İntiharlar." M.A. Thesis, Ordu Üniversitesi, 2015.

Hatipoğlu, Nevin et al. "Kızamık." *JOPP Derg* 5 (2013): 105-13.

Hökelekli, Hayati. "İntihar." *DİA* 22 (2005): 351-3.

Jakowitz, Sharon and Vincent Egan. "The Dark Triad and Normal Personality." *Personality and Individual Differences* 40 (2006): 331-9.

Kılıç, Rüya. "Gerçeklik ve Kurgu Olarak Osmanlı'dan Cumhuriyet'e İstanbul'da İntihar." *Modern Türklük Araştırmaları Dergisi* 10, no. 4 (2013): 44-70.

———. *İntiharın Tarihi: Geç Osmanlı ve Erken Cumhuriyette İstemli Ölüm Halleri.* İstanbul: Kitap Yayınları, 2018.

Konya Kadı Sicili 47 (1128-1129/1716-1717). ed. İzzet Sak. Konya: Konya Büyükşehir Belediyesi Yayını, 2014.

Lee Heon-Jeong and Kim Yong-Ku. "Serum Lipid Levels and Suicide Attempts." *Acta Psychiatrica Scandinavica* 108 (2003): 215-221.

MacDonald, Michael and R. Terence Murphy. *Sleepless Souls: Suicide in Early Modern England.* Oxford: Clarendon Yayınları, 1993.

Malinowski, Bronislaw. *Büyü, Bilim ve Din*, 2. edition, translated from the English by Saadet Özkal. İstanbul: Kabalcı Yayınları, 2000.

Minois, Georges. *İntiharın Tarihi: İstemli Ölüm Karşısında Batı Toplumu*, translated by Nermin Acar. Ankara: Dost Kitabevi, 2008.

Mulo, Marco. "Epilepsi ve Depresyon: Klinik Problemler ve Terapötik Yaklaşımlar." *Epilepsi* 18 (2012): 4-5.

Nisbett, E. Richard. *Düşüncenin Coğrafyası*, translated from the English by Gül Çağalı Güven. İstanbul: Varlık Yayınları, 2005.

Orat Akyüz, Jülide. "Avarız Vergisi Üzerine Bir Çalışma: 18. Yüzyıl Başlarında Ankara Uygulamaları." *Uluslararası Sosyal Araştırmalar Dergisi* 5, no. 22 (2012): 219-32.

Paulhus, L. Delroy and M. Kevin Williams. "The Dark Tirad of Personality: Narcisisism, Machiavellianism, and Psychopathy." *Journal of Research in Personality* 36 (2002): 560-3.

Pierce, Leslie. *Ahlak Oyunları: 1540-1541 Osmanlı'da Ayntab Mahkemesi ve Toplumsal Cinsiyet*, translated from the English by Ülkün Tansel. İstanbul: Tarih Vakfı Yurt Yayınları, 2005.

Rauthmann, F. John and Kolar P. Gerald. "How 'Dark' Are the Dark Triad Traits? Examining the Perceived Darkness of Narcissism, Machiavellianism, and Psychopathy." *Personality and Individual Differences* 53 (2012): 884-9.

Sahlins, Marshall. *Batı'nın İnsan Doğası Yanılsaması*, translated from the English by Zeynep Demirsü and Emine Ayhan. İstanbul: BGST Yayınları, 2012.

Söğüt, Salim. "Ölü." *DİA* 34 (2007): 31-32.

Şenol, Nurullah. "Arşiv Belgeleri Işığında Osmanlı Toplumunda İntihar." *Toplumsal Tarih* 110 (2003): 52-5.

————. 2003. "Suicidal Tendencies: Culture of Self-destruction in Ottoman Society." M.A. Thesis, Boğaziçi Üniversitesi.

Taş, Hülya. "Osmanlı Şehrinde 'Mahalleli'nin Ortak Sorumluluğu Nasıl Değerlendirilebilir?" *XVI. Türk Tarih Kongresi Bildirileri* 4, no. 1, 535-43. Ankara: Türk Tarih Kurumu Yayınları, 2010.

————. *XVII. Yüzyılda Ankara*, Ankara: Türk Tarih Kurumu Yayınları, 2014.

Tatlılıoğlu, Kasım. "Sosyal Bir Gerçeklik Olarak İntihar Olgusu: Sosyal Psikolojik Bir Değerlendirme." *AİBÜ Sosyal Bilimler Enstitüsü Dergisi* 12, no. 2 (2012): 135-58.

Tok, Özen. "Kayseri Kadı Sicillerindeki Yaralanma ve Ölüm Vakalarıyla İlgili Keşif Raporları (1650-1660)." *Erciyes Üniversitesi Sosyal Bilimler Enstitüsü Dergisi* 22(2007): 327-47.

Tutar Yürekli, Ayşe. "16 Numaralı Konya Şer'iye Sicili (1083-1083/1672-1673) Değerlendirme ve Transkripsiyon." M.A. Thesis, Selçuk Üniversitesi, 2018.

Tülüveli, Güçlü. "Mikro-Tarihçilik ve Kaynak Kullanımı Problemi: Trabzon Kadı Sicilleri Örneği." *Tarih Yazımında Yeni Yaklaşımlar*, İstanbul: Tarih Vakfı Yayınları, 2000: 271-87.

Verma, Sandeep et al. "Serum Lipid Profile in Suicide Attempters." *Indian Journal of Psychiatry* 41, no. 4 (1999): 300-6.

Vernon, Philip A. et al. "A Behavioral Genetic Investigation of the Dark Triad and the Big 5." *Personality and Individual Differences* 44 (2008): 445-52.

Yakut, Esra. "Tanzimat Dönemi'ne Kadar Osmanlı Hukuku'nda Taziri Gerektiren Suçlar ve Cezaları." *Türk Hukuk Tarihi Araştırmaları* 2 (2006): 25-40.

Yüksel, Nevzat. "İntiharın Nörobiyolojisi." *Klinik Psikiyatri* 2 (2001): 5-15.

CHAPTER THREE

From the Marshes to the Qadi's Court: The Trials and Tribulations of a Village with Divane Hamza*

Fırat Yaşa

Introduction

In the period between 1577 and 1590, while the Ottoman Empire initiated a series of conflicts with Iran in the East, there was an increase in various forms of illegal activities amongst ordinary people in Bursa, as in many different regions of Anatolia. At such times, the social control networks would be more fragile, and discipline and public order would be prey to corruption. Protracted wars meant worsening living conditions for the villagers. Usually, ordinary people would be the ones most affected by wars, natural disasters, economic crises, and famines. In 16th century Bursa, when common people did not utilize currency, transactions continued to be in kind, as in other regions of the empire. The villagers who were obligated to work the soil would give part of the crop they produced to the *timar* holder as *öşür* (tithe), and the *timar* holder would in turn feed the armed soldiers called '*cebelü*'.[1] *Cebe/cebelü* soldiers lived in many villages. Hamza, a soldier and the subject of this study, was part of the *timar* system as well.

Hamza lived in Bursa's Evciler village. In the 1521 census register, this village was listed among the *waqf* villages during the reign of Murad II; however, the number of households in the village was not specified in the census. In 1573, seven years before Hamza was tried in the *qadi*'s court, a new census was done. This census declared that there were five households in the village.[2] When we take into

---

*   Bursa, 1580

1   Feridun Emecen, "Cebelü," *DİA* 7 (1993): 189. For the *timar* system see Halil İnalcık, "Timar," *The Encyclopaedia of Islam* 10 (2000): 502-7; Douglas Arthur Howard, "The Ottoman Timar System and its Transformation, 1563-1656," Ph.D. dissertation, Indiana University, 1989.

2   Raif Kaplanoğlu, "Tahrir Defterlerine Göre Sultan II. Murad'ın Bursa Vakfı Köyleri," in *Sultan II. Murad ve Dönemi*, ed. Ismail Yaşayanlar (Bursa: Gaye Kitapevi, 2015), 509.

FIGURE 3.1 A section of the map for the Hüdavendigâr County. *166 Numaralı Muhâsebe-i Vilâyet-i Anadolu Defteri (937/1530).* Eds. A. Özkılınç et al. (Ankara: T.C. Başbakanlık Devlet Arşivleri Genel Müdürlüğü Osmanlı Arşivi Daire Başkanlığı Yayınları, 1995).

consideration that an average of four or five individuals lived in each household,[3] we can say that there were approximately twenty to twenty-five people who lived in the Evciler village in 1573. After seven years, with the new marriages, the number of households in the village must have increased to eight or nine.

As seen on the map, the village was quite distant from the center of Bursa. In Bursa, as in the rest of the empire, no institutional building housed the court, and the *qadi*'s residence was used as the courthouse. Towards the end of the 16th century, the *qadi*'s court was in the city center where the Ulu Camii, Covered Bazaar and commercial buildings were also located.[4] The circumstances of the period meant that the distance between the Evciler village and the *qadi*'s residence could not be covered in a single day. This then made access to the court relatively difficult.[5]

3   Nejat Göyünç, "Hane Deyimi Hakkında," *Istanbul Üniversitesi Edebiyat Fakültesi Tarih Dergisi* 32, (1979): 346.

4   Özer Ergenç states that the *qadi* resided in the Ibrahim Paşa neighborhood, and that the Ibrahim Paşa bathhouse was recorded as a neighborhood bathhouse in the registries. Özer Ergenç, *16. Yüzyıl Sonlarında Bursa* (Ankara: Türk Tarih Kurumu, 2014), 31.

5   For the concept of distance see Cemal Çetin, "Osmanlılarda Mesafe Ölçümü ve Tarihî Süreci," in *Tarihçiliğe Adanmış Bir Ömür Prof. Dr. Nejat Göyünç'e Armağan,* eds. Hasan Bahar et al. (Konya: Selçuk Üniversitesi Türkiyat Araştırmaları Enstitüsü, 2013), 443-66.

Hamza was born in Evciler village. He was a single man and probably lived with his parents. In the court records, Hamza's mother's name is not mentioned at all, and only once it is mentioned that he was the son of Dedebali. Later he was registered in the records with the nickname 'Divane' (Mad). It is certain that the villagers did not call him Divane, at least, not to his face. He had no other titles such as *Çelebi, Efendi, Ağa, El-Hâc, Seyyid* or *Şeyh*. Due to his crimes, the scribes had registered the nickname 'Divane' next to his name in the records.

The *qadi* wanted to put Hamza on trial because of the many complaints against him. For a long time, however, it remained impossible to apprehend him. Ultimately, following his final crime, Hamza was caught in the marshes where he was hiding. The inhabitants of Evciler village breathed a sigh of relief and started one after another to head for the court. Each one wanted to show up as a witness to the crimes Hamza had committed, to voice complaints and to claim their rights. In this way, they would prevent Hamza from returning to the village, for the only way to ensure peace in the village was to get rid of him.

Dancing with Fire: Hamza and the Villagers

The autumn months of 1580 also happened to be the end of the three holy months for Muslims. The months of *Rajab* and *Shaban* had passed, and *Ramadan* had arrived. Throughout the empire, in all the Muslim neighborhoods and villages, people fasted and waited for *Eid*, the religious festival. In times like these, the workload of the courts lightened[6] since incidents such as beatings, thefts, rapes and fornication would decrease in frequency. In Evciler, however, the situation was somewhat different since Hamza was intent on denying the villagers any relief.

One evening, during the *tarawih* prayer, Hamza broke into the village mosque. He beat to death a man called Ali from the village congregation. Neither the full identity of this man nor the type of enmity between him and Hamza were known. While the villagers stopped praying and fled in fear, they did not even think of saving Ali. Out of a fear of Hamza, they avoided going back into the mosque. After Hamza was arrested, they made their report in the presence of the *qadi*.[7]

The mosque attack was not the only crime Hamza committed. Earlier, he had secretly entered the house of Oruç bin Yusuf, one of the village inhabitants. He

---

6   Ümit Ekin, "17. Yüzyılın Son Çeyreğinde Rodosçuk Örneğinde Bir Osmanlı Mahkemesinin İş Yükü," *Ankara Üniversitesi Dil ve Tarih-Coğrafya Fakültesi Dergisi* 55, no. 1 (2015): 291.

7   *Bursa Court Records (BCR)*, A 119, 170.

FIGURE 3.2 A Woman and man caught by the officers (Ahmed I Album, TSMK, B. 408).

probably intended to rape Oruç's wife. To avoid being caught, Hamza had jumped out of the window and fled. Oruç bin Yusuf heard this incident from his wife and other women in the village and requested the court to punish Hamza for attempting to taint his honor. Hamza, accused of committing such a serious crime, naturally denied it. The crime needed to be proven. The *qadi,* in line with Islamic jurisprudence, could not punish Hamza without the necessary evidence (*beyyine*). Some of the villagers testified: 'We heard it as such from those present in the village and from our wives, however, we did not see anything'.[8] Because the witnesses were acting on hearsay, the case could not be concluded in favor of the plaintiffs. In such situations, the oath of the woman as the victim of attempted rape and the opinions of the neighbors and villagers could have been effective.[9] It is curious that the *qadi* neither asked for the neighbors' opinions of Hamza, nor did he request an oath from the woman whom he tried to rape. Under normal circumstances, the

---

8   BCR, A 119, 169.

9   Zübeyde Güneş Yağcı, "Osmanlı Taşrasında Kadınlara Yönelik Cinsel Suçlarda Adalet Arama Geleneği," *Kadın Araştırmaları Dergisi* 4, no. 2 (2005): 51-81.

ones who serve the state like Hamza would be punished with a minimum of five years of hard labor.[10]

Hamza was known to be a member of the cavalry and a gunner and had various 'military equipment' in his possession. He was therefore able to intimidate the villagers easily, and to gain more and more power. He made friends from the surrounding villages who, like him, were renegades. He almost became their leader. Starting with Hamza, Evciler and the surrounding villages soon became the target of small acts of banditry in 1580. Was Hamza the first of his kind or not? This can be determined by examining the court records to identify whether other people engaged in similar acts. Nevertheless, it was apparent that he abused his position and spread terror in the Evciler village.

There were many reasons for why the *Sipahi*, cavalry and gunners who actively worked in the provinces, resorted to banditry instead of ensuring order in their area, as was expected of them. Lengthy wars played a large role. Besides, naval infantry running rampant, famine, drought and natural disasters also played a role in the escalation of acts of banditry.[11] It would be simplistic to try to tie the acts of individuals like Hamza to a single cause. Researchers state that a multitude of factors from changes in government to the changes in climate affect peoples' lives in direct or indirect ways, and that bandits usually appear in such instances.[12] Some of the members of the military with titles such as *sipahi*, cavalry or gunner would join the army, but some of them would remain in the villages. This situation paved the way to the emergence of petty bandits such as Hamza.

We cannot overlook the role of the circumstances on the ground in aiding Hamza's illegal acts. In Bursa, government officials such as the *qadi* and the *subaşı* who were tasked with maintaining social order were rather distant from the Evciler village. To

---

10   Dror Ze'evi, "Changes in Legal-Sexual Discourses: Sex Crimes in the Ottoman Empire," *Continuity and Change* 16, no. 2 (2001): 237.

11   In the early modern period, the bandits in Ottoman society have been the subjects of various studies. For some of these see Mustafa Akdağ, *Türk Halkının Dirlik ve Düzenlik Kavgası Celâlî İsyanları* (İstanbul: Yapı Kredi Yayınları, 2013); Karen Barkey, *Bandits and Bureaucrats The Ottoman Route to State Cantralization* (New York: Cornell University Press, 1994). It is also known that in the beginning of the seventeenth century bandits on a small scale appeared in Bursa and increased in number towards the middle of the century. Tahsin Şahin, "Celali Kuşatması Altında Bursa," M.A. Thesis, Uludağ Üniversitesi 2017, 37, 60.

12   The following sources can be consulted on the subject: Sam White, *The Climate of Rebellion in the Early Modern Ottoman Empire* (Cambridge, New York, Melbourne: Cambridge University Press, 2011); Zafer Karademir, *İmparatorluğun Açlıkla İmtihanı: Osmanlı Toplumunda Kıtlıklar (1560-1660)* (İstanbul: Kitap Yayınevi, 2014).

a certain extent, the distance from the court expanded Hamza's range of movement. Even if complaints were made against him, he needed to be caught first before he could be tried. Arresting Hamza and those from the military who gathered around him would have meant that both Evciler and the surrounding villages would regain their peace and order. In any case, the punishment for illegal acts for state officials was heavy. Halil İnalcık, basing his argument on legal codes, states that death penalty was the due punishment for the *sipahi*, the cavalry and the gunners with military equipment who intimidated and bullied the villagers as well as disturbed the peace. Each provincial village had one *yiğitbaşı* (leader of the youth) tasked with capturing and arresting the individuals defined as 'rebel' or 'despot' in the Ottoman legal code.[13] In the case of Evciler, too, it was the village's *yiğitbaşı* that arrested Hamza and brought him to court. On that day, Hamza met 'with four soldier comrades and armed with his military equipment' in his own village to teach Mehmed bin Ali and his wife their lesson. As Mehmed and his wife Şems were working the soil in their orchard, Hamza suddenly appeared. With his men, he first cracked Mehmet's head open. According to Mehmet's testimony, Hamza tried to rape his wife in front of him. Şems cried for help as much as she could. *Yiğitbaşı* Ahmed bin Latif who was nearby at the moment rushed to the orchard, together with three villagers, Mehmed bin Abdi, Hasan bin Cafer, and Mustafa bin Nasuh. They witnessed how Hamza and his men surrounded Mehmed and had attacked him. A Christian Janissary boy who was among Hamza's followers had beaten Şems and fled. The villagers who arrived at the location of the incident managed to shoo Hamza away. He fled and hid in the marshes in the vicinity of the orchard.[14]

The Grasshopper Will Hop Once, Hop Twice: Hamza at the Qadi's Court

Hamza, having attacked Şems and her husband Mehmed, hid in a deserted, secluded marshland. As his criminal record was lengthy, he probably knew the fate that awaited him. Although he tried, he could not escape. The *Yiğitbaşı* and his company followed him and caught him at his hiding place. The *qadi* of Bursa, via the village *imam*, had previously sent correspondence to Hamza, ordering him to appear in court. When Hamza was captured and brought to court, the *qadi* first asked: "Did your *imam* Abdi not read the correspondence sent to you invoking the way of the *sharia*, and why have you not obeyed the honored religious law and come?" Hamza replied cautiously: "I saw the correspondence that said, 'come to court' and the *imam* read it, but I did

---

13   Halil İnalcık, "Adâletnâmeler," Belgeler 2, no. 3-4 (1965): 70.

14   *BCR*, A 119, 165.

not come; it was before this'. However, he said more than what was recorded in the testimony. The *imam* Abdi and the villagers who witnessed the incident expanded on Hamza's testimony. When notified that he was being summoned, Hamza, had apparently said: 'I will ruin the wives of both the one who brought me the order and the one who sent it'.[15] He was threatening both the *qadi* and the *imam*. And since the *imam* and one of the villagers had witnessed the incident, there was no need for additional evidence.

In addition to his crimes, Hamza was involved in a complicated relationship not permitted by Islamic law or approved by society. He had seduced and entered a relationship with a woman who was not yet divorced. The incident happened while Topçu Musli, a village warden and the husband of Ayşe bint-i Ahmed, was on night guard duty. Ayşe admitted Hamza into the house. The records describe the incident as follows: 'While Topçu Musli from the aforementioned village was on guard duty, the aforementioned Hamza engaged in relations with his wife Ayşe bint-i Ahmed in ways contrary to the honorable *shari'a* law and may this be investigated.'[16] When the *qadi* interrogated both Hamza and Ayşe, Ayşe claimed that Musli had divorced her; she was trying to lighten her likely punishment for the illicit relationship she had with Hamza. She knew that, legally, there were differences between a single woman having sexual relations with someone and a married woman doing the same.[17] Moreover, she did not disregard the 'marriage contract' (*nikah*) or the 'period of delay' (*iddet*) after the divorce went through. This period corresponded to a minimum of three menstrual cycles after divorce.[18] That is to say, only after the law ensured that a woman was not pregnant with her ex-husband's child that she was permitted to remarry. Ayşe's situation was different in one other way. She might have had marital discord with her husband Musli, but since her husband had not divorced her yet, she could not marry her new suitor Hamza. The *qadi* listened first to Ayşe's, then to Hamza's testimonies. Ayşe testified that she and Hamza got married after her husband divorced her. When it was Hamza's turn to be interrogated, the scope of the trial changed, because the *qadi*

---

15 *BCR*, A 119, 172.

16 *BCR*, A 119, 167.

17 Colin Imber, "*Zina* in Ottoman Law," *Turcica III: Contributions à l'histoire économique et sociale de l'Empire Ottoman* (1983): 67.

18 For an example of these studies, see Nurcan Abacı, "Koca Olsun Bu Gece Olsun: Kırk İki Günde Üç Kez Âdet Gören Bursalı Fatma'nın Hikâyesini Kurgulamak (17. Yüzyıl)," in *Âb-ı Hayât'ı Aramak, Gönül Tekin'e Armağan*, eds. Ozan Kolbaş-Orçun Üçer (İstanbul: Yeditepe Yayınevi, 2018), 689-99.

wanted to know who officiated the marriage. Under normal conditions, at least in theory, the couple that wanted to get married, after the approval of their family members, would need to get a document called the 'letter of permission'. This document showed that there were no objections to the groom and bride getting married.[19] Hamza had serious intentions and wanted to marry Ayşe. As the *imam* would not give permission to their marriage, they resorted to a different method and had a 'so-called' marriage among themselves. Hamza in the trial explained this marriage with the statement: 'The lady said 'I have been divorced and now I am married to you' and I too said 'I take you', and thus our marriage happened".[20] This statement can be interpreted as a sign of how people bend the law to their own advantage; for even if they cannot avoid criminal charges, they can hope for a lighter punishment by presenting the case as one of extenuating circumstances. Indeed, Ayşe and Hamza opted for such a path as well.

On Hamza's last trial, the plaintiff was Şems, whose husband he had beaten up in the orchard and who herself was a victim of assault with 'an intent to rape'. However, her lawsuit was based on a different issue. Şems stated that she had inherited some landed property when her father had died a few years ago, and she filed a complaint against Hamza, claiming that he was using her property illegally. When the *qadi* interrogated Hamza, he said: "As for the house and orchard and roof and storeroom mentioned before, I have not entered or harmed them in any way, however as the woman says, I have a right to them, but from now on I renounce them."[21] As it turns out, Hamza had seized someone else's property. And the fight had resulted because Şems and her husband rejected Hamza's claim of ownership. Hamza's trial at the *qadi*'s court ended with this last hearing.

Hamza's Fate

Court records generally contain information on various issues such as the challenges faced by the residents of an area or the crimes they committed; as narratives, however, they are monotonous. The issues between the parties were discussed thoroughly at the court, yet there was usually no mention of the factors that led to the incident being recorded. Forced to fit into a mechanical narrative, the *qadi* court records do not give as many details as the ecclesiastical court records in Europe. Moreover, in most

---

19   Svetlana Ivanova, "Muslim and Christian Woman Before the Kadı Court in Eighteenth Century Rumeli: Marriage Problems," *Oriento Moderno* 18, no. 79 (1999): 163.

20   *BCR*, A 119, 168.

21   *BCR*, A 119, 171.

cases, not even the sentence given is mentioned in the records.[22] The scholar might make guesses about the likely sentences, however it usually is not possible to arrive at definitive conclusions. So much so that one could deduce several possible sentences while consulting books of jurisprudence, *fatwas* from the *Şeyhülislam* and legal codes.

Hamza would receive his first sentences for seizing property and beating people, as in these incidents his crimes were proven. Similarly, the mosque attack had happened in public and did not require further evidence. Lastly, the incident of threatening the *imam* and the *qadi* was clear, beyond any doubt. The people committing such crimes would be sentenced to '*tâ'zir-i şedîd*' or '*darb-ı şedîd*'.[23] Hamza would be beaten until he came to his senses and could be locked up in prison for a duration; and a fine could be imposed on him as well.[24] Another option was to banish him from his place of residence. However, the residents of the Evciler village who were present at Hamza's trial did not make any such request.

It is highly probable that Hamza was bastinadoed and imprisoned based on his crimes mentioned above. However, we should note that he broke into someone's house and attempted to rape his wife. Even though the woman told as much to her husband and next-door neighbors, Hamza would not receive a heavy sentence due to the lack of eyewitnesses. In Islamic law, at least in the 1580s, prosecution of crimes of a sexual nature such as this one was rather difficult. The villagers had stated that they had heard from others in village the story of Hamza entering the house and attempting to rape the woman. The fact that there were no eyewitnesses would result in dismissal. In which case, the village residents' opinions of Hamza would determine how the *qadi* would mete out his sentence.[25] When we survey the Bursa *qadi* registers of the years after the incident, Hamza is never mentioned again. It is highly probable that he was sentenced

---

22 Dror Ze'evi, "Osmanlı Şer'i Mahkemesi Kayıtlarının Ortadoğu Sosyal Tarihi Açısından Kullanımı: Yeniden Değerlendirme," translated from the English by Erol Patan, *Vakıflar Dergisi* 32 (2010): 225-6.

23 Uriel Heyd, *Studies in Old Ottoman Criminal Law* (Glasgow-New York: Oxford University Press, 1973), 273-4.

24 Mehmet Âkif Aydın, "Ceza," *DİA* 7 (1993): 478.

25 Nurcan Abacı, "Osmanlı Kentlerinde Sosyal Kontrol: Araçlar ve İşleyiş," in *Şinasi Tekin'in Anısına Uygurlardan Osmanlıya*, eds. Günay Kut, Fatma Büyükkarcı Yılmaz (İstanbul: Simurg Yayıncılık, 2005), 107; Özen Tok, "Kadı Sicilleri Işığında Osmanlı Şehrindeki Mahalleden İhraç Kararlarında Mahalle Ahalisinin Rolü (XVII. ve XVII. Yüzyıllarda Kayseri Örneği)," *Erciyes Üniversitesi Sosyal Bilimler Enstitüsü Dergisi* 18 (2005): 164; Cemal Çetin, "Osmanlı Toplumunda Mahalleden İhraç Kararları ve Tatbiki: Konya Örneği (1645-1750)," *History Studies* 6, no. 6 (2014): 47; Işık Tamdoğan-Abel, "Osmanlı Döneminden Günümüz Türkiye'sine Bizim Mahalle," *İstanbul Dergisi* 40 (2002): 69.

FIGURE 3.3 A section from Pieter Bruegel's painting, The Blue Cloak

to hard labor in a distant land. In addition to all these crimes, there was also an interesting marriage that defied social norms.

Hamza and 'A Marriage Under the Broomstick'

The Dutch painter Pieter Bruegel completed "The Blue Cloak" in 1559, in which he depicted approximately one hundred Flemish proverbs.[26] One of these proverbs is 'to marry under the broomstick', as can be seen in **FIGURE 3.3**. In the early modern world, in almost every society, a relationship defying social norms was perceived as a crime, and through penalties, societies would strive to prevent these types of relationships from becoming prevalent.[27] When feelings such as love, desire and passion overtook one's body and soul, yet the relationships were carried out 'in the dark and in secret,' they were tolerated. However, when illegitimate relationships deemed improper according to the customs and conventions of the society were exposed, they usually caused serious problems. The relationship that Hamza had in Bursa, in 1580, bore similarities to the 'marriage under the broomstick.'

In Ottoman society, the groom had to pay a certain amount of *mihr* to the bride, which enabled him to have a legitimate sexual relationship with his spouse.[28] A woman, if divorced, would be paid the alimony and subsistence money by her ex-husband until the period of delay (*iddet*) was completed. The *imam* could not marry her off to another person until the end of this period, by when it would be determined whether she was pregnant with her ex-husband's baby. A woman had to option to present herself to the court three times during the forty-two days following her divorce to prove

---

26   Kenneth C. Lindsay, "Mystery in Bruegel's Proverbs," *Jahrbuch der Berliner Museen* 38 (1996), 64.

27   For some examples see Lindsay Moore, "Single Women and Sex in the Early Modern Atlantic World," *Early Modern Women* 5 (2010): 223-7; Laura Gowing, "Women's Bodies and the Making of Sex in Seventeenth-Century England," *Signs* 37, no. 4 (2012): 813-22; Lisa Vollendorf, "Good Sex, Bad Sex: Women and Intimacy in Early Modern Spain," *Hispania* 87, no. 1 (2004): 1-12; Monica Chojnacka, "Women, Charity and Community in Early Modern Venice: The Casa delle Zitelle," *Renaissance Quarterly* 51, no. 1 (1998): 68-91.

28   Imber, "Zina in Ottoman Law," 60; Also see Fikret Yılmaz, "The Line Between Fornication and Prostitution: The Prostitute Versus the Subaşı (Police Chief)," *Acta Orientalia Academiae Scientiarum Hung* 69, no. 3 (2016): 262.

that she menstruated, so that she could remarry.[29] Otherwise, she would have had to wait for the duration of three menstrual cycles specified as the period of delay (*iddet*).

Given the normal marriage procedures, how do we evaluate the relationship between Hamza and Ayşe, who claimed that her husband Musli divorced her? When the court received notice of a single girl's sexual relationship, she could be married off before the incident took on the proportions of the crime of adultery. We know that when Muslim men impregnated the daughters of Dimitri, a non-Muslim living in Bursa, their story ended with marriage.[30] It is possible to give even more examples, but the principal issue at hand is preventing the escalation of love affairs to adultery. In Hamza and Ayşe's marriage, the person who appealed to the court was not Musli. This then makes us think that the divorce between him and Ayşe may have actually taken place. This fact must have changed the course of the trial. Since the *imam* refused to grant consent to performing the marriage ceremony, we can infer that Hamza requested to get married. In cases where the incident was or thought to be difficult to prove as adultery, because it required the testimonies of four eyewitnesses. Colin Imber cites the *fatwas* of *Şeyhülislam* Ebussuud Efendi, and emphasizes the power of the word in marriage contracts, and states that a marriage is valid if a woman simply asks, 'Will you marry me?' and for the man to accept the proposal.[31] In Hamza's case, given the difficulty of proving the crime of adultery in Islamic law, it was highly probable that Ayşe and Hamza were not heavily punished. When he was convinced that Musli and Ayşe were divorced, the *qadi* might have drawn out a sentence for Hamza and Ayşe. Their marriage, being improper in terms of legal and social norms, was probably not approved by the court. In light of sentences given for similar crimes in different parts of the empire, it was possible that Hamza was sentenced to hard labor in a distant land, and Ayşe was exiled to another city.[32]

---

29   Abacı, "Koca Olsun Bu Gece Olsun," 694-5.

30   Nurcan Abacı, "Bir Tarih Metni Nasıl İnşa Edilir? (Dimitri'nin Kızlarını Kim Hamile Bıraktı?)," in *Tarih Nasıl Yazılır? Tarihyazımı İçin Çağdaş Bir Metodoloji*, Ahmet Şimşek, ed., (Istanbul: Tarihçi Kitabevi, 2011), 259-79; at the court of Ayıntab a similar event is said to have taken place. For the story of Fatma who became pregnant while single, see Leslie Peirce, *Morality Tales: Law and Gender in the Ottoman Court of Aintab* (Berkeley, Los Angeles, London: University of California Press, 2003), 351-74.

31   Colin Imber, *Ebu's-su'ud: The Islamic Legal Tradition* (Stanford, California: Stanford University Press, 1997), 166.

32   For the punishments of hard labor that the bandits received, see Esra Yakut, "Osmanlı Hukukunda Bir Suç Olarak Eşkıyalık ve Cezalandırılması," *Kebikeç* 33 (2012): 21-34. For the banishment of women from the places they lived in, see Yılmaz, "The Line Between Fornication and Prostitution," 257-8; Yağcı, "Osmanlı Taşrasında Kadınlar," 63.

Instead of a Conclusion

In this study, I employed the method of 'thick description' to construct and discuss Hamza's story within a narrative framework. It appears that in his orbit, Hamza had managed to escape the ordinary, and often crossed the boundaries of village life, defying social norms. The big picture shows that as a soldier he was the product of the *timar* system. He needed to protect peace where he lived, to maintain public order, and to join the military in times of emergency. Yet, Hamza stayed in the Evciler village in Bursa throughout the 1580s when the Ottoman State engaged in prolonged conflicts with Iran in the east. Evciler was far from the center of Bursa. Without a doubt, the issues that arose in such distant locations took a long time to reach the court. In reality, when Hamza caused problems in the village, the complaints of the villagers ensured that the *qadi* was informed. Living far from administrators would mean laxed supervision and intervention, as we can see from Hamza's steady involvement in one crime after another. The mechanisms of safety and supervision that worked much more slowly in the provinces also made it easier for Hamza to indulge in banditry; consequently, in deed and in reputation, he escaped ordinariness.

When we analyze this incident from the perspective of oral cultures and ethical norms, it is remarkable that neither Hamza nor Ayşe repudiated the marriage. We cannot know whether their verbal nuptials took place or not, or whether the *qadi* of Bursa confirmed the marriage either. None of the circumstances accords with the regular rules for marriage: the uncertainty concerning Ayşe's divorce from her ex-husband, the absence of a period of delay (*iddet*), the lack of an *imam* officiating or there being no *mehr* or witnesses while Hamza was married, and the lack of a mention of the marriage in the records. The couple's 'marriage under the broomstick' arrangement is a tactic to persuade the *qadi* against the charge of adultery, or at least, to issue a lighter sentence.

Bibliography

Archival Sources

Bursa Şer'iyye Sicili (BŞS), A 119.

166 Numaralı Muhâsebe-i Vilâyet-i Anadolu Defteri (937/1530). eds. A. Özkılınç et al., Ankara: T.C. Başbakanlık Devlet Arşivleri Genel Müdürlüğü Osmanlı Arşivi Daire Başkanlığı Yayınları, 1995.

Secondary Sources

Abacı, Nurcan. "Osmanlı Kentlerinde Sosyal Kontrol: Araçlar ve İşleyiş." in *Şinasi Tekin'in Anısına Uygurlardan Osmanlıya*, eds. Günay Kut, Fatma Büyükkarcı Yılmaz, 101-11. İstanbul: Simurg Yayıncılık, 2005.

————. "Bir Tarih Metni Nasıl İnşa Edilir? (Dimitri'nin Kızlarını Kim Hamile Bıraktı?)" in*Tarih Nasıl Yazılır? Tarihyazımı İçin Çağdaş Bir Metodoloji*, ed. Ahmet Şimşek, 259-79. İstanbul: Tarihçi Kitabevi, 2011.

————. "Koca Olsun Bu Gece Olsun: Kırk İki Günde Üç Kez Âdet Gören Bursalı Fatma'nın Hikâyesini Kurgulamak (17. Yüzyıl)." in *Âb-ı Hayâ't'ı Aramak, Gönül Tekin'e Armağan*, eds. Ozan Kolbaş and Orçun Üçer, 689-99. İstanbul: Yeditepe Yayınevi, 2018.

Akdağ, Mustafa. *Türk Halkının Dirlik ve Düzenlik Kavgası Celâlî İsyanları*. İstanbul: Yapı Kredi Yayınları, 2013.

Aydın, Mehmet Âkif. "Ceza." *DİA* 7 (1993): 478-82.

Barkey, Karen. *Bandits and Bureaucrats The Ottoman Route to State Cantralization*. New York: Cornell University Press, 1994.

Chojnacka, Monica. "Women, Charity and Community in Early Modern Venice: The Casa delle Zitelle." *Renaissance Quarterly* 51, no. 1 (1998): 68-91.

Çetin, Cemal. "Osmanlılarda Mesafe Ölçümü ve Tarihî Süreci." in *Tarihçiliğe Adanmış Bir Ömür Prof. Dr. Nejat Göyünç'e Armağan*, eds. Hasan Bahar, Mustafa Toker, M. Ali Hacıgökmen, H. Gül Küçükbezci, 443-66. Konya: Selçuk Üniversitesi Türkiyat Araştırmaları Enstitüsü, 2013.

————. "Osmanlı Toplumunda Mahalleden İhraç Kararları ve Tatbiki: Konya Örneği (1645-1750)." *History Studies* 6, no. 6 (2014): 43-70.

Ekin, Ümit. "17. Yüzyılın Son Çeyreğinde Rodosçuk Örneğinde Bir Osmanlı Mahkemesinin İş Yükü." *Ankara Üniversitesi Dil ve Tarih-Coğrafya Fakültesi Dergisi* 55, no. 1 (2015): 283-303.

Ergenç, Özer. *16. Yüzyıl Sonlarında Bursa*. Ankara: Türk Tarih Kurumu, 2014.

Emecen, Feridun. "Cebelü." *DİA* 7 (1993): 188-89.

Gowing, Laura. "Women's Bodies and the Making of Sex in Seventeenth-Century England." *Signs* 37, no. 4 (2012): 813-22.

Göyünç, Nejat. "Hane Deyimi Hakkında." *İstanbul Üniversitesi Edebiyat Fakültesi Tarih Dergisi* 32 (1979): 331-48.

Heyd, Uriel. *Studies in Old Ottoman Criminal Law*, Glasgow-New York: Oxford University Press, 1973.

Howard, Douglas Arthur. 1987. "The Ottoman Timar System and Its Transformation, 1563-1656." Ph.D. dissertation, Indiana University.

Imber, Colin. "Zina in Ottoman Law." *Turcica III: Contributions à l'histoire économique et sociale de l'Empire Ottoman* (1983): 59-92.

————. *Ebu's-su'ud: The Islamic Legal Tradition*. Stanford, California: Stanford University Press, 1997.

Ivanova, Svetlana. "Muslim and Christian Woman Before the Kadı Court in Eighteenth Century Rumeli: Marriage Problems." *Oriento Moderno* 18, no. 79 (1999): 161-76.

İnalcık, Halil. "Adâletnâmeler." *Belgeler* 2, no. 3-4 (1965): 49-161.

———. "Timar." *The Encyclopaedia of Islam* 10 (2000): 502-7.

Lindsay, Kenneth C. "Mystery in Bruegel's Proverbs." *Jahrbuch der Berliner Museen* 38 (1996): 63-76.

Kaplanoğlu, Raif. "Tahrir Defterlerine Göre Sultan II. Murad'ın Bursa Vakfı Köyleri." in *Sultan II. Murad ve Dönemi*, ed. İsmail Yaşayanlar, 499-539. Bursa: Gaye Kitapevi, 2015.

Karademir, Zafer. *İmparatorluğun Açlıkla İmtihanı: Osmanlı Toplumunda Kıtlıklar (1560-1660)*. İstanbul: Kitap Yayınevi, 2014.

Moore, Lindsay. "Single Women and Sex in the Early Modern Atlantic World." *Early Modern Women* 5 (2010): 223-7.

Peirce, Leslie. *Morality Tales: Law and Gender in the Ottoman Court of Aintab*. Berkeley-Los Angeles-London: University of California Press, 2003.

Şahin, Tahsin. 2017. "Celali Kuşatması Altında Bursa." M.A. Thesis, Uludağ Üniversitesi.

Tamdoğan-Abel, Işık. "Osmanlı Döneminden Günümüz Türkiye'sine Bizim Mahalle." *İstanbul Dergisi* 40 (2002): 66-70.

Tok, Özen. "Kadı Sicilleri Işığında Osmanlı Şehrindeki Mahalleden İhraç Kararlarında Mahalle Ahalisinin Rolü (XVII. ve XVII. Yüzyıllarda Kayseri Örneği)." *Erciyes Üniversitesi Sosyal Bilimler Enstitüsü Dergisi* 18 (2005): 155-73.

White, Sam. *The Climate of Rebellion in the Early Modern Ottoman Empire*. Cambridge-New York-Melbourne: Cambridge University Press, 2011.

Vollendorf, Lisa. "Good Sex, Bad Sex: Women and Intimacy in Early Modern Spain." *Hispania* 87, no. 1 (2004): 1-12.

Yağcı, Zübeyde Güneş. "Osmanlı Taşrasında Kadınlara Yönelik Cinsel Suçlarda Adalet Arama Geleneği." *Kadın Araştırmaları Dergisi* 4, no. 2 (2005): 51-81.

Yakut, Esra. "Osmanlı Hukukunda Bir Suç Olarak Eşkıyalık ve Cezalandırılması." *Kebikeç* 33 (2012): 21-34.

Yılmaz, Fikret. "The Line Between Fornication and Prostitution: The Prostitute Versus the Subaşı (Police Chief)." *Acta Orientalia Academiae Scientiarum Hung.* 69, no. 3 (2016): 249-64.

Ze'evi, Dror. "Changes in Legal-Sexual Discourses: Sex Crimes in the Ottoman Empire." *Continuity and Change* 16, no. 2 (2001): 219-42.

———. "Osmanlı Şer'i Mahkemesi Kayıtlarının Ortadoğu Sosyal Tarihi Açısından Kullanımı: Yeniden Değerlendirme." translated from the English by Erol Patan. *Vakıflar Dergisi* 32 (2010): 215-29.

CHAPTER FOUR

The Guiles of Men Outsmart Mâryem: Prostitution, Murder and Social Control in 18th Century Konya[*]

Cemal Çetin

A Murder is Committed, And Remains a Secret

Early one October night in 1736, in Konya's[1] Muhtar neighborhood,[2] in a room of the house that later would be discovered and registered as belonging to Maderos,

---

[*] Konya, 1736

[1] The place where the events took place is the city of Konya, capital to the Anatolian Seljuks and the principality of Karaman, and where the princes and the governor of Karaman resided in the Ottoman era. Konya was located on an extremely functional and busy central artery, called the right Anatolian branch according to the Ottoman system of roads. In addition to the functions of the right Anatolian branch in terms of transportation, communication and military logistics, the fact that it was the road to Hajj also contributed to its importance and recognition. Tuncer Baykara, "Konya," *DİA* 26 (2002): 182-7; Doğan Yörük, "XVI. Yüzyılda Konya Şehir Ekonomisi," *SUTAD* 42 (2017): 355. Konya was a large Anatolian city at that period. Suraiya Faroqhi, *Osmanlı'da Kentler ve Kentliler*, translated from the English by Neyyir Kalaycıoğlu [İstanbul: Tarih Vakfı Yurt Yayınları, 2000], 17. In a dissertation on the Tulip Period, the population of Konya in the first half of the 18th century had been given as 22.235 people using official data. The same dissertation also claimed that the population of Konya at the time should have been larger. Yusuf Küçükdağ, "Lâle Devrinde Konya", Ph.D Dissertation, Selçuk Üniversitesi, 1989, 78). In Konya, the military, the scholars, the dervishes, the notables, the merchants, the shopkeepers, the Sufis, the *haji* and the *hoja*, the imams, the insane, the drunk, the thieves, the victorious, the rich, the poor, the honest and ordinary middle class and the prostitutes all lived together. In this context, in the town of Konya that was located on a busy artery and had diverse types of people, there was, in addition to legal, beautiful and righteous acts, no lack of cursing, beating, wounding, battery, mugging, robbery, adultery, rape, slander, prostitution and murder. (Dana Sajdi, *Şamlı Berber, 18. Yüzyıl Biladü'ş-Şam'ında Yeni Okuryazarlık*, (*The Barber of Damascus: Nouveau Literacy in the Eighteenth-Century Ottoman Levant*, Stanford UP, 2013) translated from the English by Defne Karakaya [Istanbul: Koç Üniversitesi Yayınları, 2017], 29). On the social structure and typology of humans in 18th century Konya, see Küçükdağ, *Konya*, 73-180.

[2] According to the data from the year 1642, the Muhtar neighborhood was a neighborhood that was comprised of 40 real households and 3,5 *avarız* households. There were no *dhimmi* in the neighborhood during the time in question. *BOA MAD. 3074*, 64. The

the Head Furrier Artin bin Kesbir was eating, drinking, and chatting with his friends, Tekfus and Moskov. In this convivial setting where the wine flowed freely, the brawl that would erupt shortly would soak the dining table in blood. The argument that at first started as a small disagreement soon grew into a fight. When it was over, Artin, stabbed in the back and in the throat, fell over and breathed his last in front of his wife Mâryem bint-i Ağya, who had come from the next room after hearing the commotion. Those who stabbed Artin and killed him, without allowing his wife Mâryem to even scream, silenced her with a threat: 'Do not talk about this to anyone or we will murder you too'. They disposed of the evidence by digging a hole in the middle of the room and burying the body in it. However, somehow, two months after the murder was committed, the governor of Konya got wind of the incident – most probably via an informant – and on December 1, 1736, assigned Mevlana Ahmed Efendi and Hacı Mehmed Ağa the task of investigating the crime scene. Throughout the investigation, some villagers acted as witnesses. Under the supervision of the bailiff Hacı Mehmed Ağa, the body of the furrier Artin was found inside the hole in the floor of the house. The examination of the body found two stab wounds, one in the back and the other in the throat.[3] The whole investigation process was observed and recorded by Mevlana Ahmed.[4]

After the investigation concluded, the wife of the deceased, Mâryem, was called to the court to testify about this murder.[5] Ultimately the only person who knew how Artin was murdered, other than the perpetrators of the crime, was his wife. Regarding the manner and cause of death, Mâryem's testimony and the findings of the investigating officials overlapped. While being interrogated, at first glance Mâryem gave the impression of a desperate woman, whose husband was murdered

---

study on the Konya of the Tulip Period states that the Muhtar neighborhood was not registered. See Küçükdağ, *Konya*, 82, 87. According to the distribution register dated 1792s here were 20 real houses ın the Muhtar Neighborhood. *D.MKF. 31015.*

3   In some cases of murder, graves were opened and bodies and bones were examined. Özen Tok, "Kayseri Kadı Sicillerindeki Yaralanma ve Ölüm Vakalarıyla İlgili Keşif Raporları (1650-1660)," *Erciyes Üniversitesi Sosyal Bilimler Enstitüsü Dergisi* 22, (2007): 329; Alexandre Toumarkine, "Adli Doktorlar, Ruh Doktorları ve Şeyhler: Kummerau Olayı (1880) ve Bilirkişilik Meselesi," in *Osmanlı'da Asayiş, Suç ve Ceza 18.-20. Yüzyıllar*, Noemi Levy-Alexandre Toumarkine, ed. (İstanbul: Tarih Vakfı Yurt Yayınları, 2007): 96-115.

4   *Konya Court Registers (KCR)*, 53, 206, 1.

5   It is common to request the statement of the next of kin for the victim. Indeed, requesting information from those closest to the deceased is a common process in investigations. Sibel Kavaklı, "Ölüm ve Yaralanma Olaylarıyla İlgili Keşif Hüccetlerinin Değerlendirilmesi: Onyedinci Yüzyıl Amasya Şer'iyye Sicillerinden Örneklerle," *History Studies* 7, no. 3, (2013): 140.

and one who was silenced with threats. By making sure the records showed that she was only filing complaints for Tekfus and Moskov and no one else, she wished to spare first and foremost the neighborhood residents, but also other people in the city, from being implicated in the murder.[6]

According to Mâryem's court testimony, the murder was committed by two people. The two stab wounds on the body of the deceased, one in the front and one in the back, supported the claim that two people killed Artin. Mâryem spoke of her deceased husband as *mezbûh-ı mesfûr*[7] and the scribe who composed the in-

FIGURE 4.1 A female figure (Acâibü'l-Mahlûkât ve Garâibü'l-Mevcûdâd, TSMK, Hazine 20 No: 401, vr. 272).

vestigation document used the expression 'stabbed in the throat with a knife', and both indicate that the cut in the victim's throat was large and deep. It was probably this wound that caused Artin's death.

In Mâryem's testimony, there is no mention of a pre-existing hostility between her deceased husband and his murderers. Whatever happened transpired at the table and the argument that started there turned into a fight, and the fight into murder. When we consider the subsequent developments on this killing, we can say that a part of the narrative is probably Mâryem's fictionalized account. However, in order to even construct this fiction, she must have heard or seen what happened.

In the Ottoman legal system, there was no public law in the contemporary sense, and proceedings on incidents of death and injury or records of such cases were only possible if they were reported to *qadi*'s court or to another authority. Local administrators like the *beylerbeyi, sancakbeyi* or *mütesellim* would request an investigation only when they were informed of an incident or received a report.[8] Within this framework, someone must have reported Artin's death.

---

6   Indeed, one of the primary functions of the investigation records is to prevent implicating the residents of the neighborhood in which the murder took place. Suraiya Faroqhi, "Bursa'da Cinayet: Bir Cui Bono Vakası," in *Osmanlı'da Asayiş, Suç ve Ceza 18.-20. Yüzyıllar,* Noemi Levy-Alexandre Toumarkine, ed. (İstanbul: Tarih Vakfı Yurt Yayınları, 2007), 76.

7   Mezbûh: Slaughtered, immolated. See Ferit Devellioğlu, *Osmanlıca-Türkçe Ansiklopedik Lûgat* (Ankara: Aydın Kitabevi, 2001): 640.

8   Kavaklı, "Keşif Hüccetleri," 121.

It is unlikely that, for two months, no one felt the absence of Artin, the head of the furriers' guild or that no one inquired after him. Some people probably asked about him but the answers they were given did not raise suspicion, so they did not inquire further. Even though it is difficult to identify who provided those answers, two different case records from December 18 and December 22, 1737, carry some information that shed light on this question. Both recorded cases are against Mâryem. According to the testimonies of the plaintiffs and the defendants, the governor Karaman Memiş Paşa (at the time of the trial he is mentioned as 'the former governor') had Mâryem imprisoned for the crime of killing her husband or having him killed. In other words, Mâryem must have hidden the murder not because of the threat from the murderers, as she stated in the court earlier, but because she herself was involved in the incident. This seems a more reasonable explanation for how the murder was covered up for two months. It was probable that when someone asked for the Head Furrier Artin for any reason, his wife Mâryem would come up with lies and was able to dispel any suspicion concerning his absence. However, after a certain point, the lies must have stopped working, as someone found out that Artin was killed and whispered it into the ear of the governor of Konya. The investigation team dug into the floor of the house where the murder was committed and found the body easily.

Behind the Scenes of a Murder

The court registers in Konya, include a total of three documents on the *dhimmi* (Armenian) woman called Mâryem bint-i Ağya living in the Muhtar neighborhood. The first document is on the death investigation, the second is a debt warrant, and the third is a verdict for exile. These records summarize what Mâryem experienced throughout one year. However, a small detail in these records casts some doubt as to whether they speak of the same Mâryem or the same victim. In the official record of the death investigation, dated December 1, 1736, Head Furrier Artin veled-i Kesbir is identified as the person who was stabbed in the throat and in the back and buried in one of the rooms of the house. However, in the debt warrant, dated December 18, 1737, Mâryem's husband, who was killed in the same manner, is identified as Yasef, without any reference to his father's name. The third document, dated December 22, 1737, also identifies the victim as Yasef. To determine whether the three documents refer to the same victim, or to two different people, we need to take a closer look at them and consider some possibilities. If we assume that the records are correct, the first possibility is that Mâryem married three times, first Maderos, then Artin, and lastly Yasef, and that, in the span of a single year, she killed her second and third husbands, or arranged for their murder, and that she hid both in holes dug in the floor of one of the rooms of her house. The data at hand would suggest the existence of a serial killer with specific methods and rituals, yet this possibility – though fascinating – does not seem probable. The other possibility is that there were two women by the same name, born from fathers by the same name, and they had the same religious affiliations, lived in the same neighborhoods, and went about killing their husbands and burying them by using the same method. However, there are no other findings or documents supporting this scenario. In which case, even though the differences in the spelling of the aforementioned names are clear and rule out the possibility of misspellings, we need to assume that the name entered with the job title and the father's name was correct, but that the name Yasef is probably erroneously entered.[9]

After acknowledging that Artin and Yasef were most likely the same person, we need to address another issue as well: On what grounds the governor of Karaman, Memiş Paşa, had Mâryem imprisoned. According to the statements of prominent figures from the Armenian community[10] who appeared in court with debt claims, Memiş Paşa detained Mâryem and had her imprisoned because, 'You previously murdered your husband Yasef and buried his corpse in your house.'[11] In this case, the murderer of the husband was Mâryem herself. In the third document, the statement, 'having had her husband Yasef murdered and having had him buried in her house,' indicates that Mâryem was not a murderer but an instigator. Based on the documentary evidence, we can safely say that Mâryem was not innocent, but we cannot confirm her exact role in the murder. Indeed, when faced with her creditors in court, she would not/could not object to the accusations aimed at her – or at least this is what the documents reflected – and she confessed her crime. It is

---

9   Suraiya Faroqhi, "18. Yüzyıl Anadolu Kırsalında Suç, Kadınlar ve Servet," in *Modernleşme Eşiğinde Osmanlı Kadınları*, ed. Madeline C. Zilfi (İstanbul: Tarih Vakfı Yurt Yayınları, 2000), 15.

10   In the related document, it is defined as the 'Armenian group'. *KCR*, 54, 39-1, 39-2. The Armenians and Greeks in Konya had *kethüda* (chamberlains) who followed the official business between them and the *ehl-i örf*. In 1730 the chamberlain for the Armenians was veled-i Azostor. Küçükdağ, *Konya*, 72. Although there is no official data on the number of non-Muslims living in Konya in the 18th century, we can say that Armenians were more numerous than Greeks. According to the statement of Niebuhr who came around 1760, 300 of the 11.000 houses in Konya belonged to the Armenians, and 50 to the Greeks. Nejat Göyünç, "Niebuhr ve 1766 Sonlarında Konya," *Yeni İpek Yolu* I (1998): 4. According to the population data for the year 1841, there were 5.471 Muslim, 68 Greek and 136 Armenian households in the city of Konya. Baykara, "Konya," 187.

11   *KCR*, 54, 39-1.

not known whether Head Furrier Artin had a guardian or relative who would ask for ask for Mâryem to be executed in retaliation or accept blood money from the murderer. However, the fact that Mâryem was imprisoned instead of either receiving retaliation or being forgiven by paying blood money reinforces the possibility that she was not the perpetrator but the instigator.[12] The ones who committed the crime were probably Tekfus and Moskov who Mâryem instigated. In this situation, the law of retaliation must have applied, and the two were sentence to death. The statement that Artin was killed as a result of the fight that erupted at the dinner table reflects the truth. As for the start of the fight, it must have been a part of the murder plan, not the result of a natural course of events. We need to consider that Artin was the victim of a setup and that the fight did not erupt randomly.

Based on Mâryem's testimony alone, it is not possible to determine why Artin, Head of the Furrier Guild,[13] would be murdered. The absence of clear information necessitates making certain inferences. Among the reasons for women in the Ottoman Empire to murder their husbands were falling in love with another man or freeing oneself from physical violence and abuse.[14] It is highly probable that the major causes of Artin's murder are not those. Artin was killed most probably because Mâryem was running a brothel, something that must have created a conflict of power or prestige between the two. Yet one more possibility exists. Taking into account the sources of this period, we can confirm that Artin made furs out of the pelts of martens, foxes and cats with a high profit margin, and that he was in very good financial standing.[15] The fact that his business was highly profitable makes us think that, quite possibly, the issue of money was involved and that the murder was committed to confiscate

---

12 On abetting or participating in murder, see Mehmet Boynukalın, "Suç," *DİA* 37, (2009): 457; Although there are different opinions between scholars of Islamic jurisprudence, according to the Hanefi school, the main convict in a case of murder is the perpetrator and the law of retaliation should be applied to him. A strong tazir punishment would be recommended for the abettor. Halid Özkan, "Ceza Hukukunda Azmettirme," Ph.D dissertation, Selçuk Üniversitesi, 2013, 33. According to the *fatwa*s of Ebussuud Efendi "The question: If Zayd sends his attendants to Amr, saying 'I will kill you', and has him killed with a sharp object, what should be done to Zayd and his attendants according to shari'a? The answer: The attendants should be retaliated. Zayd would stay in prison for many years." Ertuğrul M. Düzdağ, *Kanunî Devri Şeyhülislâmı Ebussuud Efendi Fetvaları* (Istanbul: Kapı Yayınları, 2012), 195.

13 Özer Ergenç, *XVI. Yüzyılda Ankara ve Konya* (İstanbul: Tarih Vakfı Yurt Yayınları, 2012), 36.

14 Ebru Aykut, "Osmanlı'da Zehir Satışının Denetimi ve Kocasını Zehirleyen Kadınlar," *Toplumsal Tarih* 194 (2010): 59-62.

15 Küçükdağ, *Konya*, 151.

Artin's cash.[16] The fact that Mâryem married Artin a short time after her ex-husband Maderos died, and that her new husband was also the victim of a murder, makes Maderos's death suspicious as well. Based on all this, we can say that Mâryem was a suspicious character, and probably meddled in the Head Furrier Artin's affairs, interfered with his life and had him murdered to confiscate his assets.

One wonders how Mâryem convinced Tekfus and Moskov to commit this murder. By promising them property and cash, or by seducing them with her feminine charms?[17] Naturally, instigation was not the only method to get her husband killed. Mâryem could easily have had her husband killed by poisoning; in fact, this method would have been easier and less risky.[18] However, could we explain Artin's murder with a scenario where someone was trying to persuade him about something, and, failing at that, ended up fighting him and cutting his throat? Of course, this, too, is a legitimate question. Another possibility is that her husband was an honorable man and did not know of his wife's dealings, and upon learning about them, wanted to stop her and therefore was eliminated.

The statements of the prominent figures of the Armenian community and the residents of the victim's neighborhood form a clearer body of knowledge. According to those statements, Mâryem had been a prostitute for a long time and arranging meetings of prostitutes with bandits at her house. Her imprisonment for having her husband murdered did not correct her behavior. In fact, she lost control even more and some of her behavior was so bad as to be damnable. This information shows that Mâryem, after being released, did not refrain from committing crimes, and moreover, had close relations with people who were in the habit of committing crimes.

Mâryem's House: Private, Public or Collective

The house in which Mâryem resided, and where the murder was committed, belonged to her ex-husband Maderos who died while she was married to him. While Maderos's time of death is unknown, the death investigation document for the

16 Ebru Boyar-Kate Fleet, *Osmanlı İstanbul'unun Toplumsal Tarihi*, (*A Social History of Ottoman Istanbul*. Cambridge, 2010) translated from the English by Serpil Çağlayan (İstanbul: Türkiye İş Bankası Kültür Yayınları, 2014), 138.

17 Stephen Kern, *Nedenselliğin Kültürel Tarihi Bilim, Cinayet Romanları ve Düşünce Sistemi*, (*A Cultural History of Causality: Science, Murder Novels, and Systems of Thought*. Princeton, 2004) translated from the English by Emine Ayhan (İstanbul: Metis Yayınları, 2008), 215-26.

18 Düzdağ, *Fetva*, 197, 203. For further information see Colin Imber, "Why You Should Poison Your Husband: A Note on Liability in Hanafi Law in the Ottoman Period," *Islamic Law and Society* 1, no. 2 (1994): 206-16.

murder of Head Furrier Artin, mentions his name as 'the registered owner', which is curious. Maderos was most probably still fresh in social memory and Mâryem was remembered as his widow.[19] In fact, like any woman who lived by herself and needed to confirm at the court her name and address, Mâryem, too, could have given her name and her father's neighborhood as proof of her identity and address.[20] It is therefore reasonable to deduce that the house was still linked to Maderos who had recently died. However, if our goal is not to focus on another deceased ex-husband of Mâryem's, an alternative explanation could be that the transfer of registration for the house had not occurred yet.

Another detail that we notice is that after getting married to the Head Furrier Artin, Mâryem did not move in with him and instead continued to reside in her ex-husband's house. Her decision must have been due to her desire to maintain the social networks she had built through the house in question. Indeed, moving to another neighborhood might have harmed the social networks she had built and through which she had gained a certain amount of immunity—and maybe customers as well. The fact that she was a prostitute and ran a brothel, the possibility that she was caught quickly through the social control mechanisms of another neighborhood, or that she was unable to integrate into the new neighborhood at all are details that should not be ignored.

Except for her court appearances, none of Mâryem's actions happened in the public space, i.e., on the streets. All the crimes attributed to her happened inside her house, that is, in a private space. Under normal conditions in an Ottoman society, we know that it was men who commanded public spaces, and women the private spaces. However, marginal women fell somewhat outside the range of this condition and tended to be more visible and influential in the public sphere. In fact, separating places into two categories such as private and public can sometimes lead to wrong interpretations.[21] According to the claims of the Armenian community and the neighborhood residents, the house in question was a place where prostitutes and bandits came together – of course with Mâryem's skills – and engaged in illegal and unethical acts. Despite all of this, the house was not a public space, yet

---

19 Dina Rizk Khoury, "Slippers at the Entrance or Behind Closed Doors: Domestic and Public Space for Mosuli Women," In *Women in the Ottoman Empire: Middle Eastern Women in the Early Modern Era*, ed. Madeline C. Zilfi (Leiden: Brill, 1997), 105-127.

20 *KCR*, 12, 151-3; *KCR*, 13, 103-1.

21 Turan Açık, "Toplumsal Cinsiyet Bağlamında Osmanlı Hukukunda Kadından Eşkıya Olup Olamayacağına Dair Bir Tartışma: Havva Hatun Örneği," *Karadeniz Araştırmaları Enstitüsü Dergisi* 1, no. 1 (2015): 38.

it also lost the identity of an intimate space where the privacy of the family and of a woman was protected, and it had become a collective space (a brothel). Because of the functions of this house, Mâryem acquired a certain amount of power and influence. With the possibilities her house presented, she was able to manipulate the public sphere and to pursue some initiatives to rebuild her life. Her penetration into the Armenian community to evade prison is also an act that she followed through while imprisoned. Even from enclosed spaces, Mâryem could easily manage the streets and the spaces that men dominated, yet there was no evidence of her personal appearance in the public sphere.[22]

In addition, what is more remarkable is how after Artin was murdered, his body was hidden by burial in one of the rooms of the house – possibly a large room where guests were received. Throughout the period until the body was dug up by the *ehl-i örf*, Mâryem must have continued to live there; and since there is no information to the contrary, we can assume that the house was still her residence. There is no clear evidence of acts of prostitution taking place in this house in the period we mentioned. However, according to the allegations against her, nothing could keep Mâryem from engaging in and facilitating prostitution.[23] In this sense, aside from the irony and strangeness of engaging in acts of prostitution and merriment in a room where a body is buried, the calm composure and psychological state of those participating in these frivolities, even though the nature of the incident was well known, is astonishing. It is a mystery how the neighborhood residents – especially the women and children - felt, behaved, and spoke when they learned that someone had been murdered in a house they passed by or saw from the street every day, and how they felt as they recalled this incident years later as a memory. This house must have been sold after Mâryem was exiled from the city. Did the murder committed in it delay the sale of the house or lead to its sale for a price well below its value? Did those who bought the house recall this memory from time to time and shudder? The fact that there is no information to answer these questions necessitates leaving the fictional narrative to the reader's imagination.

---

22 Women who take up too much space in the public sphere, and who 'disturb the peace of men' who are the true owners of these spaces would receive harsh reactions. Even though we can rarely access data on this in the Ottoman documents, what little we know points to the existence of this phenomenon. Sultan, who received capital punishment one generation previously, and possibly even before Mâryem was born (H. 1701), had a quite lengthy criminal record. *KCR*, 39, 103-1.

23 *KCR*, 54, 39-2.

The Price of Freedom or The Adventure of Coming out of Prison

Mâryem who acted the role of an innocent and grieving widow at the court could not sustain her position for too long; for in a short while her ruse was exposed and therefore with the decision of the *qadi* of Konya and the order of Memiş Paşa, she was imprisoned as an accessory to murder. For Mâryem, who was used to social gatherings with libations and seeing cheerful and fun-loving people around her, this life of imprisonment was worse than death itself. She had to get out of prison at all costs. To have them pay her bail and release her from prison, she contacted people with whom she was on good terms: people such as Derviş veled-i Kiragos, Kaysar Hatırbali, Kabril veled-i Tavid and Ağya veled-i Girgor from the Armenian community to which she belonged. Not every member of the community cared for Mâryem's plea. At her house in the Muhtar neighborhood, she facilitated acts of prostitution by bringing together shady men from bandit groups and prostitutes. Innumerable people went in and out of her house. As for the Muslims in her neighborhood, although fed up with her, they were also fearful, and because of this they could not go to court, let alone react in any way. Some of Mâryem's actions and behavior had harmed the community as well, and for this reason she was warned from time to time. Although they did not feel much sympathy for Mâryem, the neighbors nevertheless did not see it appropriate to abandon a woman from their own community in prison. Consequently, a group that included five individuals, Yanos, Sergez, Sikender, Sergez and Haçır, went to meet her in prison. During the meeting, Mâryem told them that 2.500 *kuruş* had to be paid for her release, and that she would pay this money back as soon as she was out of prison. As it turned out, however, the 'fine for the crime of murder'[24] and the expenses associated with Mâryem's imprisonment exceeded the previously estimated amount. After consulting among themselves and deciding that Mâryem could pay this money back, the neighbors spent the required 4.000 *kuruş* and bailed her out of prison.

Mâryem's bail was a very large amount. Around this time, the blood money to be paid ranged between 70[25] to 100[26] *kuruş*, and in 1736, the amount paid for civil peace attained through blood money payments was 170 *kuruş*.[27] Also in the

---

24 Yusuf Halaçoğlu, "Cürm ü Cinâyet," *DİA* 8 (1993): 138-9. For the importance of criminal penalties in the Ottoman state system, see Yunus Koç and Murat Tuğluca, "Klasik Dönem Osmanlı Ceza Hukukunda Yargılama ve Toplumsal Yapı," *Türk Hukuk Tarihi Araştırmaları* 2 (2006): 13-4.

25 *KCR*, 50, 17-1.

26 *KCR*, 50, 213-1.

27 *KCR*, 53, 60-2.

same period the amount of money paid for bailing four people out of prison was 300 *kuruş*.[28] It is therefore necessary to analyze the amounts mentioned at the trial as they show Mâryem's financial power and her ability to mobilize the people who would pay the high amounts. Mâryem testified that she gave instructions for 800 *kuruş* to be paid, whereas the prominent figures of the community stated that 2.500 *kuruş* were spent for the testimonies of the witnesses; yet the total cost ended up being as much as 4.000 *kuruş*. Assuming that the amount quoted by the prominent figures of the community is correct, we need to acknowledge that they knew about Mâryem's financial power, and they trusted her to pay it back. It is understood from witness testimonies during the debt action that 2.500 *kuruş* were paid to bail Mâryem. Setting aside the 4.000 *kuruş* that the prominent figures of the Armenian community claimed they were owed,[29] 2.500 *kuruş* would have already been a small fortune in that period.

While we do not completely understand the nature and legal basis of the fee that the governor ordered Memiş Paşa to pay as Mâryem's bail, this amount was probably paid to cover the expenses made on her account while she was imprisoned for the 'crime of murder'.[30] While this fee should have a legal basis and justification, the situation is not clear.[31] Indeed, between the 15th and the 19th centuries, records show that the prison sentence was often used as a tool for political manipulation

---

28 *KCR*, 50, 187-3.

29 Suraiya Faroqhi, "18. Yüzyıl Anadolu Kırsalında Suç, Kadınlar ve Servet," in *Modernleşme Eşiğinde Osmanlı Kadınları* (*Women in the Early Modern Ottoman Empire*), 15. In Galata's register of the year 1789, the wealthiest non-Muslim woman, Armenian Serpuhi daughter of Maderos had assets amounting to 154.520 *akçes* (approximately 1.288 *kuruş*). Fatma Müge Göçek and Marc David Bear, "18. Yüzyıl Galata Kadı Sicillerinde Osmanlı Kadınlarının Toplumsal Sınırları," in *Modernleşme Eşiğinde Osmanlı Kadınları* (*Women in the Early Modern Ottoman Empire*), 49. Based on the number of rooms, the location and the size, the prices of houses had a range between 60 *kuruş* and 350 *kuruş*. The amount that was paid by the Konya township for the annual *imdadiye* campaign tax of Karaman's governor was 3.500 *kuruş*. *KCR*, 54, 3-4. It is known that in the centuries in question, the prostitutes living in Europe's large cities would not receive monetary fines due to their poverty, and would be imprisoned, beaten and banished for their crimes. Mery E. Wiesner-Hanks, *Erken Modern Dönemde Avrupa 1450-1789*, translated from the English by Hamit Çalışkan (Istanbul: Türkiye İş Bankası Kültür Yayınları, expanded 3rd edition, 2014), 427.

30 Gültekin Yıldız, *Mapusâne Osmanlı Hapishanelerinin Kuruluş Serüveni (1839-1908)* (İstanbul: Kitabevi, 2012), 18-25.

31 Due to a rumor claiming that a bribe called a present was given to the wardens of the citadel or other government officials to free someone from jail, the officials in question had to testify in court that they did not receive presents. *KCR*, 48, 17, 1.

and reckoning, where the 'honorable *shari'a*' and the law were overlooked, rather than as a punishment to ensure that the criminal would 'correct their behavior', and this indicates the arbitrariness of the prison charge. Data of this kind also make us question whether Mâryem's imprisonment process depended on the whims of Memiş Paşa.

As there were no standard imprisonment terms for any crime in the Ottoman Empire, the length of the imprisonment appropriate for Mâryem was not clear. In line with the usual practices, she would probably be staying in prison until she 'corrected her behavior', that is, until it was decided that she regretted the crime she committed.[32] However Mâryem must have wanted to get out of prison before she "corrected her behavior", as she did not hesitate in securing 2.500 *kuruş*, which, as stated earlier, equaled a small fortune. As she was a woman, it is very difficult to determine the location of Mâryem's imprisonment either from the data on imprisonment practices in the Ottoman Empire in the pre-modern period or from the data specific to Konya.[33] In Istanbul, a separate section in the Baba Cafer Prison was reserved for female prisoners. The *imam*'s house near Ağa Kapısı or even some leased buildings also functioned as women's prisons.[34] Additionally, the data[35] suggest that women throughout the Ottoman Empire were kept in the *imam*'s house, the *qadi*'s mansion or another secure and prominent location. This makes us think that Mâryem was also locked away in a similarly appropriate location.

No Knowing If She Will Return: Mâryem is Exiled

After getting out of prison, Mâryem was free. It was time for her to send for her ladies and go back to working, as in the past. The women in her retinue were extremely famous, and her house never lacked visitors who arrived to be entertained by these women. These were usually armed and troublesome bandits. However, from time to time wealthy and reputable people would also come to her house. The latter would naturally insist on privacy due to their standing in society. Owing to her patrons, some of whom instilled fear in her, and some who secretly supported her,

---

32 Yıldız, *Mapusâne*, 36.

33 We know that men who received this punishment in Konya were imprisoned in an appropriate location in the citadel or in a dungeon (*KCR*, 48, 17, 1; *KCR*, 31, 122, 1); however, we cannot access the information on where women prisoners were kept.

34 Ali Karaca, "XIX. Yüzyılda Osmanlı Devletinde Fahişe Hatunlara Uygulanan Cezalar: Hapis ve Sürgün," in *Hapishane Kitabı,* Emine Gürsoy Naskali and Hilal Oytun Altun, ed.s, (İstanbul: Kitabevi, 2010), 153-4.

35 Yıldız, *Mapusâne*, 18-25.

Mâryem was not afraid of the community for the time being. She delayed paying back her debt to Derviş veled-i Kiragos, Kaysar Hatırbali, Kabril veled-i Tavid and Ağya veled-i Girgor; and even when they sent word to her demanding payment, she ignored them. It was only when she was summoned to appear in court on a cold winter's day, on the 15th of *Şaban* (December 18), did she realize that the debt issue was serious. In court, she faced her creditors, who had brought along five witnesses, yet she still refused to pay a part of the sum. Mâryem listened to the complaints made about her and confirmed their agreement but defended herself: "I had asked these people to pay 800 *kuruş* for my bail, and since I did not know whether they had that much savings, I did not ask them for 2500 *kuruş*.' However, after the witnesses' testimonies in favor of the plaintiffs, Mâryem's words no longer had much value. The *qadi* of Konya must have thought that just as Mâryem was lying to avoid paying some of her debt, other Armenians were trying to get extra cash from her. Therefore, he ruled that the total amount specified in the contract made between the two sides, 2.500 *kuruş*, should be paid.

The complaints about Mâryem did not stop here. Four days later, fourteen *dhimmi*—Artin veled-i Agob, Murat veled-i Toç, Uğurlu veled-i Kirkor, Sergiz veled-i Evidik, Manik veled-i Gülaş, Evidik veled-i Arab, Bali veled-i Medrük, Karabet veled-i Medik, Haçır veled-i Epe, İbrahim veled-i Artin, Karabet veled-i Bağdeser, Kaysar veled-i Hatar, Kazar veled-i Kirkor and Ağya veled-i Asvazator—appeared in court, sued her on account of 'bad behavior' and petitioned for her to be exiled from the city.[36] In the presence of the *qadi*, they listed many of her crimes and misdemeanors. They each said that she was not whom she said she was: that she engaged in and facilitated prostitution; that had been imprisoned because she had her ex-husband murdered and buried at her house; and that as the Armenian community they were put in a difficult position and had to pay fines on account of her actions. Despite their many attempts at admonishing her, she never paid attention to their words and did not reform her ways. The Armenian community asked the court to banish her from the city after interviewing her Muslim neighbors. According to the statements of Muslims whose names were not specified in the trial records but who lived in the Muhtar neighborhood and knew of her situ-

---

36   Even though in similar cases, one person's complaint would be sufficient for suing, (*KCR*, 45, 102-3) in this case, the number of plaintiffs is fourteen. The large number of plaintiffs could be because she was a feared person. It could also be due to the efforts of prominent figures in the Armenian community to psychologically manipulate the *qadi* of Konya, as they wanted to quickly get rid of Mâryem who harmed their reputation and caused damage. They did this in order not to leave things to chance and to invite the verdict of exile found in the legal codes.

ation, Mâryem was a famous prostitute and besides, facilitated prostitution at her house. With the Muslims declaring her *su-i hal* (bad behavior) as specified,[37] the trial court, on December 22, 1737, decided to banish her.[38]

It looks like the process that resulted in Meryem's banishment had started on the day she asked the Armenian community to pay the money the governor requested to bail her out. If she had not denied her debt and had paid it on time, the case against her would most probably never have been opened and she would not have been exiled from the city. The accusations against her during the trial on the above mentioned date were not related to her recent actions. In the eyes of society, Mâryem's credit was used up since she had already been coded into social memory as a bad person.[39]

By the time of the final ruling that sent the Armenian woman Mâryem to exile, we can say that a total of twenty-six *dhimmi* men, consisting of one victim, two murderers, four creditors, fourteen plaintiffs and five witnesses, were directly affected. The fact that fourteen *dhimmi* plaintiffs asked the court to exile Mâryem from the city gives us the impression that some people from the Armenian community were mobilized with a resolve to banish her from the city.

While there is no information on the location of Mâryem's exile, it is probable that she was sent to a city such as Kayseri, Niğde, or a similar nearby town. Was it possible for her to avoid exile? According to the Ottoman legal system, Mâryem could have returned to her neighborhood if an honorable neighbor vouched for her, or if she repented and the neighborhood residents trusted her repentance and

---

37   According to Muslims pronouncing her *su-i hal*, Mâryem was a prostitute and facilitated prostitution. According to Ottoman legal codes, thievery and prostitution are behaviors that warranted banishment from the neighborhood and being exiled from the city. Çetin, "Mahalleden İhraç," 51.

38   Concerning cases of banishment from the neighborhood in Konya in the years 1645-1750, one of the two who were banished and exiled to a different land with the declaration of *su-i hal* was Mâryem. The Muslim woman named Havva was exiled due to an appeal sent to the center, and as for Mâryem, the Konya Court made the ruling for her exile. Çetin, "Mahalleden İhraç," 55-70.

39   Peirce claims that in the Ayntab society of the 16th century, the prestige of a person could be calculated. According to her statements, the negative remarks about a person in the collective memory of the neighborhood or in the court records, and the data describing the reasons for the negative remarks, are benchmarks for his/her prestige. Leslie Peirce, *Ahlak Oyunları 1540-1541 Osmanlı'da Ayntab Mahkemesi ve Toplumsal Cinsiyet, (Morality Tales: Law and Gender in the Ottoman Court of Aintab,* University of California Press, 2003) translated from the English by Ülkün Tansel (İstanbul: Tarih Vakfı Yurt Yayınları, 2005), 149.

requested the court to rescind its ruling and let her return.[40] However, given the contents of the complaints about her, we see that a person whom even imprisonment could not reform would not be convincing. Moreover, when we look at how she lost her major social networks—at least her connections to law-abiding individuals some of whom might have been willing to take her under their wings—it does not seem possible for her to return to Konya and to her neighborhood.

With her exile to another city, one might think that the residents of Muhtar neighborhood, the Armenian community of Konya and even the

ŞEKIL 4.2 Social gathering (Tercüme-i Miftâh-ı Cifru'l-Câmi, TSMK, Bağdad, No: 373, vr. 243).

whole Konya community rid themselves of the prostitution and other evils that Mâryem perpetrated. Indeed, regarding prostitution, the neighborhood residents would not only fear being implicated before the law[41] but also pass their days and nights in unease due to the shady people frequenting Mâryem's house. When we think of the tradition in the capital, Istanbul to isolate famous prostitutes from social life before the month of Ramadan,[42] we might conclude that the Muhtar neighborhood residents, having expelled such an evil from their neighborhood four days before the month of Ramadan, likewise significantly eased their conscience. As for Mâryem, it would be unrealistic to think that she came to her senses in exile, when we consider the conditions under which people were sent to exile in Ottoman society. Other than experiencing some difficulty because she was removed from the social network that used to protect her, it is highly probable that in exile Mâryem resumed her old lifestyle in the quickest way possible. Indeed, being banished from one's neighborhood or city inevitably affected the extent to which ordinary people adapted to their new community and pushed them once again to the margins.[43]

---

40 On the verdicts and their implementation in the legal codes, see Çetin, "Mahalleden İhraç," 51.

41 Ergenç, *Ankara ve Konya*, 68-9.

42 Karaca, "Fahişe Hatunlara Uygulanan Cezalar," 153.

43 Faroqhi, "Bursa'da Cinayet," 73, 75-6.

Instead of a Conclusion

When investigating the administrative, financial and legal structures and social codes in Ottoman society, the circumstances surrounding a non-Muslim woman having had her husband killed, the ensuing events, and the emergent relations and patterns are no less valuable than data about wars or similar large-scale events.

During the same period as the event unfolding in Konya, the main items on the agenda for government officials concerned the campaigns carried out in Russia and Austria. As for the residents of Konya, besides paying their share of taxes (to support the logistics and financing of the campaigns) and pricking up their ears to war rumors, they must have focused mostly on their daily chores, financial struggles and events around them, leaving the worries about the cost, strategy and general course of the distant war to the military.[44] We can presume that historians, similar to government officials, focused on ongoing wars against Austria and Russia, the military units that carried them out, and the events revolving around these wars. Because the organization of military campaigns involved an extremely complicated bureaucratic process to mobilize and carry out logistics on an imperial scale, there is an abundance of data about campaigns in state archives. Additionally, wars play a significant role in the lives of states and clearly explains why historians mostly gravitate towards military history. Because the state mainly focused on the major events and produced extensive documentation on them, it is only natural that these events remained central on the stage of history, both at the time they happened as well the one in which they were recorded. As for the actions of ordinary people, they remained either in the periphery of the stage or outside of it altogether.[45]

A choice made by powerful decision-makers at the center can certainly pave the way to major and rapid changes in the course of history. In this framework, the powerful figures and the events unfolding around them become more distinguishable, and the lives of ordinary people who, through their work and taxes, support the state, may seem undifferentiable and do not necessarily attract attention, especially when seen from a distance. However, a closer look will reveal that the lives of these 'modest crowds' and the individuals in them are not one and the same. When we consider the details of their lives, the environmental factors, the condi-

---

44 For the camels requested for the Moscow Campaign and the order for the campaign that was sent so that the governor of Karaman, along with his entourage, could start preparations for a campaign in order to join the army in the month of March, see *KCR*, 53, 168-1; 262-1; 275-2.

45 The concepts of the center and periphery of the stage have been inspired by Ahmet Hamdi Tanpınar's novel *Sahnenin Dışındakiler*.

tions of the period and the rhythms of social life,[46] we might claim that their lives reflect the realities of the period much more accurately. They might even provide more accurate data on the state's power and authority, the precision and operation of the justice mechanism and the effect of these mechanisms on each member of the society. They were indeed the quantitative majority, spread on a large area and shaping daily life.[47] Specifically the lives of ordinary people and the reflexes that the state and society developed as a reaction can be indicators and parameters of the state's power and authority. In fact, as in the example of Mâryem, biopsies conducted on cross-sections of the social tissue will give important clues about the social structure. It is crucial to keep an eye on the harmony and the disharmony between the part and the whole; otherwise, it is highly probable that some truths go unnoticed, or may deviate.[48]

The murder of Head Furrier Artin and the events that follow show us how the social control mechanisms had no standard applications and were in some way influenced by the individual's social standing and social networks--even in a city where these mechanisms were supposed to have been precise and functional due to its central and administrative position on the Holy Pilgrimage Route since ancient times. The chief function of the mechanisms was to purge the public living spaces of evil and its sources, to protect the community that was harmed, and to correct the behavior of criminals by making them regret their actions. In this way, evil and evildoers could not set roots in a place, and society was given an important message: that evil end evildoers could never avoid punishment.

Bibliography

Archival Sources
A- *Başbakanlık Osmanlı Arşivi (BOA)*
1- MAD. 3074,
2- D.MKF. 31015.
B- *Konya Şer'iyye Sicilleri (KŞS)*
1- 12, 13, 31, 39, 45, 48, 50, 51, 53, 54.

---

46 Nuri Adıyeke, "Kuantum Tarih Kurgusu (Makroskobik Tarihten Mikroskobik Tarihe)," in *Türkiye'de Tarih Yazımı*, Vahdettin Engin-Ahmet Şimşek, ed., (İstanbul: Yeditepe Yayınları, 2011), 376.

47 Christian Meier, "Makro ve Mikro Tarih İlişkisi Üzerine Notlar", translated from the English by Doğan Gün, *Memleket ve Siyaset Yönetimi* 7, no. 8 (2012): 104.

48 For a similar view, see Adıyeke, "Kuantum Tarih Kurgusu," 379-80.

Secondary Sources

Açık, Turan. "Toplumsal Cinsiyet Bağlamında Osmanlı Hukukunda Kadından Eşkıya Olup Olamayacağına Dair Bir Tartışma: Havva Hatun Örneği." *Karadeniz Araştırmaları Enstitüsü Dergisi* 1, no. 1 (2015): 35-93.

Adıyeke, Nuri. "Kuantum Tarih Kurgusu (Makroskobik Tarihten Mikroskobik Tarihe)." in *Türkiye'de Tarih Yazımı*, eds. Vahdettin Engin-Ahmet Şimşek, 369-82. İstanbul: Yeditepe Yayınları, 2011.

Aykut, Ebru. "Osmanlı'da Zehir Satışının Denetimi ve Kocasını Zehirleyen Kadınlar." *Toplumsal Tarih* 194 (2010): 58-64.

Baykara, Tuncer. "Konya." *DİA* 26 (2003): 182-87.

Boyar, Ebru and Kate Fleet. *Osmanlı İstanbul'unun Toplumsal Tarihi*, translated from the English by Serpil Çağlayan. İstanbul: Türkiye İş Bankası Kültür Yayınları, 2014.

Boynukalın, Mehmet. "Suç." *DİA* 37 (2009): 457.

Çetin, Cemal. "Osmanlı Toplumunda Mahalleden İhraç Kararları ve Tatbiki: Konya Örneği (1645-1750)." *History Studies* 6, no. 6 (2014): 43-70.

Devellioğlu, Ferit. *Osmanlıca-Türkçe Ansiklopedik Lûgat*. Ankara: Aydın Kitabevi, 2001.

Ergenç, Özer. *XVI. Yüzyılda Ankara ve Konya*. İstanbul: Tarih Vakfı Yurt Yayınları, 2012.

Faroqhi, Suraiya. "18. Yüzyıl Anadolu Kırsalında Suç, Kadınlar ve Servet." in *Modernleşme Eşiğinde Osmanlı Kadınları*, ed. Madeline C. Zilfi, 7-26. İstanbul: Tarih Vakfı Yurt Yayınları, 2000.

———. "Bursa'da Cinayet: Bir Cui Bono Vakası." in *Osmanlı'da Asayiş, Suç ve Ceza 18.-20. Yüzyıllar*, eds. Noemi Levy and Alexandre Toumarkine, 68-79. İstanbul: Tarih Vakfı Yurt Yayınları, 2007.

———. *Osmanlı'da Kentler ve Kentliler*. translated from the English by Neyyir Kalaycıoğlu. İstanbul: Tarih Vakfı Yurt Yayınları, 2000.

Göçek, Fatma Müge and Marc David Bear. "18. Yüzyıl Galata Kadı Sicillerinde Osmanlı Kadınlarının Toplumsal Sınırları." in *Modernleşme Eşiğinde Osmanlı Kadınları*, ed. Madeline C. Zilfi, 47-62. İstanbul: Tarih Vakfı Yurt Yayınları, 2000.

Göyünç, Nejat. "Niebuhr ve 1766 Sonlarında Konya." *Yeni İpek Yolu* 1 (1998): 3-5.

Halaçoğlu, Yusuf. "Cürm ü Cinâyet." *DİA* 8 (1993): 138-39.

Imber, Colin. "Why You Should Poison Your Husband: A Note on Liability in Hanafi Law in the Ottoman Period." *Islamic Law and Society* 1, no. 2 (1994): 206-16.

Karaca, Ali. "XIX. Yüzyılda Osmanlı Devletinde Fahişe Hatunlara Uygulanan Cezalar: Hapis ve Sürgün." in *Hapishane Kitabı*, eds. Emine Gürsoy Naskali-Hilal Oytun Altun, 152-63. İstanbul: Kitabevi, 2010.

Kavaklı, Sibel. "Ölüm ve Yaralanma Olaylarıyla İlgili Keşif Hüccetlerinin Değerlendirilmesi: Onyedinci Yüzyıl Amasya Şer'iyye Sicillerinden Örneklerle." *History Studies* 7, no. 3 (2013): 117-42.

Kern, Stephen. *Nedenselliğin Kültürel Tarihi Bilim, Cinayet Romanları ve Düşünce Sistemi.* translated from the English by Emine Ayhan. İstanbul: Metis Yayınları, 2008.

Khoury, Dina Rizk. "Terlikler Kapıda mı, Kapalı Kapılar Ardında mı: Ev İçinde ve Kamusal Mekânda Musullu Kadınlar." in *Modernleşmenin Eşiğinde Osmanlı Kadınları*, ed. Madeline C. Zilfi, translated from the English by Necmiye Alpay, 101-21. İstanbul: Tarih Vakfı Yurt Yayınları, 2000.

Koç, Yunus and Murat Tuğluca. "Klasik Dönem Osmanlı Ceza Hukukunda Yargılama ve Toplumsal Yapı." *Türk Hukuk Tarihi Araştırmaları* 2 (2006): 7-24.

Peirce, Leslie. *Ahlak Oyunları 1540-1541 Osmanlı'da Ayntab Mahkemesi ve Toplumsal Cinsiyet.* translated from the English by Ülkün Tansel. İstanbul: Tarih Vakfı Yurt Yayınları, 2005.

Sajdi, Dana. *Şamlı Berber, 18. Yüzyıl Biladü'ş-Şam'ında Yeni Okuryazarlık*, translated from the English by Defne Karakaya. İstanbul: Koç Üniversitesi Yayınları, 2017.

Tok, Özen. "Kayseri Kadı Sicillerindeki Yaralanma ve Ölüm Vakalarıyla İlgili Keşif Raporları (1650-1660)." *Erciyes Üniversitesi Sosyal Bilimler Enstitüsü Dergisi* 22 (2007): 327-47.

Wiesner-Hanks, Mery E. *Erken Modern Dönemde Avrupa 1450-1789*, translated from the English by Hamit Çalışkan. İstanbul: Türkiye İş Bankası Kültür Yayınları, 2014.

Yıldız, Gültekin. *Mapusâne Osmanlı Hapishanelerinin Kuruluş Serüveni* (1839-1908). İstanbul: Kitabevi, 2012.

Yörük, Doğan. "XVI. Yüzyılda Konya Şehir Ekonomisi." *SUTAD* 42 (2017): 353-79.

CHAPTER FIVE

Partnership in Mischief in the 16th century: An Entire Family of Thieves*

Saadet Maydaer

In 16th century Ottoman society, there were of course those who stole others' property. However, both the deterrent of punishments and the social solidarity formed against theft and similar crimes made life difficult for those inclined to theft. The neighborhood consciousness in Ottoman society, with the help of joint guarantee, ensured public awareness of any sound that came from the street and even neighboring houses, or any sign that pointed to an extraordinary situation. In this society, a woman could go outside on her own to find the source of the commotion in a house on her street, eavesdrop on the doors one by one, and upon realizing that a fight had erupted, have the door opened, go inside and save the life of her neighbor who was being strangled during a robbery.[1]

Joint guarantee, that is, the shared responsibility of neighbors in the case of a crime committed in the neighborhood, had a big role in how the residents were

---

*   Bursa, March 1584

1   *Bursa Şer'iyye Sicilleri (BCR)*, A 32, 141b. "...müşarun ileyh Mahmud mecruh olan Abbas'ı idüb? Hacı Hayyat'ın evinde kiraya oturan Mustafa ve şakirdi Memi yanlarına iledib mezkûr Mahmud kapı önünde tecessüs için durub mezbureyn Mustafa ve Memi için Hacı Abbas'ı katl idüb akçesini almak kasdına bogazlamak dileyib kavga oldukda bogazlayamayıb, bogazını şah damarından bıçakla vurub ahali-i mahalleden kavgaların Hesna? bint-i Yusuf istima edib tefahhüs edib taşra çıkıb Mahmud'u kapı önünde bulub bu kavganız hangi evden gelir deyu sual edib Mahmud bilemezem deyüb, mezbur Hesna? mahallede olan kapılara kulak urub zikr olunan Mahmud'un önünde durdugu kapıdan gelüb ardından kilitli bulub, açtırıb içerüye geleni şengülî gönderib mezbur avrat içeri vardıkda mezbureyn Mustafa ve Memi, mezkur Abbas'ı basıb bogazlar görüb feryad edib, mezbur Hesna muttali olıcak ... edib mezburan Mustafa ve Memi kaçıb ehl-i mahalle haber verilib mecruhun üzerine varıb sual olundukda mezbur Abbas mağribi? eyitti ki: 'Zikr olunan Mahmud beni Mustafa ve Memi ile 'kebab yiyelim' deyu ayardıb anda iledib Mahmud kapıyı bend eyleyib Mustafa ve Memi bana yapışıb bogazlamak kasd edib feryad eyledim feryadıma mezbure avrat geldi eğer gelmese beni katl eylediler idi.'"

so sensitive towards each other and to all kinds of sounds in a neighborhood.[2] Additionally, the neighborhood consciousness in Ottoman society urged all individuals in a neighborhood to consider responsible and socially aware behavior as normal, ordinary conduct. Likewise, even a woman who was unarmed and alone, and who clearly lacked the physical strength to fend off two or three men, knew that just by screaming she could gather all neighborhood residents around her, and therefore was able to confront criminals without hesitation. Undoubtedly, this was a deterrent for criminals. However, the deterrent element meant neither a complete lack of crime in Ottoman society, nor the recognition of the signs or the prevention of these kinds of ploys at all times. One of the common crimes, theft, is understood to have taken place in a wide range of locations: stealing a rug from the mosque,[3] a waistcloth from the bathhouse[4] or stripping the lead off the shop roofs.[5] In the Ottoman Bursa of the classical period, 25.71% of thefts took place in houses.[6] This is because houses usually were deprived of the security measures that markets, inns and the like had, as they were usually easily broken into, yet did not fail to provide loot.

According to our research on public order in 16th century Bursa, 25% of those who engaged in stealing from houses were women, 64.28% were men, and 10.72% were unidentified in terms of gender. In addition to those who worked by themselves, there were also situations where two or more persons committed organized robbery. Besides, it was possible to encounter husband-and-wife pairs engaged in robbery as well.[7] Since marriage means building a shared life, this situation can be seen as the natural consequence of couples having the same outlook or similar lifestyle and showing common effort in both good and bad times. Even when one person in the marriage engaged in thievery as an occupation, the lives of both parties would be troubled to a large extent. Murad bin Abdullah, whose thievery had been recorded in the month of *Dhu al-Hijjah* 991/January 1584 in Bursa, would hide the goods he stole in his house. Upon his arrest, his wife Ayşe bint-i Mustafa was summoned to court and interrogated as to whether she knew about her husband's activities. Denying knowledge of them, she stated that her husband Murad brought

---

2   Saadet Maydaer, *Osmanlı Klasik Döneminde Bursa'da Bir Semt: Hisar* (Bursa: Emin Yayınları 2009), 29.

3   *BCR*, A 108, 141a.

4   *BCR*, A 70, 110a.

5   *BCR*, A 145, 52b.

6   Saadet Maydaer, *XVI. Yüzyılda Bursa'da Asayiş* (Bursa: Emin Yayınları, 2016), 83.

7   Ibid, 86.

the stolen goods into his house.[8] It is natural at this point to ask: 'What was Ayşe's opinion of her husband's actions?' or 'Was she really unaware of his deeds?' Ayşe's statement suggests that she was not pleased with this situation, although we should also note that she turned a blind eye to the stolen goods being stored at her house. Ayşe probably knew that her husband engaged in theft, was feeling uncomfortable yet did not utter a word. For Murad, having a spouse who did not approve of his deeds, therefore who could at any moment report him certainly meant an insecure relationship and potential distress.

Two families: Partners in Theft

Some couples could choose to work together. In fact, as can be gleaned from the documents in Bursa dated *Rabi' al-awwal* 992/March 1584, Hacı İbrahim bin Hüseyin and Bünyad bin Ali, both professional thieves, were acting in partnership with their wives Ayşe, Raziye and Zülfü.[9] Bünyad, who apparently harassed the neighborhood inhabitants, had two wives; and both of his wives were accused of theft alongside him. As for Hacı İbrahim, he was monogamous and the 'Hacı' before his name was probably not a title used to denote his status as having performed the *Hajj*. In the Bursa Court Records, the title used for this purpose was "el-Hâc".[10] Therefore "Hacı" must have been his first name.[11]

These people had broken into several houses in the neighborhood to rob them and had harassed the neighborhood residents. Because of this they were denounced, and upon a search, many stolen goods were found in their houses. Some of the goods carefully identified in court records were returned to their rightful owners.[12]

The reports prepared on robbery accusations in Ottoman society show that the person whose property was stolen, provided that they knew the identity of the thief for certain, could go to court and file a complaint by directly naming the accused.[13]

---

8 *BCR*, A 121, 35b.

9 *BCR* A 121, 49b.

10 In the Bursa Court Record no. A153 that was transcribed into the Latin alphabet, the word "el-Hâc" was used in 1209 different places to denote someone who had performed the *Hajj*. As for the word Hacı, it was used 300 times as a title in front of first names. See *A 153 Nolu Bursa Şer'iyye Sicili*, M. Asım Yediyıldız, Saadet Maydaer, İlhami Oruçoğlu, ed.s, (Bursa: Bursa Büyükşehir Belediyesi Yayınları, 2010).

11 It is known that the word 'Hacı' was used as a name as well in Ottoman society. Rafet Metin, "XVI. Yüzyılın İkinci Yarısında Bozok Sancağında Kullanılan Erkek Şahıs İsimleri," *Kastamonu Eğitim Dergisi* 21, no. 2 (2013): 550, 557.

12 *BCR*, A 121, 49b-51a.

13 *BCR*, A 145, 75b.

Otherwise, they could request an investigation into the situation by saying[14] "Such and such person is a suspect".[15] Sometimes public safety officials such as the *zaim*, *subaşı* and the like could, probably upon receiving a report about the situation, accuse a person of theft.[16] Naturally there also emerged people who abused this situation and in order to harass someone they disliked, would incriminate them by reporting them to the *subaşı* and requesting that their houses be searched.[17] Clearly, however, such a person whose house was wrongfully searched would not refrain from filing a complaint as well.

Sometimes, the person whose property was stolen would recognize it in the hands of another, and claiming that he was the rightful owner, would appeal to the court. In the month of Ramadan 995/August 1587, Emine bint-I Hüseyin who lived in the Darbhane neighborhood of Bursa, claimed that approximately a year ago a thief broke into her house and stole some of her belongings. What was her reason to report this crime more than a year later?

The explanation was that Emine bint-i Hüseyin had seen the fabric materials— she called them light overshirt—and a pan in the house of her namesake Emine bint-i Ahmed approximately a year later, and therefore went to court and sued her.[18] However, Emine bint-i Ahmed, the accused, claimed that her sister Ayşe gifted these items to her. Her sister Ayşe corroborated the claim, stating: "I had given Emine [bint-i Hüseyin] the two pieces of light clothing and one footed pan. They were my property. Now the woman claims that the items are hers and that they were stolen from her house. Her claim is groundless." Emine bint-i Ahmed thus escaped being implicated in theft. However, the dispute between these women was not limited to this case only. In another trial, Emine bint-i Hüseyin had hunted down her 'large rug' that she had again claimed was stolen during the same rob-

---

14 The word 'mazanne/mazınne' comes from the root 'zann' in Arabic and is used to mean 'the purported, the supposed/suspected'. Here it has the meaning of 'the person suspected to be the thief'. Şemseddin Sami, *Kamus-ı Türkî* (İstanbul: Çağrı Yayınları, 1996), 1365; Ferit Devellioğlu, *Osmanlıca-Türkçe Ansiklopedik Lûgat* (Ankara: Aydın Kitabevi Yayınları, 1996), 589.

15 "Sebeb-i tahrir-i kelimat budur ki İlyas b. Şaban nâm Yahudi meclis-i şer'a Hundi bint-i Hoşkadem nâm avratı ihzar ettikde takrir-i kelam edib 'Evimden hayli esbabım sirka olundu. Mezbur Hundi'nin güveyisi? Mustafa b Abdullah mazannemdir, evi aransın,' dedikde ..." *BCR*, A 35, 334b. Also see *BCR*, A 143, 185a; *BCR*, A 145, 143a; *BCR*, A 153, 123b, 126b; *BCR*, A 44, 43b; *BCR*, A 67, 689; *BCR*, A 121, 43.

16 *BCR*, A 70, 151.

17 *BCR*, A 145, 85a.

18 *BCR*, A 145, 117a.

bery, and she accused Ayşe bint-i Ahmed.[19] However, Ayşe rejected this accusation, stating that she bought the rug in question from Muhammad Bey, Emine bint-i Hüseyin's husband, by paying him 1500 *akçe*s. Ayşe went a step further, and to portray Emine as a liar and a slanderer, she asked: 'Does anyone in the neighborhood know that the house was broken into?' When no one with such knowledge came forward, Emine bint-i Hüseyin could not prove her claim. This second case illustrates that there were clearly hostilities among Emine bint-i Hüseyin and the sisters Ayşe and Emine. Naturally, the court records do not mention how these women had met, their shared history and what led to their disputes. However, one can make educated guesses by reading between the lines.

For instance, Emine bint-i Hüseyin's animosity seems to have been mainly towards Ayşe. Indeed, given the order of the trials in the court records, we see that the first person Emine bint-i Hüseyin sued was Ayşe, and that the material value of the rug was greater than that of the other goods she would later claim were her property. Ayşe somehow knew Emine's husband Muhammed as well. He was probably a distant relative, a family friend, or an acquaintance. When he was claimed to have sold the rug without the knowledge of his wife, no one came forward to say, "Ayşe and Muhammed have nothing to do with each other.' Failing to even prove that her house was robbed, Emine bint-i Hüseyin then sued Ayşe's sister too, claiming that some items she saw in Emine bint-i Ahmed's possession belonged to her. If we look closely, we see that, unlike her sister, Emine bint-i Ahmed did not request witnesses for the robbery of the claimant's house. However, nor could she say, 'These items belong to me'. Emine bint-i Ahmed's acquaintances and neighbors knew that the items in question did not belong to her which suggests that the items must have arrived at her house later. At the same time, she had to explain their origin to acquit herself of the charges, and therefore she claimed that these goods were given to her by her sister Ayşe.

Which prompts us to ask: where had Ayşe bint-i Ahmed acquired the disputed items. The records make it clear that the rug and the other items originally belonged to the claimant Emine bint-i Hüseyin. Her husband Muhammed must have gifted the other items to Ayşe just as he sold her the rug. Because he removed the items from the house without his wife's knowledge, Emine bint-i Hüseyin must have thought they were stolen. Seeing the items a year later with Emine bint-I Ahmet, she filed her charges. As to why Muhammed, the husband, would gift or sell these items to Ayşe, we can surmise that either Muhammed had run out of money and

---

19   *BCR*, A 145, 117a.

started selling items from his house, or he had a close relationship with Ayşe bint-i Ahmed such as friendship, kinship, acquaintanceship or an illicit relationship, the nature of which we cannot ascertain from the documents. We certainly do not have the means to find out the exact reason for Muhammad's behavior.

The case about Emine bint-i Hüseyin's rug does not end here. Emine saw the same rug at the house of Kerime bint-i Hacı Ahmed and sued her by claiming that it belonged to her. She repeated her claims: 'A year ago during the month of Holy Ramadan, my house was broken into and some of my belongings were stolen. I found one of those stolen goods, a rug, in the hands of Kerime. It should be investigated'. How did the same rug move from the house of Ayşe bint-i Ahmed to the house of Kerime? Kerime answered: 'The woman called Ayşe from the Nalband neighborhood pawned the large rug in question to me by taking 800 *akçes* from me as a benevolent loan.' The case once more returns to Ayşe bint-i Ahmed. When asked about how the rug again ended up in her hands, Ayşe repeated her earlier claim: "The large rug in question is my property. I had purchased it from Muhammed Bey, Emine's husband, for 1500 *akçes*. Taking 800 *akçes* from the aforementioned Kerime, I pawned that large rug in return." The court, instead of summoning Muhammed Bey to confirm whether such a purchase took place or not, requested Emine to prove that the rug belonged to her. Emine presented the testimonies of a total of four witnesses, one male and three females, and proved that the rug belonged to her. To reclaim the rug, however, a second step was needed: to prove that she did not sell or gift the rug to her husband Muhammed Bey. Emine did not have any witnesses who could prove that such a transaction had not taken place. Consequently, Emine was ordered to take an oath which, in turn, rendered void the purchase supposedly initiated by her husband Muhammed Bey.[20]

To sum up, we can say that sometimes, there would be different reasons behind what look like allegations of theft. In some cases, the person accused of theft would confess their crime.[21] If the person accused of theft did not accept the charge, and if there was no evidence or witness regarding the crime, the alleged thief would be asked to name a guarantor whose duty was to prevent the accused from escaping until proven innocent or guilty.[22] If someone failed to provide a guarantor, the suspect was held in jail until truth of the matter was revealed.[23]

---

20 *BCR*, A 145, 123b.

21 *BCR*, A 67, 689; *BCR*, A 153, 42a, 87b; *BCR*, A 108, 141a, *BCR*, A 42, 46b; *BCR*, A 121, 33a, 46a, *BCR*, A 145, 116a; *BCR*, A 44, 44a.

22 *BCR*, A 32, 165; *BCR*, A 121, 61b.

23 *BCR*, A 121, 61b; *BCR*, A 32, 173; *BCR*, A 145, 88b.

There were also situations in which those who committed theft were not accused or were caught red-handed or known by everyone to be thieves. In this case the major concern was to find the stolen items as well as the identities of their real owners by having the thieves' houses searched. Indeed, in the trials concerning the families of Hacı İbrahim and Bünyad mentioned above, a similar process took place when the men along with their wives, Ayşe, Raziye and Zülfü, were brought to the court.[24] Even though the records do not specify how each person was related, we know that Raziye and Hacı İbrahim lived in different houses, Hacı İbrahim did not refer to Raziye as 'my spouse', and various other details suggest that Ayşe was Hacı İbrahim's wife, and Bünyad had two wives called Raziye and Zülfü.[25] Raziye was widely known as a thief. As was the custom in the Ottoman legal system, enough 'neutral' individuals, that is, those known to have no previous disagreements with or hostility towards the accused, were sent into the houses of the two families (who turned out to have engaged in theft as partners in Rabi al-awwal 992/March 1584), located the items and registered them one by one. With the exception of some, the stolen items were sorted by location: 'The items found in Hacı İbrahim's chest'; 'The items found in Raziye's chest.'

In the Ottoman times, valuable belongings, such as precious textiles, money, and jewelry, were kept locked in chests at peoples' homes.[26] Therefore such chests would be the first target for thieves.[27] Similarly, those who engaged in robbery also used the chests to store the stolen items in their houses.[28] However, if the thieves were accused or caught, chests made it easier to find the stolen goods and use them as evidence against them, therefore chests were not always preferred. More reliable hiding methods used by thieves included transferring the items to someone else's house or selling them immediately to get them off their hands.[29] Raziye and Ibrahim preferred to hold some of the stolen items in chests at their house. When their houses were searched and the chests opened, the found items were matched with their owners, who had identified their belongings in their formal complaint. Consequently, Raziye and Ibrahim were confirmed as thieves.

The stolen items recorded in the documents also reveal which goods the thieves considered as "light in load yet heavy in value," in the 16th century. According to the documents, the most popular item that one would wish to steal was, predict-

---

24 *BCR*, A 121, 49b.
25 *BCR,* A 121, 49b-51b.
26 *BCR*, B 140, 144a.
27 *BCR*, B 104, 27a.
28 *BCR*, A 121, 49b.
29 *BCR*, B 136, 39a; A 121 21b.

ably, jewelry—as in all periods. However, we see that the goods that Ibrahim and Raziye stole in the largest quantities were textiles and clothing. This may not make sense in light of the stealing practices of our times, but it clearly illustrates the need to evaluate a past event in the context of its own period.

The Items Found in the Houses of Hacı İbrahim and Raziye

The court records solely listed, but did not give any information on, the material value of the stolen items found in the houses of Hacı İbrahim and Raziye. However, we can assess their value by consulting related records, such as the testimonies of the actual owners:[30] "A month before the written date, Ibrahim broke into my house in daytime and stole 5 embroidered macramé cloths worth 90 *akçes* each, red sandals worth 500 *akçes*,[31] a satin caftan, 5 new yellow garments worth 50 *akçes* each,[32] and a pan worth 60 *akçes*."[33] In the case of Hacı İbrahim and Raziye, however, the principal goal was not to compensate a particular plaintiff but to identify and return to the rightful owners all the stolen items found in the possession of people known to be thieves. For this reason, the court felt no need to appraise the value of said items, and the victims were able to retrieve them by proving that the goods belonged to them.[34] There were nine such victims who were able to retrieve the stolen items: Hacı Osman bin Hacı Ali, Mustafa Çelebi bin Budak, Nasuh bin Abdullah, Şemsi Hatun bint-i Yusuf, Muslihuddin bin Muhyiddin, Ömer bin Hacı Balı, Ahmed bin Yusuf, Hüseyin bin Pir Ali, Müderris Mevlana Balı Çelebi bin Mustafa and Mehmed. As we can see, only one of them was a woman. One of the male victims was a teacher. There is no data to guide us on the social or financial standing of the others.

The victims presented the court with two witnesses each and proved which items among the stolen property belonged to them. We see that two of the witnesses, Mehmed bin Mustafa and Mustafa bin Mehmed, testified for two different people at the same time.[35] One of these was Muslihuddin bin Muhyiddin, and the other, Şemsi Hatun bint-i Yusuf. Şemsi Hatun did not appear in person and instead sent Muslihuddin bin Mehmed as a proxy. In this case, the two people probably lived with each other, as their witnesses were the same as well. Maybe they were rela-

---

30   *BCR*, B 20, 138a; *BCR*, B 104, 27a.

31   A type of aromatic tree brough from India. Şemseddin Sami, *Kâmûs-ı Türkî*, 834.

32   A type of silk. Sir James W. Redhouse, *Turkish and English Lexicon* (İstanbul: Çağrı Yayınları, 2006), 881. Devellioğlu, *Osmanlıca-Türkçe Ansiklopedik Lûgat*, 166.

33   *BCR*, B 104, 27a.

34   *BCR*, A 121, 49b-51a.

35   *BCR*, A 121, 50b.

tives who lived in the same house. The witnesses for the others were a variety of individuals. In the end, a small number of the stolen items were returned to their owners, while the owners of most of the items remained unknown.

CHART 5.1. The stolen items that victims were able to retrieve

The name of the stolen item	The owner	Estimated value
Navy blue *çuha* wrap with dark green lining[36]	Hacı Osman bin Hacı Ali	31 akçes[37]
One glass bowl	Mustafa Çelebi bin Budak	20-91 akçes[38]
One blue caftan	Mustafa Çelebi bin Budak	122-273 akçes[39]
One pink? Macramé	Mustafa Çelebi bin Budak	6-41 akçes[40]
Old underpants	Mustafa Çelebi bin Budak	6-25 akçes[41]
Macramé towel	Mustafa Çelebi bin Budak	6-41 akçes[42]
One boy's shirt	Mustafa Çelebi bin Budak	5-200 akçes[43]
One white skullcap[44]	Mustafa Çelebi bin Budak	20-142 akçes[45]
One waistcloth for the bathhouse	Mustafa Çelebi Bin Budak	36 akçes[46]
Some pieces of clothing	Mustafa Çelebi bin Budak	26-53 akçes[47]
Red *çuha* bodysuit with crisscross buttons	Nasuh bin Abdullah	140 akçes[48]
White plain long sleeve	Nasuh bin Abdullah	31 akçes[49]
Multicolored	Nasuh bin Abdullah	129 akçes[50]
Cut Eye-of-Nightingale	Şemsi Hatun bint-i Yusuf	430 akçes[51]

36   Dark green; of dark green color, petroleum colored. Devellioğlu, *Osmanlıca-Türkçe Ansiklopedik Lûgat*, 818.

37   *BCR*, A 167, 68b.

38   *BCR*, A 167, 17a, 67b.

39   *BCR*, A 167, 44b, 47a.

40   *BCR*, A 167, 33b, 29a, 51b, 58a, 57a, 46b, 48a, 51b, 44a, 29b, 68a.

41   *BCR*, A 167, 47a, 57a, 68b, 68a, 59a, 48a, 67b.

42   *BCR*, A 167, 33b, 29a, 51b, 58a, 57a, 46b, 48a, 51b, 44a, 29b, 68a.

43   *BCR*, A 167, 59a, 67a, 51b, 58a, 68b, 68a, 63b, 20b, 59a, 46b, 43a, 67b, 46b, 47a.

44   The name of the felt cap worn by dervishes. Şemseddin Sami, *Kâmûs-ı Türkî*, 934. *Arakiyye* comes from the word *arak* in Arabic, meaning sweat. It was worn under the main headgear to absorb perspiration. Reşad Ekrem Koçu, *Türk Giyim, Kuşam ve Süslenme Sözlüğü* (Ankara: Başnur Matbaası, 1967), 14.

45   *BCR*, A 167, 59a, 44a, 58a, 23b. 33b.

46   *BCR*, A 167, 47a.

47   *BCR*, A 167, 23b.

48   *BCR*, A 167, 67a.

49   *BCR*, A 167, 68b.

50   *BCR*, A 167, 7b.

51   *BCR*, A 31, 99.

The name of the stolen item	The owner	Estimated value
Sewn Eye-of-Nightingale	Şemsi Hatun bint-i Yusuf	430 akçes[52]
Beige lining	Şemsi Hatun bint-i Yusuf	32-48 akçes[53]
Dark green fabric[54]	Şemsi Hatun bint-i Yusuf	53-60 akçes[55]
Purple wool	Şemsi Hatun bint-i Yusuf	250 akçes[56]
Second-hand black çuha	Muslihuddin bin Muhyiddin	232-470 akçes[57]
Cut green fabric	Ömer bin Hacı Balı	53-60 akçes[58]
Brocaded belt	Ömer bin Hacı Balı	90 akçes[59]
Seven feet of voile	Ahmed bin Yusuf	100? akçes[60]
Black long-sleeved çuha gown with crosswise buttons	Hüseyin bin Pir Ali	232-748 akçes[61]
Blue fabric	Müderris Mevlana Balı Çelebi bin Mustafa	95 akçes[62]
Navy blue çuha	Müderris Mevlana Balı Çelebi bin Mustafa	748? akçes[63]
Nezkeb[64]	Müderris Mevlana Balı Çelebi bin Mustafa	10-47 akçes[65]
Blue çuha headscarf	Müderris Mevlana Balı Çelebi bin Mustafa	125 akçes[66]
One small bowl	Mehmed nâm dürzî	11-75 akçes[67]
Hindi	Mehmed nâm dürzî	33 akçes[68]

52 *BCR*, A 31, 99.

53 *BCR*, A 167, 72a, 17b, 33b.

54 Bogasi: A loosely woven cloth used for the lining. It was similar to gray cotton cloth or canvas and was woven from cotton yarn. Koçu, *Türk Giyim, Kuşam ve Süslenme Sözlüğü*, 41.

55 *BCR*, A 167, 17b.

56 Maydaer, *Hisar*, 244.

57 Ibid, 251.

58 *BCR*, A 167, 17b.

59 Maydaer, *Hisar*, 250.

60 *BCR*, A 153, 128a.

61 Maydaer, *Hisar*, 251; *BCR*, A 167, 33b.

62 Maydaer, *Hisar*, 251.

63 *BCR*, A 167, 33b.

64 Nezkeb: The gold-studded headdress worn by women, headscarf. Derleme Sözlüğü, http://www.tdk.gov.tr/index.php?option=com_ttas&view=ttas&kategori1=derlay&kelime1=nezkep. (Accessed on 06.19.2018).

65 *BCR*, A 167, 48a, 68b, 58a, 59a, 51b, 57a.

66 *BCR*, A 167, 59a.

67 *BCR*, A 167, 57a, 29a, 9b, 29b, 29a, 48a, 63b, 22a, 29b, 59a, 20b.

68 Maydaer, *Hisar*, 251.

Even though the records do not include data on the value of the items taken out of the house of Raziye and Ibrahim, effort was given to provide estimate values by determining the highest and lowest prices for similar items in the *tereke* (estate) accounts during the same period.[69] In this way, it is possible to get an idea of both the sum of monetary damage to the victims and the value of the items that thieves considered as valuable.

Among the victims who retrieved their belongings by proving that they were the rightful owners, Mevlana Balı bin Mustafa's belongings were of the highest value. Court documents on the robbery provide no information except his occupation: teacher in the Lale Şahin *Madrasa*.[70] Consistent with his occupation, he must have owned valuable clothing worth stealing by the thieves. With the exception of two bowls, textiles made up most of the stolen items. As fabrics in that period were completely handcrafted and produced through a long and arduous process, they were quite expensive. The clothes sewn with these fabrics, already quite expensive, would increase even more in value when they were custom-made in special styles by the dressmakers. In other words, clothing oneself in the 16th century was quite costly, and even simple pieces of fabric or macramé napkins were attractive to thieves. We can understand this better by looking at food prices of the period. In early 16th century Bursa, one *akçe* could buy 700 *dirhams*[71] (approximately 2240 grams) of bread, 250 dirhams (800 grams) of meat in the winter, 300 *dirhams* (900 grams) of lamb meat in the summer, 1 *okka*[72] (approximately 1282 grams) of carp and 600 *dirhams* (1920 grams) of saltwater fish, and 150 *dirhams* (2480 grams) of cherry.[73]

According to the price list that Barkan compiled for the Süleymaniye soup kitchen in Istanbul based on the accounting records in 1585/1586, one *okka* (ap-

---

69　Although there are different opinions as to whether the *tereke* registers should be used to determine prices in the period in question, due to their status as official documents, the *qadis* had to evaluate prices realistically and did not venture outside of official prices. Mustafa Öztürk, "Osmanlı Dönemi Fiyat Politikası ve Fiyatların Tahlili," *Belleten* 55, no. 212 (1991): 98.

70　Mefail Hızlı, *Osmanlı Klasik Döneminde Bursa Medreseleri* (İstanbul: İz Yayınları, 1998), 30.

71　One *dirham* is the equivalent of approximately 3,20 grams.

72　One *okka* is the equivalent of approximately 1282 grams.

73　*Kanunnâme-i İhtisab-ı Bursa* (Ankara: Türk Standartları Enstitüsü, 2004), 1, 2, 3, 4, 11. For the price list of foodstuff in Bursa between the years 1674 and 1864 see Şevket Pamuk, *İstanbul ve Diğer Kentlerde 500 Yıllık Fiyatlar ve Ücretler 1469-1998* (Ankara, T.C. Başbakanlık Devlet İstatistik Enstitüsü, 2000), 174-176.

proximately 1285 grams) of lamb meat cost 3 akçes.[74] Since the prices in Bursa were always higher than in Istanbul, and one could buy 50 dirhams less in Bursa than in Istanbul for the same price,[75] approximately 1125 grams of lamb meat would have cost 3 akçes in Bursa. In other words, around the end of the 16th century in Bursa, 1 akçe could purchase approximately 375 grams of lamb meat. What this calculation also shows is that, in the span of a century, the price of lamb meat had almost doubled. Mustafa Akdağ has claimed that a period of inflation started in the years 1585-95, and the prices of some items increased twofold or more in the course of the century.[76] The most important reason for this is undoubtedly the reduction of valuable metal content of coins, in other words, debasement.[77]

When looking at the income levels during the same period, for instance, at the wages earned by the Lala Şahin madrasa teacher who was one of the robbery victims, we see that it was 20 akçes per day.[78] Although the wage scales varied between waqfs, we can infer that imams were normally paid 3 akçes and the muezzins 2 akçes/dirhams per day.[79] However, wages paid by the waqfs did not change significantly across centuries. Even though the salaries seemed to become more meager, in practice, the waqf employees at both mosques and in the service of education had supplementary income beyond this fixed daily wage due to duties they took on as reciters of the Qur'an at several different waqfs. Besides, at several waqfs payments in kind (wheat and the like) were also made. These payments in kind sometimes reached amounts far more than fixed salaries.[80]

When we look at the purchasing power of construction workers in Istanbul in the 16th century, we see that the daily wages of a common construction worker could purchase 2 kilograms of lamb meat, 8 kilograms of bread or 2.5 kilograms of rice.[81] Skilled construction workers were able to earn an income 1.5-2 times that of the common ones. In 1581, in Istanbul, a common construction worker was able to earn

74 Ömer Lütfi Barkan, "XVI. Asrın İkinci Yarısında Türkiye'de Fiyat Hareketleri," *Belleten* 34, no. 136 (1970): 566.

75 *Kanunnâme-i İhtisab-ı Bursa*, 3.

76 Mustafa Akdağ, "Osmanlı İmparatorluğu'nun Kuruluş ve İnkişafı Devrinde Türkiye'nin İktisadi Vaziyeti," *Belleten*, 43, no. 51 (1949): 531.

77 Pamuk, *Fiyatlar ve Ücretler 1469-1998*, 34.

78 Hızlı, *Bursa Medreseleri*, 28.

79 Maydaer, *Hisar*, 83, 87, 89.

80 Salih Pay, *Kuruluşundan Günümüze Yeşil Külliyesi* (Bursa: Bursa Büyükşehir Belediyesi Yayınları, 2010), 262.

81 Pamuk, *Fiyatlar ve Ücretler 1469-1998*, 64.

7.5 *akçes* a day, while in 1586 this number had reached 10 *akçes*. Between the same years, the daily wages of a skilled increased from 10.4 *akçes* to 16.7 *akçes*.[82] When we keep in mind that the wages in Bursa and Istanbul were comparable, we can calculate that a construction worker in the period in question would have to work for at least 2 days to purchase a shirt of average quality, 4-5 days to purchase an ordinary caftan, and 20-25 days to purchase a velvet quilt. If he wished to become a homeowner, of course allowing for variations according to the qualities of the house, a house in average condition in Hisar, the most popular residential area in Bursa in the 16th century, would have cost 3000 *akçes/dirhams*. At the same time, one could become a homeowner even with 700 akçes/dirhams.[83]

Other Items Found in the Homes of Thieves Hacı İbrahim and Bünyad

The items found in the homes of the thieves in question did not consist solely of the items listed above; several other items including jewelry and Qurans with unknown owners were also found. Most of those other items were again textile garments of various kinds. Even though we have no data on their value, the fact that they were made of expensive materials indicates that they had significant value. In a similar robbery, a young thief broke into the house of a woman living alone in the Temenyeri Neighborhood of Bursa in broad daylight and stole goods, mostly varieties of fabrics, worth 1260 *akçes*. The thief stated that he sold the caftan worth 500 *akçes* for 245 *akçes*, an amount less than half of its original price.[84] Of course, selling stolen items for far below their value is a practice that does not change across time and place. Since those who dealt in stolen property were usually known, a thief had to sell off a stolen item as soon as possible, and any sale of an item acquired for free naturally results in a profitable transaction.

Jewelry

The stolen jewelry found in Hacı İbrahim and Raziye's chests consisted of two gold rings, two silver rings, a pair of gold earrings, one threaded pearl, several pearls, a silver bracelet and various silver accoutrements. When we try to estimate the value of the jewelry in question from the *tereke* registers of the same years, we see

---

82 Pamuk, *Fiyatlar ve Ücretler 1469-1998*, 69. For the daily wages of construction workers in Ottoman towns between the years 1489 and 1914 see Pamuk, *Fiyatlar ve Ücretler 1469- 1998*, 79-82.

83 Maydaer, *Hisar*, 221.

84 *BCR*, B 104, 27a.

that a ring was worth anywhere between 10 and 180 *akçes*.[85] Earrings were usually more expensive, and their price would range between 57 and 540 *akçes*.[86] Pearls were an expensive type of jewelry used with care by Ottoman women and could be priced between 271-370 *akçes*.[87] Always highly valuable, the gold items, we can easily guess, were worth a great deal. Also light in load yet heavy in value, jewelry was much coveted by thieves. However, we see that Hacı İbrahim and Bünyad did not have plenty of precious jewelry in their homes. It is possible to think that they either had already sold the jewelry off or, a case of bad luck, they could not find any in the houses they entered.

Textiles

In the 16th century Ottoman society, textiles were valuable items and for this reason were in high demand by thieves. In the homes of Hacı İbrahim and Bünyad there were plenty of fabrics of several colors and types as well. These were very precious fabrics embroidered by golden and silver threads. They were entered in the court records as textiles found in both of the thieves' homes: Golden, tapered macramé, *kemha* in several colors and amounts,[88] red *kemha* with flag, purple *çuha*, two Chinese silks, beige lining, an old black *dimi*,[89] beige lining torn from its caftan, two pieces of raw silk, four pieces of voile,[90] colored cotton quilt, purple old worn wool, dark navy silk, cotton silk, blue silk, unsewn *bogasi* with its lining, navy blue *çuha* with flag,[91] navy

---

85   *BCR*, A 167, 58a, 68b, 7b, 59a.

86   *BCR*, A 167, 68b, 51b, 44a, 29a.

87   *BCR*, A 167, 58a; Maydaer, *Hisar*, 248.

88   *Kemha* is the name given to a silk dress fabric embroidered with gold and silver threads, and especially used for caftans. The richest, most valuable and oldest Turkish *kemha* were woven in Istanbul and Bursa. Koçu, *Türk Giyim, Kuşam ve Süslenme Sözlüğü*, 153. Devellioğlu, *Osmanlıca-Türkçe Ansiklopedik Lûgat*, 506.

89   *Dimi* is a cotton or woolen fabric or cloth woven on a gusset or a similar type of fabric. Şemseddin Sami, *Kamus-ı Türkî*, 645.

90   A type of silk fabric. Devellioğlu, *Osmanlıca-Türkçe Ansiklopedik Lûgat*, 1136.

91   *Çuha* is the name given for woolen textiles, and to dresses made from woolen fabrics. Çuha would be used to make overcoats for women, and would be used mostly for men's suits, vests, cloaks, shalwars, jodhpurs, coats and raincoats. It would usually be imported from Europe. As in all fabrics, the price of *çuha* would be calculated by the skeins of wool used, and prices would vary according to the color. In the markets of Istanbul the most preferred type was red *çuha*. All *kapıkulu* soldiers were given one layer of outfits made from *çuha* annually. The military had blue *çuha* outfits that were woven in Salonica. For further information see Koçu, *Türk Giyim, Kuşam ve Süslenme Sözlüğü*, 82.

blue satin *çuha*, in addition to two navy blue *çuha* pieces, red *çuha*, almond-like red *çuha* with flag, nightingale's eye wool and a Yanbolu[92] coat.

Cut Fabrics

Some of the fabrics found in the homes of Hacı İbrahim and Bünyad were cut to make clothing. These included a cut piece of wool (with flag), a nightingale's eye weave and green cambric. From time to time, whole pieces of fabric that customers gave to dressmakers could become the target for thieves; it is quite interesting to see that Hacı İbrahim and Bünyad had also stolen cut fabrics.[93] Maybe these were stolen as intact by the thieves and cut later. We do not have clear information on this subject.

Tailor made Clothes

In the Ottoman classical period, women and men wore shirts as light upper garments. Prices of shirts, of different varieties such as mottled, voile and embroidered, changed according to the type of fabric.[94] According to the 16th century records, shirts priced between 10 and 200 *akçe*s were worth 20-25 *akçe*s on average.[95] The buttonless *dolama* worn over the shirt and usually made of *çuha*, was held together with a belt tied on top of it, and it was among the most widely used types of clothing by both men and women in that period. *Dolama*s made from *kemha* and embroidered fabrics were usually worn by the janissaries.[96] Even though its price varied by type, a *dolama* would on average be worth 30-67 *akçe*s.[97] Among the items found in the house of Ibrahim or Raziye, there were three *dolama*s, two of them small, and three shirts, one of them small and one white.

As for the *zıbın*, a cotton, sleeveless bodysuit worn under the caftan in the winter, it could be sold anywhere from 20 *akçe*s to 140 *akçe*s.[98] In Raziye's chest, three such *zıbın*s made from navy blue *çuha* were found. The one found in Ibrahim's chest was described as 'old and worn'. As for the red *çuha zıbın* crisscrossed with

---

92 The name of a city in southeastern Bulgaria, situated in a fertile valley by the Tunca river, at an altitude of 135 meters above sea level. It was known for its production of a thick and coarse fabric called *kebe*. This type of fabric, known in Thrace and the Balkans as the "Yanbolu kebesi", was in high demand in the Ottoman markets. Machiel Kiel, "Yanbolu," *DİA* 43 (2013): 314.

93 *BCR*, A 112, 88a.

94 Maydaer, *Hisar*, 242.

95 *BCR*, A 167, 59a, 67a, 51b, 58a, 68b, 68a, 63b, 20b, 59a, 46b, 43a, 67b, 46b, 47a.

96 Koçu, *Türk Giyim, Kuşam ve Süslenme Sözlüğü*, 93.

97 *BCR*, A 167, 68b; Maydaer, *Hisar*, 247.

98 Koçu, *Türk Giyim, Kuşam ve Süslenme Sözlüğü*, 251; *BŞS*, A 167, 44b, 67a, 68b, 46b, 72a, 59a.

buttons, it is not clear where it was found. Also recorded was an 'old and mottled' caftan, which is usually made from the most precious fabrics. The object called a *kaftan sancağı* must have been a type of clasp used to bring together the two sides of the caftan.[99] The phrase 'White simple long sleeved' probably referred to a shirt.

Undergarments

The underpants and undershirts worth anywhere between 10 and 70 akçes,[100] were found in the chests of both Raziye and Ibrahim.

Bath Materials

In this period, there was an established bath culture in Bursa. The accessories such as towel, waistcloth, or bowls brought to the bathhouse were symbols of wealth and would be selected with care. A bath set was called *silki*. One worth between 21 to 52 akçes was found in the chest of Raziye. Also recorded in Raziye's chest were one complete *silki*,[101] a towel described as 'fringed,' and other bathhouse accessories of unspecified nature. The roster of found items also included a felt mat, a waistcloth, two bath bowls and a white bath towel without any information on where they were found.

Bundles

In the Ottoman society of the 16th century, clothing and other fabrics were usually wrapped up in bundles called *bohça* and stored in chests or cabinets. Young girls usually would bring their trousseau in bundles when getting married; in other words, the bundles often contained important home goods usually made from precious cloths and decorated with various embroideries. In Ibrahim's chest, there were a total of three bundles, one small, two of unspecified size, and in Raziye's chest, there were four bundles of unspecified size. A Yemeni bundle was also recorded without information on where it was found.

Macramé and Handkerchiefs

Macramé, tablecloths and covers with embroidered borders as well as and *destimal*s that were kerchiefs used as dishtowels and hand towels were elaborately embroidered

---

99 Sancak: Hairclip, hairpin. *Türkiye Türkçesi Ağızları Sözlüğü* (Erişim Tarihi: 19.06.2018), http://www.tdk.gov.tr/index.php?option=com_ttas&view=ttas&kategori1=derlay&keli me1=sancak

100 *BCR*, A 167, 68b, 17b, 56a, 57a, 68a.

101 Silk: A lineup, a kit, a set. *Örnekleriyle Türkçe Sözlük* IV (İstanbul: Milli Eğitim Bakanlığı Yayınları, 2004), 2552.

items found in every home in Ottoman society.[102] We see that such items made from precious fabrics were also recorded among the stolen items found in the houses of Ibrahim and Raziye. Two Indian macramé and white macramé of unknown origin were found in Raziye's chest. In Ibrahim's chest, an unspecified macramé of unknown quality and another type of macramé called *döğme* were found. Aside from these, six macramé of unspecified type with three of them old and worn, two white, one mottled, and one *döğme* macramé were recorded without information on where they were found. In addition, there was also the mention of a 'woman's macramé', which was a kind of scarf tied on the head by women.[103] As for the kerchiefs used as washcloths, there were four: One blue, one fringed, and two mottled.

Futa

From the *futa* that the shopkeepers usually wore, there was one found in Ibrahim's chest, and there were two in Raziye's.[104]

Pieces of Fabric

Among the items found in the houses of Ibrahim and Raziye, there were old pieces of fabric as well. These were most probably without much value, used by the thieves to bundle up the items stolen from houses and to throw them out of the window or over the wall. They were recorded as "Old white cloth," "scrap cloth," "white worn cloth," "pieces of cloth,"…etc.

Headwear

In Ottoman society, people would wear various types of headwear that marked their social class. Some of these could be quite ornate and valuable. The *arakiyye*s, dervish felt caps, worth 20-142 *akçe*s[105] in the records were a lot more valuable than the *nezkeb*, tall headpiece for women's, priced between 8-47 *akçe*s[106] and therefore

---

102 Devellioğlu, *Osmanlıca-Türkçe Ansiklopedik Lûgat*, 575, 179; Koçu, *Türk Giyim, Kuşam ve Süslenme Sözlüğü*, 178.

103 Devellioğlu, *Osmanlıca-Türkçe Ansiklopedik Lûgat*, 575.

104 *Futa* is defined in the *Kamus-ı Türki* as the silk cloth tied to the waist while working or in the bathhouse. (Şemseddin Sami, *Kamus-ı Türki*, 1008). Reşad Ekrem disagrees and states that it was a widely known fact that not all waistcloths were made from silk, and therefore there was a phrase called 'silk *futa*'. He discusses how the futa (waistcloth) tied to the waist in social life for hundreds of years had become a talisman and a marker of skill, expertise, luck and health for all shopkeepers and artisans. Koçu, *Türk Giyim, Kuşam ve Süslenme Sözlüğü*, 119.

105 *BCR*, A 167, 44a, 59a, 58a.

106 *BCR*, A 167, 48a, 68b, 58a, 68a, 59a, 51b, 57a, 67b, 47a, 46b.

the former were more attractive items for thieves. Naturally, both in Raziye's and Ibrahim's chests, gold filigree *arakiyye* were found.[107] There were also three pieces of *çuha* and four old *arakiyye*s found in Raziye's chest. Several old and new tiara-like *çember*,[108] three pieces of muslin and 'an old blue *nezkeb*' were also among the items of headwear found in the house of the thieves.

Belts

In the clothing styles of the Ottoman Classical Period, the clothes worn on the lower part of the body such as *shalwar* or trousers would be fixed to the waist with a thin cloth drawstring, or regular belts threaded through the waist section.[109] An Indian belt was among the items found in Raziye's chest; another drawstring with no address attached was also found in one of the houses.

Linens

A total of six linens were among the items found in the chests: One in Raziye's chest, three in Ibrahim's, and two of unknown location. One of these was recorded as 'mottled' meaning 'of multiple colors', and the other as 'old'. Another was used as a duvet cover.

Yarn

Cotton yarn was found in Ibrahim's chest, and the records mention that in Raziye's chest there was some *kılabdan,* gold filigreed silk thread.[110]

Kitchenware

The stolen kitchenware items found in Raziye and Ibrahim's houses consisted of pots of several sizes, pans, bowls and trays. The average value of each ranged from 20 to 80 *akçes*.[111] Two large pots called *kebir*s, one small pot, two footed bowls, one bowl with lid, two footed pans, a bowl of unknown type, a glass bowl, a footed tray, two small trays and one pastry tray were recorded as kitchenware among the stolen goods.

---

107 Ibrahim had two golden arakiyyes. This was probably due to his status as the chief of the gang.

108 *Çember*: Kerchief, headscarf. *Yeni Tarama Sözlüğü*, Cem Dilçin, ed., (Ankara: Türk Dil Kurumu Yayınları, 1983), 52.

109 Koçu, *Türk Giyim, Kuşam ve Süslenme Sözlüğü*, 236.

110 *Kılabdan*: Silk or cotton thread coiled with a spinning wheel. Şemseddin Sami, *Kâmûs-ı Türkî*, 1077.

111 Maydaer, *Hisar*, 232-235; BCR, A 167, 22b, 44a, 22b, 58a, 30a, 59a, 22a, 57b, 57a, 67a, 23b, 33b, 7b, 63b, 19a, 22a, 29a, 20b.

Miscellaneous

Among the items found in Ibrahim's chest was a Holy Qur'an, the material value of which was not specified. In the 16th century, the average value of a copy of the Holy Qur'an would range from 250 to 400 *akçes*.[112] However, one could also come across very cheap or very expensive copies ranging from 28 to 36000 *akçes*.[113] Among these, especially the valuable ones were targets for thieves. As a matter of fact, in the year 976/1586, a Holy Qur'an was stolen from the Ulu Cami. Later, the *subaşı* caught the thieves and returned the Qur'an to where it belonged.[114]

A type of pouch carried diagonally on the torso called *'Hamayil'* (sic) or 'Hamaylı',[115] another pouch of unknown type, and a pair of scissors called *mikras*[116] were found in Ibrahim's chest. As for Raziye's chest, a mirror, a mask, an Indian *mahbes* (sic), and some trinkets in a box were found. Lastly, items called "Yemenî *sumat* (sic)" and "black *çulgar* (sic)" were also located among the stolen items.

Who was the Head of the Gang?

Ibrahim and Raziye were professional thieves. They worked in partnership with their spouses and others and would share the loot. In organized incidents, usually one of the thieves would open the doors, two watchmen would check the surrounding area, and one would enter the house and steal whatever he/she could find that was light in weight yet heavy in value.[117] Later they would share the money or items they stole or store it in a place they considered safe or look for ways to sell them off.[118] In reality, the more scrupulous of the shopkeepers knew the identity of those who dealt in stolen goods, and this situation would raise complaints from time to time. For

---

112 Ali İhsan Karataş, "Tereke Kayıtlarına Göre XVI. Yüzyılda Bursa'da İnsan-Kitap İlişkisi," *Uludağ Üniversitesi İlahiyat Fakültesi Dergisi* 8, no. 8 (1999): 325.

113 Karataş, "Bursa'da İnsan-Kitap İlişkisi," 324, 325.

114 Hikmet Turhan Dağlıoğlu, *1558-1589 On Altıncı Asırda Bursa* (Bursa: Bursa Vilâyeti Matbaası, 1940), 85.

115 *Hamayil/hamail* is the name given to the cylindrical box hung on the neck and in which charms and amulets were kept. *Hamaylı* comes from the Arabic "hamail". It is used as a strap hung diagonally from the shoulder, as a sword *hamail* and aiming *hamail*. The amulets and lucky charms hung in the same way were also called *hamail*. The pouches hung on the shoulders of schoolchildren diagonally, along with the diagonal strap, were also called *hamaylı*. Koçu, *Türk Giyim, Kuşam ve Süslenme Sözlüğü*, 126.

116 *Mikras* means scissors, or a tool used for cutting. Devellioğlu, *Osmanlıca- Türkçe Ansiklopedik Lûgat*, 647.

117 *BCR*, A 93, 57a.

118 *BCR*, A 121, 52b; *BŞS*, B 136 39a; *BŞS*, A 93 57a.

instance, in the month of *Shawwal* 1035/June 1626, the woolen drapery sellers of Gelincik Bazaar applied to the court with their *yiğitbaşı*, and voiced their concern that some of the proprietors were buying and selling stolen goods for cheap.[119] The shopkeepers were disturbed by the ill-gotten gains from immoral practices of those who traded in stolen goods. Moreover, these unscrupulous people would not obey their *yiğitbaşı* and refuse to pay their share of *tekâlif-i örfiyye,* a kind of tax divided equally between the shopkeepers.

The stolen items could be sold most easily in flea markets where second-hand goods were traded. It is known that in Bursa before the 18th century there was a 'Flea Market Bazaar'.[120] Some of these shopkeepers would work together with the thieves and even personally participate in house robberies.[121] In addition to the vendors who dealt in stolen items in the Bursa bazaar, vendors also arrived from other cities as itinerant salesmen.[122] Thieves frequently used the method of transferring a stolen item to other cities to prevent it from being recognized by its owner; thus, an item stolen in Bursa could resurface in Istanbul or Manavgat.[123]

Ibrahim and Raziye, the subjects of our study, operated within the system of thievery, and worked in an organized fashion. Hacı İbrahim bin Hüseyin, Bünyad bin Ali and their wives Ayşe, Raziye and Zülfü were those who were brought to the court with the charges of "breaking into houses, confiscating garments and engaging in robbery".[124] However, Ibrahim and Raziye were named as the only owners of the chests that had been used as safe boxes when their houses were searched by court order.

One might ask: "Were all of the items found at the houses of the thieves and registered in court records stolen property? Might not some of these be the personal items of the thieves?" Yes, this is possible; however, if they were, the thieves would at least claim ownership and even try to prove it, as some thieves had in similar incidents.[125]

---

119 *BCR*, B 45, 121a.

120 This bazaar had been destroyed by two fires before the 18th century and the shopkeepers there had to move to the Yeni Hallaçlar Bazaar. Kamil Kepecioğlu, *Bursa Kütüğü* I, Hüseyin Algül, Osman Çetin, Mefail Hızlı, Mustafa Kara, M. Asım Yediyıldız, ed.s, (İstanbul: Bursa Büyükşehir Belediyesi Yayınları, 2009), 203.

121 *BCR*, A 121, 52b.

122 *BCR*, A 32, 136.

123 *BCR*, B 136, 39a; *BŞS*, A 5, 153a.

124 *BCR*, A 121, 49b.

125 *BCR*, A 145, 116a; *BŞS*, A 93, 57a.

Ibrahim and Raziye's names are mentioned in another incident. In that instance, Raziye met with Alaaddin and Kara Mehmed by a mosque in the Ibrahim Paşa Neighborhood. They had stolen goods with them, and Ibrahim testified that these items made up a portion of the stolen items that were recorded.[126] We therefore can answer our previous question of whether any of the recorded items were personal belongings of the thieves. Indeed, all of them were stolen.

When Raziye met with these men by the mosque, three people who each had robbed different locations had come together to divide the stolen goods among themselves. We can also infer from the records that Hacı İbrahim had also agreed to meet with them by the mosque. However, in his confession at the court, he claimed that he 'happened to run into them" while they had the stolen items in their possession. "I did not even come with them," he had said, to suggest that he himself did not engage in the robbery with the group.[127]

All these stories show us that we are dealing with a network of thieves. The married couples among them were either previously engaged in robberies and decided to get married to work better together, or they were already married and decided to assimilate into their criminal environment. One of the two people with whom they partnered was identified as a *suhte,* a medrese student. It is known that in the Ottoman Classical period, some *suhte*s were involved in such illegal activities.[128] One of them was notorious enough to have earned the nickname 'Black.'

Then who was the leader of this network of thieves? Although we have no clear information, the court records and reading between the lines suggest that Hacı İbrahim was the leader. His name is mentioned in all the court records pertaining to this case. Besides, he was the last to join the meeting near the Ibrahim Paşa mosque, and he had no stolen goods with him. This suggests that while he had not participated in the robbery itself, he had come to claim a portion of the loot. This supports the idea that he was the leader of the network. He tried to insist on his innocence by pointing out that he didn't have any stolen items with him, but his claim did not help explain all the stolen items found in the chest at his house. After Ibrahim, the most active and influential member of this organized network was Raziye; she did not shy away from engaging in robbery on her own and meeting with the rest of the members of the network by herself at street corners to claim her share of the loot. Other thieves had a certain amount of respect for her due to her

---

126 *BCR,* A 121, 51b.
127 *BCR,* A 121, 51b.
128 Maydaer, *Asayiş,* 46, 51, 54, 55, 56, 60.

reputation and would follow her advice. The great amount of valuable items found in Raziye's chest was proof of this. Moreover, only two of the seven known members of the network had their chests searched and recorded by the court. Also, we see that the items found in her chest were no less valuable in quality or quantity than those found in Ibrahim's chest. It is therefore reasonable to conclude that Ibrahim and Raziye played lead roles in this network.

What Became of Them?

The documents do not give us information on the fate of these thieves. What kind of punishment would have been adequate for people who clearly were members of an organized network of thieves? Were they given a *hadd* or did they receive a *tazir*? Were they put in jail, sentenced to the galley or exiled? Or did they pay a monetary fine?

As we know, in Islamic jurisprudence, even if a particular crime requires the *hadd* but there is the slightest doubt about the evidence or the nature of the crime, the accepted norm was the suspension of *hadd*. Likewise, any procedural errors found before punishment is executed--even if the sentence has been given--will render the *hadd* null and void.[129] For example, if someone confesses to having stolen 100 *akçes* from Ahmed but later says, 'I was wrong, I had stolen 100 *akçes* not from Ahmed but Mehmed', and if there is no other evidence, the *hadd* punishment cannot be carried out.[130] Nor can it be carried out if the accused thief claims that the property belongs to him, or that he left the item with the plaintiff in trust or as a deposit, or that he had bought the item, or that someone donated it to him, or that someone allowed him to take the item.[131] As the experts of Islamic jurisprudence widely agree, the punishment is not implemented unless the crime is proven beyond any doubt since later there would be no turning back.[132]

The preponderance of circumstances that could nullify the *hadd* punishment for stealing ended up limiting its implementation. Ottoman legal codes concerning stealing generally include statements such as 'may the *qadi* decide on *tazir* if

---

129 Ömer Menekşe, "XVII-XVIII. Yüzyılda Osmanlı Devleti'nde Hırsızlık Suçu ve Cezası," Ph.D dissertation, Marmara Üniversitesi, 1998, 45.

130 Ömer Nasuhi Bilmen, *Hukuk-ı İslamiyye ve Istılahat-ı Fıkhiyye Kamusu* 3 (İstanbul: İstanbul Üniversitesi Yayınları, 1950), 295.

131 Menekşe, *Hırsızlık Suçu ve Cezası*, 48.

132 Menekşe, *Hırsızlık Suçu ve Cezası*, 45. For situations that led to an abatement in incidents of robbery see Bilmen, *Istılahat-ı Fıkhiyye Kamusu* 3, 295-8, 303-5, also see Menekşe, *Hırsızlık Suçu ve Cezası*, 45-51.

the hand is not cut'.[133] The types of *tazir* punishment suggested in the penal code were: death sentence, prison term,fines, galleys, imprisonment in a fortress, and exile.[134] Concerning the thieves who are the subject of this study, we do not have specific information about which of these *tazir* punishments they received--i.e. on the basis of the stolen items, their quantity and the method of stealing. Although recognized as thieves, they never were caught red-handed, and they returned the items they stole, which makes us think that they must have been punished with at least one of the *tazir* penalties and not the *hadd*. Indeed, there are documents showing that only *tazir* penalties would be carried out in cases where thieves returned the items they stole.[135] We also know that usually small-scale house burglaries such as this one merited the punishment of exile.[136] Another mystery is whether Raziye, İbrahim and the other thieves were given the same punishment or not, since we get the impression that their roles in the crime were not the same. If they were exiled, did they change their behavior, that is, renounce their ways and lived as honest and good people? Or as we see in several other cases, did they also fail to change their ways, and continue to organize robberies wherever they went?

Instead of a Conclusion

At least for now, we cannot answer these questions because the limited number of official documents we can access on these individuals say very little on the subject. The format of the legal documents makes their interpretation even more difficult. Be that as it may, in this study we evaluated different aspects of comparable cases and tried to fill the gaps through interpretation and reading between the lines, in order to take a closer look at the life of an organized network of thieves made up of two families in the 16th century. New data that we hope to obtain in the future on the same individuals might enable us to answer the questions we articulated above.

---

133 Ahmed Akgündüz, *Osmanlı Kanunnâmeleri ve Hukukî Tahlilleri 4. Kitap, Kanunî Devri Kanunnâmeleri, I. Kısım Merkezî ve Umumî Kanunnâmeleri* (İstanbul: Fey Vakfı Yayınları, 1992), 368, 425.

134 Menekşe, *Hırsızlık Suçu ve Cezası*, 117.

135 Menekşe, *Hırsızlık Suçu ve Cezası*, 116.

136 For examples of those exiled due to the crime of robbery, see Ali İhsan Karataş, *Osmanlı Dönemi Bursa Sürgünleri (18-19. Asırlar)*, (Bursa: Emin Yayınları, 2009), 188-94.

Bibliography

Archival Sources

Bursa Şer'iyye Sicilleri A 70, A 108, A 32, A 121, A 145, A 143, A 153, A 44, A 67, A 70, A 42, A 32, B 140, B 104, B 136, B 20, A 167, A 31, A 93, B 45, A 5.

Secondary Sources

A 153 Nolu Bursa Şer'iyye Sicili. eds. M. Asım Yediyıldız, Saadet Maydaer, İlhami Oruçoğlu. Bursa: Bursa Büyükşehir Belediyesi Yayınları, 2010.

Akdağ, Mustafa. "Osmanlı İmparatorluğu'nun Kuruluş ve İnkişafı Devrinde Türkiye'nin İktisadi Vaziyeti." *Belleten* 13, no. 51 (1949): 497-564.

Akgündüz, Ahmed. *Osmanlı Kanunnâmeleri ve Hukukî Tahlilleri, 4. Kitap, Kanunî Devri Kanunnâmeleri, I. Kısım Merkezî ve Umumî Kanunnâmeleri*. İstanbul: Fey Vakfı Yayınları, 1992.

Barkan, Ömer Lütfi. "XVI. Asrın İkinci Yarısında Türkiye'de Fiyat Hareketleri." *Belleten* 34, no. 136 (1970): 557-607.

Bilmen, Ömer Nasuhi. *Hukuk-ı İslamiyye ve Istılahat-ı Fıkhiyye Kamusu*. İstanbul: İstanbul Üniversitesi Yayınları, 1950.

Dağlıoğlu, Hikmet Turhan. *1558-1589 On Altıncı Asırda Bursa*. Bursa: Bursa Vilâyeti Matbaası, 1940.

Devellioğlu, Ferit. *Osmanlıca-Türkçe Ansiklopedik Lûgat*. Ankara: Aydın Kitabevi Yayınları, 1996.

Hızlı, Mefail. *Osmanlı Klasik Döneminde Bursa Medreseleri*. İstanbul:İz Yayınları, 1998.

Derleme Sözlüğü. Accessed on 19.06.2018. http://www.tdk.gov.tr.

Kanunnâme-i İhtisab-ı Bursa. Ankara: Türk Standartları Enstitüsü, 2004.

Karataş, Ali İhsan. "Tereke Kayıtlarına Göre XVI. Yüzyılda Bursa'da İnsan-Kitap İlişkisi." *Uludağ Üniversitesi İlahiyat Fakültesi Dergisi* 8/8 (1999): 317-28.

———. *Osmanlı Dönemi Bursa Sürgünleri (18-19. Asırlar)*. Bursa: Emin Yayınları, 2009.

Kepecioğlu, Kamil. *Bursa Kütüğü*, eds. Hüseyin Algül, Osman Çetin, Mefail Hızlı, Mustafa Kara, M. Asım, Yediyıldız. İstanbul: Bursa Büyükşehir Belediyesi Yayınları, 2009.

Kiel, Machiel. "Yanbolu." *DİA* 43 (2013): 313-5.

Koçu, Reşad Ekrem. *Türk Giyim, Kuşam ve Süslenme Sözlüğü*. Ankara: Başnur Matbaası, 1967.

Maydaer, Saadet. *Osmanlı Klasik Döneminde Bursa'da Bir Semt: Hisar*. Bursa: Emin Yayınları, 2009.

———. *XVI. Yüzyılda Bursa'da Asayiş*. Bursa: Emin Yayınları, 2016.

Menekşe, Ömer. 1998. "*XVII-XVIII. Yüzyılda Osmanlı Devleti'nde Hırsızlık Suçu ve Cezası.*" Ph.D dissertation, Marmara Üniversitesi.

Metin, Rafet. "XVI. Yüzyılın İkinci Yarısında Bozok Sancağında Kullanılan Erkek Şahıs İsimleri." *Kastamonu Eğitim Dergisi* 21, no. 2 (2013): 543-60.

Örnekleriyle Türkçe Sözlük. İstanbul: Milli Eğitim Bakanlığı Yayınları, 2004.

Öztürk, Mustafa. "Osmanlı Dönemi Fiyat Politikası ve Fiyatların Tahlili." *Belleten* 55, no. 212 (1991): 87-100.

Pamuk, Şevket. *İstanbul ve Diğer Kentlerde 500 Yıllık Fiyatlar ve Ücretler 1469-1998*. Ankara: T.C. Başbakanlık Devlet İstatistik Enstitüsü, 2000.

Pay, Salih. *Kuruluşundan Günümüze Yeşil Külliyesi*. Bursa: Bursa Büyükşehir Belediyesi Yayınları, 2010.

Redhouse, Sir James W. *Turkish and English Lexicon*. İstanbul: Çağrı Yayınları, 2006.

Şemseddin Sami. *Kamus-ı Türkî*. İstanbul: Çağrı Yayınları, 1996.

CHAPTER SIX

The Case of Gülpaşa of the Gurbet Taifesi at Bor in the 16th Century*

Emine Dingeç

Introduction

Without a doubt, one of the groups that have remained on the margins of Ottoman historiography is the Roma.[1] In the Ottoman documents of the 16th century, this group is usually identified as *Çingene* or 'the Copts'. The community has also been described, in different times and places, as *"ehl-i fesad"* and *"gurbet taifesi"*. These expressions essentially carry different meanings. *Ehl-i fesad* refers to those who would incite trouble, disturb public order and engage in banditry.[2] As for *'Gurbet Taifesi'*, *taife* is a group noun while the word *'Gurbet'* entails feelings of nostalgia, otherness and estrangement experienced while being far away from one's country, one's homeland.[3] Although the Ottoman society included multiple ethnic communities, the term *gurbet* has usually been associated with the Roma.[4] *Gurbet*

---

*   Bor, Niğde, 1529

1   The term *Çingene* (Gypsy) in this article is used in line with the historical documents.

2   For further information see Faika Çelik, "Exploring Marginality in The Ottoman Empire: Gypsies or People of Malice (Ehl-i Fesad) as Viewed by the Ottomans," (Badia Fiesolana: Europen a Institute, 2004).

3   "İlhan Ayverdi, *Misalli Büyük Türkçe Sözlük* 1 (İstanbul: Kubbealtı Neşriyat, 2006), 1099-100. In the *mühimme* records as well, the word gurbet is used in the phrase "Gurbet ve Çingân tâifesi". See. *3 Numaralı Mühimme Defteri* (Ankara: Başbakanlık Devlet Arşivleri Genel Müdürlüğü, 1993), Hk. 1280; BOA, MD, C.27, 345, Hk. 828.

4   In the *Tarama Sözlüğü* the word "gurbet" is defined as Gypsy. See *Tarama Sözlüğü* 3 (Ankara: Türk Dil Kurumu, 1963), 1835. Ali Rafet Özkan states that the name "Gurbeti" originated in Afghanistan and spread through the Balkans up to Western European countries. Sampson, who conducts research on the accents of the Roma, separates the Roma into two branches based on the language they used: He called the ones who moved southeast after Iran the Ben, and the ones who went west the Phen. He states that within the Southeastern branch, those in northern Syria and Iran were called the Gurbeti. See Ali

FIGURE 6.1 The Roman woman (İBB Atatürk Library Postcards Archive)

points to the melancholy and pain that homesickness carries. The Roma or *gurbet taifesi* have also at times been associated with activities disapproved of by society. Since differences in nomenclature reflect the perspectives of state and society towards this group, we should analyze archival sources in terms of the language used in them. This study will focus on the case of Gülpaşa who was charged with fornication and tried in the *qadi*'s court in Bor, in central Anatolia. Through the short official report where the name of Gülpaşa is mentioned, we will address the widespread prejudices regarding Romany women who were usually associated with 'fornication and prostitution'. In addition, we will try to illustrate how historical reality can be constructed in various forms by interpreting one document from different angles.

Gülpaşa in Bor

In Ottoman society, the nomadic Roma would usually set off in the month of April and travel for almost six months. Not all of them followed the same route.

Rafet Özkan, *Türkiye Çingeneleri* (Ankara: Kültür Bakanlığı Yayınları, 2000), 77. Today, the Roma found in Cyprus are also called Gurbet.

For example, some moved from the northern Balkans to Anatolia, while others traveled further north of the Balkans. They would return to their homestead at the beginning of October.[5] Gülpaşa and her group most probably did likewise. We don't know exactly the origin of the Roma group who arrived in Bor. However, it is certain that they visited several cities during their travels.[6] According to the court records, Gülpaşa and company reached Bor probably around the beginning of August.

Bor was a medium-sized settlement larger than a village and smaller than a city. Connected to the Niğde *sanjak*, Bor was a small place that had been steadily growing.[7] The Hacı İsmail Mescidi neighborhood had been added that year to the already existing neighborhoods of Veled Seydi Mescidi, Hacı Muhsin Mescidi, Celal Mescidi, Vüsta Mescidi, Hacı Kemal Mescidi, Akkız Oğlan Mescidi, Sufiyan Mescidi, İlyas Fakih Mescidi, Uğurlu Mescidi, Hacı Pir Ahmed Mescidi and Cami, bringing the number of neighborhoods to thirteen.[8] The addition of neighborhoods, of course, indicated increase in population. This was important for Gülpaşa and company, as they wanted to sell the goods they produced. They made a living through producing and selling while on the road and would roam from place to place in order to reach more people.

Bor was one of the quiet towns in Anatolia. Not a lot happened that required court intervention. No more than twenty people per month would appear before the qadi.[9] This meant that on some days no one came knocking at the *qadi*'s door. Most of the

---

5   Alexandre G. Paspati lived with both the settled and the nomadic peoples in the 19th century in order to write his work on the language of the Roma. Paspati included his observations of the Roma in the foreword to his dictionary. See Alexandre G. Paspati, *Etudes Sur Ies Tchinghianes ou Bohemiens De L'empire Ottoman* (Osnabrück, 1973), 10.

6   The Puşiyan (Poşa), the group that made a living by selling sieves and sifters in the 18th century, travelled from Sivas to Aydın. Some of the places they stopped at during these travels were Kütahya and Karahisar-ı Sahip. This group had been recorded in the Kütahya Court Records on May 2, 1762, due to a tax issue. See *Kütahya Şer'iyye Sicili*, 2/73a.

7   While Bor was still a village in 1507, it became a township in 1518. See Rafet Metin, "XVI. Yüzyılda Niğde ve Kırşehir Sancaklarında Mahalle Yapılanması," *Karadeniz Araştırmaları* 20 (2009), 47.

8   Metin, "XVI. Yüzyılda Niğde ve Kırşehir Sancaklarında Mahalle Yapılanması", 53.

9   In the court records where Gülpaşa was registered, the three-year average was a monthly sum of 14 to 19. See Selma Tarakçı, "Bir Orta Anadolu Kazası: Bor H. 936-937-938 Tarihli Bor Şer'iyye Sicilinin Tarih Yazıcılığında Kullanımı Denemesi," Ph.D Dissertation, Ankara Üniversitesi, 2006, 15.

issues referred to the court were inheritance,[10] how to divide inheritance, price setting,[11] custody, indemnity, receivables and payables, and marriage and divorce. However even in Bor, people would trample on the rights of others and would commit crimes. The court also reviewed cases such as murder, battery, profanity, adultery, fornication and rape.[12] Women who lived in this small place would also knock on the door of the *qadi* without hesitation and would be present at the court.[13] After spring, the court cases would increase.[14] As a woman, Gülpaşa was taken to court for an incident of fornication. Gülpaşa's crime was recorded in the registers of the *qadi* of Bor on August 29, 1529. The record was extremely plain and did not give any details: "Let the record stand that Emirze el-Hâc at the *sharia* court, willingly and with consent, without any compulsion, admitted and confessed, saying, 'I and those called Mehmed bin Mahmud and Hacı İsa bin Mustafa and Cihan Şah brought over the woman called Gülpaşa from the *Gurbet* community[15] and committed fornication.' The testimony was recorded as such in the register as a legal admission and valid confession. At the end of *Dhu al-Hijjah*, year 935. Witnesses present: Bi mahzar-ı Emir Çelebi bin Hasan, Salih bin Musa, Nasuh bin Muhiddin, Ahmed bin Mustafa, Ali bin Sufi Dede and Budak, Veli bin Mehmed, Hüseyin bin İsa."[16]

The court record was unbiased. Gülpaşa was neither slandered nor acquitted. The silence of the Bor court records and the lack of detailed information on the incident beg for a multidimensional interpretation of the case. Most probably, the *subaşı* of Bor brought the individuals to the court with the indictment of fornica-

---

10   According to the Ottoman legal system, the document in which the property of the deceased was recorded. See Tahsin Özcan, "Muhallefât," *DİA* 30 (2005): 406.

11   The price ceiling set by the state for the prices of goods and services. See Mübahat S. Kütükoğlu, "Narh," *DİA* 32 (2006): 391.

12   Tarakçı, *Bir Orta Anadolu Kazası*, 45-6.

13   Thirty-one women appealed to the court within the same court record. See Tarakçı, "Bir Orta Anadolu Kazası," 31.

14   According to Tarakçı's research, the numbers of trials at the court in the spring and summer were more than those in the winter. See Tarakçı, "Bir Orta Anadolu Kazası," 29.

15   The communities were also called "katuna". Some communities were made up of three people, some of three hundred. Their movement as a community made it easier for them to be controlled. The word community here does not denote a unity of religious opinions. It is similar to the word *oba*, used to mean tribe. The state recognized the communities in question as the "ser cemaatleri". The relations with the state were handled by the head of the community. See Emine Dingeç, "XVI. Yüzyılın Başlarında Rumeli Şehirlerinde Çingeneler," in *Osmanlı Dönemi Balkan Şehirleri* III, Zafer Gölen, Abidin Temizer, ed.s, (Ankara: Gece Kitaplığı, 2016), 1214.

16   *H. 936-937-938 Tarihli Bor Şer'iyye Sicili*, 3.

tion and requested that they be punished. As we know, in cases of such crimes, the guilty party would be levied a *cürm-ü cinayet* tax [for those crimes as severe as murder]. The simplicity of the statement makes us think that the individuals did not come to the court of their own accord.

As stated in the document, Emirze el-Hâc Hoca, Mehmed bin Mahmud, Hacı İsa bin Mustafa and Cihan Şah 'confessed' that they took Gülpaşa with them and committed fornication. It is not clear whether Gülpaşa was present at this trial. If she was, Gülpaşa must have remained silent. We don't know if this silence is due to her denial or acceptance of guilt. We might also think that she remained silent to prevent this incident from being investigated, hoping that at least she herself would get away without a penalty.[17] Otherwise she would have faced criminal sanctions such as having her forehead painted black, walking around with animal entrails on her head, having her genitalia or face seared with a hot iron, having her house destroyed or being banished from the neighborhood. By the day of the trial, she might have already left Bor for some time[18]

We cannot understand exactly whether this incident was consensual or took place due to a threat or vested interest. If we assume that the story was true, it is important to prove that the act was adulterous. It might also have been a matter of mutual consent. On the other hand, Emirze did not give detailed information on Gülpaşa or try to slander her. The fact that the incident was not blown out of proportions in the testimony makes us think that it was based on mutual consent.

The scarcity of information makes us think that Gülpaşa and the others involved were single. If they were married, this would have in some way been specified. In Islamic jurisprudence, punishment for adultery would be *rajm*, that is, death by stoning,[19]

---

17 "Ve eğer bir avrete bir kimesne ben seni şöyle edib dürürüm dese, avret münkire olsa, avrete and vereler, eri kadı ta'zîr ede; iki ağaca ehl-i örf bir akçe cerime ala." See Ahmed Akgündüz, *Osmanlı Kanunnâmeleri ve Hukukî Tahlilleri* 3 (İstanbul: Faisal Eğitim ve Yardımlaşma Vakfı Yayınları, 1991), 425. The punishment for fornication was given to the one among the parties who admitted to the crime. See Zübeyde Güneş Yağcı, "Osmanlı Taşrasında Kadınlara Yönelik Cinsel Suçlarda Adalet Arama Geleneği," *Kadın Araştırmaları Dergisi* 6, no. 2 (2005): 53.

18 Fikret Yılmaz, "Zina ve Fuhuş Arasında Kalanlar Fahişe Subaşıya Karşı," *Toplumsal Tarih* 220 (2012): 28.

19 *Rajm* (stoning) happened in the Ottoman Empire only in the year 1680. In Istanbul, the neighborhood residents caught the wife of a janissary with the Jewish owner of a silk fabric store in her house. When the neighborhood residents testified to 'Having caught them in the act of adultery', they received the *rajm* punishment. See Abdülmecit Mutaf, "Teorik ve Pratik Olarak Osmanlı'da Recm Cezası: Bazı Batı Anadolu Şehirlerindeki Uygulamalar," *Turkish Studies* 3, no. 4 (2008): 584-85.

and for fornication, *tazir,* a lighter form of punishment.[20] Fikret Yılmaz attributes the difference in the types of punishment to marital status, stating that the marriage contract involved the payment of *mahr,* through which the man purchased the owner-ship of the woman's genitals.[21] According to Yılmaz, a similar but temporary owner-ship situation was involved in prostitution since it was based on payment by mutual consent.[22] From a legal perspective, the factor that either mitigated or aggravated the penalty was one's marital status.[23] In this regard, the court wanted to avoid interfer-ing with the rights of third persons (i.e., the spouse). *Rajm* was rarely implemented in the Ottoman Empire, as it was very difficult to ascertain the crime of adultery.[24]

In the case involving Gülpaşa, there was no mention of money. Going by Emirze's testimony, the incident falls within the scope of fornication. One of the most important differences between fornication and prostitution is that prostitu-tion was chosen as a profession, which, in turn, would increase the likelihood that the crime would be repeated. There are no other court records on Gülpaşa in the same register; if prostitution was the case, the situation might have been different.

---

20   Punishments that were not explicitly specified in Islamic jurisprudence and instead left to the discretion of the administrator or the judge, who would also oversee their imple-mentation. See Tuncay Başoğlu, "Ta'zîr," *DİA* 40 (2011): 198; In Islamic jurisprudence, fornication necessitates the *hadd* punishment. *Hadd* is a crime committed against God. For this reason, no one was given the permission to pardon it. Other than fornication, six more crimes were within this category: Libel concerning fornication, drinking alcohol, thievery, highway robbery, rebellion, and apostasy. It is significant that the libel concern-ing fornication is considered a crime as much as fornication itself. In this way, caution was taken to prevent the unjust accusation of people and their implication in a crime. The crimes committed against individuals such as murder, or battery, could be pardoned by the individual. As for the *tazir* crimes, they concerned both the public and the individual, such as bribery. See Ahmed Akgündüz, *Osmanlı Kanunnâmeleri ve Hukuki Tahlilleri* 1 (İstanbul: Fey Vakfı Yayınları, 1990), 108-9.

21   Colin Imber, "Zina in Ottoman law," *Turcica III: Contributions à l'histoire économique et sociale de l'Empire Ottoman* (1983): 60.

22   Yılmaz, "Fahişe Subaşıya Karşı," 30.

23   "Bir kimesne bir avret ile zinâ eylese, şer' ile sâbit olsa, evlü olsa üç yüz akçe cerîme alına. Ve eğer mutavassıtu'l-hâl olsa iki yüz ve fakirü'l-hâl olsa yüz akçe alına." See Akgündüz, *Osmanlı Kanunnâmeleri ve Hukuki Tahlilleri* 3, 425.

24   Mutaf, "Recm Cezası," 585. Regarding this issue, many scholars are of the same opin-ion. For example, see Yılmaz, "Fahişe Subaşıya Karşı," 26; to punish for the crime of fornication, several conditions need to be fulfilled: the perpetrators need to confess to their crime, four eyewitnesses should be present, the case should not lapse, and an unmarried person should be pregnant. See Akgündüz, *Osmanlı Kanunnâmeleri ve Hukuki Tahlilleri* 1, 108-9.

The register where Gülpaşa's case appears includes three more cases of forni-cation.[25] Only one of the cases involves the *gurbet taifesi*, of which Gülpaşa was a member. The other two women who were charged with fornication had confessed their crime. In one of those cases, Musa and Hatice were caught red-handed in the garden. That incident took place outdoors would have increased the likelihood of eyewitnesses. It is highly probable that the eyewitnesses made the issue into gossip material. In this particular case, the Amil of Bor, Ali bin Hasan brought the charges against Musa bin Durdu and Hatice bint-i Aykut, saying that they were caught red-handed while engaging in fornication in Receb's yard. It is not clear whether Ali bin Hasan was a witness to the incident or not. Three witnesses were certain that they saw Musa lying prone on Hatice.[26] Despite the existence of eyewitnesses, both Hatice and Musa denied the accusation.

Discussion of the Rumors about the women in Gülpaşa's Company

The purpose of analyzing Gülpaşa's case here is to address the prejudices about Gypsy women that were perpetuated as truths. Such prejudices are proof that his-torians are often influenced by social convictions that they do not even question. Our study is based on the fallacy of the position that associates Roma women with fornication and prostitution.

In the 16th century, during incidents that showed a breakdown in morals, the Roma were usually accused. There was a widespread belief that they engaged in fornica-tion. Mustafa Akdağ, who thinks that the Roma played a role in the degeneration of Ottoman society in the 16th century, states that in many places in Anatolia, Romany men would take beautiful women with them to facilitate prostitution, preying on young men and *madrasa* students in crowded cities. For Akdağ, the limited information on the movements of the Roma in Rumelia serves as proof of their scarcity in this area.[27] It looks like Akdağ was largely wrong on both counts. First, prostitution is not a crime specific to the Roma; therefore, one cannot claim that they were the ones responsible for disturbing social order. Second, neither is it correct that the Roma got involved in crimes more frequently than other social groups. Furthermore, recent studies prove that the Roma were more populous in Rumelia than in other regions in Anatolia.[28]

---

25   H. *936-937-938 Tarihli Bor Şer'iyye Sicili.*

26   Tarakçı, "Bir Orta Anadolu Kazası," 37.

27   Mustafa Akdağ, *Büyük Celâlî Karışıklıklarının Başlaması* (Erzurum: Atatürk Üniversitesi Yayınları, 1963), 36, 49.

28   The studies on the history of the Roma have shown that the population was most dense in Rumelia. See Emine Dingeç, "Rumeli'de Geri Hizmet Kurumu İçinde Çingeneler (XVI.

The most important documentary evidence that researchers have regarding Romany women's engagement in prostitution is the legal code of 1530 called "The Copts of the Province of Rumelia".[29] This text describes how in the Rumelia province, in Adrianapolis, Plovdiv and Sofia, Romany women who partook in illegal activities would pay a 'cut-off tax' of a hundred *akçes* per month.[30] This information does make us think that prostitution was taxed. However, according to the Ottoman law based on the *shari'a*, it is not possible for the law to permit or to tax the activity. What escapes researchers is the section where this tax is included: It is described as part of the 'crime of murder' tax.

To understand the issue better, we need to analyze it further. This tax, as its name suggests, would be collected when a crime was committed. As required by the *timar* system, or the disciplinary code, local administrators had control of this tax so that local authorities could be more efficient in establishing public order in rural areas. The taxes collected from *reaya* who committed crimes, depending on the type of the land, would either be assigned to the *sanjakbeyi* or shared between the *sanjakbeyi* and the owner of the estate. The payment of a fixed tax meant that, depending on the population, a fixed amount was specified and collected beforehand. As this revenue was not included in the state records, the amount of the tax did not quite concern the state. Thus, in most cases, the amount was recorded as if it were standard. Indeed, in the *tahrir* record books of *müsellems* from the Roma, the tax collected due to the 'crime of murder' was the same in different periods of the 16th century. Therefore, we cannot claim that this legal article legalizes prostitution. In an empire with an Islamic state tradition and that defined women's places as the

---

Yüzyıl)," Ph.D dissertation, Anadolu Üniversitesi, 2004, 88-90; Elena Marushiakova-Vesselin Popov, *Osmanlı İmparatorluğu'nda Çingeneler*, (*Gypsies in the Ottoman Empire*, Hatfield: University of Hertfordshire Press, 2000) translated from the English by Bahar Tırnakçı (İstanbul: Homer Kitabevi, 2006), 33; İsmail Altınöz, *Osmanlı Toplumunda Çingeneler* (Ankara: Türk Tarih Kurumu, 2013), 192; Dingeç, "XVI. Yüzyılın Başlarında Rumeli Şehirlerinde Çingeneler," 1216. However, the Roma scattered across Ottoman Anatolia require the attention of more detailed studies.

29　The work of Marushiakova and Popov implies that this tax was collected from frivolous women and that the fact that the fine was defined as a tax lent legitimacy to illegal proceedings. See Marushiakova and Popov, *Osmanlı İmparatorluğu'nda Çingeneler*, 53; Faika Çelik, "Exploring Marginality in The Ottoman Empire: Gypsies or People of Malice (Ehl-i Fesad) as Viewed by the Ottomans," (Badia Fiesolana: Europen University Institute, 2004), 10.

30　BOA, *TTD* No: 370, 374; Ahmed Akgündüz, *Osmanlı Kanunnâmeleri ve Hukukî Tahlilleri, Kanuni Devri Kanunnâmeleri* 6 (İstanbul: Faisal Eğitim ve Yardımlaşma Vakfı Yayınları, 1993), 512.

"harem," it is possible that the relatively more unfettered behavior and activities of the Romany women—i.e., their entering houses to sell wares, their participation in dance and entertainment or maybe fortune telling, an unapproved activity—would be perceived as unacceptable behavior. Acts of prostitution were treated as individual conduct that was kept separate, and so was its punishment.[31]

We are likely to arrive at biased interpretations if we base our analysis of the Roma solely on criminal records kept by *qadis*, on the *mühimme* registers of the *divan* as an upper-level institution above the courts, or on legal codes mainly concerned with prohibitions. Certainly, among the Roma there were '*ehl-i fesad*' (troublemakers), however, the crimes committed by these people were not due to a specific ethnicity, but of a personal nature, and so was their prosecution. In the *mühimme* record below, this stance can easily be observed.[32]

A mühimme was sent sent in the year 972/1564-65 to a few provinces. The decree describes how the '*Gurbet* and Gypsy' group have defied Islamic religious prohibitions, and orders that such illegal behavior should be forestalled. Yet at the same time, the decree includes the statement, "you should refrain from harassing those who keep to themselves, and from taking their property or clothes and thereby engaging in cruelty and injustice," emphasizing that the innocent should be spared. It is this statement that was ignored. The crime in question is of a personal nature and the innocent should be left to themselves, and not harmed.

---

31 Even though the century in question is different, Osman Köse's research clarifies this issue. Köse analyzed prostitution and the alcohol ban in the 18th century and determined that a large portion of those engaged in prostitution were Muslims. In addition, he states that the punishment stipulated for prostitution, to "reform the self", was either exile or imprisonment. Osman Köse, "XVIII. Yüzyıl Sonları Rus ve Avusturya Savaşları Esnasında Osmanlı Devleti'nde Bir Uygulama: İstanbul'da İçki ve Fuhuş Yasağı," *Turkish Studies* 2, no. 1 (2007): 107, 111, 116.

32 "Şimdiki hâlde taht-ı hükûmetinüzde ba'zı Gurbet ve Çingân tâyifesi zuhûr idüp envâ-ı muharremât ve esnâf-ı münkerâtı irtikâb idüp fısk (u) fücûr üzre fahişeleri ve alet-i lehv ü lu'b u sâzla şehirlerde ve kasabât-ı kur'ada bi'l-cümle kesret-i nâs olduğı cem'ıyyetlere ve bâzârlara varub muttasıl vilâyeti geşt idüp râst geldükleri nâsı ıdlâl ve memlekete ihtilâl virüp ve tenhâ buldukların gâlib geldüklerinde ve ebnâ-i sebîli katl ü gâret idüp dâyimâ fesâd ü şenâ'atden hâlî olmayub ol asıl müfsidlerin def'-ı mazarratı vâcib ü lâzım olmağın... Bu bâbda tamâm ihtimâm idüp emrüm üzere vilâyeti ol asıl müfsitlerden pâk ü temiz idüp eyyâm-ı adâlet-i hümâyûn ve hengâm-ı sa'âdet-makrunumda kimesneye şer'-ı şerîfe muhâlif iş ittürmekden ve bu bahâne ile kendü hâlinde olanlara dahl-ü tecâvüz olunup mâlları ve esbâbları alınup zulm ühayf olmakdan hazer idesin..." *6 Numaralı Mühimme Defteri* (Ankara: Başbakanlık Devlet Arşivleri Genel Müdürlüğü, 1995), 206.

In the Ottoman Empire, when an unwanted act or behavior emerged, the following procedure would be followed: First, *tenbih* (warning), followed by *te'kîd*, (reiteration), and if these were not effective, *'ta'zir* (admonishment), and *tekdir (stronger admonishment)'* would be issued. Those who carried the illegal act even further, to unpreventable heights, would be 'banished'. In the social context, the first two times, communities would try to solve the situation via counsel, and if they could not get results, would request the removal of the perpetrator from their group. In short, at the social level, a process that stretched between counsel and banishment would be carried out. In line with this process, both the state and the society adopted an extremely tolerant attitude. It was expected that the perpetrators of all acts of crime would be given chance to 'come to their senses' before they reached the last stage. In this respect, there are no accusations aimed at a whole community in the documents; and all legal implementations are based on individual cases. The term *"Sâ'î-bi'l-fesâd"* (agent of mischief) is both legal and social that denotes this individualism.

Instead of a Conclusion

One can witness Gülpaşa's experience in any place or period, and therefore, it would not be accurate to attribute the act of fornication to her ethnic origin and way of life. In this incident, we need to perceive Gülpaşa solely as a woman. However, it has been the case throughout history that these types of incidents, when the parties include the Roma, would result in prejudiced judgments on the community of the Roma as a whole. In the Ottoman society, Romany women in general were not linked to prostitution and fornication, and like other crimes, fornication and adultery was perceived as a personal crime. In other words, the perception of criminals in the eyes of the Ottoman state could be summarized as 'To each, his/her own.'

Bibliography

Archival Sources
H. 936-937-938 Tarihli Bor Şer'iyye Sicili
2 Numaralı Kütahya Şer'iyye Sicili
Başbakanlık Osmanlı Arşivi (BOA). Mühimme Defteri (MD). C. 27
BOA Tapu Tahrir Defteri (TTD). No: 370

Primary Sources
3 Numaralı Mühimme Defteri. Ankara: Başbakanlık Devlet Arşivleri Genel Müdürlüğü, 1993.

5 Numaralı Mühimme Defteri. Ankara: Başbakanlık Devlet Arşivleri Genel Müdürlüğü, 1994.

6 Numaralı Mühimme Defteri. Ankara: Başbakanlık Devlet Arşivleri Genel Müdürlüğü, 1995.

Secondary Sources

Akdağ, Mustafa. *Büyük Celâlî Karışıklıklarının Başlaması*. Erzurum: Atatürk Üniversitesi Yayınları, 1963.

Akgündüz, Ahmed. *Osmanlı Kanunnâmeleri ve Hukuki Tahlilleri* 1. İstanbul: Fey Vakfı Yayınları, 1990.

———. *Osmanlı Kanunnâmeleri ve Hukukî Tahlilleri* 3. İstanbul: Faisal Eğitim ve Yardımlaşma Vakfı Yayınları, 1991.

———. *Osmanlı Kanunnâmeleri ve Hukukî Tahlilleri* 6. İstanbul: Faisal Eğitim ve Yardımlaşma Vakfı Yayınları, 1993.

Altınöz, İsmail. *Osmanlı Toplumunda Çingeneler*. Ankara: Türk Tarih Kurumu Yayınları, 2013.

Ayverdi, İlhan. *Misalli Büyük Türkçe Sözlük* 1. İstanbul: Kubbealtı Neşriyat, 2006.

Başoğlu, Tuncay. "Ta'zîr." *DİA* 40, (2011): 198-202.

Çelik, Faika. "Exploring Marginality in The Ottoman Empire: Gypsies or People of Malice (Ehl-i Fesad) as Viewed by the Ottomans." Badia Fiesolana: Europen University Institute, 2004.

Dingeç, Emine. 2004. "Rumeli'de Geri Hizmet Kurumu İçinde Çingeneler (XVI. Yüzyıl)." Ph.D dissertation, Anadolu Üniversitesi.

———. "XVI. Yüzyılın Başlarında Rumeli Şehirlerinde Çingeneler." in *Osmanlı Dönemi Balkan Şehirleri* III, eds. Zafer Gölen-Abidin Temizer, 1211-23. Ankara: Gece Kitaplığı, 2016.

Güneş Yağcı, Zübeyde. "Osmanlı Taşrasında Kadınlara Yönelik Cinsel Suçlarda Adalet Arama Geleneği." *Kadın Araştırmaları Dergisi* 6, no. 2, (2005): 51-81.

Imber, Colin. "Zina in Ottoman Law." *Turcica III: Contributions à l'histoire économique et sociale de l'Empire Ottoman* (1983): 59-92.

Köse, Osman, "XVIII. Yüzyıl Sonları Rus ve Avusturya Savaşları Esnasında Osmanlı Devleti'nde Bir Uygulama: İstanbul'da İçki ve Fuhuş Yasağı." *Turkish Studies* 2, no. 1 (2007): 104-23.

Kütükoğlu, Mübahat S. "Narh." *DİA* 32 (2006): 391-92.

Marushiakova, Elena and Vesselin Popov. *Osmanlı İmparatorluğu'nda Çingeneler*. translated from English by Bahar Tırnakçı. İstanbul: Homer Kitabevi, 2006.

Metin, Rafet. "XVI. Yüzyılda Niğde ve Kırşehir Sancaklarında Mahalle Yapılanması." *Karadeniz Araştırmaları* 20 (2009): 45-58.

Mutaf, Abdülmecit. "Teorik ve Pratik Olarak Osmanlı'da Recm Cezası: Bazı Batı Anadolu Şehirlerindeki Uygulamalar." *Turkish Studies* 3, no. 4 (2008): 573-97.

Özcan, Tahsin. "Muhallefât." *DİA* 30 (2005): 406-7.

Özkan, Ali Rafet. *Türkiye Çingeneleri*. Ankara: Kültür Bakanlığı Yayınları, 2000.

Öztürk, Rıdvan. "Kıbrıs'taki Gurbetlerin Gizli Dili." http://www.ayk.gov.tr/: 1399-412.

Paspati, Alexandre G. *Etudes Sur Ies Tchinghianes ou Bohemiens De L'empire Ottoman*. Osnabrück, 1973.

Pelekani, Chryso. 2018. "The Gurbetties of Cyprus And Their Language Gurbetcha." Ph.D dissertation, Kıbrıs Üniversitesi.

Tarakçı, Selma. 2006. "Bir Orta Anadolu Kazası: Bor H. 936-937-938 Tarihli Bor Şer'iyye Sicilinin Tarih Yazıcılığında Kullanımı Denemesi." M. A. Thesis, Ankara Üniversitesi.

Tarama Sözlüğü III. Ankara: Türk Dil Kurumu, 1963.

Yılmaz, Fikret. "Zina ve Fuhuş Arasında Kalanlar Fahişe Subaşıya Karşı." *Toplumsal Tarih* 220 (2012): 22-31.

CHAPTER SEVEN

Have Some Mercy, Sir!: The Suffering of Selim the Slave*

Zübeyde Güneş Yağcı

What happens when slaves, expected to show complete loyalty and obedience, do not abide by these principles? Or what becomes of the female or male slaves who do not serve a merciful master? I ask these questions to address the human (or humanity's) feelings of mercy in the context of the master-slave relationship. From our contemporary perspective, making humans into slaves, purchasing and selling them as if they were property, passing them down as inheritance, or including them as assets in contracts or partnerships, or leasing them to someone who benefits from their labor, are all unacceptable acts and incidents.[1] However, in the face of wars that have existed since the earliest ages in history, we are forced to seek an answer to the question: what became of the prisoners of war. The history of slavery started when the powerful needed a labor force and exploited the societies they perceived as their inferior—or even their equal—and defeated through warfare. This practice eventually brought about the slave laws and the regulations aimed at creating the framework of master-slave relations.

Taking this idea as my starting point, I will discuss the experiences of Selim the Slave, who lived in mid-19th century in the Ottoman Empire. Selim was not tied to one person only; he belonged to the slave merchant Mehmed. Given that Mehmed was still in the market after the Istanbul Slave Bazaar was officially closed is proof

---

*   Manisa, 19th Century

1   According to Islamic jurisprudence, the slave, being subject to proprietary and legal processes, is considered as property. When viewed from this perspective, the slave can be purchased and sold, inherited, and owned in partnership. In the case of worship, he has full authority and obligations. The responsibility in a crime committed by the slave is half that of a free person. On the other hand, he has no property ownership rights. Mehmet Akif Aydın- Muhammed Hamidullah, "Köle," *DİA* 16 (2002): 230-41; Also see Şafak Baran, "Felsefenin Gözüyle Kuran'da Kölelik ve Câriyelik," Ph.D dissertation, Selçuk Üniversitesi, 2006, 91-107.

that the business of slave trading was still going on. Selim lived in Manisa which, until the rise of Izmir in the 18th century, was one of the most important *sanjak*s and cities of the empire in Western Anatolia, and the place where princes would assume governorship of the *sanjak* until the time of Ahmed I (1603-17). However, when Sultan Mehmed III, the father of Ahmed I, refused to send his sons there, it lost its former prominence. Despite these developments, Manisa remained an unquestionably significant city through the period when Selim the Slave lived, because of its agricultural importance even if it was no longer the region's administrative center. Historical documents do not make it clear whether Esirci Mehmed, the slave trader, bought Selim to sell him or to use his labor, engaged as he was in agriculture in addition to slave trading. I believe that he bought Selim to have him at his service: in a court testimony, he stated that he punished Selim due to Selim's attempt on his life, property, and honor. The allegation indicates that Selim must have stayed at his house, if not for a long time, at least for a sufficient duration.

Let me pause here to offer an overview of the history of the master-slave relationship since Selim was obviously not the only slave who was subjected to violence in either in Ottoman society or in human history. The long tradition of corporal punishment practiced on slaves will help us evaluate what Selim went through.

The Sumerian and Hammurabi laws, the first written legal codes in the world, contain articles on the regulation of master-slave relationships as well as rules concerning the cases in which the master's punishment of his slave would be warranted. According to these rules, when slaves escaped, it was assumed that they were disobedient and that they had to be violently punished. Usually, this punishment would consist of cutting the slave's ear.[2] Assyrian law allowed the master to punish a disrespectful slave by burning his mouth by filling it with a unit of salt. The Hittites had a heavier punishment for similar infractions: the slave would be thrown in a boiler.[3]

Concerning Roman law, the basis of modern-day laws, the terms were no different. Roman law specified heavy punishments for slaves who did not obey the orders of their masters. In cases like Selim's, Roman law corporal punishment as the appropriate sanction for a slave who attempted to escape or, when his master claimed, made attempts on his honor and his life.[4] The law was binding not only

---

2   Yusuf Kılıç and Suzan Akkuş Mutlu, "Çivi Yazılı Hukukta Kölelere Verilen Cezalar," *Turkish Studies* 8, no. 3 (2013): 289.

3   Turgut Yiğit, "Çivi Yazılı Kanunlarda Kölelik," *Türkiye Sosyal Araştırmalar Dergisi* 3, no. 2 (1999): 67.

4   Özlem Söğütlü Erişgen, "Vekâlet Sözleşmesi Bağlamında Noxal Sonuçlu Sözleşme- Hırsız Köle Olayı," *Ankara Üniversitesi Hukuk Fakültesi Dergisi* 51 (2002): 85. Even in the time

for the slaves but also for their children. Because it was assumed that slaves would tell the truth only under torture, violent forms of punishment were allowed when a slave, never mind attempting an escape or threatening his master, merely defied his master's orders. Even if the slave was spared punishment on the first escape attempt, he would be corporally punished when the slave tried a second time, to make sure he could not escape. The lightest corporal punishment was cutting behind the knees. The severest was crucifixion.[5] Another way of preventing the slave's escape was either branding him or fitting him with an iron collar that only a blacksmith could remove.[6] Of course, killing the slave meant economic loss.

Was there a similar understanding of punishment in Islamic societies? The religious teachings recommended freeing the slaves after a set period, and even as recompense for certain sins. However, what were the rules concerning slaves who committed crimes and ran away? The answers to these questions will provide the basis on which we can interpret the procedures in the Ottoman State, an Islamic state, the framework of the master-slave relationship, and Selim's own experiences. To fully understand the Islamic position, we need to first review the position of the previous Abrahamic religions concerning slavery. Slavery was an important element when Judaism first emerged, since at the time that Moses became a prophet, the Jewish people were slaves in Egypt. The prophethood of Moses paved the way to their escape from Egypt and their liberation, yet it did not end the practice of slavery. The requirement for slaves to blindly obey their masters continued in Judaism. It was the norm to punish the slave who disobeyed his master, and the choice

---

of the Emperor Constantius (306-37 AD), there would be no criminal sanctions when the master punished his slave, or even when the slave died during the punishment. This was seen as the master's right and not considered an unjust act. Cahit Güngör, "Çağdaş Tefsirde 'Kölelik' Yorumu," Ph.D dissertation, Ankara Üniversitesi, 2005, 11-2; Ahmed Akgündüz, *İslâm Hukukunda Kölelik- Câriyelik Müessesesi ve Osmanlı'da Harem* (İstanbul: Osmanlı Araştırmaları VakfıYayınları, 1995), 75; Ali Bakkal, "Hz. Peygamber'in Kölelere Verdiği Değer ve İslâm'ın Köleliğe Bakışı," in *I. Kutlu Doğum Sempozyumu Hz. Peygamber ve İnsan Sevgisi, 21-22 Nisan 2007*, Musa K. Yılmaz, ed., (Urfa 2007), 221.

5   Robert Garland, *The Other Side of History: Daily Life in the Ancient World* (Virginia: The Great Courses, 2012), 159. The abuse of slaves led to slave revolts in the Roman Empire. The largest and most well-known of these is the Spartacus Revolt (73-71 BC). For further information, see Brent D. Shaw, *Spartacus and The Slave Wars, A Brief History with Documents* (Boston: Bedford Press, 2001).

6   Gürkan Ergin, "Roma Toplumunda Kölelik Eleştirisi ve Kölelere Empati," *Cedrus* 2 (2014): 369; Hasan Malay, *Çağlar Boyu Kölelik* (İstanbul: Gündoğan Yayınları, 2010), 197-8; Halûk Çetinkaya, "Roma ve Bizans İmparatorluklarında Yoksulluk ve Din Etkisi," in *IV. Uluslararası Felsefe Kongresi Yoksulluk, Dayanışma ve Adalet*, Mehmet Fatih Elmas-Metin Becermen, ed.s, (Bursa: 2016), 287.

FIGURE 7.1 A black slave (Mecmuâ-i Eş'âr, TSMK, Hazine 20, No: 796, vr. 142).

of punishment was left to the master's conscience. Legal institutions, by not getting involved in this situation, also acknowledged the master's authority in enforcing the rules. As Judaism is based on the idea of 'the chosen people' and the honor of a free Jewish person is held above everything, slaves were naturally assigned a lower social standing. A Jew who became a slave due to reasons such as debt retained his low standing for a maximum of 6 years.[7] At the end of this period, he immediately became free.[8] However in the case of other races, not only did the slave status go on for a lifetime, but the children born to the slave were also considered to be slaves. For this reason, a master or another free man killing a slave, regardless of the motive, did not warrant any punishment. That a free man could not be punished on account of a slave was a rule based on the idea of the Jews as the chosen people. It is here that the proprietary right of the master came into play.[9]

---

7   Other than being in debt, a Jewish person could also enter slave status by trading themselves or their offspring due to poverty. Gül Akyılmaz, "Osmanlı Hukukunda Köleliğin Sona Ermesi ile İlgili Düzenlemeler ve Tanzimat Fermânının İlanından Sonra Kölelik Müessesesi," *Gazi Üniversitesi Hukuk Fakültesi Dergisi* 9, no. 1-2 (2005): 215. If in such a situation the slave ran away, he was considered to be free in the place to which he had escaped. Hamza Üzüm, "Tanah ve Talmut'ta Kölelik," *Kafkas Üniversitesi Sosyal Bilimler Enstitüsü Dergisi*" "12 (2013): 170; Gülnihal Bozkurt, "Eski Hukuk Sistemlerinde Kölelik," *Ankara ÜniversitesiHukukFakültesiDergisi*" "38, no. 1-4 (1981): 82.

8   Salime Leyla Gürkan, "Yahudilikte İhtida Meselesi," *İslam Araştırmaları Dergisi* 7 (2002): 37.

9   When the master kills his slave by beating the punishment can change according to the time the slave was killed. If the slave dies immediately, an unspecified penalty would be mentioned, yet if the death takes place a day later, there is no proposed penalty. Sevda Yaman, "Tevrat'a Göre İnsan Hayatı ve Onurunun Kutsallığı," *İnsan ve Toplum Bilimleri Dergisi, Yahudilik Özel Sayısı7*, no. 2 (2016): 347.

Christianity, spreading among slaves most rapidly when it first appeared, was not very different in its approach.[10] It did not question the slaves' absolute obedience towards their masters; and neither did it dwell on what kinds of punishments could be given to slaves for disobedience. This shows the outlook of the period regarding the master-slave relationship, and how the master viewed his slave. One of the best examples of this is how for a period the papacy perceived the slaves as animals.[11] This mindset gave the owners the opportunity to behave as they willed with their slaves.

As with other Abrahamic religions, when Islam emerged, slavery had been already in existence. Islam did not abolish slavery yet saw taking war prisoners as the only legitimate basis for slavery, and additionally, it encouraged manumission even if only in the name of Allah.[12]

The biggest change introduced by Islam in the context of master-slave relations is the acknowledgement of slave rights. While the master can punish his slave, the slave in any situation has the right to appeal to the court, and the intentional killing of the slave even by his master necessitates criminal sanctions.[13]

The Prophet Muhammad—whose teachings and practices are perceived as exemplary—did not punish masters who beat up their slaves yet at the same time advocated manumission. He did so even in an incident that involved a slap on the face.[14] and, most crucially, without investigating whether the slave was guilty

---

10 Kürşat Demirci, "Hıristiyanlık," *DİA* 17 (1998): 332; Mehmet Ali Ünal, *Osmanlı Sosyal ve Ekonomik Tarihi* (İstanbul: Paradigma Yayıncılık, 2012), 38.

11 Hannah Barker, *Egyptian and Italian in the Black Sea Slave Trade, 1260-1500*, Ph D. Thesis Colombia University, 2014, 21.

12 The Koran, al-Nur 3, al-Baqarah 177, an-Nisa 92. In the Koran, in cases of *zihar* (a type of divorce), accidental murder or breaking of an oath, the master was ordered to free his slave. Al-Mujadila 1-4, al-Ma'idah 89.

13 The most basic rights of slaves are the right to life and the right to sustenance. The willful murder of a slave was a crime that required *qisas* (retaliation). Ömer Nasuhi Bilmen, *Hukuki İslamiyye ve Istılahatı Fıkhiyye Kamusu* 3 (İstanbul: Bilmen Yayınevi, 1950), 65. There were slaves who appealed to the court because their masters did not provide sustenance. İzzet Sak, "Şer'iye Sicillerine Göre Sosyal ve Ekonomik Hayatta Köleler (17. ve 18. Yüzyıllar)," Ph.D. dissertation, Selçuk Üniversitesi, 1992, 67-9.

14 When the Prophet Muhammad heard that a master had slapped his slave, he ordered the slave to be manumitted without asking for the reason. Hasan Tahsin Fendoğlu, *İslam ve Osmanlı Hukukunda Kölelik ve Cariyelik* (İstanbul: BeyanYayınevi, 1996), 233. In another incident, the slave warned his master. The event unfolded in the following way: "Ebû Mes'ûd el-Bedrî did not refrain from whipping his slave, let alone from beating him. When he saw the incident, the Messenger of God immediately stepped in and shouted at

or what kind of a crime he might have committed. Islamic jurisprudence, treating Mohammad's actions as precedent, prohibited the punishment of slaves and imposed sanctions on this matter. Another incident which the Prophet witnessed involved Ebû Zer el-Gıfârî, one of the Prophet's companions, who addressed Bilal al-Habashi as "O İbnissevda, the son of the black woman".[15] Mohammad warned him with the words: 'O Abu Zar! You still have residues of the *jahiliyya* in you. Those slaves are your brethren. Allah the Almighty put them in your hands, and from now on, feed them from your own food, clothe them with your own clothes, and don't order them to do anything that they will be incapable of, and if you do, help them."[16] This admonition by the Prophet has been considered as a proof that one ought to perceive the slaves as trusts from Allah, and even if they err, to kindly warn them.[17] It would not be wrong to say that Islamic jurisprudence took these two examples as fundamental norms.[18] Concerning both pre-Ottoman and Ottoman history, our view is supported by several documents and court records on manumission that were granted for a variety of reasons.[19] Be that as it may, slaves surely had responsibilities and duties towards their masters. First and foremost came obedience and loyalty. Being good to their master would result in gaining their favor, and the master would in turn show his favor to his slaves, doing whatever he could to ensure that the slaves lived comfortably.[20]

In the Ottoman court records on slaves, the verdicts that occurred most frequently are those on manumission.[21] In such cases, it was the owners and not the slaves who appealed to the court. Most often, the slaves appealed to the court when the master

---

Ebû Mes'ûd el-Bedrî in anger, and said: 'Know that God has more power over you than you have power over him." Bakkal, "Hz. Peygamber'in Kölelere Verdiği Değer," 247.

15   Bakkal, "Hz. Peygamber'in Kölelere Verdiği Değer," 248.

16   Bilmen, *Hukuki İslamiyye*, 531-2; Mehmet Nadir Özdemir, "İnsan Hakları Bağlamında Hz. Peygamber'in Köleliğe Yaklaşımı," *Bilimname* 19, no. 2 (2010): 79.

17   Bakkal, "Hz. Peygamber'in Kölelere Verdiği Değer," 245-246.

18   An incident that took place during the Umayyad period can serve as an example. A slave appealed to the court and declared that his master was beating him, whereupon the *qadi* decided that the slave should be manumitted. A. Mez, "Orta Zamanda Türk-İslam Dünyasında Köleler," *Ülkü* 11, no. 63 (1938): 222.

19   Ahmet Şamil Gürer, "Osmanlı Kölelik Tarihi Araştırmaları İçin Veri Kaynağı Olarak Itıknâmeler ve 1822 Tarihli Bir Itıknâme Örneği," *Türklük Bilgisi Araştırmaları Şinasi Tekin Armağanı* 32, no. 1 (2008): 251-5.

20   Bilmen, *Hukuki İslamiyye*, 532.

21   See İzzet Sak, "Sosyal ve Ekonomik Hayatta Köleler," 87-130; Mustafa Akbel, "Osmanlı Başkentinde Kölelerin Durumu ve Azatları: Galata Örneği (1718-1730)," *Journal of History and Future* 3, no. 1 (2017): 223-8.

attempted to renounce manumission, or, when the master's heirs refused to honor the court's decision.[22] There are also court records about the direct, in-person appeal of slaves due to the injustices they experienced, or to regain their rights. From time to time, slaves would also appeal to the court due to the physical violence they experienced and would request that their owners be punished. Consistent with Mohammad's teachings we discussed above, the publications of *fatwa* would emphasize the importance of treating the slaves well. The clearest examples of this are contained in the *fatwa*s of Ebussuud Efendi. Ebussuud Efendi decreed that if a master wounded his slave, the master would, in addition to being punished in the afterlife, receive a *tazir* punishment determined by the *qadi*.[23] Another scholar, Feyzullah Efendi, approximately a century later, gave a *fatwa* to the same effect.[24] The same position also applied to eunuchs, male slaves assigned to the *harem* in Islamic states. Eunuchs, whose duty was to protect the women in the *harem*, and who acted as the link to the outside world, were brought to Islamic states from abroad.[25] In Islam, it was forbidden to castrate a human being. However, the demand created a supply. Ebussuud Efendi at this point invokes the matter of human will.[26] A master

---

22   Mehmet Canatar, "Şer'iyye Sicillerinde Köle Ticareti ve Kölelik Muâmelatı Çerçevesinde Düzenlenen Belgeler," *Arşiv Dünyası* 12 (2009): 38-41.

23   Question: If Zayd gouged out the eye of his slave Amr, what should be done to Zayd? Answer: A great torment in the afterlife, and a severe *tazir* punishment in this life. Mehmet Ertuğrul Düzdağ, *Şeyhülislâm Ebussuud Efendinin Fetvâları Işığında 16. Asır Türk Hayatı* (İstanbul: Enderun Kitapevi, 1972), 120.

24   "If Zayd's slave Amr knowingly wounds and kills him with a sharp tool, what should be done to Amr? Answer: Retaliation. If Zayd's slave Amr knowingly wounds Zayd with a blow to the head with a large club and his other slave Bekir knowingly cuts him with a knife and both of them wound and murder Zayd, would Zayd's successors be authorized to retaliate against Amr and Bekir? The answer: They would. The person who killed his slave would even receive a *tazir* punishment and a prison sentence. If Zayd murders the mother of a Hind without any rights, what punishment should be given to Zayd? The answer: A severe *tazir* punishment and a prison sentence. If Zayd murders his concubine Hind, which punishment should be given to Zayd? The answer: A severe *ta'zir*." Şeyhülislam Feyzullah Efendi, *Fetâvâ-yı Fevziye*, Süleyman Kaya, ed., (İstanbul: Klasik Yayınları, 2009), 449-50, 616.

25   Aydın Taneri, "Hadım," *DİA* 15 (1997): 1-3.

26   The slaves Cafer and Gazanfer were sold after being captured by pirates. Somehow, they entered Prince Selim's palace and befriended him; however, they had to consent to being castrated when Selim ascended the throne. For several years they served in positions where they had access to the private life of the Sultan. Maria Pia Pedani, "Erken Modern Dönemde Osmanlı İmparatorluğu'nda Venedikli Köleler," in *Osmanlı Devleti'nde Kölelik, Ticaret, Esaret, Yaşam*, Zübeyde Güneş Yağcı, Fırat Yaşa, Dilek İnan, ed.s, (İstanbul: Tezkire Yayınları, 2017), 124.

who castrated a slave against his will was considered a sinner. By contrast, a slave who consented to being castrated fell outside the scope of the prohibition.[27] In any event, Islamic jurisprudence and the publication of *fatwa*s within this framework unequivocally forbid the master from subjecting the slave to violence.[28]

What happens to a good slave when bound to a cruel master, or in the event of a most minor infraction, or when the master believed that his 'owner's right' entitled him to acts of verbal or physical abuse? When these and similar questions arose, slaves were able to appeal to the court to claim their rights. It is known that slaves would sometimes attempt to run away to be emancipated, and other times they ran away as they could not stand the torture inflicted by their masters, and they would also face the consequences. In the Ottoman Empire, the provisions on how to treat runaway slaves had been specified in detail. In this context, the goal was to first return these slaves to their masters.[29] Very few of the documents at hand allow us to reveal how the runaway slave was received upon his return. Selim serves

---

27　Rahmi Yaran, "Hadım," *DİA* 15 (1997): 3.

28　"The question: If Zayd cuts the manhood of his slave Amr without consent and castrates him, would he be considered a sinner? The answer: He would." Mehmet Ertuğrul Düzdağ, *Şeyhülislâm Ebussuud Efendinin Fetvâları Işığında 16. Asır Türk Hayatı* (İstanbul: Enderun Kitapevi, 1972), 120; The only exception to this would be if a slave entered the harem, i.e., the private bedchamber of his master to make an attempt on his life and honor. If the master killed his slave at that moment, this act might not have even been considered as murder. Fırat Yaşa, "Efendi Köle İlişkisi Bağlamında Şeyhülislâm Fetvaları," in *Osmanlı Devleti'nde Kölelik, Ticaret, Esaret, Yaşam,* eds. Zübeyde Güneş Yağcı et al. (İstanbul: Tezkire Yayınları, 2017), 222. However, this decree should not be interpreted only in the context of slaves. Even today, any move against someone who enters the bedroom of a person with a weapon - even if without the aim of murder- is considered as an act of self-defense.

29　For the process of the capture and delivery of the runaway slave to his master, see Zübeyde Güneş Yağcı-Emre Ataş, "Osmanlı Devleti'nde Kaçak Köleler: Abd-ı Abık," in *Osmanlı Devleti'nde Kölelik, Ticaret, Esaret, Yaşam,* Zübeyde Güneş Yağcı, Fırat Yaşa, Dilek İnan, ed.s, (İstanbul: Tezkire Yayınları, 2017), 303-12. In the court registers of Üsküdar the records on runaway slaves add up to a large amount. Yvonne J. Seng, "Fugitives and Factotums: Slaves in Early Sixteenth-Century Istanbul," *Journal of the Economic and Social History of the Orient* 49, no. 2 (1996): 136-69; Ekrem Tak, 1513-1520 Tarihli Üsküdar Kadı Siciline Göre Kaçkın Köleler," in *Üsküdar Sempozyumu II, 12-13 Mart 2004 Bildiriler* I, Zekeriya Kurşun-Ahmet Emre Bilgili, ed.s, (İstanbul 2005), 19-28; Zübeyde Güneş Yağcı, "Kölelerin Kaçtıkları Mekân Üsküdar (XVI-XVIII. Yüzyıllar)," in *Uluslar arası Üsküdar Sempozyumu VIII, 21-23 Kasım 2014 Bildiriler* II, Coşkun Yılmaz-Cengiz Tomar, ed.s, (İstanbul 2015), 267-83; Suraiya Faroqhi, *Osmanlı İmparatorluğu'nda Yollara Düşenler,* translated from the English by Zulal Kılıç (İstanbul: Kitap Yayınevi, 2016), 192-198.

as a rare example. So does another slave who was also subjected to great cruelty; he was tortured by his master who went as far as gouging out the slave's eye. Like Selim's master, his master also received hard labor as punishment. Cruelty did not only lead to corporal punishment such as in the case of Selim the Slave and Ferah the Concubine. Going against such teachings as "Feed your slaves from your own food and clothe them with your own clothes," starving the slaves was seen as one of the greatest acts of cruelty. A slave trader by the name of Hamza was one of those who engaged in such cruelty. When he did not give sufficient food to the slaves he brought over from Tripoli, some starved to death, and some even had to eat the rats they caught.[30]

In this context, we need to discuss the circumstances that led to Selim's fate and that of several other slaves. Although it is very difficult to pinpoint where Selim came from, it is known that he was black, and he was brought from Africa to Manisa by a slave trader. If the historical document specified his place of origin or his ethnicity, we could have said that he was from Ethiopia, Sudan or Chad; however, it is not possible to ascertain this. Was he brought over by Mehmed, who himself was a merchant in the international slave trade, or did Mehmet purchase him from another slave trader or even someone else? We do not know. Was Selim the son of a slave? Or was he a free man and made a slave by a slave hunter? Whatever the case, if he or his family had endured a long and arduous journey by land and was brought to the Mediterranean shores, like many other slaves, he must have embarked on a journey from there to Crete via North Africa, and from there to Izmir (Smyrna).[31] He must have met his buyers in Izmir. It is possible that Mehmed the Slave Trader, who purchased him could not pronounce his name

---

30   A concubine was among the deceased; for the interrogation of Hamza, see: *BOA A.MKT. UM.*, nr. 235/17, Lef 4, 22 Şaban 1272, Hamza and his partner in crime were sent to prison, and the well-being of the slaves was ensured in a safe place. *BOA A.MKT.UM.*, nr. 235/17, Lef 3, 22 Shaban 1272 (April 28, 1856). Some of the slaves of the Slave-holder Hami fell ill due to starvation. Ömer Şen, *Osmanlı'da Köle Olmak* (İstanbul: Kapı Yayınları, 2007), 87-97. Slaves who were starved would attempt to run away to live under better conditions from time to time. Kutlu Zaman, a concubine of Russian origin, and Ivan, a slave of Georgian origin, were two runaways. When they were caught and brought before the *qadi*, they stated that their master starved them and kept them naked, and that they ran away to be sold to someone else. See Fırat Yaşa, "Desperation, Hopelessness, and Suicide: An Initial Consideration of Self-Murder by Slaves in Seventeenth-Century Crimean Society," *Turkish Historical Review* 9, no. 2 (2018): 204.

31   Ehud R. Toledano, *Osmanlı Köle Ticareti (1840-1890)* (*The Ottoman Slave Trade and Its Suppression, 1840- 1890*, Princeton: Princeton University Press, 1982), translated from the English by Y. Hakan Erdem (İstanbul: Tarih Vakfı Yayınları, 2000), 16-28.

given at birth and named him Selim. As he knew how to appeal to the court, Selim must have lived for a long time either in Manisa or in another Ottoman city. We should also assume that he knew Turkish enough to get by. In the end, Selim was not someone who could accept slavery. This was due to the humiliating nature of slavery as well as the cruel behavior of his master, Mehmed. When Selim ran away, Mehmed asked the authorities to find him. Once found, Selim was delivered back to Mehmed, as it was the custom. Mehmed cut Selim's hands and penis off with a hatchet. Selim did not bleed to death and his wounds healed. We don't know whether, after the incident, Mehmed was remorseful and took him to the doctor, or whether Selim, despite everything he went through, managed to escape again, and was treated back to health with the help of the community. What we do know is that he must have recovered within the four months between the incident and the time when he came to the court and made his appeal. In the intervening months, we can surmise, he was treated well after his tragic experience. However, we will never know who took care of him, who helped him, or whether Mehmed, regretting his actions, tried to help him heal by doing what was necessary. Slave Trader Mehmed claimed at the court that Selim was disobedient and unruly. According to him, Selim even abducted women, and eventually, he even made an attempt on the property and life of his master. Despite these claims, the law enforcement officers put Mehmed in jail.[32] This was because corporal punishment of a slave by his master was unacceptable, regardless of what transpired, or whether the master considered it proper to torture and punish him harshly.

At the trial, Mehmed had to confess his crime. That there were witnesses to Mehmed's crime must have helped Selim's case. Selim did not turn down his master's monetary offer during the trial. The price for his suffering was 500 *kuruş*.[33] By paying the 500 *kuruş*, Mehmed managed to regain his freedom. However, the incident eventually came to the attention of Meclis-i Vâlâ (Supreme Council of Judicial Ordinances). We do not know how the news of the incident made its way to Istanbul. What we know is that even though seven years had passed, the case was not closed. Meclis-i Vâlâ requested a written report from the governor of Izmir. Ali Paşa who, after describing the incident briefly, stated that Selim and his master made their peace in exchange for the payment of 500 *kuruş*. Yet Selim's

---

32 Another slave who attempted to kill his master was Uzun Abdullah who attacked his master Mustafa Ağa with a hatchet. Mustafa Ağa was barely able to escape from his slave. The slave was sentenced to hard labour. According to a high order, he was sent to Istanbul to serve out his sentence. *BOA KK.d.*, nr. 5660, vr. 3a, hk. 1.

33 *BOA İ.DH.*, nr. 272/17071, Lef 1, 11 Zilkade 1262 (31 October 1846).

treatment by his master was still reviewed in the Meclis-i Vâlâ and acknowledged to be inhumane; accordingly, the council concluded that the fact of a truce agreed by the parties did not lessen the gravity of the situation. The Council repeatedly emphasized that the Sultan's justice would not permit such inhumane atrocity. Ultimately the Council ruled that Slave Trader Mehmed should be put in shackles in Izmir, and the sultan ratified the ruling.[34]

A few years after what happened to Selim, Slave Trader Rahmetullah beat his concubine Ferah, and went as far as to take her right eye out. Rahmetullah was sentenced to hard labor, and Ferah was sent to prison as a ward of the state.[35] Since he was given a three-year sentence, we can assume that one or two years into his sentence, Rahmetullah must have shown remorse and asked for a pardon, and the incident was brought up once more. When Rahmetullah was set free, there emerged the problem of what to do with the concubine. As it was not possible to return the concubine to her owner, she would have to be either manumitted or sold to someone else. In their opinion, official authorities raised concern that if the concubine was sold to another person, Rahmetullah would not leave the new owner alone. In that case, the most appropriate solution would be the manumission of the concubine Ferah. This indicates that Ferah was still perceived as Rahmetullah's property. For his part, it does not seem that Rahmetullah approved of manumitting his concubine free of charge. Consequently, the authorities decided that the only way to rescue Ferah from her master would be to pay her price. To determine her price, the chamberlain of the slave traders and a few other slave traders were consulted, and they deemed the concubine to be worth 3.500 *kuruş*. However, the court was able to make a less pricey deal with Slave Trader Rahmetullah, for 3.000 *kuruş*. The court also decided that the money would be paid out of the district's alms and charity fund.[36] In this way Ferah was both emancipated and saved from the possible wrath of Rahmetullah.

Under which circumstances did the court grant a slave's appeal? At a time when beating was the norm and seen as a part of education and life, where would the boundary be drawn? Did a limb or organ have to be harmed, as in the case of Selim the Slave and Ferah the Concubine? Mercan the Black, who lived in the village of Analiyonda of the Dağ jurisdiction of Cyprus, was subjected to beating, though not to the extent

---

34   *BOA İ.MVL.*, nr. 274/10645, Lef 1, Ramazan 1269 (June-July 1853).

35   In Istanbul, there were the dungeons of Tersane, Baba Cafer and Yedikule. See: Zübeyde Güneş Yağcı-Esra Nalbant, "İstanbul Tersane Zindanı," in *Osmanlı İstanbul'u* IV Feridun Emecen, Ali Akyıldız, Emrah Safa Gürkan, ed.s, (İstanbul 2016), 86.

36   *BOA İ.MVL.*, nr. 471/21316, Lef 1, 2, 3, 5 Şaban 1278 (5 February 1862).

of Selim and Ferah. His master Hüseyin broke his arm. When the incident reached the court, Hüseyin attempted to deny it, but the testimonies rendered his denial null and void. The *qadi* ruled that Hüseyin would be put in shackles for six months.[37]

This incident does not help us in our quest to answer the questions listed above either. However, in another incident that took place in Cyprus, the court's decision in favor of the slave did not necessarily take into consideration beating or bodily harm. The incident involved a black child. Those who appealed to the court were two men named Yakup from Nicosia and Hasan. Hasan and Yakup asserted that Arif slandered the black slave child by claiming he engaged in theft and he even cursed at the child. On the testimonies of Hasan and Yakup, the case was seen as closed and the court sent Arif to jail.[38] In this incident, it is possible to see society's reaction to injustice against slaves. A similar example concerns the slave trader Hasan who had both beaten and shackled his concubine Black Nevres. Authorities acted upon an informant's report and underlined the fact that such behavior was considered a crime according to the 203rd clause of the Imperial Legal Code. In his testimony, Slave Trader Hasan stated that Nevres had ran away a few times and when she was caught by the authorities and returned to him, he put shackles on her feet as a measure of last resort. The investigation found that Nevres had been the slave of Zeki Paşa and had recently been sold to slave trader Hasan for 900 *kuruş*. Nevres could not stand being sold and despite all coercive measures she attempted to run away. The Meclis-i Vâlâ suggested that 900 *kuruş* should be taken from Zeki Paşa and given to Hasan; yet later, the money for the slave trader was paid out of the alms and charity fund. Thus, Nevres was emancipated.[39]

Like Selim, Nevres had the status of a runaway slave. Nevres's master stated that she committed no crimes other than being a runaway slave, and that she did not make an attempt on his life or property. Since ancient times, a slave's escape had been one of the biggest crimes. In the Ottoman Empire the slave was expected to obey his master.[40] Aside from doing the work her master demanded, her escape attempt was interpreted

---

37 Güven Dinç and Cemil Çelik, "Kıbrıs'ta Kölelik 1800-1878," *Uluslar arası Sosyal Araştırmalar Dergisi* 5, no. 23 (2012): 193.

38 Celâl Erdönmez, "Şer'iyye Sicillerine Göre Kıbrıs'ta Toplum Yapısı (1839-1856)," Ph.D dissertation, Süleyman Demirel Üniversitesi, 2004, 21.

39 *BOA İ.MVL.*, nr. 512/23102, Lef 1, 2, 3, 17 Zilhicce 1280 (24 May 1864)

40 For example, in Istanbul a *dhimmi* called Parsam appealed to the court claiming that his slave Ohan (?) was disobedient. He requested a court decision to admonish the slave and ensure that his slave would obey him. In the presence of the master, the court issued a warning to the slave to be obedient. "Osmanlı Toplum Yaşayışı ile ilgili Bilgi ve Belgeler-Kölelik," *Tarih ve Toplum* 1 (1984): 60.

as destroying all good will. Mustafa Âli of Gelibolu, whose work, *Mevâidü'n-Nefâis fî Kavâidi' l-Mecâlis,* helps us understand the world of the 16ᵗʰ century, stresses that disobedience of slaves was not an acceptable conduct; furthermore, if a slave who had not suffered any torture or oppression ran away, this was unforgivable. He believed that, for the slave, the duty of service to his master had to come before his worship.[41] Obeying the master could even pave the way to becoming a master himself in the future and could initiate the process that led to marriage. As for running away, it was the biggest act of disobedience that erased all of this good will. Mustafa Âli of Gelibolu does not provide any guidance on how masters should treat slaves who ran away.[42] Nevertheless, it was known that slaves who intended to run away or who did run away and were caught would lose their value significantly. Despite all of this, the court records on runaway slaves do not mention any interrogation regarding their reason for running away. Or perhaps, their answers were not recorded. For this reason, it is not possible to arrive at definitive conclusions regarding the master-slave relationship based solely on the cases of runaway slaves brought to the court before the 19ᵗʰ century.[43] This much is clear, however: a slave's crime could not be a valid reason for the master to torture him. Indeed, a slave by the name of Reyhan had stolen cash from her master, slave trader Ahmed Efendi, and stated that she gave the money to her previous master Süleyman. When the incident was brought to court, it was discovered that Ahmed Efendi got Reyhan to confess by beating her. The court punished Reyhan with four months of shackles for theft, and Ahmed Efendi with two months of imprisonment for torturing a slave.[44] Another incident took place in the Edremid jurisdiction of the Karesi *sanjak.* A slave who stole gold worth 10.000 *kuruş* from his master was transferred from his location to Istanbul to be thrown in jail.[45]

Instead of a Conclusion:

This discussion of master-slave relationship by way of Selim's case shows us that masters could not wilfully punish their slaves. The *fatwa*s issued and the rulings by the court corroborate our finding. Masters who tortured their slaves to the extent

---

41 Mehmet Şeker, *Gelibolulu Mustafa Âli' ve Mevâ'idü'n-Nefâis Fî-Kavâ'ıdi'l-Mecâlis* (Ankara: Türk Tarih Kurumu Yayınları, 1997), 171.

42 Y. Hakan Erdem, "Osmanlı Toplumunda Köle Kimliğini Kuşatan Uygulama ve ZihniyetYapıları," *Tarih Eğitimi ve Tarihte "Öteki" Sorunu* (1998): 179-80.

43 Zübeyde Güneş Yağcı, "Kölelerin Kaçtıkları Mekân Üsküdar (XVI-XVIII. Yüzyıllar)," 267-83.

44 "Osmanlı Toplum Yaşayışı ile ilgili Bilgi ve Belgeler- Kölelik," 58-60.

45 *BOA A.MKT.DV.*, nr. 7/51.

of cutting their limbs, gouging out their eyes and breaking their arms could not escape punishment. Nevertheless, we do not have a clear understanding how and how often the slaves were able to reach the court in such situations. Several slaves like Selim were able to appeal to the court; yet it is impossible to recover the stories of those who were unable to make such an appeal.

Bibliography

Archival Sources

BOA A.MKT.DV., nr. 7/51.

BOA A.MKT.UM., nr. 235/17.

BOA İ.DH., nr. 272/17071.

BOA İ.MVL., nr. 274/10645, 471/21316, 512/23102.

BOA KK.d., nr. 5660.

Secondary Sources

Akbel, Mustafa. "Osmanlı Başkentinde Kölelerin Durumu ve Azatları: Galata Örneği (1718-1730)." *Journal of History and Future* 3, no. 1 (2017): 212-38.

Akgündüz, Ahmed. *İslâm Hukukunda Kölelik-Câriyelik Müessesesi ve Osmanlı'da Harem.* İstanbul: Osmanlı Araştırmaları Vakfı, 1995.

Akyılmaz, Gül. "Osmanlı Hukukunda Köleliğin Sona Ermesi ile ilgili Düzenlemeler ve Tanzimat Fermanının İlanından Sonra Kölelik Müessesesi." *Gazi Üniversitesi Hukuk Fakültesi Dergisi* 9, no. 1-2 (2005): 213-38.

Aydın, M. Akif-Muhammed Hamidullah. "Köle." *DİA* 26 (2002): 237-46.

Bakkal, Ali. "Hz. Peygamber'in Kölelere Verdiği Değer ve İslâm'ın Köleliğe Bakışı."in *I. Kutlu Doğum Sempozyumu Hz. Peygamber ve İnsan Sevgisi 21-22 Nisan 2007*, ed. Musa K. Yılmaz (2007): 219-61.

Baran, Şafak. 2006. "Felsefenin Gözüyle Kuran'da Kölelik ve Câriyelik." Ph.D dissertation, Selçuk Üniversitesi.

Bilmen, Ömer Nasuhi. *Hukuki İslamiyye ve Istılahatı Fıkhiyye Kamusu* 3. İstanbul: Bilmen Yayınevi, 1950.

Bozkurt, Gülnihal. "Eski Hukuk Sistemlerinde Kölelik." *Ankara Üniversitesi Hukuk Fakültesi Dergisi* 38, no. 1-4 (1981): 65-106.

Canatar, Mehmet. "Şeriye Sicillerinde Köle Ticareti ve Kölelik Muâmelatı Çerçevesinde Düzenlenen Belgeler." *Arşiv Dünyası* 12 (2009): 38-41.

Çetinkaya, Halûk. "Roma ve Bizans İmparatorluklarında Yoksulluk ve Din Etkisi." in *IV. Uluslararası Felsefe Kongresi Yoksulluk, Dayanışma ve Adalet*, eds. Mehmet Fatih Elmas-Metin Becermen, 286-94. Bursa: Asa Kitapevi, 2016.

Demirci, Kürşat, "Hıristiyanlık." *DİA* 17 (1998): 328-40.

Dinç, Güven and Cemil Çelik. "Kıbrıs'ta Kölelik 1800-1878." *Uluslararası Sosyal Araştırmalar Dergisi* 7, no. 23 (2012): 185-96.

Düzdağ, M. Ertuğrul. *Şeyhülislâm Ebussuud Efendinin Fetvâları Işığında 16. Asır Türk Hayatı*. İstanbul: Enderun Kitapevi, 1972.

Erdem, Y. Hakan. "Osmanlı Toplumunda Köle Kimliğini Kuşatan Uygulama ve Zihniyet Yapıları." *Tarih Eğitimi ve Tarihte "Öteki" Sorunu*, 171-81. İstanbul, 1998.

Erdönmez, Celâl. 2004. "Şer'iyye Sicillerine Göre Kıbrıs'ta Toplum Yapısı (1839-1856)." Ph.D dissertation, Süleyman Demirel Üniversitesi.

Ergin, Gürkan. "Roma Toplumunda Kölelik Eleştirisi ve Kölelere Empati." *Cedrus* 2 (2014): 355-76.

Faroqhi, Suraiya. *Osmanlı İmparatorluğu'nda Yollara Düşenler*, translated from the English by Zulal Kılıç. İstanbul: Kitap Yayınevi, 2016.

Garland, Robert. *The Other Side of History: Daily Life in the Ancient World*. Virginia: The Great Courses. 2012.

Güneş Yağcı, Zübeyde. "Kölelerin Kaçtıkları Mekan Üsküdar (XVI-XVIII. Yüzyıllar)." in *Uluslar arası Üsküdar Sempozyumu VIII, 21-23 Kasım 2014 Bildiriler* 2, eds. Coşkun Yılmaz and Cengiz Tomar, 267-83. İstanbul, 2015.

Güneş Yağcı, Zübeyde and Esra Nalbant. "İstanbul Tersane Zindanı." in *Osmanlı İstanbul'u* IV, eds. Feridun M. Emecen, Ali Akyıldız, Emrah Safa Gürkan, 83-113. İstanbul, 2016.

Güneş Yağcı, Zübeyde and Emre Ataş. "Osmanlı Devleti'nde Kaçak Köleler: Abd-ı Abık." in *Osmanlı Devleti'nde Kölelik, Ticaret, Esaret, Yaşam*, eds. Zübeyde Güneş Yağcı, Fırat Yaşa, Dilek İnan. 297-323. İstanbul: Tezkire Yayınevi, 2017.

Güngör, Cahit. 2005. "Çağdaş Tefsirde 'Kölelik' Yorumu." M. A. Thesis, Ankara Üniversitesi.

Gürkan, Salime L. "Yahudilikte İhtida Meselesi." *İslam Araştırmaları Dergisi* 7 (2002): 31-55.

Gürer, Ahmet Ş. "Osmanlı Kölelik Tarihi Araştırmaları İçin Veri Kaynağı Olarak Itıknâmeler ve 1822 Tarihli Bir Itıknâme Örneği." *Türklük Bilgisi Araştırmaları Şinasi Tekin Armağanı* 32, no. 1 (2008): 251-55.

Kılıç, Yusuf and Suzan Akkuş Mutlu. "Çivi Yazılı Hukukta Kölelere Verilen Cezalar." *Turkish Studies* 8, no. 7 (2013): 283-92.

Malay, Hasan. *Çağlar Boyu Kölelik*. İstanbul: Gündoğan Yayınları, 2010.

Mez, A. "Orta Zamanda Türk-İslam Dünyasında Köleler." *Ülkü* 11, no. 63 (1938): 220-4.

"Osmanlı Toplum Yaşayışı ile ilgili Bilgi ve Belgeler: Kölelik." *Tarih ve Toplum* 1 (1984): 57-63.

Özdemir, Mehmet N. "İnsan Hakları Bağlamında Hz. Peygamber'in Köleliğe Yaklaşımı." *Bilimname* 29, no. 2 (2010): 75-98.

Sak, İzzet. 1992. "Şer'iye Sicillerine Göre Sosyal ve Ekonomik Hayatta Köleler (17. ve 18. Yüzyıllar)." Ph.D dissertation, Selçuk Üniversitesi.

Seng, Yvonne J. "Fugitives and Factotums: Slaves in Early Sixteenth-Century Istanbul." *Journal of the Economic and Social History of the Orient* 49, no. 2 (1996): 136-69.

Shaw, Brent D. *Spartacus and The Slave Wars, A Brief History with Documents*. Boston: Bedford Press, 2001.

Söğütlü Erişgen, Özlem. "Vekâlet Sözleşmesi Bağlamında Noxal Sonuçlu Sözleşme-Hırsız Köle Olayı." *Ankara Üniversitesi Hukuk Fakültesi Dergisi* 51, no. 4 (2002): 83-98.

Şanlıbayrak, Hakan. 2007. "III. ve VI. Yüzyıllar Arasında Avrupa'da Kölelik." Ph.D dissertation, Fırat Üniversitesi.

Şen, Ömer. *Osmanlı'da Köle Olmak*. İstanbul: Kapı Yayınları, 2007.

Şeyhülislam Feyzullah Efendi. *Fetâvâ-yı Fevziye*, ed. Süleyman Kaya. İstanbul: Klasik Yayınları, 2009.

Tak, Ekrem. "1513-1520 Tarihli Üsküdar Kadı Siciline Göre Kaçkın Köleler." in *Üsküdar Sempozyumu II, 12-13 Mart 2004 Bildiriler* I, eds. Zekeriya Kurşun and Ahmet Emre Bilgili, 19-28. İstanbul: 2005.

Taneri, Aydın. "Hadım." *DİA* 15 (1997): 1-3.

Ünal, Mehmet Ali. *Osmanlı Sosyal ve Ekonomik Tarihi*. İstanbul: Paradigma Yayınları, 2012.

Üzüm, Hamza. "Tanah ve Talmut'ta Kölelik." *Kafkas Üniversitesi Sosyal Bilimler Enstitüsü Dergisi* 12 (2013): 163-182.

Yaman, Sevda, "Tevrat'a Göre İnsan Hayatı ve Onurunun Kutsallığı." *İnsan ve Toplum Bilimleri Dergisi, Yahudilik Özel Sayısı* 5, no. 2 (2016): 338-54.

Yaran, Rahmi. "Hadım." *DİA* 15 (1997): 3.

Yaşa, Fırat. "Efendi-Köle İlişkisi Bağlamında Şeyhülislâm Fetvaları." in *Osmanlı Devleti'nde Kölelik, Ticaret, Esaret, Yaşam*, eds. Zübeyde Güneş Yağcı, Fırat Yaşa, Dilek İnan, 209-226. İstanbul: Tezkire Yayınları, 2017.

———. "Desperation, Hopelessness, and Suicide: An Initial Consideration of Self-Murder by Slaves in Seventeenth-Century Crimean Society." *Turkish Historical Review* 9, no. 2 (2018): 198-211.

Yiğit, Turgut. "Çivi Yazılı Kanunlarda Kölelik." *Türkiye Sosyal Araştırmalar Dergisi* 3, no. 2 (1999): 53-69.

SECTION TWO

The Operations of Ottoman Bureaucracy: Helpful or not?

CHAPTER EIGHT

Alaeddin from Üsküp (Skopje): From Captivity to Mülazemet[*]

Yasemin Beyazıt

> *The path of knowledge includes significant distress and*
> *disasters and follows a thousand lies and laments.*[1]

Ottomans, who built and operated the largest *ilmiye* (learning) organization in Islamic history, trained the labor force necessary for it in the *madrasas*. Students graduating from the *madrasa* could be employed in areas such as law, the judiciary, religion, education and teaching, and could take up positions such as *müderris, mufti, qadi, imam* or *muezzin*. If the student did not want to follow the path of the *ilmiye*, it was also possible for him to work as a scribe or bureaucrat in the Ottoman offices. The graduates would sometimes gravitate towards the Sufi path and turn down any jobs they were offered. Regardless of the assignment they carried out, the education they received at the *madrasa* included a significant amount of religious learning. With the knowledge they gained, they would perform the most crucial tasks in society, and true to the Prophet's hadith 'The *ulama* are the inheritors of the prophets,' they would earn considerable respect. They were exempt from taxes, controlled the income of wealthy *waqfs* and their children could inherit their property as well as professional status, all of which made them a privileged class among other groups in the *askeriye*.[2] Given the prospect of such attractive occupations, the Muslim youth among the Ottoman subjects would develop a passion for scholarship and become students, striving to attain first the novice rank of *suhte* then *dânişmend* and finally, *mülâzemet*.[3] The Ottoman State

---

[*] Skopje, 2nd half of 16th Century

[1] This expression was used for the poet from Bursa, Selman. Beyânî, *Tezkiretüʾş-Şuarâ*, Aysun Sungurhan, ed. (Ankara: Kültür ve Turizm Bakanlığı Yayınları, 2017), 94.

[2] Ahmet Yaşar Ocak, "Dini Bilimler ve Ulema," in *Osmanlı Uygarlığı* I, Halil İnalcık and Günsel Renda, ed.s, (Ankara: Kültür ve Turizm Bakanlığı Yayınları, 2004), 244-54.

[3] It is generally held that the *Mülazemet* system might have emerged during the process of centralization that started during the reign of Mehmed II (the Conqueror). The Ottoman

conducted an apprenticeship system of *mülazemet,* by assigning specific positions[4] in the service of high-ranking *müderris* and *molla*s. Alaeddin from Üsküp (Skopje), the subject of our study, also found himself in the middle of this educational and career network in the second half of the 16th century. It came to our attention that even though there are significant number of studies on the Ottoman *ulama*, the institutions of *ilmiye* and the occupation itself, there are very few focusing on *tâlib*, the students and the pupils

---

administration wanted to keep the *ilmiye* class in check, both its size and its mindset. One strategy was the efficient use of existing posts and the appointment of known figures to these posts, approved by the *ulama* and authorized by the state. With the emergence of the *mülazemet* system, a selective process was established for those who wanted to enter the profession. From then on, it was no longer sufficient for the students to have completed their *madrasa* education. They would also need to be schooled by high ranked *ulama*s, work in their service and receive their approval. In this way, high ranked *ulama,* could open the doors to the profession for them. The student gained knowledge and experience while in service to the *ulama,* such as the *şeyhülislam* and the *kadıasker*s, and the *qadi*s of Istanbul, Edirne, Bursa, as well of Egypt, Damascus, Aleppo, Mecca, Medina and Baghdad. The student would also enter the service of the *muderris* who taught at the *madrasa*s and carried the rank of "Dâhil". When the service period ended, the student would earn the right to enter the profession through the posts allocated for his teacher. Yasemin Beyazıt, *Osmanlı İlmiye Mesleğinde İstihdam* (Ankara: TTK Yayınları, 2014), 32.

4   The path of the *mülazemet* and its posts assumed its classical form in the middle of the 16th century. The most important condition for the *ulama* to grant *mülazemet* was the event of a movement, or a reassignment, through the ranks of the *madrasa*s and the *mevleviyyet*. There were rules about the posts and the number of people the *ulama* granted *mülazemet* to. In the entrance to the *ilmiyye* the assistant teachers had a distinguished status. *Muderris* who worked in *madrasa*s with the minimum of a "Dâhil" ranking were able to open the doors of the *ilmiye* to their assistants. When the *muderris* were appointed to another *madrasa,* to the post of *qadi,* or retired, they were granted the right to incorporate their assistant at their former *madrasa* into the *ilmiye*. Those who entered the *ilmiye* in this way were called "muîdlikten" or "iâdeden". When the ulama were appointed to another post or received promotion, they were granted a cadre called "teşrîf". At this stage, the number of students that the *ulama* could incorporate into the *ilmiye* was in direct proportion to their own position. In addition to the path of *teşrîf,* the *şeyhülislam* used the post of "bailee of the *fatwas*", and the *kadıasker* that of secretary to incorporate one of their students every six months into the *ilmiye* class. The post called "Müstakillen" (Distinguished) had a privileged status, and was presented due to the students' distinguished service and success or their special status, say, as children of the *mullah* and the *şeyh*s. At times, the *ulama* incorporated some students whose service they were pleased with into the *ilmiye* in this manner as well. Another staffing pattern was the *nevbet*. The *nevbet* openings had predetermined times, but also could be announced in times of military victory, the ascension of a new Sultan to the throne, imperial festivities, and the production of an important work by one of the *ulama*. The time of openings ranged from three years to nine years. During the *nevbet,* the rules specified which *ulama* could add their students to the *ilmiye,* and the number of students to be added as well. Beyazıt, *Osmanlı İlmiyye Mesleği,* 52-3.

themselves. Therefore, in the study below, we will try to contribute to the history of students with a micro example, namely, Alaeddin from Üsküp.

Üsküp as Homeland, Edirne (Adrianople) as the Door to the Ilmiye

Our only source of information for the life of Alaeddin from Üsküp[5] is

FIGURE 8.1 The mülazemet record of Mevlana Alaeddin (NOK, RKR, 5193/3, 6b).

the record written by Bostanzade Mehmed Efendi[6] in the *mülazemet* register that he kept during his first time as the *kadıasker* of Rumelia. From this document, first we learn that he was the son of Mustafa from Üsküp. We do not have information on his family or the occupation of his father. As there are no honorifics in the record such as *efendi* or *bey*, Mustafa was probably a commoner; that is to say, Alaeddin came from a family that was not already part of the *askeriye*.

The document[7] shows that in the year 981 (1573/1574) Alaeddin was studying under Mahmud Beğ Efendi, a teacher at the Sultan Bayezid *madrasa*. Even though

---

5   For a study on another individual from Üsküp (Skopje), see Cemal Kafadar, "Mütereddid Bir Mutasavvıf: Üsküplü Asiye Hatun'un Rüya Defteri," *Kim Var İmiş Biz Burada Yoğ İken* (İstanbul: Metis Yayınları, 2009), 123-91.

6   Nevizâde Atâi, *Hadâ'iku'l-Hakâ'ik fî Tekmileti'ş-Şakâ'ik* 1, Suat Donuk, ed., (İstanbul: Türkiye Yazma Eserler Kurumu Başkanlığı Yayınları, 2017), 1116-23.

7   Nuruosmaniye Kütüphanesi (NOK), *Rumeli Kadıaskerliği Ruznamçesi* (RKR), 5193/3, vr. 6b. The transliteration of the document is as follows:

"Mevlana Alaeddin bin Mustafa el-Üskübî.

Mevlana-yı mezbûr kazâ-i Bağdad'dan mütekâ'id iken vefât iden merhûm Mahmud Beğ Efendi dâ'ilerine dokuz yüz seksen bir târîhinde cenâb-ı cennetmekân Sultân Bayezid Hân medresesinde irtibât idüb eski dânişmendlerinden olub mevlânâ-yı müşârünileyhe mahmiyye-i mezbûre 'inâyet buyuruldukda sılasında bulunub ardınca Bağdad'a gitmek niyeti ile Selaniğe gelüb sefineye girüb Şam Trablusuna müteveccih oldukda kazâ ile kâfire esîr olub yedi yıldan sonra bahâ ile halâs olub her vechle mazlûm dâ'ileri olduğundan mâ'ada kânûn-ı kadîm-i pâdişâhî bade'l-vefât altı ay tevakkuf iken merhûm salifü'z-zikrin mülâzımları müddet-i mu'ayyeneden akelde alınmağla mevlânâ-yı mezkûr mazlûm mahrûm olub târîh-i mezbûrdan vefâtına gelince müşârünileyhden munfasıl olmayub eski dânişmendi olduğuna eşrâf-ı müderrisîn ve a'yân-ı kuzâttan mahzarı ve mute'addid

we do not have information on his education before his arrival in Edirne, it is possible that he was schooled in Üsküp. In that period, Üsküp was one of the important cities in the Balkans, with a mostly Muslim population, a crossroad of trade and culture, and in Kemalpaşazade's comparison, it was the 'Bursa of Rumelia'.[8] This comparison was undoubtedly inspired by the fact that Üsküp was an important cultural center. Kâtip Çelebi, in his work titled *Cihannüma*, written in the mid-17th century, describes Üsküp as *"ma'den-i ulemâ ve fuzalâ"*, the source and cradle of scholars and the virtuous ones. In addition, he specifies that the *qadi*s on duty and those who had been dismissed, as well as many of the *qadi*s who worked at the office of the *Kadıasker* of Rumelia, chose to live in Üsküp.[9] Evliya Çelebi, approximately one hundred years after Alaeddin's student days, states that Greek historians refers to Üsküp as *"Mazenderân-ı Rûm"* and mentions that the residents of Üsküp were welcoming towards dervishes, poets and the poor.[10] Growing up in such a cultural environment, Alaeddin from Üsküp must have been in his twenties in those years as he became a student of a high-ranked scholar in the years 1573/1574 and started his education in a *madrasa* of the sultan. The anonymous author of *Hırzü'l-mülûk* states that the age ranges of the *mülazım* were between 25 and 30.[11] Thus we can say that Alaeddin was born around the beginning of the second half of the 16th century.

During this period the Ottoman *madrasa* system consisted of two main groups called *Harici* (External) and *Dahili* (Internal).[12] External *madrasa*s were arranged according to their levels such as *yirmili* (Twenties), *otuzlu* (Thirties), *kırklı* (Forties), *ellili* (Fifties). External fifties *madrasa*s were built by Muslim administrators of state, rulers and the members of the ruling family that came before the Ottomans. The *madrasa*s built by Ottoman viziers were also included in this group.[13] As

---

temessükâtı olmağın 'avâtıf-ı 'aliyye-i hüsrevâniyyeden zerre 'inâyet mazhar olub mülâzım alınması içün pâye-i serîr-i ma'dalet masîre 'arz olundukda sadaka buyurulub kaydolundu."

8   Mehmet İnbaşı, "Üsküp," *DİA* 42 (2012): 378.

9   Djuneis Nureski, "Osmanlı Kaynaklarına Göre Kültür Merkezi Konumundaki Makedonya Şehirleri ve Özellikleri," *Balkan Araştırma Enstitüsü Dergisi* 3, no. 1 (2014): 71.

10   Nureski, "Makedonya," 73-4.

11   Anonim, *Hırzü'l-Mülûk*, *Osmanlı Devlet Teşkilâtına Dair Kaynaklar, Kitâb-ı Müstetâb, Kitâb-ı Mesâlihi'l Müslimin ve Menâfi'il Mü'minîn, Hırzü'l-Mülûk*, Yaşar Yücel, ed., (Ankara: Türk Tarih Kurumu Yayınları, 1988), 195.

12   Cornell H. Fleischer, *Tarihçi Mustafa Âli: Bir Osmanlı Aydın ve Bürokratı, (Bureaucrat and Intellectual in the Ottoman Empire: The Historian Mustafa Ali (1541–1600).* (Princeton, NJ: Princeton University Press, 1986) translated from the English by Ayla Ortaç (İstanbul: Tarih Vakfı Yurt Yayınları, 1996), 24.

13   *Künhü'l-Ahbâr*, 80.

for the internal *madrasa*s that were above these, they were built by the Ottoman sultans and the ruling family. Above the internal *madrasa*s was the Sahn *madrasa*, and above Sahn, there were the institutions of education called the 'sixties' that also included the Süleymaniye *madrasa*s – completed in the year 1559.[14]

The *madrasa*s in the Ottoman Empire in the 16th century were scattered across the lands. Approximately half of the *madrasa*s were in the cities called the *bilad-ı selase*, the three capital cities of Bursa, Edirne and Istanbul. As their levels advanced, the percentage of *madrasa*s located in the three centers increased, and most of the highest ranked madrasas accumulated in Istanbul, Edirne and Bursa. This

FIGURE 8.2 Müslim Çelebi and his student (Âşık Çelebi, Meşâirü'ş-Şuara, c. 2, haz. Filiz Kılıç, 807).

spatial distribution naturally affected the movements of the students and the *ulama*. Students, as they progressed in their education, would have to go to the large urban centers. Among the three cities, 71% of the *madrasa*s were in Istanbul, 15% in Edirne, and 14% in Bursa. The data above indicates that Istanbul was a large center of education and culture. Another feature of the *madrasa*s was that the three capital cities were identified as 'internal provinces' and the *müderris* who worked in these cities would have a higher rank compared to those in other cities. Only the *müderris* who worked in the 'internal provinces' would have the right to *mülazemet*. Students who received their education outside of these three cities had to go to the *madrasa*s in these cities and train as the students of prominent *müderris* or *qadis* who were entitled to the *mülazemet*.[15]

Alaeddin must have progressed through the stages of education mentioned above. In 16th century Üsküp, there were the twenties, forties and fifties *madrasa*s. Hüseyin Şah *madrasa* was twenties level, Hacı Hüseyin *madrasa* was forties level,

---

14   *Künhü'l-Ahbâr*, 71.

15   Beyazıt, *Osmanlı İlmiye Mesleği*, 237-8.

Ishak Paşa and Isa Bey *madrasa*s were fifty *akçe madrasa*s.[16] Around Üsküp, in Kratova and İştib there were twenties *madrasa*s as well.

It is most likely that Alaeddin, after having received an education in the *sıbyan* (elementary) schools and the *buka madrasa*s, frequented the high-level *madrasa*s in Üsküp. According to the *madrasa* tradition, he probably took the *kutub-ı mu'tebere* (the respected books) with him, as well as the *temessuk* document that listed the books he had read. With it in hand, he went from one *madrasa* to another,[17] completing his education in the Ishak Paşa and Isa Bey *madrasa*s of the fifties level. Isa Bey *madrasa* had ten cells and each student was given a daily allowance of one *akçe*.[18] As the *müderris* also acted as the *mufti*, we can say that this *madrasa* was the most highly respected one in Üsküp. Both *madrasa*s had extensive libraries.[19]

Did Alaeddin join the *suhte* movements seen around Üsküp during his final days in the city? How did he look at these events? Even though we don't know how he viewed the riots, we know that in the second half of the 16th century when, along with the rise in population, the interest in the *ilmiye* occupations rose. It became popular to be a student in small *madrasa*s in towns due to the esteem and the tax exemptions it brought. When we compare the number of students entering the *ilmiye* between mid-16th century and the years 1587-88, we see a 177% increase. This situation caused a tremendous bottleneck at the entrance to the *ilmiye,* and there was thus an extended wait period for assignment to duties.[20] In the same period there were several *suhte* riots, and Üsküp got its share of uprisings as well.[21]

If Alaeddin wanted to be a member of the Ottoman *ilmiye* class, he would have to enter a higher-level *madrasa* and work to become a *mülazım*. This was possible only by going to the capital cities (internal provinces). With these thoughts, Alaeddin looked for a teacher in Edirne, the former capital, who could open the doors to the

16 Cahit Baltacı, *XV-XVI. Yüzyıllarda Osmanlı Medreseleri* 1 (İstanbul: İFAV Yayınları, 2005), 490-4.

17 "Kanunnâme-i Ehl-i İlm," *Osmanlı Kanunnâmeleri ve Hukuki Tahlilleri* 4, Ahmet Akgündüz, ed., (İstanbul, FEY Yayınları, 1992), 662.

18 Ekrem Hakkı Ayverdi, Aydın Yüksek et al., *Avrupa'da Osmanlı Mimari Eserleri* 3 (İstanbul: İstanbul Fetih Cemiyeti Yayınları, 2000), 252.

19 Ljutfı Nedzıpı, "XV. ve XVI. Yüzyıllarda Makedonya'da Kültür ve Medeniyet," Ph.D. dissertation, Marmara Üniversitesi, 2006, 37-40.

20 Beyazıt, *Osmanlı İlmiye Mesleği*, 40.

21 Halil İnalcık, "Kazasker Defterine Göre Kadılık," translated from the English by Bülent Arı, *Adalet Kitabı* (Ankara: Adalet Bakanlığı Yayınları, 2007), 122; Mustafa Akdağ, "Medreseli İsyanları," *İstanbul Üniversitesi İktisat Fakültesi Mecmuası* 11, no. 1-4 (1949-1950): 379-80.

ilmiye for him. His choice of Edirne might have been inspired by this city's proximity when compared to Istanbul and the recommendations of his teachers in Üsküp. We do not have clear information on who Alaeddin's teachers were in Üsküp. To the extent of what we can confirm, the earliest assignment record is from the year 1581, and for this reason we do not know which *muderris* was on duty in Üsküp during the period that Alaeddin was a student. Unfortunately, biographical works are silent on this matter.

A new journey from Üsküp towards hope must have thrilled Alaeddin. He was ultimately headed to the ex-capital and thought that he would attain his goal by what he would learn in the *madrasa* and the relationships he would develop.

The *Madrasa* of Sultan Bayezid II was a building complex that the Sultan had commissioned while embarking upon his campaigns of Kili and Akkerman. It was part of a large social complex by the Tunca River, and included a mosque, a soup kitchen, a bathhouse and a hospital. According to the endowment, the *madrasa* was a fifties one,[22] yet became an Internal sixties *madrasa* in the second half of the 16th century. After the *madrasa* of Selimiye, it was one of the most highly respected and ranked institutions in Edirne.

The Bayezid *madrasa* in Edirne was a perfect fit for Alaeddin. In this *madrasa* with eighteen cells, he both lived and received his education. His sustenance was provided for by the soup kitchen, he made use of the library, and he also received a daily allowance of two *akçes* from the *madrasa* foundation.[23]

Upon starting his *madrasa* education, he became one of the students of the *müderris* Mahmud Beğ Efendi. According to information given by Atâi, Mahmud Beğ Efendi was of Hungarian origin and while at the service of Hüsrev Paşa from the entourage of Grand Vizier Sokullu Mehmed Paşa, he took an interest in scholarship and upon receiving *mülazemet* from Ebussuud Efendi, the greatest scholar of the time, entered the *ilmiye*. After holding office in the *madrasa*s of Hoca Hayreddin, Merdümiyye, Atik Ali Paşa, Bursa Sultaniyesi and Sahn, Mahmud Beğ Efendi was assigned to the *madrasa* of Bayezid in Edirne, in the month of Ramadan in the year 979 (January-February 1572).[24] His assignment there continued until the month of Safer in the year 983 (May-June 1575). If Alaeddin was the student of Mahmud Beğ Efendi in the year 981 (1573/1574), approximately

---

22 Baltacı, *Osmanlı Medreseleri*, 760.

23 İ. Aydın Yüksel, *Osmanlı Mimarisinde II. Bayezid Yavuz Selim Devri* 7 (İstanbul: İstanbul Fetih Cemiyeti Yayınları, 1983), 103, 105, 120.

24 Nevizâde Atâi, *Hadâ'iku'l-Hakâ'ik*, 905.

two years must have passed since Mahmud Beğ's arrival in Edirne. The *müderris* Mahmud Beğ Efendi had gotten accustomed to life in Edirne and a circle of students had formed around him. As he was working in a sixties level *madrasa* of the sultan, he was also expecting to be appointed to a good *qadi* post. After his work as *müderris*, he could advance in the path of being a *qadi* that would take him to the highest levels of the *ilmiye*. Perhaps, even if he started off with lower level *qadi* positions, he could end up with the positions in Mecca, Medina, Bursa, Edirne and Istanbul, and would be able to rise to the highest ranks of the *ilmiye*, i.e. those of the *kadıasker* and even, potentially, of the *Şeyhülislam*. After serving in Edirne for approximately three and a half years, Mahmud Efendi was assigned to the position of *qadi* in Baghdad.

The Road to Baghdad Ends in Captivity

At the time of Mahmud Efendi's Baghdad appointment, Alaeddin had been his student for approximately two years. For Alaeddin, the main story that would shape his life started here. Mahmud Beğ Efendi was appointed at a time when Alaeddin was in his hometown, and he learned of this development upon returning to Edirne. When his teacher assumed duty in Baghdad, he had two paths in front of him: either he would follow his teacher, or he would join the student circle around a new *müderris*. As the second option would push him back on the path to *mülazemet*, Alaeddin must have chosen the first path and following his teacher and set off for Baghdad. When a scholar adopted another's student without an *ijaza* (Permission), it was frowned upon. This situation, also described in the legal codes, would be called 'luring a student'."[25]

Alaeddin was possibly both happy and sad about the news of the assignment. On the one hand, as the good fortune of the teacher meant the good fortune of the student, he saw himself one step closer to the *mülazemet;* on the other, travelling to his teacher's side may have preoccupied him. If Alaeddin had a fearless and adventurous personality, he might have seen this process as a once in a lifetime opportunity to get to know new lands and a new culture.

Following his assignment to Baghdad, Mahmud Beğ Efendi must have given *mülazemet* to honor his most senior student and assistant at the *madrasa*.[26] It is also clear that Alaeddin was not one of his outstanding students. If he were his assistant or one of the outstanding students, he could have attained *mülazemet* through the

---

25 "Kanunnâme-i Ehl-i İlm," 663.

26 Beyazıt, *Osmanlı İlmiyye Mesleği*, 55, 65.

honor roll. As this did not happen, we can assume that he was a novice in the path to *mülazemet*. The legal codes frequently warned the *müderris* about the quick progression of their students. They were told to not settle for one book from each science and one chapter from each book, and instead to have their students read important books in their entirety.[27] We can assume that Mahmud Beğ Efendi also possessed such sensitivities.

When travelling to Baghdad, Alaeddin chose the faster sea route, and embarking in Salonica, wanted to reach Tripoli. However, he was not able to, and in the language of the document, had been captured by 'the infidels'. As the Mediterranean in this period saw intense pirate activity, Alaeddin also had his share of it and remained in captivity for seven years. Even though we don't know his whereabouts during that time and what he experienced, we do know that he went through difficult times and tried to procure his ransom money. He wrote petitions[28] to his family, his acquaintances, his teacher, administrators, and even to the members of the dynasty and Sultan Murad III, all to secure his release from captivity, and that he bent over backwards to find the amount required for the ransom.

We can assume that Alaeddin was freed from captivity by paying his ransom after seven years, and had returned to Üsküp. He was deeply affected by his captivity while pursuing *mülazemet* and trying to become a *qadi* or *müderris*. Once he recovered in Üsküp, he might have inquired about his teacher and perhaps tried to find him. As for Mahmud Beğ Efendi, he was dismissed only after one year in his new post, when he issued a verdict against one of the *ocak beyi*, whose complaint triggered the dismissal. Mahmud Beğ Efendi retired in the month of *Rabi ul awwal* in 984 (May/June 1576), with a daily allowance of forty *akçe*s. We do not know why he preferred retirement. Serving as a *qadi* might have overwhelmed him and felt very different from the life of a *müderris*. Being a *qadi* was, in the words of Taşköprülüzade, a life-draining occupation.[29] It would even haunt one's dreams and cause nightmares.[30] *Qadi*s, in addition to serving as judges, also had financial,

---

27 "Mevâli-i İzâm ve Müderrisîn-i Kirâmın Tedrîse Muvâzebetleri İçin Nişân-ı Hümâyun," *Osmanlı Kanunnâmeleri ve Hukuki Tahlilleri* 4, Ahmet Akgündüz, ed., (İstanbul: FEY Yayınları, 1992), 667-8.

28 For letters and petitions, see Uğur Demir, "Esir/Esire Mektupları ve Arzuhalleri (1700-1750)," *Uluslararası Türk Savaş Esirleri Bildiri Kitabı* (İstanbul 2017), 53-94.

29 Aslı Niyazioğlu, "On Altıncı Yüzyıl Sonunda Osmanlı'da Kadılık Kâbusu ve Nihânî'nin Rüyası," *Journal of Turkish Studies* 31, no 2 (2007): 137.

30 Taşköprülüzâde İsâmuddin Ebu'l-Hayr Ahmet Efendi, *eş-Şakâiku'n-Numâniyye fî Ulemâi'd-Devleti'l-Osmaniyye*, Muharrem Tan, ed., (İstanbul: İz Yayıncılık, 2007), 379.

administrative, and municipial duties. His retirement undoubtedly affected his students as well. As he could no longer rise in rank in his career, he could not choose new *mülazemet* except in cases of occasion or death. And for these, his students needed to wait patiently.

From Captivity to Mülazemet

Mahmud Beğ Efendi stayed in the *qadi*ship of Baghdad for exactly one year. When Alaeddin was probably freed from captivity around the years 1581-82, six years had passed since his teacher's retirement. As a retired teacher would be neither favored nor assigned additional staff, Alaeddin might have given up hopes of attaining *mülazemet*. While in captivity, he had missed the vacancies announced in the years 987 (March-April 1579) and 990 (1582-83),[31] when his teacher's senior student must have entered *ilmiye*. The prospect of seeking another teacher to enter *ilmiye* must not have appealed to him due to his ordeals in captivity or because of the lengthy wait time it would have required. He might have also taken up other jobs and to secure a new livelihood. As the graduate of a *madrasa* unable to attain *mülazemet*, he might have worked as teacher, preacher, substitute judge, scribe or in various posts in *waqf*s, and it is possible that his disappointment led him to go into the family business.

Mahmud Beğ Efendi passed away five or six years after Alaeddin's release from captivity. We do not know the extent to which Alaeddin maintained the teacher-pupil relationship with his teacher after captivity. The *mülazemet* record indicates that until his teacher's death, Alaeddin remained his student. However, this was probably not an active studentship; it was rather a designation to maintain the connection between them.

The news of his teacher's death might have both saddened and relieved Alaeddin. While he might have put his life in order and gotten used to it, not having reached his goal probably hurt him. The news of the death of his teacher also would have reignited his hope for becoming a *mülazım*, because the death of a highly ranked *müderris* or *qadi* who had *mülazemet* could pave the way to *mülazemet* for the student who was left behind. "*Mülazemet* from death", or "*mülazemet* from the deceased "[32]

---

31 Beyazıt, *Osmanlı İlmiyye Mesleği*, 74.

32 The number of *mülazemet* to be granted by the *ulama* was specified for assistantships, *teşrifen*, the bailiff of *fatwa*s, secretary and *nevbet*. However, *mülazemet* appointments due to the death of the ulama could pose difficult questions for the *ilmiye* bureaucracy. Sometimes, a teacher could leave behind 30-40 students. If all of his students were incorporated into the *ilmiye,* the number of *mülazım* waiting to be appointed increased drastically, creating bottlenecks. For this reason, examiners appointed by the *kadıasker* from among the *müderris*

was, perhaps, his last chance. A confusion regarding the date of death for Mahmud Beğ Efendi comes to our attention. Atâl cites 997(1588-1589) as the year. However, the *mülazım* record in the *ruznamçe* register gives the date as first of Jumada al-Awwal in 996 (March 29-April 7,1588).[33] Since this record was made after the examination and inspection of Mahmud Efendi's student, and the inspection was done before the requisite waiting period of six months after death, we can assume that Mahmud Beğ passed away at the beginning of the year 996 (December 1587-January 1588). By then, five or six years had passed since Alaeddin's release from captivity.

Mahmud Beğ Efendi's records of *mülazemet* due to death cannot be found in the *ruznamçe* registers that have survived until today. For this reason, we don't know how many students he had or how many succeeded in becoming *mülazım*. The record on Alaeddin mentions another personal misfortune in addition to captivity. Since the student of Mahmud Beğ Efendi was illegally registered before the required six-month waiting period was over, Alaeddin was not able to register as a *mülazım* in the right time. As a last chance, Alaeddin requested documents from prominent *qadis and müderrises* to prove that he was a former student of Mahmud Beğ Efendi, and that he had not abandoned his education. With these proofs, he appealed to the *kadıasker,* requesting the position of *mülazım*. The *kadıasker* of Rumelia, Bostanzade Mehmed Efendi, saw this request as reasonable and presented it to the sultan, and thereby opened the door of the *ilmiye* to Alaeddin.

It is apparent that Alaeddin's *mülazemet* was delayed due to captivity and due to his teacher's retirement. From the research on the *ruznamçe* registers of the period, we could not confirm whether or not he was assigned to any posts after becoming *mülazım*. This is possibly because the records in question did not survive in their entirety, or because Alaeddin chose neither the path of the *qadi* nor that of the *müderris*. If he wanted to work in the *ilmiye* profession, he must have completed

---

of Süleymaniye or Sahn, would be tasked with determining how many and which student could be granted *mülazemet*. The examiner would perform a process called "tahrir" (registration) or "teftiş" (inspection), six months after the death of the scholar. The students would prove their scholarship through certificates and letters given to them previously by their teacher. In addition to these documents, the examiners would also take the testimonies of distinguished and prominent *müderris* (eşrâf-ı müderrisîn) and *qadis* (ayân-ı kuzât) into account. After the inspection, the prominent students of the deceased scholar would be singled out as "asil", "intihaben" or "müncezen", and receiving *mülazemet* directly, enter the *ilmiye*. Those left behind,"umum", would have to toil away at the *buka madrasa* for several years, before they might be appointed to a 'twenties' *madrasa*. Sometimes they would not be granted *mülazemet* and would have to wait for the *nevbet* to enter the *ilmiye* or would be sent to the service of other *ulama*. Beyazıt, *Osmanlı İlmiyye Mesleği*, 42-43, 75-81.

33 *NOK, RKR*, 5193/3, 6b.

the waiting period of two to three years[34] before attaining the *mülazemet*, and subsequently received an assignment to a post as *qadi* or *müderris*.

Instead of a Conclusion: The Moral of the Story for the Historian

The *ruznamçe* register that provides us with a view into the life of Alaeddin, gives us important clues about the systems of education and the system of *mülazemet* that enabled access to the *ilmiye* profession. A *mülazım* candidate who applied the theoretical knowledge gained at the *madrasa* would, in the *qadi*'s court, expand his knowledge and skills through both assisting the *qadi* in his duties and being a witness to the rulings of the court. As Alaeddin fell into captivity while still on this path, his life took a new direction, and before he could complete the process of *mülazemet* he got separated from the *ilmiye,* yet he was later reconnected to the system. He waited patiently for *mülazemet* and finally could attain it due to his teacher's death. Even though he missed the registration for students, he was familiar with the existing system, and he sought his rights by showing the early student registration as his reasoning. This shows that Alaeddin was following the develop-ments in Istanbul; the fact that he was able to obtain documents such as petitions and vouchers from prominent *qadi*s shows us that he maintained his relationship with them. Due to his experiences, Alaeddin became a *mülazım* through death, which was a less esteemed path when compared to other paths such as assistant-ship, honor appointment, or clerkship that were, without a doubt, respected more. *Hırzü'l-mülûk*, written by an anonymous *timar* holder in the time of Murad III, gives us this impression. The author requests the *kadıasker*s to assign posts due to merit, and to refrain from accepting bribes and from telling anyone, 'You are a *mülazım* due to death' or 'You have very little time'.[35] 'Mülazemet due to death' was valued less mainly because it was open to misuse. Mustafa Âli of Gelibolu states that the family of the deceased scholar would seize the opportunity to trade the post off and would put down the names of whoever bribed them as students from the teacher's register.[36] Such acts must have been undeniably widespread to make their way into the treatise.

---

34 This waiting period was approximately three years in the 16th century and seven years in the middle of the 18th century. Ali Aslan, "XVIII. Yüzyıl Osmanlı İlim Hayatından Bir Kesit: Sıdkî Mustafa Efendi'nin Günlüğü ve Mülazemet Yılları," Ph.D. dissertation, İstanbul Üniversitesi, 2015, 30.

35 Hırzü'l-mülûk, 195.

36 Gelibolulu Mustafa Âlî, *Siyaset Sanatı Nushatü's-selâtin*, Faris Çerçi, ed., (İstanbul: Büyüyen Ay Yayınları, 2015), 140.

Alaeddin was set apart from his peers when he fell into captivity as a student who was advancing on the regular path to the profession of *ilmiye*. To what extent did falling into captivity and the fear of it pose threats for individuals in the 16th century Ottoman Empire? Within the Ottoman domains, being caught by pirates was a nightmare scenario for sea travelers. The Mediterranean teemed with pirates: those affiliated with Venice; Uskoks under the patronage of the Austrian Habsburgs; the Knights of Saint Jean who went to Malta after the conquest of Rhodes; Spanish pirates, The Knights of the Order of Saint Stephen under the patronage of Tuscany;[37] the British who only recently had started to make their presence felt in the Mediterranean; and the *levent*s who were Ottoman subjects.[38] After the conquest of Cyprus and the Battle of Lepanto, piracy replaced naval warfare in the Mediterranean. This transformation was mostly due to the heavy financial burden that naval warfare put on states.[39] Piracy took place especially along the Alexandria-Rhodes-Istanbul and the Cyprus-Istanbul routes.[40] Cyprus and the area around Crete were highly favorable locations to take captives.

Alaeddin was neither the first nor the last member of the *ilmiye* to fall into captivity. Among the scholars who shared Alaeddin's fate were Abdülgaffar,[41] the *qadi* of Vlorë (1589); Haşim,[42] the qadi of Hırsofi in Cyprus (1591); and Macuncuzade Mustafa Efendi,[43] the *qadi* assigned to Paphos, Abdurrahman Efendi, the *qadi* of Ajloun, and Sinan Efendi, the *qadi* of Güğercinlik, all of whom fell into captivity in the same year (1597).[44]

---

37 Mikail Acıpınar, "XVII. Yüzyılın İlk Yarısında Toskana Grandukalığında Türk Esirler," *Tarih İncelemeleri Dergisi* 27, no. 1 (2010): 15-38.

38 Emrah Safa Gürkan, "Batı Akdeniz'de Osmanlı Korsanlığı ve Gaza Meselesi," *Kebikeç* 33 (2012): 173-4; Serap Mumcu, "Akdeniz'de Korsanlık ve Osmanlı-Venedik İlişkilerinde Bir Esir Alma Krizi: Arap Emiri Kızı Zemre'nin Kaçırılışı," in *Osmanlı Devleti'nde Kölelik Ticaret-Esaret-Yaşam*, Zübeyde Güneş Yağcı, Fırat Yaşa, Dilek İnan, ed.s, (İstanbul: Tezkire Yayınları, 2017), 155-6.

39 Emrah Safa Gürkan, "Osmanlı-Habsburg Rekabeti Çerçevesinde Osmanlılar'ın XVI. Yüzyıl'daki Akdeniz Siyaseti," in *Osmanlı Dönemi Akdeniz Dünyası*, Haydar Çoruh, M. Yaşar Ertaş, M. Ziya Köse, ed.s, (İstanbul: Yeditepe Yayınevi, 2011), 16.

40 Mikail Acıpınar, "Güney Anadolu Kıyılarında Hristiyan Korsanlar (1604-1608)," *Akademik Bakış*, 21 (2017): 184.

41 *MA, RKR*, 182/5, 38.

42 *NOK, RKR*, 5193/4,7b.

43 İsmet Parmaksızoğlu, "Bir Türk Kadısının Esaret Hatıraları," *Tarih Dergisi* 8 (1953): 77-8.

44 Mâcuncuzâde Mustafa Efendi, *Malta Esirleri Ser-Güzeşt-i Esîrî-i Malta*, Cemil Çiftçi, ed., (İstanbul: Kitabevi Yayınları, 1996), 22-3.

FIGURE 8.3 The record of Mevlana Bedri's assignment to the post of Qadi (NOK, RKR, 5193/4, 33a).

Besides Alaeddin, we know of one other student who fell captive, Bedri, the eventual *qadi* of Yacağac. His personal records dated 28th of *Jumādā al-ʾĀkhir* in 1000 (April 11, 1592) indicate[45] that he was the student of Molla Ahmed Efendi and had suffered captivity in the hands of the infidels for several years. Upon returning from captivity, he attained *mülazemet*, and by imperial edict, he was assigned to Yacağac for 35 *akçe*s. Even though the records do not specify where Bedri was traveling from when taken captive, the assignment locations of his teacher Molla Ahmed Efendi present two options. The first was Damascus where Molla Ahmed Efendi served as the *qadi* between the dates of *Jumada al-Awwal* 989 and *Rabiʿ al-Akhir* 991 (June/July 1581- April/May 1583). The second one was Egypt where he was the *qadi* between the dates of *Muharram* 996 and *Zilqad* 998 (December 1587- September 1590).[46] Since' Bedri's captivity lasted for several years, we can estimate that he was captured sometime between his teacher's travel to Damascus and one of the trips the teacher and pupil might have taken together. After being freed from captivity, Bedri was able to become a *mülazım* while his teacher was still alive, and he was assigned to the *qadi*ship by an imperial edict.

The other two students who shared the same fate with Alaeddin were Muharrem and Abdülbaki Efendi, both among the students of Kemal Beğzade Mehmed Efendi.

---

45   *NOK, RKR*, 5193/4, 33a.

46   Nevizâde Atâi, *Hadâ'iku'l-Hakâ'ik*, 1194.

Kemal Efendi served as *qadi* in Egypt, then in Edirne, and lastly Eyüp, where he passed away on the 18th of Shawwal, 1007 (May 14,1599).[47]

Muharrem traveled to Egypt with his teacher (*Zilqad* 998/ September 1590). Kemal Efendi was eventually dismissed from his duty there, at the beginning of the year 1000 (1591). As for Muharrem, he fell captive while he was on his way out of Egypt, following his teacher. After staying in captivity for several years he had escaped with the help of God, and with the favor of Sinan Paşa, and he was able to become a *mülazım* on his return from captivity, in June 1599.[48] It has been determined that after Kemal Efendi's death, his student was identified and recorded in the *ruznamçe* register by the *müderris* of Sultaniye, Mustafa Efendi, on the 10th of *Jumada al-Akhir* in 1008 (December 28, 1599). Of Kemal Efendi's thirty-two students, Mustafa Efendi wanted five to be *mülazım*, and the rest to be registered by fours during shifts.[49] It is remarkable that Muharrem, possibly with the aid of Sinan Paşa, was admitted to *mülazemet* without having to wait for his teacher's students to be registered.

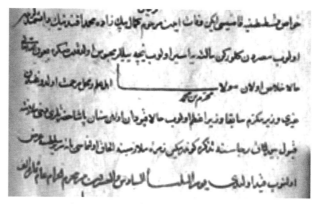

FIGURE 8.4 The record of Mevlana Muharrem's mülazemet (MA, RKR, 184/7, 4).

We can infer from another *ruznamçe* record that Muharrem did not fall captive alone.[50] Elmalılı Abdülbaki, one of the prominent students of Kemal Beğzade Efendi, was held in captivity in Malta for ten years, and upon his teacher's death and the en-

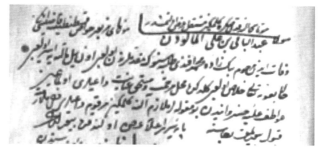

FIGURE 8.5 The record of Mevlana Abdülbaki's mülazemet. (MA, RKR, 184/7 45)

---

47   Nevizâde Atâi, 1133.

48   *MA, RKR*, 184/7, 4.

49   *MA, RKR*, 184/7, 22.

50   *MA, RKR*, 184/7, 45.

suing student reassignment, was also admitted in October, 1600 to the *mülazemet* through an independent offer.

Comparing Alaeddin's experience with other students who fell into captivity such as Bedri, Muharrem and Abdülbaki is important to understand his student days. First, we see that all of them stayed in captivity for a long time. The period varied between seven and ten years. Two of them fell captive on their way to Egypt, one of them on the way to Damascus, and the other on the way to Baghdad, all via sea route. Two of them fell captive in Malta, while the location of captivity for the other two is unknown. We can say that in the 16ᵗʰ century, due to the treaty between states, captives could be sent back to their countries via repatriation-exchange agreements, or in exchange for a ransom, and that in this process, ambassadors, consuls, and merchants played important roles. The state tried to help release the captives by sending an official in some cases, and by promising rewards for those who rescued the captives in others.[51] We know that Alaeddin was released with the payment of a 'price', i.e. ransom money. As for the others, there is no information on how their releases were secured. The document states that Muharrem and Abdülbaki were freed with the help of God, but it is not clear exactly how.

We can say that Bedri, Muharrem and Abdülbaki were luckier compared to Alaeddin. Their teachers were able to attain higher ranks than Alaeddin's teacher, Mahmud Beğ, and therefore had closer relationships with the central administration. When the imperial edict on Bedri was issued, we see that Sinan Paşa acted as an intermediary for Muharrem, and that Abdülbaki attained the post of *mülazım* through an independent petition, on the initiative of the *kadıasker*. When compared with their cases, the fact that Alaeddin could not immediately become a *mülazım* upon his return, and that he had to wait for his teacher's death to achieve *mülazım* status can be seen as an indication that Alaeddin had not established, or was unable to establish, strong networks of affiliations.

While in captivity, Alaeddin, sent letters to his loved ones, his family and the authorities, and following his return saved these as mementos. He must have narrated his experience in detail, several times, to those around him. Even though we do not have information on Alaeddin's captivity period, his letters and memories, that is, the literature of captivity, make us wonder whether or not he published his memories as an adventure or had a personal journal. Did Alaeddin have letters like those of Abdi Çelebi who fell captive to pirates in the Mediterranean and those

---

51 Ahmet Önal, "XVI. Yüzyılda Osmanlı Esirlerin Kurtarılması," *Marmara Türkiye-Almanya Araştırmaları Dergisi*, 4/1-2 (2015): 41-53.

written to Hamza the son of Erdoğmuş[52] who fell captive to the Florentines? Did he have poems that he wrote and sent to members of the dynasty, the elders or his teacher? Did he have memories of captivity like those of the *qadi* Macuncuzade Mustafa Efendi[53] who while going to the post in Paphos fell captive to the pirates of Malta, or those of Osman Ağa from Temeşvar? If we could have gotten a hold of these sources mentioned – that is, if they exist – we would have been able to know Alaeddin better, along with his joy, his sadness, his hopes and his fears.

Osman Ağa from Temeşvar who, in the wars following the second siege of Vienna during when Üsküp was also burned and destroyed, fell captive to Austrians between the years 1688 and 1700. In his memoir about his captivity, he writes the following to specify that he did not describe his memories in their entirety, but merely summarized them: 'Now, until today several events have happened and if we had to write down and report each one, we would have to prolong the story we are writing…'[54] If we could have access to Alaeddin's memories of captivity like those of Osman Ağa, we would have much more to write, and this article would not have ended here.

Bibliography

Archival Sources

Bab-ı Meşihat Şeyhülislamlık Arşivi, *Rumeli Kadıasker Ruznâmçeleri*, 182/5, 184/7.

Nuruosmaniye Kütüphanesi, *Rumeli Kadıasker Ruznâmçeleri*, 5193/3, 5193/4.

Primary Sources

Anonim, Hırzü'l-Mülûk. *Osmanlı Devlet Teşkilâtına Dair Kaynaklar, Kitâb-ı Müstetâb, Kitâb-ı Mesâlihi'l Müslimîn ve Menâfi'il Mü'minîn, Hırzü'l-Mülûk*, ed. Yaşar Yücel. Ankara: TTK Yayınları, 1988.

Aşık Çelebi. *Meşâirü'ş-Şuarâ* II, ed. Filiz Kılıç. İstanbul: İstanbul Araştırma Enstitüsü Yayınları, 2010.

Beyânî. *Tezkiretü'ş-Şuarâ*, ed. Aysun Sungurhan. Ankara: Kültür ve Turizm Bakanlığı Yayınları, 2017.

---

52 Halil Sahillioğlu, "Akdeniz'de Korsanlara Esir Düşen Abdi Çelebi'nin Mektubu," *Tarih Dergisi* 13, no. 17-18 (1963): 241-56; Mikail Acıpınar, "Floransalılara Esir Düşen Erdoğmuş Oğlu Hamza'ya Yazılan Türkçe Bir Mektup (1576)," *Erdem Dergisi* 66 (2014): 5-18.

53 Mâcuncuzâde Mustafa Efendi, *Malta Esirleri*, 19-99; Parmaksızoğlu, "Bir Türk Kadısının Esaret Hatıraları," 77-84.

54 Harun Tolasa, *Kendi Kalemiyle Temeşvarlı Osman Ağa Bir Osmanlı Türk Sipahisi ve Esirlik Hayatı* (Ankara: Akçağ Yayınları, 2004), 38.

Gelibolulu Mustafa Âlî. *Künhü'l-Ahbâr* II, ed. M. Hüdai Şentürk. Ankara: Türk Tarih Kurumu Yayınları, 2003.

———. *Siyaset Sanatı Nushatü's-selâṭîn*, ed. Faris Çerçi. İstanbul: Büyüyen Ay Yayınları, 2015.

"Kanunnâme-i Ehl-i İlm," *Osmanlı Kanunnâmeleri ve Hukuki Tahlilleri* 4, ed. Ahmet Akgündüz, 662-5. İstanbul, 1992.

Mâcuncuzâde Mustafa Efendi, *Malta Esirleri Ser-Güzeşt-i Esîrî-i Malta*, ed. Cemil Çiftçi. İstanbul: Kitabevi Yayınları, 1996.

"Mevâli-i İzâm ve Müderrisîn-i Kirâmın Tedrîse Muvâzebetleri İçin Nişân-ı Hümâyun." *Osmanlı Kanunnâmeleri ve Hukuki Tahlilleri* 4, ed. Ahmet Akgündüz, 667-72. İstanbul, 1992.

Nevizâde Atâi. *Hadâ'iku'l-Hakâ'ik fî Tekmileti'ş-Şakâ'ik* 1, ed. Suat Donuk. İstanbul: Türkiye Yazma Eserler Kurumu Başkanlığı Yayınları, 2017.

Tarih-i Raşid 4. İstanbul, 1282.

Taşköprülüzâde İsâmuddin Ebu'l-Hayr Ahmet Efendi. *eş-Şakâiku'n-Numâniyye fî Ulemâi'd-Devleti'l-Osmaniyye*, ed. Muharrem Tan. İstanbul: İz Yayıncılık, 2007.

Secondary Sources

Acıpınar, Mikail. "Floransalılara Esir Düşen Erdoğmuş Oğlu Hamza'ya Yazılan Türkçe Bir Mektup (1576)." *Erdem Dergisi* 66 (2014): 5-18.

———. "Güney Anadolu Kıyılarında Hristiyan Korsanlar (1604-1608)." *Akademik Bakış* 21 (2017): 183-208.

———. "XVII. Yüzyılın İlk Yarısında Toskana Grandukalığında Türk Esirler." *Tarih İncelemeleri Dergisi* 25, no. 1 (2010): 15-38.

Akdağ, Mustafa. "Medreseli İsyanları." *İstanbul Üniversitesi İktisat Fakültesi Mecmuası* 11, no. 1-4 (1949-1950): 361-87.

Aslan, Ali. 2015. "XVIII. Yüzyıl Osmanlı İlim Hayatından Bir Kesit: Sıdkî Mustafa Efendi'nin Günlüğü ve Mülazemet Yılları." M. A. Thesis, İstanbul Üniversitesi.

Ayverdi, Ekrem Hakkı, Aydın Yüksek et al. *Avrupa'da Osmanlı Mimari Eserleri* 3. İstanbul: İstanbul Fetih Cemiyeti Yayınları, 2000.

Baltacı, Cahit. *XV-XVI. Yüzyıllarda Osmanlı Medreseleri* 1. İstanbul: İFAV Yayınları, 2005.

Beyazıt, Yasemin. *Osmanlı İlmiye Mesleğinde İstihdam*. Ankara: Türk Tarih Kurumu Yayınları, 2014.

Demir, Uğur. "Esir/Esire Mektupları ve Arzuhalleri (1700-1750)." *Uluslararası Türk Savaş Esirleri Sempozyumu Bildiri Kitabı*. İstanbul 2017, 53-94.

Fleischer, Cornell H. *Tarihçi Mustafa Âli Bir Osmanlı Aydın ve Bürokratı*, translated from the English by Ayla Ortaç. İstanbul: Tarih Vakfı Yurt Yayınları, 1996.

Gürkan, Emrah Safa. "Batı Akdeniz'de Osmanlı Korsanlığı ve Gaza Meselesi." *Kebikeç* 33 (2012): 173-204.

————. "Osmanlı-Habsburg Rekabeti Çerçevesinde Osmanlılar'ın XVI. Yüzyıl'daki Akdeniz Siyaseti." in *Osmanlı Dönemi Akdeniz Dünyası*, ed. Haydar Çoruh, M. Yaşar Ertaş, M. Ziya Köse, 11-50. İstanbul: Yeditepe Yayınevi, 2011.

İnalcık, Halil. "Kazasker Defterine Göre Kadılık," translated from the English by Bülent Arı. *Adalet Kitabı*. Ankara: Adalet Bakanlığı Yayınları, 2007, 117-37.

İnbaşı, Mehmet. "Üsküp." *DİA* 42, (2012): 377-81.

Kafadar, Cemal. "Mütereddid Bir Mutasavvıf: Üsküplü Asiye Hatun'un Rüya Defteri." *Kim Var İmiş Biz Burada Yoğ İken*, 123-91. İstanbul: Metis Yayınları, 2009.

Mumcu, Serap. "Akdeniz'de Korsanlık ve Osmanlı-Venedik İlişkilerinde Bir Esir Alma Krizi: Arap Emiri Kızı Zemre'nin Kaçırılışı." in *Osmanlı Devleti'nde Kölelik Ticaret-Esaret-Yaşam*, eds. Zübeyde Güneş Yağcı, Fırat Yaşa, Dilek İnan, 155-85. İstanbul: Tezkire Yayınları, 2017.

Nedzıpı, Ljutfi. 2006. "XV. ve XVI. Yüzyıllarda Makedonya'da Kültür ve Medeniyet." M. A. Thesis, Marmara Üniversitesi.

Niyazioğlu, Aslı. "On Altıncı Yüzyıl Sonunda Osmanlı'da Kadılık Kabusu ve Nihânî'nin Rüyası." *Journal of Turkish Studies* 31, no. 2 (2007): 133-43.

Nureski, Djuneis. "Osmanlı Kaynaklarına Göre Kültür Merkezi Konumundaki Makedonya Şehirleri ve Özellikleri." *Balkan Araştırma Enstitüsü Dergisi* 3, no. 1 (2014): 63-102.

Ocak, Ahmet Yaşar. "Dini Bilimler ve Ulema." in *Osmanlı Uygarlığı I* eds. Halil İnalcık, Günsel Renda, 242-65. Ankara: Kültür ve Turizm Bakanlığı Yayınları, 2004.

Önal, Ahmet. "XVI. Yüzyılda Osmanlı Esirlerin Kurtarılması." *Marmara Türkiye-Almanya Araştırmaları Dergisi* 4, no. 1-2 (2015): 39-56.

Parmaksızoğlu, İsmet. "Bir Türk Kadısının Esaret Hatıraları." *Tarih Dergisi* 5, no. 8 (1953): 77-84.

Sahillioğlu, Halil. "Akdeniz'de Korsanlara Esir Düşen Abdi Çelebi'nin Mektubu." *Tarih Dergisi* 13, no. 17-18 (1963): 241-56.

Tolasa, Harun. *Kendi Kalemiyle Temeşvarlı Osman Ağa Bir Osmanlı Türk Sipahisi ve Esirlik Hayatı*. Ankara: Akçağ Yayınları, 2004.

Yüksel, İ. Aydın. *Osmanlı Mimarisinde II. Bayezid Yavuz Selim Devri* 5. İstanbul: Fetih Cemiyeti Yayınları, 1983.

CHAPTER NINE

Voting and Election Practices of the Greek Community in the Ottoman Classical Period: The Demogerontia Elections[*][1]

Filiz Yaşar

It was 1697. In the island of Chios off the coast of Anatolia in the Aegean, the long and humid summer months had ended, and the resin of mastic trees, or *pistacia lentiscus*, the most special of the scrubs, had been picked and dried in the fall, and the long-awaited winter season had finally arrived. Unlike in other regions, the inhabitants of Chios in the classical period viewed the dreaded winter months as a time of rest, spent in the company of wine and *ouzo*, made from the grapes they had harvested in the summer. In the island of Chios that managed to stay green throughout all seasons with its pine forests, scrubs, shrubberies, vineyards, olive and almond trees, the lightening of chores in the winter did not mean fewer responsibilities. They had a duty to fulfill before spring came: To determine the governance of the community for the year.

Chios, like many Mediterranean islands, was a place where Hellenic culture endured. During the Iron Age, Ionians who escaped from middle Greece due to the Dorian invasion (End of 11th century BC- beginning of 10th century BC) had laid the foundations of the culture that has largely survived to this day. Since the times when Ionians arrived on the island, it had an entrenched cultural structure. The island inhabitants were, over time, ruled by the governance of strong political sovereigns such as the Romans, the Byzantine, the Genoese, and the Ottomans But still, they managed to preserve their culture by adhering to their traditions. The Ottomans had conquered the island in 1566 during Süleyman the Magnificent's

---

[*]   Chios Island, Greece, 1697

[1]   This essay based on of the author's Ph.D dissertation titled "Bir Osmanlı Adasında Toplum ve Ekonomi (XVI. Yüzyıldan-XVIII. Yüzyıla Sakız)" written in 2013 at the History Department of the Social Sciences Institute at Hacettepe University under the supervision of the Ph.D. advisor, Prof. Dr. Mehmet Öz.

Szigetvár campaign. The mastic-perfumed island remained under Ottoman rule until the First Balkan War in 1912.

In February of 1697, as in every year, a systemic ritual that the residents of Chios inherited from their great grandfathers would take place. On the morning of February 28, the last Sunday service of the month had taken place; yet Father Nikolas was not done for the day. After the church service, like the rest of the community, he went to the village square with excitement. The notables and other residents of the village had congregated in the square. The notary, the legal representative of the community, was there as well. He caught the eyes of Michales Protopsaltes (son of Stefanos), Giannes Kritakes and Georges (son of Nikolas). The square was buzzing with expectation. Presently, the new leaders of the community would be elected.[2]

Demogerontia was a type of system of local governance that managed to survive under both Genoese and Ottoman rule. In this study, we analyze the 1697 *demogerontia* election in the Kalamoti village, documented in the community records of Chios Island in the Aegean Sea. The aim of the study is to evaluate Ottoman social structure through the analysis of an event at the micro level. The main research question is: how in the Ottoman Empire the elections to ensure community representation were conducted and what their function was within the social structure.

The Ottoman social structure had an organizational model based on religion. The residents of the Chios Island were of the Greek Orthodox group, or, in other words, belonged to the Greek Orthodox community. In this social structure, non-Muslims had their own communal system regarding education, matters of religion, social structure, and security. In addition, they had the opportunity to continue their traditional practices in areas of family law, inheritance law and private law.[3]

---

2   The section so far has been constructed using a record in the Codex no.69 at the Chios Archives under the General Archives of Greece (GAK). *GAK*, N. Chiou, Notariakos Kodikas Kalamotis, fakelo: 69, filo: 13v, 28.02.1697.

3   For further information on the status of non-Muslims in the Ottoman social structure, see Halil İnalcık, "Greeks in Ottoman Economy and Finances, 1453-1500," in *Studies in Honor of Speros Vryonis*, eds. Jr. J.S. Allen et al. (New York: Aristide D. Caratzas, 1993), 307-19; Halil İnalcık, "The Status of the Greek Patriarch under the Ottomans," *Turcica* 21-23 (1991): 411-28; Nuri Adıyeke, "Islahat Fermânı Öncesinde Osmanlı İmparatorluğu'nda Millet Sistemi ve Gayrimüslimlerin Yaşantılarına Dair," *Osmanlı Ansiklopedisi* 4 (1999): 255-61; Gülnihal Bozkurt, *Gayrimüslim Osmanlı Vatandaşlarının Hukuki Durumu* (Ankara: Türk Tarih Kurumu, 1989); Kemal Çiçek, "Cemaat Mahkemesinden Kadı Mahkemesine Zımmilerin Yargı Tercihi," in *Pax Ottomana Studies in Memoriam Prof. Dr. Nejat Göyünç*, Kemal Çiçek (Harlem-Ankara: Sota&Yeni Türkiye Yayınları, 2003), 31-49; Yavuz Ercan, *Osmanlı Yönetiminde Gayrimüslimler, Kuruluştan Tanzimat'a Kadar Sosyal, Ekonomik ve Hukuki Durumları* (Ankara: Turhan Kitabevi,

Among those who shared the responsibility of protecting this traditional structure were social leaders as well.[4]

The primary material used in this study are the records in a register found in the communal archive of the village of Kalamoti in Chios. In the Ottoman era, communal law was conducted through notaries in some Aegean islands. These people also kept the communal records for Chios, in codices called *notariaka*. Those that survived till today are stored in the regional archives at the State National Archives in Greece. These codices are Ancient Greek manuscripts, and include records on marriage, engagement, inheritance, commerce and loans as well as elections. The election of 1697 that we discuss here was recorded in the codex no. 69 of the Kalamoti village in Chios.

In the Ottoman administrative system, Kalamoti was attached to the township (*nahiye*) with the same name. When we consider the number of taxpayers in the census records (*tahrir*) of the Classical period, we can say that it was one of the largest villages in Chios, with approximately 270 households.[5] Besides, this was one of the villages that produced mastic gum. According to the tax records included in the census conducted after the conquest of the island, the village had the largest mastic gum production on the island.[6]

2001); Bilal Eryılmaz, *Osmanlı Devletinde Gayrimüslim Tebaanın Yönetimi* (İstanbul: Risale Yayınları, 1996).

4   The competency of the leaders assigned with this task increased in direct proportion to its importance. Baki Tezcan observes that in the early modern and modern periods, the administrative power of some social classes increased. In the 17th and 18th centuries, when the sultan's authority weakened, social elements that influenced the state's decisions and politics gained prominence in the imperial administration. Baki Tezcan, *The Second Ottoman Empire: Political and Social Transformation in the Early Modern World* (Cambridge, New York: Cambridge University Press 2010), 4-10, 232. Starting with the 18th century, we see the growing influence of rural notables and gentry in the administration. The same was true for the Christian subjects as well. The Christian notables in the rural areas gained as much importance as those in the Muslim community, albeit in a less official way. Antonis Anastasopoulos, Elias Kolovos, Marinas Sariyiannis, "The Ottoman Empire and The Greek Lands," in *Ottoman Architecture in Greece*, Ersi Bourskari, 23-45 (Athens: Hellenic Ministry of Culture, 2008), 39.

5   Nejat Göyünç, "Hane Deyimi Hakkında," *İstanbul Üniversitesi Edebiyat Fakültesi Tarih Dergisi* 32, (1979): 346; Halil İnalcık, "Timar," *The Encyclopaedia of Islam* 10 (2000): 502-7. For a detailed evaluation of production and demographic structure in Chios based on the *tahrir* registers, see Filiz Yaşar, "Bir Osmanlı Adasında Toplum ve Ekonomi (16. Yüzyıldan 18. Yüzyıla Sakız)," Ph.D dissertation, Hacettepe Üniversitesi (2013), 35-55.

6   Yaşar, "Bir Osmanlı Adasında," 71-2.

Demogerontia: A Provincial Organization

The Ottoman state considered the subjects under its rule as communities based on their religious, sectarian, cultural or ethnic origins. The Ottoman subjects in the Classical period had identities as part of the communities they belonged to. The Greek Orthodox community was one of them, which, in the simplest terms, meant that the community adopted the Orthodox sect of Christianity and that it was subject to the Phanariot Patriarchate. Greeks, Bulgarians, Serbs and Romanians were members of this group. These different elements had come together in the partnership of religion-sect-patriarchate. They were members of the same community due to this partnership yet manifested differences in terms of social structure. *Demogerontia* was one of the areas of difference.

Demogerontia, communal governance or communal leadership, was a sociocultural organization in the Greek-speaking Orthodox society. However, this term was not used throughout the Greek Orthodox community. The Greek-speaking Orthodox people had a comparable sociocultural organization that were called by different names in some places. *Demogerontia* was implemented in mostly the Aegean islands and some regions in the area that is modern-day Greece. This system was traditional in character. Throughout Ottoman rule, Greeks preserved their traditional cultural structure; even when they relocated beyond the Ottoman borders, they took their traditions along with them. For example, it is known that the Greeks who settled in Hungary since the classical period carried on with their traditional structure in those lands as well.[7]

The Ottomans, consistent with their relations with other non-Muslim communities in their realm, did not interfere with the social structure in Chios either. Consequently, the *demogerontia* system that originated well before Ottoman times continued to function. The island, even under Ottoman rule, did not completely move away from its order and tradition.

The Christian (Orthodox) leaders of the community were mostly called *demogerontes* by the Byzantine and the Genoese, *deputati* by the Romans, and *kocabaşı*

---

7   See studies on the Greek settlers in Hungary who had brought along their traditional structure. Ö. Üves, "Το πανεπιστημιακό τυπογραφείο της Βούδας και οι Έλληνες της διασποράς στην Ουγγαρία," Μακεδονικά 19, no. 1 (1979): 159-67; Ιωάννης Κ. Χασιώτης, Όλγα Κατσιαρδή-Hering, Ευρυδίκη Α. Αμπατζή, Οί Έλληνες στην Διασπορά (Ατήνα: Βουλή των Ελλήνων 2006); László Sasvári-György Diószegi, "Τα κυρία χαρακτηριστικά της ιστορίας των ελληνικών κοινοτήτων της Ουγγαρίας του 17ου -19ου αιώνα στον καθρέφτη της ορθοδοξίας του Miskolc, Szentendre, Tokaj κατ Vác," Ελληνική Ορθόδοξος Διασπορά στην Ουγγαρία 17ος-19ος Αιώνας (Budapest: Budapesti Történeti Múzeum, 2009): 43-71.

by the Ottomans.[8] In fact, the terms used to define the leaders of this community differ according to the region. Terms such as *demogerontes, proestoi, kantzilieris, epitropos* were used for the Aegean islands; Philadelpheus, in his study on Athens in the Ottoman period, states that the Athenians were called *archontes, epitropoi, proestotes, demogerontes, gerontes, vekilides*.[9] The Ottoman administration called the leaders of the Chios community by their customary names, *demogerontas*, in addition to *kocabaşı*.[10] *Demos–geron* (δήμος–γέρων), a word that survived from the ancient period, means "the eldest of the folk". The singular is *demogerontas*, the plural *demogerontes* (δημογέροντας–δημογέροντες). As much as we can tell from the records, in the colloquial and in practice, *gerontas/gerontes* were also used. In the notary codices we studied, the term *gerontas/es* was used more frequently. Another local name was *archontas/archontes* (άρχοντας\άρχοντες).[11] The council of elders, a type of administrative and social structure consisting of *demogerontas*, was identified as the assembly of *demogerontia* (δημογεροντία) or *gerontes*.

Demogerontia consisted of *demogerontas* (also called assemblies of *Gerontas*), *epitropi* and the members. *Demogerontas*, regarded by the Ottomans as *leader and representative of the community*, were the most competent individuals in this institution and the community. They came to power through elections. Their most important mission was to protect and look after their community. In the Chios records, we see that there was a group of representatives working together with the *demogerontas* called *epitropi* (board/assembly of representatives). The representatives, like the *demogerontas*, would come to power through elections, and worked together with the *demogerontas* in all the service they were tasked with overseeing. These individuals, who formed a type of advisory council, had the same authority and responsibilities as the *demogerontas*. Apart from these, *demogerontia* organization included another

---

8 Κωνσταντίνος Σγουρός, *Ιστορία της Νήσου Χίου Από τον Αρχαιότατων Χρόνων μέχρι του 1700 μ.χ.* (Αθήνα: Τύποι Πυρσού, 1937): 336. In the Byzantine period these were called protevontes (πρωτεύοντες), protogerontes (πρωτογέροντες), vouleftes (βουλευτές), dekouriones (δεκουρίωνες), dekemouir (δεκέμουιρ), dekanoi (δεκανοί), dekaprotoi (δεκάπρωτοι), novilissimoi (νοβιλίσσιμοι), kandidatoi (κανδιδάτοι), sakellarioi (σακελλάριοι). See Αντώνιος Χαροκόπος, *Ο θεσμός της Δημογεροντίας εν Χίω επί Τουρκοκρατίας* (Χίος, 1960): 41; Σγουρός, *Ιστορία της Νήσου Χίου*, 336.

9 For further information see Θ.Ν. Φιλαδελφεύς, *Η Ιστορία των Αθηνών επί τουρκοκρατίας Από του 1400 μέχρι του 1800* (Αθήνα: Καραβία, Δ.Ν.-Αναστατικές Εκδόσεις, 1991).

10 Αλ. Βλαστός, *Χιακά ήτοι ιστορία της νήσου Χίου από των Αρχαιοτάτων Χρόνων Μέχρι Της Έτει 1822 Γενομένης Καταστροφής Αυτής Παρά Των Χίων. Β›.* (Ερμούπολη,1840): 119; Σγουρός, *Ιστορία της Νήσου Χίου*, 341; Γεωργός Ζολώτας, *Ιστορία της Χίου. Τόμοι, Γ-Ι* (Αθήνα: Τύπος Π. Δ. Σκελλάριου, 1921-28), 341.

11 Κωνσταντίνος Κανελάκης, *Χιακά Ανάλεκτα* (Χίος: Έκδοση Χίος Ημερολόγιο, 1890): 378.

group, called the members. It is known that members also were elected to their positions. However, in the codex we analyzed, only the elections for *demogerontas* and *epitropi* were recorded. There is no information on the members. Yet we know that in the elections in Chios, members were elected. For example, in an election done in Chios (*chora* – downtown), the community elected the members in addition to five *demogerontas,* and, in all, a committee of thirteen people was formed.[12] Apparently, as Kalamoti was a village, the three elected *demogerontas* and two *epitropi* were sufficient for the business to be conducted. Therefore, in village settlements like Kalamoti, we can presume that these people also assumed the duties of members.

"Mezas" (Μέζας)[13] was the place where all business, meetings and bureaucratic procedures were conducted. We also know that for some of the duties the group went out on the field. For example, for the tax collection, one of their most important duties, they would not sit at the *mezas* but would visit the villagers' homes. *Demogerontas* were the greatest aides to the state officials in the collection of the *jizya, bâd-ı hevâ* and product taxes.[14] They also collected the community taxes. For example, on the island of Hydra, the leaders of the community called *prokritoi* would collect community taxes (taxes specific to boat ownership and sailing) from the boat owners and the seamen.[15]

Demogerontas would keep records of all kinds of community operations. A scribe tasked with this job was responsible for all secretariat business, and we could not identify a permanent official apart from that. The notary officials worked in coordination with the *gerontes* assemblies. Indeed, the notary records we analyzed include the decisions made at the *gerontes* assemblies in addition to the legal procedures. We can even say that the notary officials thus worked as if they were members of the *gerontes* assembly. Certainly, from an institutional viewpoint the two had different duties, but because both were local administrative elements trying to protect the communal order, they formed several partnerships in their operations. The provincial practices of these two structures were mutually intertwined, carried out

---

12 Αντώνιος Χαροκόπος, *Ο θεσμός της Δημογεροντίας εν Χίω επί Τουρκοκρατίας* (Χίος: 1960): 48.

13 Α. Κοράης, *Άτακτα* (Παρίσι, 1835): 202.

14 In Evangelia Balta, in her study on the *jizya* tax in the Island of Samos, reveals how this tax was collected by the leaders of the community (proesti). The *jizya* tax of the years 1633-42 in Samos were collected by the community leaders in each village. Evangelia Balta, "Açıl Susam, Açıl," *Osmanlı Araştırmaları* 19 (1999): 40, 43.

15 Αποστ. Βακαλόπουλος, Ιστορία του νέου ελληνισμού Στ´ Η μεγάλη Ελληνική Επανάσταση *(1821-1829)*-Η εσωτερική κρίση *(1822-1825)*, (Θεσσαλονικη: 1982): 896.

in tandem and in coordination with each other. For this reason, the information gathered from notary records allowed us to collect significant information on the operation of the *gerontes* assemblies.[16]

A Traditional Legacy: Demogerontia Elections

The studies done so far are unable to answer the question of how the *demogerontia* system came into being. While the origins of this structure are unknown,[17] it is nevertheless a fact that such urban or rural communities existed before Ottoman times, in the Byzantine Empire.[18] The same was also true for regions under Roman rule such as the Genoese-Venetian.[19] Adamantia Pollis shows how a local system that had their community leaders elected in rural areas in Cyprus endured in the Ottoman era as well.[20] In the lands they conquered, the Ottomans kept the sociocultural structure intact as long as it did not run counter to their system. The social organization in the empire was shaped on the axis of property and land administration and, within the framework of rules determined by the central administration, according to local traditions. In this way, not only was the existing social structure preserved, but it facilitated the adaptation of the residents of the conquered areas to the Ottoman system. On the other hand, the continuity of the social structure in these lands was ensured in exchange for some obligations.[21] We need to discuss *Demogerontia* in this context

---

16 For the analysis of the notary codices in Chios and the details of the *demogeronti* system gleaned from the codices, see Yaşar, "Bir Osmanlı Adasında," 104-22.

17 Δημήτρης Γεωργόπουλος, Το Αρχείο της Επαρχιακής Δημογεροντίας Ναυπλίου *(1828-1829)* (Ναυπλίος: Υπουργείο Παιδείας & Θρησκευμάτων Γενικά Αρχεία του Κράτους Αρχεία Νομού Αργολίδος, 2015), 20; Σ. Αντωνιάδης, Τα Δημοτικά (Αθήνα: 1842), 133.

18 Α. Βακαλόπουλος, "Οι Κοινότητες," Ιστορία του Ελληνικού Έθνους, τ. Ι΄, Αθήνα (1975): 150-155. On Greek social organization and its history, see Γ.Δ. Κοντογιώργης, Κοινωνική δυναμική και πολιτική αυτοδιοίκηση. Οι ελληνικές Κοινότητες της τουρκοκρατίας (Αθήνα: 1982), 30-38. Nikolas Oikonomides, in his study on the Athos mountain, the meeting place of Christian monks, states that in the Byzantine period (10th century) there was a council of monks called *gerontes*. Nicolas Oikono- mides, "Mount Athos: Levels of Literacy," *Dumbarton Oaks Papers* 42 (1988): 168.

19 The Island of Chios entered Ottoman rule after Genoese rule. According to Alexander H. De Groot, after the conquest of Chios by the Ottomans, the administration of the island was entrusted to the state officials along with the *demogerontes*. Alexander H. De Groot, "The Historical Development of The Capitulatory Regime in The Ottoman Middle East from The Fifteenth to The Nineteenth Centuries," Oriente Moderno, Nuova serie, Anno 22 (83), no. 3, *The Ottoman Capitulations: Text And Context*, (2003): 583.

20 Adamantia Pollis, "Intergroup Conflict and British Colonial Policy: The Case of Cyprus," *Comparative Politics* 5, no. 4 (1973): 575-99.

21 Αντωνιάδης, Τα Δημοτικά, 125-26.

too. *Demogerontia* of the *gerontes* assemblies were a part of the social organization, however one should keep in mind that the Ottoman state did not acknowledge them as official institutions. Yet this does not mean that they were not recognized at all; indeed, Islamic law had a jurisdiction structure that did recognize these institutions.[22]

The leader and members of *Demogerontia* were determined by election. Antonis Anastasopoulos, among the sources he analyzed for his dissertation, has found a 1765 correspondence that refers to a community leader being elected to his office in one of the villages of Karaferye. According to the records, a religious functionary was appointed as the person responsible for administrative duties in the village, and the one to represent its inhabitants.[23] Unfortunately, sources on this subject are scarce and their contents significantly limited, therefore there aren't many examples. Antonis Anastasopoulos and Eleni Gara, who studied the same region, made a similar observation. In her research on 17th century court records, Eleni Gara states that respected individuals represented the village and town residents as a whole. However, she adds that there is no information on how subsequent representatives were elected or appointed.[24] It is known that the tradition of elections is deep-seated in Greek culture. The method of voting had been in practice since 750 BC in Sparta among the Greek city-states. However, in that era, only aristocrats enjoyed a political voice. In the periods where direct democracy was implemented, the members of the assemblies of *apella* and *gerousia* would be determined through elections and an official voting process that involved all citizens.[25] In the ancient periods, similar structures existed under different names in the Athenian *polis* and other city-states.

---

22 Eleni Gara, "In Search of Communities in Seventeenth Century Ottoman Sources: The Case of the Kara Ferye District," *Turcica* 30 (1999): 136.

23 The religious functionary was elected as the representative of the community and had assigned two people as collectors. See Antonios Anastasopoulos, *Imperial Institutions and Local Communities: Ottoman Karaferye, 1758-1774*, unpublished Ph.D dissertation, Cambridge University, (Cambridge: 1999), 75.

24 In addition, she states that with a few exceptions, the court proceedings referred to these people were by their own names instead of titles. Eleni Gara, *In Search of Communities*, 143.

25 E.S. Staveley, *Greek and Roman Voting and Elections* (Thames and Hudson: Britain, 1982), 18, 20, 22, 31. Gerousia was one of the common characteristics of Greek city life in the Hellenistic and the Roman periods. Unfortunately, we do not have sufficient information on their functions or structure. M.A.H. El Abbadi emphasizes two different opinions on the function and structure of the Gerousia Assemblies in Egypt in the Roman period. First, they were a public institution that managed religious affairs and sometimes participated in the city administration. Second, they were a social organization that was neither official nor public. Gerousia assemblies have been found in Oxyrhynchus, close to Alexandria and Al Bahnasa in Egypt. See M.A.H. El-Abbadi, "The Gerousia in Roman Egypt," *The Journal of Egyptian Archaeology* 50 (1964): 164 vd. Aristotle defines

We see that etymologically, the Gerousia Assembly in the ancient period is derived from the same roots as the assemblies of *demogerontia* or *gerontes*. Both terms mean council of elders. Yet it would not be correct to say that *demogerontia* was based on the *gerousia* of the ancient period. There is not sufficient evidence to prove such a long continuity. *Gerousia* and *gerontia* (*demogerontia*) were very different from each other in terms of authority and institutional character. The assemblies of *gerousia* in the *polis* city-states were higher judicial bodies that prepared resolutions and sent them to the people's assembly. The members of the assembly were distinguished individuals, older than 60 and appointed "as long as they were alive".[26] In contrast, the authority and duties of the *demogerontia* were much weaker. The people in *Demogerontia* were 'civilian' representatives tasked with ensuring public order and safety. Their institutional features had not been clarified.

In the election that took place in Kalamoti on the 28th of February in 1697, the records document the fact that the village dignitaries and all village folk had congregated at the square for the election.[27] In the Ottoman period, in places where this system was implemented, the elections for *demogerontia* would be conducted by starting from the smallest administrative units, villages and neighborhoods. If there was anything that called the election into question, the election would be repeated.[28] There were no such incidents at that election in Kalamoti. The election had successfully taken place, and afterwards no objections made their way to the records.

In 1697, one of the candidates in the village square was Father Nikolas (Papas Nikolas) who had put forward his candidacy for the *demogerontia* administration for the year. The *Gerontes* assemblies would come to power through "democratic ways". All of the community[29] would vote in the election.[30] In the 19th century,

---

it as a structure made up of wealthy and strong Spartan families. Philip Davies, "Kalos Kagathos' And Scholarly Perceptions Of Spartan Society," *Historia: Zeitschrift für Alte Geschichte*, Bd. 62, H. 3 (2013): 270. In a study on the Gerousia assemblies of Roman Sparta, it has been proven that they were composed of 23 members. Nigel M. Kennell, "IG V 1, 16 and the Gerousia of Roman Sparta," *Hesperia: The Journal of the American School of Classical Studies at Athens* 61, no. 2 (1992): 194, 198.

26   Bülent İplikçioğlu, *Eskiçağ Tarihinin Anahatları* II (İstanbul: Marmara Üniversitesi Yayınları, t.y.), 42; Staveley, *Greek and Roman Voting*, 76-8.

27   *GAK*, N. Chiou, Notariakos Kodikas Kalamotis, fakelo: 69, filo: 13v, 28.02.1697

28   Γιάννης Τσάρας, "Εκλογές για μουχταροδημογεροντία στο Μπλάτσι της Κοζάνης (1888)," Μακεδονικά 14, no. 1 (1974): 52-3.

29   "Γερής και γέροντες και ο κοινός λαός (The elderly, the council of elders and the public)."

30   The elections in the ancient period were open to everyone, yet not all citizens could vote. Those who participated had to fulfill certain conditions. For example, in the Gerousia elections of the Athenian city-state, four conditions needed to be met in order to vote.

the *demogerontia* candidates would be expected to pay a tax to the public treasury. However, there is no information on the amount.[31] The Chios records do not make any mention of this requirement. In other words, we cannot know whether the candidates for the *demogerontia* made any payments before or after elections.

Demogerontas and the committee (*epitropi*) assignments would be determined according to majority vote. In the *gerousia* elections of city-states, there were fewer participants when compared to the Ottoman era, and the voters would be allowed to speak one by one, that is, casting a voice vote. A chairman chosen to supervise the election would moderate the voice vote, write down the voter's choice, count the votes and announce the results.[32] In the Ottoman era, it goes without saying that the tradition of asking voters for their opinions one by one as in the city-states would have been impossible.

The candidates would be chosen from among the community members who were in good standing, educated, trustworthy and believed to work honestly. Rather than commoners, these would usually be members of wealthy, prominent families and most frequently, clergymen. Indeed, Father Nikolas also belonged to the clergy, an affiliation that made him a much stronger candidate than the others. The eligibility criteria were not quite strict, and most importantly, being literate was a significant privilege since it was very difficult to find literate people within the village boundaries. Under the circumstances of the period, and thanks to the church-centered education system, the clergymen were among the most educated and knowledgeable people. It was therefore commonplace for the clergymen to be elected as the *gerontas*. In addition to the clergymen, people from the wealthy and powerful families would be among the *demogerontas*. This does not necessarily mean that only the elite or the clergy won the elections. Ordinary members of the community would also be elected to this committee.[33] As a matter of fact, the main criterion was well-rounded competence since the *demogerontas* were tasked with keeping all official records including the list of the community members, dealing with the Ottoman officials, working in

---

The first was being a citizen of Athens, the second, having turned 18, third, having been born of Athenian parents, and the fourth, being male. R. Last, "The Election of Officers in the Corinthian Christ-Group," *New Testament Studies* 59, no. 3, (2013): 365-81.

31 Τσάρας, "Εκλογές για μουχταροδημογεροντία," 52-53.

32 Voting in the assemblies in the first periods was done with pebbles called *psefos*. The voters would leave the pebble in front of the candidates they supported. Later, voting took pace by 'hand raising'. Staveley, in his evaluation of these practices, underlines how a secret ballot was not practiced in those periods. He also states that these practices, rather than reflecting individual preferences, favored the choice of the majority. Staveley, "Greek and Roman Voting," 77-78, 83-84.

33 For examples of this issue, see Yaşar, *Bir Osmanlı Adasında*.

coordination with officials and even, as needed, representing the community at the level of state authority. For this reason, they were preferably experts at social decorum, literate, knowledgeable about Turkish even if a little—in short, the notables of the community. These criteria favored Father Nikolas at the 1697 election. Once the candidates were identified, they would be presented to the village folk for the election. First the *demogerontas* would be elected, then the *epitropi* immediately afterwards or on the next day. For example, in the Kalamoti elections held the following year (April 1698), the *demogerontas* then the *epitropi* were determined on the same day.[34]

It is not possible for us to trace the entire history of the *demogerontia* election system and the changes throughout. When we compare the scholarly literature on this subject with the sources we have obtained, we see no major changes during the Ottoman era.[35] However we cannot say that everything remained the same either. For example, we notice differences in the number of the *demogerontas*. In a study about the same period and drawing from the records the number of elected *demogerontes* is specified as five.[36] Additionally, M.O. Eneman, who visited the island in the 18th century and witnessed a *demogerontas* election, observes that only two people were elected.[37]

It is equally impossible to give a precise number of members on the *demogerontia* committee that was made of community representatives and the council members. The *demogerontia* committee usually seated 12 people and was therefore called the Assembly of the Twelves. However, it is difficult to claim that this number was fixed since the number of members in the committee ranged from 10 to 13.[38] Frankly, it is not unusual that the number of *demogerontia* members varied in different centuries or in different regions. Even in the Kalamoti codex records that we analyzed, there are differences in the numbers of *demogerontas*. **CHART 9.1** lists the names of those elected to the *demogerontas* between the years 1695 and 1710 in Kalamoti. This list is drawn from the notary codex of the Kalamoti village. The list shows that in a 15-year period, the number of elected *demogerontas* ranged between two and four.

---

34 For the Epitropos election see *GAK*, N. Chiou, Notariakos Kodikas Kalamotis, fakelo: 69, filo: 19r, 11.04.1698. For the Demogerontes election see *GAK*, N. Chiou, Notariakos Kodikas Kalamotis, fakelo: 69, filo: 18v, 11.04.1698.

35 For a study on the Demogerontes elections of the Island of Chios, see Χαροκόπος, "Ο θεσμός της Δημογεροντίας εν Χίω," 47-57.

36 Χαροκόπος, "Ο θεσμός της Δημογεροντίας εν Χίω," 48.

37 Φιλίππου Αργέντης-Στιλπνός Κυριακήδος, *Η Χίος παρά τοις Γεωγράφοις και Περιηγηταίς από τον Όγδοου μέχρι του Εικοστού Αιώνος* 3, (1946): 1593.

38 For examples see Χαροκόπος, "Ο θεσμός της Δημογεροντίας εν Χίω," 47-57; Philip Argenti, *Chius Vincta Occupation of Chios by the Turks (1566) &Their Administration of the Island (1566-1912)* (Cambridge Press, 1941): clxxxi-clxxxv.

CHART 9.1. The list of demogerontas elected between the years 1695 and 1710 in the village of Kalamoti

Date	Demogerontas	Demogerontas	Demogerontas	Demogerontas
1695[39]	Kazas	Kostas Maistros	Papas Ioannes son of Stefanos	
1696[40]	Michales Kazas	Kostas Maistros	Papas Ioannes son of Stefanos	
1697[41]	Papas Nikolas Amires	Michales Protopsaltes	Giannis Kritakes	Georges son of Nikoles
1698[42]	Papas Nikolas Chrisolouras	Papas Kostas Kritis	Kostas Mavrothires	Mastromichale Maistros
1701[43]	Papas Georges Salonikios	Unknown	Unknown	
1702[44]	Papas Georges Salonikios	Ksenos Melisinos son of Vasiles Ksenos Sefes son of Papa Ioannes		Sideros Melisinos
1705[45]	Panteles Varlas	Kostas Triteakes	Kiriakos son of Mones	Nikolas Kontaratos
1706[46]	Georgis Krites son of Nikoles	Papas Mikes Vergitzes	Kostas Kinigos	Kostas Alithinos
1708[47]	Ksenos Melisinos son of Papas Ioannes	Sideros Frangoulakes	Sideros Melisinos	Panteles Mentones

39 October: They were on duty at this time. *GAK*, N. Chiou, Notariakos Kodikas Kalamotis, fakelo: 69, filo: 9v, 13.10.1695.

40 March: They were on duty at this time. Their date of election is unknown. *GAK*, N. Chiou, Notariakos Kodikas Kalamotis, fakelo: 69, filo: 9r, 04.03.1696.

41 They were elected on February 28, a Sunday. *GAK*, N. Chiou, Notariakos Kodikas Kalamotis, fakelo: 69, filo: 13v, 28.02.1697; *GAK*, N. Chiou, Notariakos Kodikas Kalamotis, fakelo: 69, filo: 16r, 12.04.1697; *GAK*, N. Chiou, Notariakos Kodikas Kalamotis, fakelo: 69, filo: 14v, 10.03.1697.

42 They were elected on April 11, a Monday. *GAK*, N. Chiou, Notariakos Kodikas Kalamotis, fakelo: 69, filo: 18v, 11.04.1698.

43 October: They were on duty at this time. Their date of election is unknown. *GAK*, N. Chiou, Notariakos Kodikas Kalamotis, fakelo: 69, filo: 21v, 14.11.1701.

44 May: They were on duty at this time. Their date of election is unknown. *GAK*, N. Chiou, Notariakos Kodikas Kalamotis, fakelo: 69, filo: 25r-25v, 10.05.1702.

45 *GAK*, N. Chiou, Notariakos Kodikas Kalamotis, fakelo: 69, filo: 46r, 31.12.1706.

46 *GAK*, N. Chiou, Notariakos Kodikas Kalamotis, fakelo: 69, filo: 46r, 31.12.1706.

47 October: They were on duty at this time. Their date of election is unknown. *GAK*, N. Chiou, Nota- riakos Kodikas Kalamotis, fakelo: 69, filo: 70r vd, 07.10.1708.

Date	Demogerontas	Demogerontas	Demogerontas	Demogerontas
1709[48]	Gianes Vestarches	Ksenos Melisinos	Nikolas son of Stefanos	
1710[49]	Papas Georges Kazas	Georges son of Papas Lios		

In 1697, the villagers in Kalamoti did elect Father Nikolas Amires as *demogerontas*. Michales Protopsaltis, son of Stefanos, Giannes Kritakes, and Georges, son of Nikolas, oversaw the election that chose the four members of the *demogerontas* for the year.[50] However, in the same year, in one of the neighboring villages, only two people were elected as the *demogerontas*. On the morning of April 29, 1697, that is, one day after the Kalamoti elections,[51] residents in the neighboring village of Armolia in Chios also had congregated in the village square to elect their *demogerontas* for the year. Father Michales, son of Father Stefanos, and Michales Filimates from a prominent family, were elected. As can be seen, two villages in the same region in the same year elected different number of *demogerontas*. When we examine the records in the entire codex, we see that Kalamoti elected sometimes four (1698, 1702, 1705, 1706 and 1708),[52] and sometimes three people (1696, 1697, 1709 and 1710).[53] Although rare, there were also years when only two people were elected.[54]

As it happened in 1697, when Father Nikolas Amires and three others were elected to serve as the *demogerontas* for the year, a small ceremony would mark the official assumption of duties right after the election. In this ceremony, the

---

48 August: They were on duty at this time. Their date of election is unknown. *GAK*, N. Chiou, Notariakos Kodikas Kalamotis, fakelo: 69, filo: 96r, ??.09.1710.

49 October: They were elected on this date. *GAK*, N. Chiou, Notariakos Kodikas Kalamotis, fakelo: 69, filo: 96v, 18.10.1710.

50 *GAK*, N. Chiou, Notariakos Kodikas Kalamotis, fakelo: 69, filo: 13v, 28.02.1697.

51 April 29, 1698, Thursday, 11.00 in the morning. *GAK*, N. Chiou, Notariakos Kodikas Armolion, fakelo: 95, filo: 73v, 29.04.1697.

52 *GAK*, N. Chiou, Notariakos Kodikas Kalamotis, fakelo: 69, filo: 18v, 11.04.1698; *GAK*, N. Chiou, Notariakos Kodikas Kalamotis, fakelo: 69, filo: 25r-25v, 10.05.1702; *GAK*, N. Chiou, Notariakos Kodikas Kalamotis, fakelo: 69, filo: 46r, 31.12.1706; *GAK*, N. Chiou, Notariakos Kodikas Kalamotis, fakelo: 69, filo: 70r vd, 07.10.1708; *GAK*, N. Chiou, Notariakos Kodikas Kalamotis, fakelo: 70, filo: 42v-43r, 13.07.1698.

53 *GAK*, N. Chiou, Notariakos Kodikas Kalamotis, fakelo: 69, filo: 96r, ??.09.1710; *GAK*, N. Chiou, Notariakos Kodikas Kalamotis, fakelo: 69, filo: 9v, 13.10.1695; *GAK*, N. Chiou, Notariakos Kodikas Kalamotis, fakelo: 69, filo: 9r, 04.03.1696.

54 *GAK*, N. Chiou, Notariakos Kodikas Kalamotis, fakelo: 69, filo: 96v, 18.10.1710.

FIGURE 9.1 An example of the traditional clothing worn by the notables of the island of Chios before 1822 (Philip P. Argenti, *The Costumes of Chios. Their development from the XVth to the XXth century*, London: B.T. Batsford, 1953).

new *demogerontas* would take an oath and sign the election record in front of those congregated in the village square. As part of their oath, they would promise to 'work honestly' and fulfill their duties 'duly in the shadow of divine justice'. Citing the records, we can say that the 'Fear of God' was the most important mechanism for supervising these individuals.[55]

Throughout their tenure, the *Gerontas* were responsible first to God and then to their own conscience while overseeing all the business of the villagers and the village. They also had supervisory duties, such as protecting the civil peace, organizing affiliations, ensuring the continuation of production, in short, maintaining the village order through and through. From the moment they got elected, they would try to fulfill their duties to the villagers. They had given their word to the people. In the sources we analyzed, there is no mention of an obligation or responsibility towards the state.

On the day following the election, the outgoing *demogerontas* would hand over the job to the new ones. The new *demogerontas* would officially start their tenure by first visiting the island's administration, including the *müsellim,* the *qadi*, the customs official (*gümrük emini*) and various deputies (*vekilides*); afterwards, they would go to the metropolitan bishop and initiate their first official communications.[56]

Gerontas would be elected for a year. In Kalamoti, Papas Nikolas Amires, Michales Protopsaltes son of Stefanos, Giannes Kritakes and Georges son of Nikolas were elected to serve until the following February, and in Armolia, Papas Michales and Michales Filimates were elected to the village administration to serve until the fol-

---

55   μόν(ον) νά κάμουν κ(αι) αυτί με φόβον Θ(εο)ύ κ(αι) με καταστήχουν αδόλου κ(αι) καθαρού. *GAK*, N. Chiou, Notariakos Kodikas Kalamotis, fakelo: 69, filo: 13v, 28.02.1697.

56   Χαροκόπος, "Ο θεσμός της Δημογεροντίας εν Χίω," 49-50.

lowing April.[57] As long as they remained in office, the villagers would pay all the necessary expenses related the job.[58] The annual expenses would be recorded, and later, the calculated sum would be apportioned among the villagers.[59]

Since the oldest election report in the codex we analyzed belongs to the year 1697,[60] we wanted to analyze this election at the micro level. We can say that for *demogerontas* elections in Chios, a fixed date was not specified. However, there is reason to believe that in some regions this ritual was held on specific days. For example, the *demogerontia* election in the Balatsi neighborhood of the Kozani region was usually held every year either on September 23, the Feast of Agios Georgios, or on October 26, the Feast of Agios Dimitrios.[61] In the region of Kozani, located in northern Greece, winters were harsh and snowy. For this reason, the elections were not held in February and March.[62] The same was not true for Chios. In fact, the election we analyzed had taken place at the end of February. Since the village folk gathered in the village square, we infer that there was no inclement weather that prevented the elections from happening.

After the election, the village notary would record the ritual in its entirety in the registers and write the names of the new officials in the codex. However, the bureaucracy did not end there. The names of the new *demogerontas* would be sent to the *qadi* for his approval, only after which the roles of these individuals would become official. It was imperative for the *qadi*, the highest administrative and judiciary official on the island, to certify the election and the appointments. Until the elected candidates received the *hüccet,* that is, the qadi's certification, they would not be considered to have officially started their job. This would most definitely be acknowledged in the reports of the notary records. As a matter of fact, the election reports of both villages included the statement, "They should obtain *hüccet* from the presiding *qadi*".[63] Since there is no mention whether the certification was granted,

---

57 *GAK*, N. Chiou, Notariakos Kodikas Kalamotis, fakelo: 69, filo: 13v, 28.02.1697; *GAK*, N. Chiou, Notariakos Kodikas Armolion, fakelo: 95, filo: 73v, 29.04.1697.

58 *GAK*, N. Chiou, Notariakos Kodikas Kalamotis, fakelo: 69, filo: 13v, 28.02.1697.

59 *GAK*, N. Chiou, Notariakos Kodikas Kalamotis, fakelo: 69, filo: 18v, 11.04.1698.

60 As we can see in membership chart, the demogerontas from the previous years were identified, yet the election reports could not be found. For former demogerontas see *GAK*, N. Chiou, Notariakos Kodikas Kalamotis, fakelo: 69, filo: 9v, 13.10.1695; *GAK*, N. Chiou, Notariakos Kodikas Kalamotis, fakelo: 69, filo: 9r, 04.03.1696.

61 Τσάρας, "Εκλογές για μουχταροδημογεροντία," 52.

62 Τσάρας, "Εκλογές για μουχταροδημογεροντία," 52.

63 "και πηήσουν και χουγγέτην ης του ευρισκόμενου καδίν" *GAK*, N. Chiou, Notariakos Kodikas Kalamotis, fakelo: 69, filo: 13v, 28.02.1697; *GAK*, N. Chiou, Notariakos

FIGURE 9.2 Chios in the 17th century (Bibliothèque nationale de France Archives).

we cannot ascertain the result of the procedure, yet we see that the *qadi* was the final decision mechanism. Starting in the 17th century local agents began to gain administrative and political strength;[64] however, we need to acknowledge that this trend did not become prevalent easily. Non-Muslims were relatively free in their self-governance yet still not free from the scrutiny of the state. The residents could elect their own local administrator and delegate all internal affairs to him. However, at the same time, officials of the central government who were assigned to the provinces controlled the whole process. The *demogerontas* as the local representatives and community leaders were, through the *hüccet* obtained from the *qadi*, officially recognized by the

---

Kodikas Armolion, fakelo: 95, filo: 73v, 29.04.1697. Antonios Anastasopoulos's Ph.D. dissertation has the same findings. It emphasizes how the leader of the community in Karaferye needed to get an approval from the *qadi*'s court. See Antonis Anastasopoulos, *Imperial Institutions and Local Communities: Ottoman Karaferye*, 55. The scribes would put down the names determined by the election in court records, and a *hüccet* on this subject would be issued for the *demogerontas*. Χαροκόπος, "Ο θεσμός της Δημογεροντίας εν Χίω," 49. For an example of Hüccet in Chios see Χρίστος Μαυρόπουλος, Ιστορίαν της Χίου–Τουρκικά Έγγραφα. (Αθήνα: Τυπογραφείου Πετράκου, 1920): 113.

64   For findings on this issue see Tezcan, *The Second Ottoman Empire*.

state.[65] Given that the *demogerontas* were constantly in communication with central authority and personally tasked with official duties such as tax collection, it was important for these individuals to be recognized by the state. For this reason they would receive an official endorsement from the civil-administrative supervisor they were working under.

Before the reforms of the Tanzimat era, an official title for the *demogerontas* had not been specified. We see that in the 19th century, when the office of *muhtar* was established, the *demogerontas* became *muhtar*s and their status was thereby formalized. In his article based on the report on a *demogerontia* election in 1888, Tsaras states that the elected members would be called *muhtarodemogerontas* (*muhtar demogerontas*). We infer from this

FIGURE 9.3 A Greek woman from Chios (IBB Atatürk Library Postcard Archive).

document that during the elections, the district governors and directors were also present.[66] The participation of civil authority at the township elections ratified the legitimacy of the process and of those elected.

Instead of a Conclusion

The Orthodox Greeks in the Ottoman Empire had deeply rooted traditions of social organization. They were able to pass it down through generations. The *demogerontia* system was an organizational model that preserved its functionality regardless of the changing regimes in the region. Although we might perceive this system as an extension of the culture of democracy inherited from Ancient Greece, it is difficult

---

65   Χαροκόπος, "Ο θεσμός της Δημογεροντίας εν Χίω," 49. Bir hüccet örneği için bkz Χρίστος Μαυρόπουλος, Ιστορίαν της Χίου–Τουρκικά Έγγραφα. (Αθήνα: Τυπογραφείου Πετράκου,1920): 113.

66   Τσάρας, "Εκλογές για μουχταροδημογεροντία," 51-2.

to verify such an extrapolation. It is more likely that the Greek community was able to retain its traditions, if not a culture of democracy.

The *demogerontia*, the elections of which we analyzed, was an important and effective structure that preserved public order in the Greek community and ensured that the community came together around a common culture. The *Demogerontia* administration/administrations ensured the continuation of a traditional order for the society on the one hand and provided the imperial government with the ability to interact with the community on the other. Owing to its effectiveness, the system successfully endured throughout different political rules. The ruling powers, instead of destroying the *demogerontia* system, chose to cooperate with it and in this way were able to control the social structure.

Another noteworthy consequence of the system is that it empowered the community. Indeed, it was the masses, or the 'public' who determined (personally elected) the *demogerontia* administration. Moreover, we see that elections were held under judicial supervision, and, remarkably, took place in a village square instead of a church. Even so, it would not be valid to claim that this community adopted a "culture of democracy" as an inheritance from Ancient Greece, since such a model was not possible in the Ottoman era either intellectually, politically, or socially. However, we can say that this system that elected its representatives by public choice was a sociocultural organization rooted in the past. An autonomous system was not formed within this sociocultural organization. On the contrary, we observe the power and influence of the central administration, like other regions of the empire. The most typical example of central authority was the necessity for the *demogerontas* to seek the *qadi*'s confirmation. Even though the *demogerontas* were administrators or rulers in the internal workings of the community, in the eyes of the state they were merely representatives. As the Ottoman state usually did not intervene in the internal workings of communities, they did not meddle with the elections of representatives or the methods of determining these representatives. However, the representative would have to go to the most competent civilian authority and obtain a certification of his position, and this would usually be the *qadi*. As the community records indicate, Father Nikolas, too, had to obtain approval from the *qadi* of the Island of Chios to validate his representative role.

The institutional aspect of this system in the classical period is debated. In the pre- Tanzimat era, 'institutional' is a notion that is hard to define. In this sense, it is also difficult to determine if the *demogerontia* had an institutional structure or not. The fact that both the structure and its elected representatives would be confirmed by the state and at the same time recognized legally and officially was important, yet still insufficient to define the demogerontia as an institution.

The system of *demogerontia,* implemented by some communities among the Greek Orthodox population preserved its traditional texture in the Ottoman era despite being subject to state authority. However, we cannot claim that the research done so far provides sufficient data to explain fully the structure of this system. To understand if the *demogerontia* system was 'institutional' or 'sociocultural' in its structure, more records need to be analyzed. For this reason, new research into the structure of the *demogerontia,* its internal workings, duties, authority, and official status is needed. Through these, we will better understand the status of the Greek Orthodox community within Ottoman social organization.

Bibliography

Archival Sources

General Archives of the State of Greece (GAK), Notebooks in the Classification of Notariaka (Νοταριακά)

GAK, N. Chiou, Notariakos Kodikas Kalamotis, fakelo: 69 (1696-1711).

GAK, N. Chiou, Notariakos Kodikas Armolias, fakelo: 16 (1692-1698).

Chiou, Notariakos Kodikas Kalamotis, fakelo: 70, filo: 42v-43r, 13.07.1698.

Secondary Sources

Adıyeke, Nuri. "Islahat Fermanı Öncesinde Osmanlı İmparatorluğu'nda Millet Sistemi ve Gayrimüslimlerin Yaşantılarına Dair." *Osmanlı Ansiklopedisi* 4 (1999): 255-61.

Anastasopoulos, Antonios. *Imperial Institutions and Local Communities: Ottoman Karaferye, 1758-1774.* unpublished Ph.D dissertation, Cambridge: Cambridge University, The Faculty Of Oriental Studies, 1999.

Anastasopoulos, A., Kolovos, E., Sariyiannis, M. "The Ottoman Empire and the Greek Lands." in *Ottoman Architecture in Greece,* ed. Ersi Bourskari, 23-45. Atina: Hellenic Ministry of Culture, 2008.

Argenti, Philip. *Chius Vincta Occupation of Chios by the Turks (1566) & Their Administration of the Island (1566-1912).* Cambridge: Cambridge Press, 1941.

Balta, Evangelia. "Açıl Susam, Açıl." *Osmanlı Araştırmaları* 19 (1999): 9-81.

Bozkurt, Gülnihal. *Gayrimüslim Osmanlı Vatandaşlarının Hukuki Durumu.* Ankara: Türk Tarih Kurumu, 1989.

Çiçek, Kemal. "Cemaat Mahkemesinden Kadı Mahkemesine Zımmilerin Yargı Tercihi." in *Pax Ottomana Studies in Memoriam Prof. Dr. Nejat Göyünç,* ed. Kemal Çiçek, 31-49. Harlem-Ankara: Sota & Yeni Türkiye Yayınları, 2003.

Davies, Philip. "Kalos Kagathos' and Scholarly Perceptions of Spartan Society." *Historia: Zeitschrift für Alte Geschichte*. Bd. 62, H. 3 (2013): 259-279.

De Groot, Alexander H. "The Historical Development of the Capitulatory Regime in the Ottoman Middle East from the Fifteenth to the Nineteenth Centuries." *Oriente Moderno, Nuova serie*, 22 (83/3), *The Ottoman Capitulations: Text And Context* (2003): 575-604.

El-Abbadi, M.A.H. "The Gerousia in Roman Egypt." *The Journal of Egyptian Archaeology* 50 (1964): 164-169.

Ercan, Yavuz. *Osmanlı Yönetiminde Gayrimüslimler, Kuruluştan Tanzimat'a Kadar Sosyal, Ekonomik ve Hukuki Durumları*. Ankara: Turhan Kitabevi, 2001.

Eryılmaz, Bilal. *Osmanlı Devletinde Gayrimüslim Tebaanın Yönetimi*. İstanbul: Risale Yayınları, 1996.

Gara, Eleni. "In Search of Communities in Seventeenth Century Ottoman Sources: The Case of the Kara Ferye District." *Turcica* 30 (1999): 136.

Göyünç, Nejat. "Hane Deyimi Hakkında." *İstanbul Üniversitesi Edebiyat Fakültesi Tarih Dergisi* 32 (1979): 331-48.

İnalcık, Halil. "Greeks in Ottoman Economy and Finances, 1453-1500." in *Studies in Honor of Speros Vryonis, Jr.*, eds. J.S. Allen, C.P. Ioannides, J.S. Langdon, S.W. Reinert, 307-19. New York: Aristide D. Caratzas, 1993.

———. "The Status of the Greek Patriarch under the Ottomans." *Turcica* 21-23 (1991): 411-28.

———. "Timar." *The Encyclopaedia of Islam* 10 (2000): 502-7.

İplikçioğlu, Bülent. *Eskiçağ Tarihinin Anahatları* II. İstanbul: Marmara Üniversitesi Yayınları, no date.

Kennell, Nigel M. "IG V 1, 16 and the Gerousia of Roman Sparta." *Hesperia: The Journal of the American School of Classical Studies at Athens* 61,no. 2 (1992): 193-202.

Kolovos, Elias. "Insularity and Island Society in the Ottoman Context, The Case of the Aegean Island of Andros (Sixteenth to Eighteenth Centuries)." *Turcica* 39 (2007): 49-122.

Last, R. "The Election of Officers in the Corinthian Christ-Group." *New Testament Studies* 59, no. 3 (2013): 365-81.

Oikonomides, Nicolas. "Mount Athos: Levels of Literacy." *Dumbarton Oaks Papers* 42 (1988): 167-78, https://www.jstor.org/stable/1291595, Accessed on: 28.12.2018.

Pollis, Adamantia. "Intergroup Conflict and British Colonial Policy: The Case of Cyprus." *Comparative Politics* 5, no. 4 (1973): 575-99, https://www.jstor.org/stable/421397, Accessed on: 28.12.2018.

Sariyannis, Marinos. "Ruler and State, State and Society in Ottoman Political Thought." *Turkish Historical Review* 4 (2013): 92-126.

Sasvári, László and Diószegi, György. "Τα κυρία χαρακτηριστικά της ιστορίας των ελληνικών κοινοτήτων της Ουγγαρίας του 17ου -19ου αιώνα στον καθρέφτη της ορθοδοξίας του Miskolc, Szentendre, Tokaj κατ Vác." in *Ελληνική Ορθόδοξος Διασπορά στην Ουγγαρία 17ος-19ος Αιώνας*, ed. Vasilios Stamatopoulos, 43-71. Budapest: Budapesti Történeti Múzeum, 2009.

Staveley, E.S. *Greek and Roman Voting and Elections*. Britain: Thames and Hudson, 1982.

Steinhauer, George. "Unpublished Lists of Gerontes and Magistrates of Roman Sparta." *The Annual of the British School at Athens* 93 (1998): 427-447, https://www.jstor. org/stable/30103800, Accessed on: 28.12.2018.

Tezcan, Baki. *The Second Ottoman Empire: Political and Social Transformation in the Early Modern World*. Cambridge, New York: Cambridge University Press, 2010.

Üves, Ö. "Το πανεπιστημιακό τυπογραφείο της Βούδας και οι Έλληνες της διασποράς στην Ουγγαρία." *Μακεδονικά* 19, no. 1 (1979): 159-67.

Yaşar, Filiz. 2013. "Bir Osmanlı Adasında Toplum ve Ekonomi (16. Yüzyıldan 18. Yüzyıla Sakız)." Ph.D dissertation, Hacettepe Üniversitesi.

Αντωνιάδης, Σ. *Τα Δημοτικά*. Αθήνα: 1842.

Αργέντης, Φιλίππου-Στιλπνός Κυριακήδος. *Η Χίος παρά τοις Γεωγράφοις και Περιηγηταίς από τον Όγδοου μέχρι του Εικοστού Αιώνος 3*, Αθήνα.

Βακαλόπουλος, Α. "Οι Κοινότητες." *Ιστορία του Ελληνικού Έθνους*. C.I, Αθήνα: 1975.

Βακαλόπουλος, Αποστ. *Ιστορία του νέου ελληνισμού Στ΄ Η μεγάλη Ελληνική Επανάσταση (1821-1829)-Η εσωτερική κρίση (1822-1825)*, Θεσσαλονικη: 1982.

Βισβίζης, Τ. Ιάκωβος. "Η Κοινοτική διοίκησης των Ελλή- νων κατά την Τουρκοκρατίαν." L' Hellénisme Contemporain: Le cinq-centieme anniversaire de la prise de Constantinople. Athenes: 1953.

Βλαστός, Αλ. *Χιακά ήτοι ιστορία της νήσου Χίου από των αρχαιοτάτων χρόνων μέχρι της έτει 1822 γενομένης καταστροφής αυτής παρά των Χίων*. Β', Ερμούπολη, 1840.

Γεωργόπουλος, *Δημήτρης. Το Αρχείο της Επαρχιακής Δημογεροντίας Ναυπλίου (1828-1829)*. Ναυπλίος: Υπουργείο Παιδείας & Θρησκευμάτων Γενικά Αρχεία του Κράτους Αρχεία Νομού Αργολίδος, 2015.

Ζολώτας, Γεωργός. *Ιστορία της Χίου*, Τόμοι, Γ-Ι, Αθήνα: Τύπος Π. Δ. Σκελλάριου, 1921-28.

Ζακυθηνός, Δ. Η. Τουρκοκρατία. Αθήνα: 1957.

Κανελάκης, Κωνσταντίνος. *Χιακά Ανάλεκτα*, Χίος: Έκδοση Χίος Ημερολόγιο, 1890.

Κοντογιώργης, Γ. Δ. *"Κοινωνική δυναμική και πολιτική αυτοδιοίκηση."* Οι ελληνικές *Κοινότητες της τουρκοκρατίας*. Αθήνα: 1982.

Κοράης, Α. *Άτακτα,* Παρίσι, 1835.

Κούκου, Ε.Ε. Οι κοινοτικοί θεσμοί στις Κυκλάδες κατά την τουρκοκρατία. Αθήνα: 1980.

Μαυρόπουλος, Χρίστος. *Ιστορίαν της Χίου – Τουρκικά Έγγραφα*. Αθήνα: Τυπογραφείου Πετράκου,1920.

Πανταζόπουλος, Ν. Ο Ελληνικός κοινοτισμός και η νεοελληνική κοινοτική παράδοση. Αθήνα: 1993.

Σακελλαρίου, Μ.Β. Η Πελοπόννησος κατά την δευτέραν τουρκοκρατίαν (1715-1821). Αθήνα: 1939.

Σγουρός, Κωνσταντίνος, *Ιστορία της Νήσου Χίου Από τον Αρχαιότατων Χρόνών μέχρι του 1700 μ.χ.* , Αθήνα: Τύποι Πυρσού, 1937.

Τσάρας, Γιάννης. "Εκλογές για μουχταροδημογεροντία στο Μπλάτσι της Κοζάνης (1888)." *Μακεδονικά,* 14(1), (1974): 52-53.

Φιλαδελφεύς, Θ. Ν. *Η Ιστορία των Αθηνών επί τουρκοκρατίας Από του 1400 μέχρι του 1800.* Αθήνα : Καραβία, Δ.Ν. - Αναστατικές Εκδόσεις, 1991.

Χαροκόπος, Αντώνιος. *Ο θεσμός της Δημογεροντίας εν Χίω επί Τουρκοκρατίας,* Χίος: 1960.

Χασιώτης, Ιωάννης Κ.- Κατσιαρδή Hering, Ό.- Αμπατζή, Ευρυδίκη Α. *Οι Έλληνες στην Διασπορά.* Ατήνα: Βουλή των Ελλήνων 2006.

CHAPTER TEN

Two Steps Forward, One Step Back: A Grand Melee in the Ottoman Provinces[*]

Özlem Başarır

In the first half of the 19th century, as a surviving legacy of much earlier eras, the Ottoman realm was home to self-interested actors, individuals or groups, who would try to make the maximum use of deadlocks in rural administration and would even dare to challenge state authority. Other, more obscure actors would not refrain from following similar methods to acquire what they wanted, even though they had a narrower mindset in terms of territory and ambitions. One such actor was Mehmed Bey from the Şeyhzâde family who lived in the city of Diyarbakır. His efforts to advance his and his family's interests at the centers of power in the heart of the province forced him to resort to unorthodox methods. His life-risking activities enabled him to stand out on a regional scale, yet compared to the gains of his peers, we see that his fate ended up being exile and expulsion. The punitive measures, rather than chastening him, impassioned him even further, although this should not be a surprising behavior for someone conditioned to reach his goals no matter what. It is at least reasonable to expect that the longstanding dialogue between the state and the provincial notables that was built on military, political and economic interests, would in turn create the grounds for the family members to seek and seize opportunities for personal gain. This study, by focusing on one of the Gordian knots in the provincial fabric, aims to provide a closer look at the 'melee'[1] staged by the role-players at the provincial center.

The urban population of Diyarbakır fought, on the one hand, epidemics like the plague and cholera as well as natural disasters such as prolonged famines, and they

---

[*]   Diyarbakır, beginning of 19th century

1   The term "Kör dövüşü" (Melee/Blind fight) is used in its dictionary meaning: "the disorganized and ill-informed efforts of people who share the same purpose yet end up blocking each other". *Türkçe Sözlük* (Ankara: Türk Dil Kurumu, 2005), 1234.

were forced, on the other hand, to continue to live under the threat of tribal bandits, most of whom were nomadic. Added to this was the abuse of the administrators in a disorderly environment due to the weakened central authority.[2] In the layout created by these circumstances, safeguarding the state's authority became the major challenge in the provinces. The trauma experienced by the central administration in the region is best illustrated by the 58 governors it had to appoint between the years 1780 and 1838. The governors remained in office for a year or even shorter periods of time, adding to the community's discontent by collecting illegal taxes for the 'rulers' entourage' and procuring goods and food items from the shopkeepers free of charge. The governors did not go to the provinces and instead fulfilled their duty through their *mütesellim*s [a deputy governor or provincial head of administration],[3] deputies who, in turn, became the most apparent driving force behind the thriving of local figures.[4] To illustrate how unstable the state of provincial administration was, we must recall how the community expelled the Governor Mehmed Şerif Paşa (1808-9) from the city by force, or how in 1817, Abdurrahman Ağa, the *mütesellim* of Diyarbakır at the time, executed Gevranlızâde Mustafa Ağa, one of the local notables, and sent his severed head to Istanbul.[5]

The unhindered behavior of local elements[6] that benefited from the disorderly atmosphere in the province gave way to two important events. The first of these

2   İbrahim Yılmazçelik, "Osmanlı Döneminde Diyarbakır'da Yönetim-Halk Münasebetleri," *38. ICANAS- Uluslararası Asya ve Kuzey Afrika Çalışmaları Kongresi (10-15 Eylül 2007),* Ankara: 3383-5.

3   It is known that in Ottoman provincial administration, the system of *mütesellim* had been used for a long time. We must state that this job entailed being the representative of the Beylerbeyi/governor and the *sancakbeyi*, and when they were away at a campaign or if they did not arrive at their place of duty, the *mütesellim* managed the province and collected the taxes on their behalf. According to usual staffing procedures, the candidate for the *mütesellim* post would be declared to the central administration at the time of application. Then upon the issuing of the edict that confirmed his *mütesellim* post, he would be able to officially assume his duty. Yücel Özkaya, "Mütesellim," *DİA* 32 (2006): 203.

4   Yılmazçelik, "Osmanlı Döneminde Diyarbakır'da Yönetim-Halk Münasebetleri," 3389- 90.

5   Suavi Aydın, Kudret Emiroğlu, Oktay Özel, Süha Ünsal, ed., *Mardin, Aşiret-Cemaat-Devlet,* (İstanbul: Tarih Vakfı Yurt Yayınları, 2000), 197.

6   In his study, Özcoşar criticizes the central/government approach to define the Ottoman/Islamic city via the city of Diyarbakır, describing the notables who expressed the 'urban will' and the roles they played in the urban administration. Özcoşar puts forward some criteria to describe this group. Among these are their economic power; being among the more established residents of the city; having settled in the city personally or as a family after having moved there for administrative work, and even after the work ended, for scholarly duties; being *seyyid*; and having achieved economic power and influence comparable to that of the prominent leaders of tribes such as Milli and Kiki. In addition, their status as

took place in 1802 when Hacı Emin Ağa, the *voyvoda** of the period, turned the mansion of the Diyarbakır *mufti*, Mesut Efendi, into barracks and created an armed force called *Otuzbir Ortası* from the soldiers in the city.[7] The second event would shape the fate of the protagonist of this study, Mehmed Bey, when in 1819[8] the urban notables, bolstered by the participation of the shopkeepers and the community in the central province, revolted, following the assignment of Behram Paşa[9] from the Milli tribe, nicknamed 'Deli', to the governorship of Diyarbakır. This appointment by the state administration was a continuation of a policy that had a lengthy history.[10] In 1791, Şeyhzâde İbrahim Paşa was positioned against Milli Timur Paşa, in an operation organized against him. And now, Behram Paşa from

---

notables depended on two other conditions: the continuation of the circumstances that afforded them this reputation, and the existence or family members who were qualified and competent enough to sustain this reputation through generations. İbrahim Özcoşar, "Şehir ve Eşrâf: Osmanlı Diyarbekir'inde Eşraf," *Elektronik Sosyal Bilimler Dergisi* 14, no. 53 (2015): 131-2. On local notables of the region in mid-18th century, also see Ercan Gümüş, "Ahkâm Defterlerine Göre 18. Yüzyıl Ortalarında Urfa/Ruha'da Yükselen Yerel Güçler ve Bunların Devlet ve Çevreleriyle İlişkileri," *Tarih Okulu Dergisi (TOD)* 36 (2018): 104-29.

*   "A term of Slavic origin that passed into Ottoman usage; in the seventeenth century, an administrator of a tax benefice often personally appointed by the beneficiary of the benefice; in the eighteenth century, an Ottoman provincial administrator of a large or aggregate set of tax farms", Ariel Salzmann, *Measures of Empire: Tax Farmers and the Ottoman Ancient Regime, 1695-1807,* Unpublished Phd. Thesis, Colombia University, 1995, xii. –tn.

7   Yılmazçelik, "Osmanlı Döneminde Diyarbakır'da Yönetim-Halk Münasebetleri," 3390- 91.

8   In the year 1819, the province of Diyarbakır and its environs were witnessing a conflict between Derviş Paşa, the warden of Van, and Selim Paşa, the *mutasarrıf* of the *sanjak* of Muş, along with significant interventions from the central administration. The high-ranking administrators in the region were told to prepare for a military to be dispatched to the region. Apparently, the local elements in the region always acted in line with their own interests and continued to be the major cause of regional threat. However, the events that developed on the arrival of Behram Paşa, appointed governor, to the city of Diyarbakır, would mean that the continuing interventions would come to a grinding halt. For more information on the Derviş Paşa Revolt see Fatih Gencer, "Van Muhafızı Derviş Paşa İsyanı," *Tarih Araştırmaları Dergisi* 29, no. 47 (2010): 197-216.

9   Behram Paşa's governorship of Diyarbakır, combined with the province of Raqqa, began in 1819 and continued for a period of five months. Abdülgani F. Bulduk, *Diyarbakır Valileri*, Eyyüp Tanrıverdi, Ahmet Taşğın, ed.s, (Ankara: Medrese Yayınları, 2007), 149. We see that Behram Paşa also worked as the governor of Sivas, Aydın, Maraş, Raqqa and Aleppo until his death in 1832/33, mostly under the title of the vizierate. Mehmed Süreyya, *Sicill-i Osmanî* 2, Nuri Akbayar, ed., (İstanbul: Tarih Vakfı Yurt Yayınları, 1996), 365. For the undated imperial decree on the exile and execution of Behram Paşa see *BOA., HAT* 503/24732; *BOA., HAT* 503/24776.

10   Aydın et al., *Mardin, Aşiret-Cemaat-Devlet*, 197.

the same tribe was being appointed to the governorate to prevent the activities of the urban notables, among them the Şeyhzâde family. This was akin to a fuse of intense strife being lit between the centers of power in the region.[11] Even though the extant narratives and interpretations on the revolt point to different reasons behind the development of the event,[12] they agree on the fact that local figures allied with the local community fought together against the governor, who represented the state.

Before moving on to the event mentioned above, it is necessary to talk about how Mehmed Bey's family, the Şeyhzâde, established itself in the region long before him. It's worth noting first that his great grandfather İsmail Ağa and grandfather İbrahim Paşa played a major role both at the level of the central administration and in keeping the family flourishing in the region. The main architect of the family's influence was İsmail Ağa. He assumed the duty of the *voyvoda* of Diyarbakır and was charged with collecting taxes and enlisting soldiers from the region in the name of the state, both of which contributed significantly to the family's influence.[13] His achievements were crowned by the career track of his son İbrahim Paşa who reached the rank of governor and served between 1809 and 1813, a lengthy term in office when compared to other governors of Diyarbakır. At the same time, the family, whose lineage could be traced back to Şeyh Yusuf-ı Velî,[14] tried to abuse the esteem and respect shown towards such religious figures in society to support their interests, or to create new opportunities for themselves.

---

11   It is known that the Ottoman state utilized the strategy of playing the actors of the region against each other for years. It is possible to see important examples of this in the conflict between the tribe and the *beys* in Mardin, or in the competition between the Çapanoğlu and the Caniklizâdeler. Aydın et al., *Mardin, Aşiret-Cemaat-Devlet*, 197; Rıza Karagöz, *Canikli Ali Paşa* (Ankara: Türk Tarih Kurumu, 2003); Özcan Mert, *XVIII. ve XIX. Yüzyıllarda Çapanoğulları* (Ankara: Kültür Bakanlığı Yayınları, 1980).

12   For a compilation of information from various sources on the subject, see Şevket Beysanoğlu, *Anıtları ve Kitâbeleri ile Diyarbakır Tarihi Akkoyunlular'dan Cumhuriyet'e Kadar* 2 (Ankara: Diyarbakır Büyükşehir Belediyesi Kültür ve Sanat Yayınları, 1998), 684-90.

13   For the nature of Şeyhzâde İsmail Ağa's duties, see the following documents: the decree dated 26 *Dhu al-Hijja* 1197 (November 22, 1783) prepared for the collection of the taxes paid by the province in full, in *BOA., C.ML.* 28535; the decree for the payment of the *eşkinci bedeliyye* of the Diyarbakır Province dated 28 *Shawwal* 1199 (September 3, 1785) in *BOA., C.DH.* 11550; the decree prepared on the collection of the *voyvodalık [aggregate tax farms in a district or province under the administration of a voyvoda]* and *jizya* taxes in Diyarbakır, dated 5 Safar 1200 (December 8, 1785) in *BOA., C.ML.* 10566.

14   For the family tree, see Ali Emirî, *Mir'âtü'l-Fevâ'id fî Terâcimi Meşâhîri Âmid Diyarbakır Ulemâ ve Eşrâfı* 2 (İstanbul: Türkiye Yazma Eserler Kurumu Başkanlığı, 2014), 235.

Mehmed Bey, who represented the last strong generation of the family[15] along with his uncle,[16] was the grandson of İbrahim Paşa through his son Tahir Bey. In the first half of the 19th century when the conditions that strengthened these local elements started to change, Mehmed Bey was the most harshly tested member of the family. He spent his life pursuing an active role in provincial administration and trying to protect the influence of the family in the region. The death of his grandfather İbrahim Paşa in 1813 while he was governor of Diyarbakır was probably the best opportunity for Mehmed Bey to achieve his goals since he had never been that close to the *mütesellim* position in provincial administration that he so fervently desired. The *qadi* [judge] of central *kaza* [the district under the *qadi's* jurisdiction] in the province of Diyarbakır immediately confiscated the property of the *paşa*, and appointed Mehmed Bey as *mütesellim*. Naturally the official letter from the *qadi* would not be sufficient for the assignment. He and his uncle Osman Bey therefore appealed to the center for both the *mütesellim* post and to inherit the confiscated assets of the paşa as the heirs. However, the reply they received was unfortunately the opposite of what they had expected. For immediately before İbrahim Paşa passed away, Emin Paşa (1813-15) had already been appointed as the governor to the province.[17] The death of the paşa before the news of the new appointment could reach the province would not change the decision.[18]

15　We see that Şeyhzâde Osman Bey was appointed to the magistracy of Mardin with the rank of *mîr-i mirân* due to his success in the conquest of Baghdad in 1832; Aydın et al., *Mardin, Aşiret-Cemaat-Devlet*, 199. A later record shows that Osman achieved the title of *pasha*, twelve years prior to the aforementioned document, ran away from Diyarbakır and went to Baghdad, and only in the middle of the year 1258 (1842/43) arrived at Diyarbakır. For the two missives penned by the Marshal of Diyarbakır, İsmail Paşa, dated 21 *Rajab* 1259 (August 17, 1843) see *BOA., İ.MVL.* 52/1005.

16　Mehmed Sadık Bey was the district governor of Saruhan and a member of the Karaosmanoğlu family, which was one of the most powerful families of notables in Western Anatolia. For his experiences due to the administrative policies of the central government, see Ferhat Berber, "Manisa'da Âyân Soyundan Son İdareci: Saruhan Kaymakamı Mehmed Sadık Bey," *Celal Bayar Üniversitesi Sosyal Bilimler Dergisi* 13, no. 3 (2015): 291-304.

17　It has been claimed that Emin Paşa was appointed to the post of governor because İbrahim Paşa was no longer able to fulfill his duties due to old age and illness. İbrahim Yılmazçelik, "Osmanlı Hakimiyeti Süresince Diyarbakır Eyaleti Valileri (1516-1838)," *Fırat Üniversitesi Sosyal Bilimler Dergisi* 10, no. 1 (2000): 283.

18　For the undated imperial decree see *BOA., HAT* 1268/49127. From the appeal that Osman Bey made later, we see that his requests for the property to be given to him were fulfilled. *BOA., C.ML.* 154/6510.

Power Struggles in a Competitive Environment

The architects of the revolt against Behram Paşa and the state authority he represented as the governor of Diyarbakır, were Şeyhzâde Mehmed Bey as well as the *mufti* of Diyarbakır, the *naib* [deputy *qadi*] of Diyarbakır, the commander-in-chief of the Janissaries. They were supported by the shopkeepers and the community at large. The Paşa accused the revolt leaders of desiring to rule the province with the *mütesellimlik* under their control. He also held the community at least as responsible as those who initiated the revolt, especially due to their vigilance in the struggle against Derviş Paşa, the Defender of Van. According to the accounts of the Paşa,[19] a revolt broke out on his fourth night in the city. Even though the residents rioted around seven o'clock, he was still awake and able to fend off the attack. While being prepared beforehand helped in the defense, the leaders of the revolt were able to attack violently, asserting: "What did that Great State do to us when we have insulted every vizier who arrived at our region in every way, and even robbed Şerif Paşa[20] down to his *harem* and shut him off? What can it say now?' Based on this experience, it is possible to presume that the Paşa's claims regarding the rebels were partially true. The lack of effective measures by the central administration against previous disruptions in the region had created an environment where the community was 'spoiled' and wanted to act as they wished.[21]

The Paşa managed to fend off the first attack, but on the eleventh night of his governorship and while everyone was asleep, a crowd of 15-20.000 rebels swarmed the Governor's palace. According to his accounts, he had not gone to sleep yet, and with the help of God, he was able to throw rebels out, shut the doors, and continued to defend. He stated that the *mufti* of the city had instigated everyone in the city – on a day that happened to be in the holy month of Ramadan – by saying, 'Break your fast, you are travelling. From now on, we obey no one.' The governor added that Mehmed Bey had armed the community and that, for sixteen days straight, the rebels had been attacking with gunfire and cannons day and night. He was offended by this violent behavior and complained that he was a newcomer and yet had not been offered even a cup of water.

On the following days of the revolt, he appealed to the central administration to ask for support, reporting that since the rebels controlled the bazaar and the

---

19 For Behram Paşa's note dated 13 *Shawwal* 1234 (August 5, 1819), the undated order of the grand vizier and the imperial decree from the Sultan, see *BOA., HAT* 508/24969.

20 The records show that the governorship of Şerif Paşa, appointed to the post in 1808, lasted for 17 days. Bulduk, *Diyarbakır Valileri*, 144-5.

21 Cevdet Paşa, *Tarih-i Cevdet* 11 (İstanbul, 1309), 22-3.

market, he and his companions had to eat everything including their horses, and that they would continue to defend until death. Adding that 29 people were killed by the rebels and 150 were wounded, he was striving to 'execute the Sultanic will' with all his might.[22] According to Behram Paşa, the ringleaders' supporters directed groups of three hundred to five hundred people and were continuing their attacks with a vengeance. Some were captured and executed by decapitation, including: Alaybeyi Selim, Turnabaşı Abdülkadir, Çelenkçi Ebubekir, Çarşı Ağası İbrahim ile Bayraktar Abuş, Kavukçu İsmail, Boyacıoğlu Hüseyin, Deli Ali and Kara Mehmed, bandit chiefs from the entourage of Mehmed Bey, and Dalmızrakoğlu Hüseyin from the entourage of Karahoca and Karakollukçu Veli from the entourage of the commander-in chief of the Janissaries.[23] In addition, by sending his soldiers to the road to Maden and Şirin Inn, and to Çermik and Mardin, the Paşa was one step closer to ensuring the safety of the city.[24]

A correspondence that most likely carried the seal of Mehmed Enver, one of the administrators in the region, offers a different perspective on the events that Behram Paşa describes. According to Mehmed Enver, Behram Paşa was also to blame for the events, at least as much as those who acted against him, due to his failure as a governor and his flawed methods. Besides, the central administration was also aware of unfavorable opinions of him, and should he be dismissed from duty, it might be deemed appropriate to appoint the talented İbrahim Paşa from Gevran in his place.[25]

Worth noting is the cautious behavior of Nurullah Paşa, the regional administrator and custodian (emin) of Maden-i Hümayun, who, among others, was expected

---

22 In the contents of the order referring to his appeal, the following points were included: Behram Paşa could act independently in punishing the rebels; more forcefully written orders would be sent to the surrounding administrators for the required provisions, military and ammunition; there should be an investigation of why Nurullah Paşa had not shown an effort to help and support; it is not appropriate to display the heads of the executed rebels in front of government offices; yet if they were thrown into the sea, the Paşa would be discouraged, and for this reason he should not be informed, and the messenger who brought the severed heads should wear a caftan. For Behram Paşa's note dated 13 Shawwal 1234 (August 5, 1819), the undated order from the grand vizier, and the imperial decree of the Sultan, see *BOA, HAT* 508/24969.

23 For Behram Paşa's note dated Selh-i Muharrem 1235 (November 18, 1819), see *BOA., HAT* 507/24947.

24 For the declaration of the undated imperial order, see *BOA., HAT* 660/32204.

25 For Mehmed Enver's communication dated 19 Zilkade 1234 (September 9, 1819) requesting the replacement of the attendant who did not dispatch Mehmed Enver's letter to the central administration, see *BOA., C.DH.* 259/12907.

to give military assistance[26] to Behram Paşa. According to him, the residents of Diyarbakır were forming alliances with the surrounding tribes and seeking collaboration. While he kept the soldiers at the ready as requested by Behram Paşa and the central administration in Ergani, he worried that if the soldiers decided to support the community, the chaos would drag on, and thus he preferred to wait. Besides, he also believed that the community's reaction grew only stronger because of the expenses[27] associated with the arrival of governors with vizier titles to Diyarbakır. For this reason, he believed the province would be administered without complaints 'only if it was assigned to a *Mîr-i mîrân*' with a lower rank. As for the former *mutasarrıf* of Çorum, İbrahim Paşa, he was cut out for this position.[28]

The rumors from the region suggested that among the reasons for the revolt was the public suffering caused by the tyranny of the Behram Paşa. However, the central administration dismissed this motive. It was known that he was not a 'conservative vizier' to begin with, and the events were sparked because the community was accustomed to freedom and rejected the stewardship of the governor, since the province had been ruled through the *mütesellim* system. Just as they had long been 'trouble and mischief-makers,' now, too, they should be seen as the main reason for the current chaos. Even if Behram Paşa might be seen as an oppressor by some, it should be acknowledged that he did not have the time to attend to this affair. The clearest proof of how the residents rejected the governors was their attitude towards them in earlier times. If the governor was replaced on the suggestion of Nurullah Paşa, the emin of the Maden-i Hümayun, this would only encourage the residents further because they were "impertinent." Even though the central administration agreed that Behram Paşa should be dismissed and replaced by İbrahim Paşa, the *mutasarrıf* of Çorum from the old '*mîr-i mîrân*', it was assumed that the city residents would not ever obey him since they had already behaved in this way previously and were used to mischief.

---

26 By sending frequent orders, the center held the local administrators responsible for supporting the Paşa and fulfilling all of his needs, ammunition and provisions being first and foremost. For the note dated 17 *Dhu al-Hijja* 1234 (October 7, 1819), and the following order dated 4 *Muharram* 1235 (October 23, 1819) see *BOA., C.DH.* 88/4367.

27 The sheer size of *kapu halkı*, the entourages maintained by the governors, had been one of the most criticized issues, because of the financial burden that the community had to shoulder. The residents of the city felt most of the distress. For example, they complained to the central administration about being unable to cover the expenses of Mehmed Paşa who came to Diyarbakır with a *kapu halkı* of three hundred people in 1803. İbrahim Yılmazçelik, *XIX. Yüzyılın İlk Yarısında Diyarbakır (1790-1840)* (Ankara: Türk Tarih Kurumu, 1995), 181, 188.

28 For the declaration of the undated imperial order see *BOA., HAT* 660/32204.

It was clear as day that the residents could be reined in because Behram Paşa was competent in 'battles and uprises,' he continued to fight without compromise, and because of his own tribal roots in Diyarbakır and Maden.[29]

Eventhough the state turned a blind eye on the residents' mistreatment of the former governors, it was determined to disallow the same against Behram Paşa. Those who instigated the revolt were described as 'nobodies', and the following precautions were deemed appropriate for the 'reinforcement of state's authority and power': the neighboring administrators would be charged with giving Behram Paşa every kind of support possible; Şeyhzâde Mehmed Bey should be exiled; utmost care and attention should be shown towards providing Nurullah Paşa with the soldiers, provisions, ammunition and similar necessities; since Maraş and Aleppo were close to Diyarbakır, their governors should be asked to assist Behram Paşa with the necessary number of soldiers; and the governor of Sivas, Lütfullah Paşa, should, in addition to supplying soldiers, and be ready to take command if necessary. If, despite everything, the residents and the notables still attempted to expel the Paşa from the province, they would have proven their disloyalty in the eyes of the central administration.[30]

In a note (kaime) Behram Paşa wrote directly to Hurşid Paşa, the Governor of Aleppo, he stated that although the rebels had finally lost their strength and started fleeing in the small hours of the morning on the 5th of Muharram, 1235 (October 24, 1819).[31] He added that the situation had relatively calmed down, although one could still not claim that the chaos was completely over. For this reason, he wanted Bilecik, Berazi and Rumkale to send military support.[32]

During Behram Paşa's struggles to gain control, the central administration did not remain idle. It initiated due process to confiscate the mukâta'a [tax revenue unit], and property from the five people who were seen as the ringleaders of the rebellion.[33] Our research determined that eight mukâta'as belonged to the mufti and

---

29 For the declaration of the undated imperial order, see *BOA., HAT* 660/32204.

30 For the declaration of the undated imperial order, see *BOA., HAT* 660/32204. In summary, the Sultan felt the need to intervene quickly in these types of incidents and was concerned that if the community got the upper hand, a widespread rebellion throughout the country was possible. For the declaration of the undated imperial order referring to this concern, see *BOA., HAT* 504/24836.

31 The preferred destinations for the fugitives were Baghdad, Mardin or Maden. The safety of the roads was threatened because they were not caught. For the declaration of the undated imperial order, see *BOA., HAT* 660/32204.

32 For the note dated 11 *Muharram* 1235 (October 30, 1819), see *BOA., HAT* 1437/59080B.

33 *BOA., AE.SMHD.II* 2/71. Some mistakes were also made in this matter. The *müderris* Mehmed Şerif Efendi from the residents of Diyarbakır was implicated due to his name

to Mehmed Bey and that there were no *mukâta'a*s or properties in the possession of Karahocaoğlu Ömer or the commander of the Janissaries Hacı Mustafa.[34] As next steps, the central administration decided that the *naib* and the *mufti* should be exiled to Anapa, and that Mehmed Bey and the commander of the Janissaries should be executed. The order also stated that, should it prove difficult to send the *mufti* and the *naib* to Anapa, they should be sent to Magosa.[35]

The sable fur garments sent to Behram Paşa and his entourage upon the suppression of the revolt[36] proved that the state was satisfied with the outcome of the operation. Seventy one residents who were presumed guilty for their involvement in the events; were banned from entering Diyarbakır, although, in approximately five years, they would be pardoned and allowed into the city. In the years that followed, governors such as Gevranlızâde Mehmed Paşa (1823), Hüseyin Paşa (1823-1824) and Ebûlubûd Mehmed Paşa[37] (1826) would unfortunately continue

---

being the same as the rebel deputy *qadi* Mehmed Şerif Efendi. In line with the confiscation of the the rebels' property and *mukâta'a*s, the *müderris' mukâta'a* share was erroneously recorded in the registry for the Imperial property. To clarify the situation and to declare that 'he had been a *mutasarrıf* for many years,' the *müderris* went to the central government with a decree from the deputy *qadi* of Diyarbakır. The center was informed of another error that the *mütesellim* of Diyarbakır committed as well. On the missive requesting further action dated 13 *Rajab* 1235 (April 26, 1820) see *BOA., C.DH.* 195/9713.

34 For a copy of the edict dated 15 *Jumada al-Awwal* 1235 (February 29, 1820) see *BOA., C.ML.* 570/23345.

35 Several officials, the *mutasarrıf* of the *sanjak* of Muş, the governor of Erzurum, the wardens of Kars and Van, the governor of Çıldır and the *mutasarrıf* of Bayezid, were all held directly responsible for the search and execution of the fugitives. For the postscript of the edict dated Evahir-i Muharrem 1235 (November 9-18, 1819), written on 22 *Rabi ul-Awwal* 1236 (December 28, 1820) see *BOA., C.DH.* 118/5879. According to Cevdet Paşa, the order regarding the death sentence and exile was dated 30 Muharram 1235 (November 18, 1819) (*Tarih-i Cevdet*, 36).

36 *Tarih-i Cevdet*, 35-36.

37 When the Paşa lived in Dimetoka, the province of Diyarbekir was assigned to him with the honor of the vizierate, and later the Raqqa province was also added. Ahmed Lûtfî Efendi, *Vak'anüvîs Ahmed Lûtfî Efendi Tarihi* 1-8, Nuri Akbayar, ed., (İstanbul: Tarih Vakfı-Yapı Kredi Yayınları, 1999), 89, 154. Lütfi Efendi states that the vizier title had been repealed from the Paşa due to complaints. However, the records kept in the vizierate's office of the scribe, state that the Paşa was punished because he and his entourage participated in sedition. It was decided that his vizierate would be withdrawn and he would reside in Tokat, while the province of Diyarbekir would be assigned to the *maden emini*. However, fearing dismissal and exile, Ebûlubûd ran away to Baghdad. The central administration had granted him permission to reside in Tokat, in deference to his old age, but his courage to rebel necessitated a harsh punishment. Whether he went to Baghdad or

to oppress the community, in fact, to an extent that necessitated their execution and exile.[38]

The Struggle to Stay in the Game: An Ambitious Runaway and Exile

Mehmed Bey, who was sentenced first to exile and then to execution, appears to have escaped following the central administration's decision to oppress and punish the rebels. We do not know the exact date of his escape from the province; however, it likely occurred around November 1819 when the orders of execution and exile for the rebels were issued. Based on his mother's appeal to the central administration asking for his son's pardon,[39] we learn that his runaway period was at least seventeen months long, and that he lived in miserable conditions in the mountains. By her account, her son was only twenty-two years old; the people who started the events in Diyarbakır tried to put the blame on Mehmed Bey to save themselves; her son was frightened of the death sentence; and his absence devastated his family in Diyarbakır, even depriving them of their daily bread. She hoped that the state would have mercy on her son because of his young age and valor, while she was old and had to care for her other children who were in misery. She asked the state to absolve Mehmed Bey on the condition that he would reside in the capital city. For the state that probably achieved its goal of breaking the influence of the family. Rescinding the death sentence[40] would not pose a problem anymore, on the condition that Mehmed Bey stayed in the capital 'permanently.'

---

to Egypt, his execution would be carried out. *Vak'anüvîs Ahmed Lûtfî Efendi Tarihi*, 211-12. The imperial decree mentioned that Ebûlubûd Paşa was "of the friends of tyranny and enmity" and included the decision to appoint Yahya Paşa of Mosul in his place. The decree also affirmed that the state would not breathe easily until it put an end to the tyranny inflicted on the community by the governors. *Vak'anüvîs Ahmed Lûtfî Efendi Tarihi*, 645. Traditionally, the state attempted to prevent administrative abuse of the community by issuing edicts of justice across all the well-protected domains. However, this created its own problems. Chief among them was the new burden placed on the community to cover the expenses and fees associated with the work animals and the officials carrying out the edicts. *Vak'anüvîs Ahmed Lûtfî Efendi Tarihi*, 645. On the edicts of justice also see Halil İnalcık, "Adâletnâmeler," *Belgeler* 2, no. 3-4 (1965), 2. edition (1993): 49-142.

38 Yılmazçelik, "Osmanlı Döneminde Diyarbakır'da Yönetim-Halk Münasebetleri," 3393-94.

39 For the undated appeal of the mother of Mehmed Bey, see *BOA., C.DH.* 118/5879.

40 *Şeref-yafte-i sudûr olan hatt-ı hümâyûn-ı merhamet-makrûn-ı şâhâne mûcebince fîmâ- ba'd Diyarbekir ve havâlisine ayak basmamak ve dâ'imî der-sa'âdetde ikâmet eylemek şartıyla 'afv ve ıtlâkıçün buyuruldu* fî 29 Rebiyülevvel 1236 (January 4, 1821) *BOA., C.DH.* 118/5879. Karahocaoğlu and the rebel janissary commander who were sentenced to death were pardoned on the condition that they relocate to Baghdad. The date of this order has been recorded as *evasıt-ı Cemaziyülevvel* 1235 (February 25-March 5, 1820). Apparently two

Once his punishment was changed to exile, it was time to figure out how to facilitate Mehmed Bey's return to Diyarbakır to rebuild the family's influence. The determining factor in convincing the state was the provincial governors' need for local forces in carrying out administrative affairs and collecting taxes. In a report (*takrir*) dated *Rajab* 19, 1238 (April 1, 1823) and written by one of the governors of Diyarbakır, possibly Hüseyin Paşa (1823-24),[41] Mehmed Bey was not held accountable for the past and Behram Paşa was blamed instead. The culture of tyranny that Behram Paşa created at the start of his term inevitably led to the confrontation with the community. It was Hüseyin Paşa's opinion that people who experienced disasters while enduring oppression and tyranny deserved compassion and a helping hand. He also believed that, since Behram Paşa caused the chaos in Diyarbakır, it was unjust to sanction the dignitaries and notables of the region who were either goaded into evil, calamity and chaos or destroyed completely. This was why Mehmed Bey had to be spared punishment, poverty, and humiliation; instead, out of 'kindness,' 'charity' and, above all, compassion for his mother who was burning with longing, he had to be pardoned and allowed to return back to the region. However, the real reason for Hüseyin Paşa's appeal was the fact that Mehmed Bey was the only '*ocak-zâde*' left in the region who could work closely with the governor to manage the state's affairs.

Mehmed Bey's return was probably accelerated by the appointed governers' inability to handle regional affairs, including issues such as safety of the roads and managing the central treasury revenues. According to Hüseyin Paşa, there was no one either to manage Mehmed Bey's affairs in the province or to look after his family which was in distress; consequently, his income was about to be depleted and his home ruined. At the same time, he was struggling with several problems in Istanbul. Hüseyin Pasha perceived the family as the strongest of the oldest dynasties of Diyarbakır and as a point of honor for the community. We do not know how much this opinion persuaded the state to show mercy; however, his explanation that no '*ocak-zâde*' other than Mehmed Bey remained to help with the management of administrative affairs must have carried greater weight. Accordingly, it appears that he was permitted to return 'on condition that he would attend to his own

---

of Mehmed Bey's accompices had been pardoned long before him; in fact, they were pardoned shortly after the rebellion was suppressed.

41 *BOA., HAT* 653/31947. Although the author of the related declaration was unnamed, similar expressions and concerns found in the following declaration of Hüseyin Paşa make us think that it was written by him as well.

affairs and reside in Diyarbakır.[42] Following the period of exile (around 1821-24) which he spent in Istanbul thanks to governor Hüseyin Paşa's interventions, it is not surprising that Mehmed Bey attempted to establish his influence immediately upon arriving in the region. So much so that already during the first governorship of Salih Paşa[43] as Hüseyin Paşa's successor and the Emin of the Maden-i Hümayun, Mehmed Bey's name would once again begin to be mentioned for the *mütesellim* —the deputy governor position he had set his eyes on from the beginning.

When the governorship was handed over to Salih Paşa, he was aware that the main goals of the state were the protection of the province and ensuring the safety of the roads. Due to the urgency of the situation, he was ordered to appoint a *mütesellim* from among various candidates, including Mehmed Bey. However, Salih Paşa was strongly opposed to Mehmed Bey, whom he saw responsible for the disorder in the region. The previous governor Hüseyin Paşa, due to his old age, had not been able to deal with the rogue elements and could not prevent them from becoming threats. Salih Paşa was therefore aware that the present chaotic environment was the perfect opportunity for Mehmed Bey, who would do anything to secure the administration of the province. Even though it seemed that Hüseyin Paşa's weakness was partly to blame, one could predict how someone who had dared to exhibit questionable conduct during Hüseyin Paşa's rule, would behave if they ever attained the post of *mütesellim*.

After extensive deliberation, Salih Paşa recognized that none of the other candidates were suitable for the post of *mütesellim,* and he therefore had to choose the best of a bad lot and appoint Mehmed Bey as *mütesellim*, on the condition that he would ensure the safety of the roads. However, since Mehmed Bey's nature was leavened with malice, he acted as if to confirm his former reputation and continued to provoke the *eşkıyâ-yı ekrâd*. It quickly became clear that he restored some kind of order by entrusting the community affairs to despotic figures such as the *kethüda* and *subaşı*, and that, with each passing day, he inflicted more hardship and cruelty on the community. Despite several warnings to correct his behavior, nothing changed. Salih Paşa believed appointing someone else to the post of *mütesellim* would be more effective. However, he was anxious that the community

---

42   For the note of Hüseyin Paşa dated 29 *Rajab* 1239 (March 30, 1824) see *BOA., HAT* 514/25150.

43   For Salih Paşa's thoughts on the damage caused by banditry in mining operations and suggestions on how to increase production, see Fahrettin Tızlak, *Osmanlı Döneminde Keban- Ergani Yöresinde Madencilik (1775-1850)* (Ankara: Türk Tarih Kurumu, 1997), 144-5.

would react adversely (as it did to Behram Paşa) since Mehmed Bey was a 'local' of Diyarbakır. Therefore he preferred that his edict to exile Mehmed Bey to Ankara or somewhere else was conveyed to him 'secretly'.[44]

It was not clear how the new term of exile would affect the position of the family in the region since the family was chiefly concerned with keeping its finger on the pulse of the times and managing the developments well in this period and its aftermath. The best option, based on previous experience, was to put oneself at the state's mercy. Therefore, a new appeal on behalf of the family came from the governor of Diyarbakır, Mehmed Emin Paşa (1826) who requested Mehmed Bey's return to Diyarbakır due to the miserable state of his 'spouse and children'. According to him, the time Mehmed Bey spent in exile should be deemed sufficient for his 'self-correction' (ıslâh-ı nefs).[45]

The central administration appears to have been aware of Mehmed Bey's erroneous conduct for a long time. We conclude this based on a report (tahrirat)[46] that was probably authored by Çötelizade İshak Paşa[47] since his governorship of Diyarbakir fell between 1832-34. Even though Mehmed Bey was sent to exile and distanced from the region more than once, such punishment and 'taming' tactics failed. Mehmed Bey's actions in the ten years since his return to the region showed that he would never change. Indeed, chief among Ishak Paşa's complaints were the facts that Mehmed Bey had always dreamt of 'secession,' (teferrüd hulyâsında) and

---

44 While the central administration was convinced by the justification and confirmed Mehmed Bey's exile to Ankara, it did not neglect to warn Nuri Paşa, the mutasarrıf of Ankara, and prohibit him from communicating with Mehmed Bey's relatives, as he was one of the notables of Diyarbakır. For the imperial decree on Salih Paşa's note dated 4 Jumada al-Awwal 1241 (December 15, 1825) see BOA HAT 508/24960.

45 BOA., HAT 503/24727. Mehmed Emin Paşa even stated in his note dated selh-i Jumada al-awwal 1242 (December 30, 1826) that, following the repeal of the decision of exile by Salih Paşa for unknown reasons, he wrote to the central administration: "There remained no reasons for Mehmed Bey to avoid returning to Diyarbakır, and his return would even be auspicious." For the order pardoning Mehmed Bey dated 23 Jumada al-Akhir 1242 (January 22, 1827) see BOA., HAT 1570/11. The period of exile began towards the end of 1825 and was completed at the beginning of 1827.

46 For the correspondence dated 23 Jumada al-awwal 1249 (October 8, 1833) see BOA., HAT 700/33720A.

47 He is from Harput. After the death of his uncle Hacı İbrahim Paşa, the governor of Diyarbakır, he became governor with the order of the vizierate, and was dismissed in 1834. Bulduk, Diyarbakır Valileri, 158; Yılmazçelik, "Osmanlı Hakimiyeti Süresince Diyarbakır Eyaleti Valileri (1516- 1838)," 265.

that he had, since the time of the former governor of Diyarbakır Yahya Paşa,[48] exploited the annual customs and *mukâta'a* taxes as well as the poor in the community. Despite his multifaceted analysis of the events and the current situation, İshak Paşa was forced to appoint Mehmed Bey as *mütesellim*, though did not mind voicing his reluctance by attributing it to the pressures of the time and the circumstances of the period *("be-hasbe'l- vakt ve'l-hâl")*.

Ishak Paşa's negative views about Mehmed Bey did not end there. He also complained that he did not follow orders, and ignored directives pertaining to the mâl of mukâta'a [the yearly income, usually nominal, on a tax farm] or any other business he was tasked with, and that he was unable to adjust his thinking when confronting problems. However, most critical for him was Mehmed Bey's search for supporters to fulfill his ambition of *teferrüd* [gain independence/obtain autonomy] in the region. Ishak Paşa reproached and blamed specifically the governor of Şehrizor, Mehmed Paşa, whom Ishak Paşa called 'my brother', for giving guidance to Mehmed Bey while he stopped in Diyarbakır on his way to Iraq. Ishak Paşa was also aware that, on his promise and assurance of support, Mehmed Paşa had taken Mehmed Bey's scribe Şerif Efendi with him as well, on the pretext that he needed the scribe for an altogether different matter. This action, Ishak Paşa warned the central administration, proved even more clearly that Mehmed Bey was 'unfit' for his office, reinforcing his opinion by pointing to the attitude of the community. In fact, the citizens were unable to escape the suffering and oppression inflicted on them by Mehmed Bey. This was the reason why, while they were not brave enough to oppose Mehmed Bey's demands, they were trying to resist his cruelty by at least informing Ishak Paşa.

The fact that he instigated *ekrâd tâ'ifesi* secretly and threatened the safety of the roads must have put a strain on Ishak Paşa concerning the very sensitive matter of regional peace and stability. Because he believed the main reason behind Mehmed Bey's strange conduct was the support he received from the governor of Şehrizor, Ishak Paşa repeatedly appealed to the central administration, requesting that he should be warned with a *'tenbîhnâme'* (letter of demerit). Additionally, he did not refrain from sending to the central administration Mehmed Bey's income and ex-

---

48   Yahya Paşa was one of the Celilizâdes in Mosul. He had come to Diyarbakır in 1829 and stayed on duty for two years. Bulduk, *Diyarbakır Valileri*, 157. The justification for his dismissal from the governorship was his supposed inadequate "qualifications and competence," which must have increased his range of movement (Yılmaz Çelik, "Osmanlı Hakimiyeti Süresince Diyarbakır Eyaleti Valileri (1516-1838)," 284).

pense register[49] for his eight month-long *mütesellim* activities, thereby revealing all kinds of 'fraud and malice' and his 'unfitness' for the job. It was clear that Mehmed Bey's survival strategy lay in his ability to manipulate the positions of power around him and the state's dependence on local figures to ensure regional stability.

For about ten years, the Ottoman documents on him remain silent, and the final piece of information on him dates back to the 1830s when he requested the assistance of the governor of Şehrizor. What made him resurface in the year 1259 (1843/44) was his conduct, along with his uncle Osman, to instigate the community and incite anarchy. The central administration reacted as expected, and after a series of events, both he and his uncle were exiled. What convinced the administration in this matter were the testimonies of both İsmail Paşa (1842-45), the marshal of the province[50] at the time, and the naib of Diyarbakır who voiced the requests of the local community.

Interestingly, during this period, the local community's negative perception of Mehmed Bey remained very much alive.[51] The residents had believed for a long

---

49 For the register dated 21 *Rabi al-akhir* 1248 (September 17, 1832) see *BOA., HAT* 700/33720B.

50 In the second quarter of the 19th century, after the formation of the *redif* (military organization) new problems arose. To solve these, new provinces were formed from 1836 onwards, with military interests in mind. High ranked officers of the Ottoman Army were appointed as marshals to these provinces. Musa Çadırcı, *Tanzimat Döneminde Anadolu Kentleri'nin Sosyal ve Ekonomik Yapısı* (Ankara: Türk Tarih Kurumu, 1997), 22. The Diyarbakır province was located within the Sivas Marshalship at first and became an independent Marshalship in 1838. This unit included the provinces of Diyarbakır and Raqqa as well as Ma'den-i Hümayun Emaneti. From then on, the governors of Diyarbakır would also begin to be called marshals. Yılmazçelik, "Osmanlı Hakimiyeti Süresince Diyarbakır Eyaleti Valileri (1516-1838)," 285.

51 The following events kept Mehmed Bey in the collective memory of the community: In 1234 (1818/19) during the time of Behram Paşa, he had instigated the *ehl-i fesâd* (mischief-makers) and had fought with the Paşa for 101 days, causing several casualties. He had fought Ebûlubûd Mehmed Paşa and forced him out of the city in 1241 (1825/26). All viziers up until Reşid Paşa (1834-36) had been *forced* to appoint him to the post of chamberlain. However, Reşid Paşa, although humiliated by his tricks, did not achieve his goal, as his main intention was revealed previously. In 1256 (1840/41) Mehmed Bey took the opportunity to instigate the rebels once more and upended the order of the city, but falling into disgrace, then plundered the house of the *dhimmi* named Tomik, a goldsmith. In 1258 (1842/43) he armed the people and left no one at peace. It was already widely known that whenever a revolt broke out in the city, it was due to Mehmed Bey's provocation. Also, wherever he worked as a *mütesellim*, the community suffered from his tyranny. For the decree of the naib dated *Mid-Rajab* 1259 (August 7-16, 1843) see *BOA., İ.MVL.* 52/1005.

time that he was predisposed to malice and fraud, and accustomed to dishonesty. According to them, he always remained close to rabblerousing liars, and by instigating chaos to animate his evil intentions, he asked to be seen as their leader. Besides, he drew to his side people without intelligence and conscience, who in turn acted as accomplices in his malice. All things considered, it was not appropriate for Mehmed Bey to stay in Diyarbakır, and the best thing to do would be to send him away from the region.

Mehmed Bey, known by such honorifics as "of the distinguished directorate of *Istabl-ı 'Âmire*"[52] and "among *vücûh* [provincial elites] of Diyarbekir," would never give up his dreams and ambitions that he had pursued from the beginning. From then on, his ultimate goal was to attain "tahsîl-i riyâset [getting ahead]" by inciting the community. One of his most well-known methods was resorting to force and behaving in line with his vested interests. According to the statements of Ismail Paşa, Mehmed Bey's uncle Osman Paşa, who troubled the administration at least as much as his nephew and had escaped to Baghdad twelve years ago, had returned to Diyarbakır in the year 1258 (1842/43) and was appointed by his predecessor Vecihi Paşa[53] as the *kaymakam* [sub-governor] of Diyarbakır.[54] Later when

---

52 The Istabl-ı Âmire organization, where the horses of the Ottoman sultan and palace dignitaries were kept, had been reorganized in the time of Mahmud II. The highest rank of the organization, the title of *mirâhur* had been abolished, and instead, the directorate of the Istabl-ı Âmire was founded. This title was given as the highest ranked title on occasion. Abdülkadir Özcan, "Istabl," *DİA* 19 (1999): 203-6. For the missive that reached the Ministry of Finance, see *BOA., A.MKT.MHM.* 18/84. In recognition of the proliferation of 'imperial gifts', the 19th century was close to being called the age of the honorary distinctions. The state-conferred distinctions or awards to people whom it could not discipline or control had been a political tool used for some time. For detailed information, see, Selim Deringil, *The Well-protected Domains: Ideology and the Legitimation of Power in the Ottoman Empire 1876-1909* (London, New York: I. B. Tauris, 1998).

53 He acted twice as governor of Diyarbakır: For nine and a half months in 1841, and for two months and two days in 1851. Bulduk, *Diyarbakır Valileri*, 164.

54 With the reorganization of 1842, the administrative structure was divided into province-*sanjak*-townships, and the duties previously fulfilled in *sanjak*s by the *mütesellim* would be taken over by the district governors. They would be directly connected to the Ministry of Interior and their duties would be assigned from there. In addition to answering to the governors, the district governors' independent decisions were significantly limited. Çadırcı, *Tanzimat Döneminde Anadolu Kentleri'nin Sosyal ve Ekonomik Yapısı*, 236-40. The district governors who could not find a role in provincial administration in the post-Tanzimat period acted as representatives and attendants of the governors. The governors and the marshals had the authority to appoint district governors. The recommended candidates were discussed at the Sublime Porte, the Ministry of Finance and the Supreme Council, and the office of the Grand Vizierate confirmed the appointment. Being

Ismail Paşa was appointed as *müşir* [field marshal] and arrived in Harput, he left all administrative officials in their posts, and Osman Paşa was permitted to stay on duty as well. However, when his term in office ended, the situation changed, and Osman Paşa's desire to remain in office led him and his nephew Mehmed Bey to resort to creating chaos in the region. Ismail Paşa did not think it was possible for them to remain in the area. He found it unacceptable that in the chaotic environment of their own making, the two were also attempting to make themselves indispensable "no matter what."[55] As a result of a briefing submitted by the Paşa, the Meclis-i Vâlâ-yı Ahkâm-ı Adliye (Supreme Council of Judicial Ordinances) agreed to review the issue, concluding that these people, having been "convicted for similar acts many times before," were "unfit men" and ruled that Mehmed Bey should be exiled to Aydın and Osman Paşa to Kütahya.[56]

Instead of a Conclusion

By his mother's account, during the revolt of 1819 Mehmed Bey was in his early twenties. In fact, his aspirations for provincial administration after the death of his grandfather in 1813 coincided with the most passionate years of his adolescence. Since he died in 1849,[57] we have been able to witness approximately thirty years of Mehmed Bey's life. In the period we discussed, the province of Diyarbakır was unstable, suffering from an atmosphere of unrest and disorder, and witnessing all kinds of wanton and recalcitrant movements led by local elements. Inevitably, compounding the difficulty of maintaining order was the administrative organization of the province—the fact that it was at times administered together with the Raqqa province or Maden-i Hümayun Emaneti, or that some field marshals within the system managed their affairs from Harput. As for the governors, their short-lived appointments, and the management of their duties through the *mütesellim* can be

---

knowledgeable on administrative and financial affairs factored into the selection of the district governor. In the formation of the new order, the *muhassıl* [the officials who collect taxes belonging to the state] and *mütesellims* of the previous period could have been left as district governors in their posts. Mehmet Güneş, *Osmanlı Devleti'nde Kaymakamlık (1842-1871)* (İstanbul: Kitabevi, 2014).

55   For the two notes written by the Marshal of Diyarbakır, İsmail Paşa, dated 21 *Rajab* 1259 (August 17, 1843), see *BOA., İ.MVL.* 52/1005.

56   For the undated missive from the Supreme Council of Judicial Ordinances, see *BOA., İ.MVL.* 52/1005.

57   For the document dated 14 *Muharram* 1266 (November 30, 1849) see *BOA., A.MKT. UM.* 3/23. The governor writes that Mehmed Bey passed away a few days before the document was written yet does not give a specific date.

seen as factors contributing to the instability. Therefore, the newly built system must have encouraged conditions that strengthened the local elements unavoidably left in the background.

Mehmed Bey's schemes to manipulate this environment for his own interests and his insatiable ambitions unfortunately led to a life of exile. His character was opportunistic to the extent that he could provoke chaos and paralyze the governors, thereby creating a need for his services in administrative affairs and in the collection of taxes. Persistent and ambitious, he would try every possible method to attain his goals. All of these had made him into a person who smartly exploited the dynamics of the period for his own ends. Yet we also see that his grandfather and great grandfather had more favorable positions in the Ottoman provinces, and that, despite his countless attempts, Mehmed Bey was unfortunately not as effective as they were. We can therefore say that the results of his lifelong striving remained confined to relatively small gains.

Bibliography

Archival Sources

Başbakanlık Osmanlı Arşivi (BOA.)

BOA., A.MKT.MHM. (Sâdaret Mektubî Kalemi Mühimme Kalemi Evrakı) 18/84

BOA., A.MKT.UM. (Sâdaret Mektubî Kalemi Umum Vilâyet Evrakı) 3/23

BOA., AE.SMHD.II (Ali Emirî Tasnifi Sultan Mahmud II Tasnifi) 2/71

BOA., C.DH. (Cevdet Dahiliye Tasnifi) 88/4367

BOA., C.DH. 118/5879

BOA., C.DH. 195/9713

BOA., C.DH. 259/12907

BOA., C.DH. 11550

BOA., C.ML. (Cevdet Maliye Tasnifi) 154/6510.

BOA., C.ML. 570/23345

BOA., C.ML. 10566

BOA., C.ML. 28535

BOA., HAT (Hatt-ı Hümâyûn Tasnifi) 503/24727

BOA., HAT 503/24732

BOA., HAT 503/24776

BOA., HAT 504/24836

BOA., HAT 507/24947

BOA., HAT 508/24960

BOA., HAT 508/24969

BOA., HAT 514/25150

BOA., HAT 653/31947

BOA., HAT 660/32204

BOA., HAT 700/33720A

BOA., HAT 700/33720B

BOA., HAT 1268/49127

BOA., HAT 1437/59080B

BOA., HAT 1570/11

BOA., İ.MVL. (İrade Meclis-i Vâlâ) 52/1005

Secondary Sources

Ahmed Lûtfî Efendi. *Vak'anüvîs Ahmed Lûtfî Efendi Tarihi* 1-8, ed. Nuri Akbayar. İstanbul: Tarih Vakfı-Yapı Kredi Yayınları, 1999.

Ali Emirî. *Mir'âtü'l-Fevâ'id fî Terâcimi Meşâhîri Âmid Diyarbakır Ulemâ ve Eşrâfı* 2. İstanbul: Türkiye Yazma Eserler Kurumu Başkanlığı, 2014.

Aydın, Suavi, Kudret Emiroğlu, Oktay Özel, Süha Ünsal, eds. *Mardin, Aşiret-Cemaat-Devlet*. İstanbul: Tarih Vakfı Yurt Yayınları, 2000.

Berber, Ferhat. "Manisa'da Âyân Soyundan Son İdareci: Saruhan Kaymakamı Mehmed Sadık Bey." *Celal Bayar Üniversitesi Sosyal Bilimler Dergisi* 13, no. 3 (2015): 291-304.

Beysanoğlu, Şevket. *Anıtları ve Kitâbeleri ile Diyarbakır Tarihi Akkoyunlular'dan Cumhuriyet'e Kadar* 2. Ankara: Diyarbakır Büyükşehir Belediyesi Kültür ve Sanat Yayınları, 1998.

Bulduk, Abdülgani F. *Diyarbakır Valileri*, eds. Eyyüp Tanrıverdi, Ahmet Taşğın. Ankara: Medrese Yayınları, 2007.

Cevdet Paşa. *Tarih-i Cevdet* 11. İstanbul, 1309.

Çadırcı, Musa. *Tanzimat Döneminde Anadolu Kentleri'nin Sosyal ve Ekonomik Yapısı*. Ankara: Türk Tarih Kurumu, 1997.

Deringil, Selim. *İktidarın Sembolleri ve İdeoloji II. Abdülhamid Dönemi (1876-1909)*, translated from the English by Gül Çağalı Güven. İstanbul: Doğan Kitap, 2014.

Gencer, Fatih. "Van Muhafızı Derviş Paşa İsyanı." *Tarih Araştırmaları Dergisi* 29, no. 47 (2010): 197-216.

Gümüş, Ercan. "Ahkâm Defterlerine Göre 18. Yüzyıl Ortalarında Urfa/Ruha'da Yükselen Yerel Güçler ve Bunların Devlet ve Çevreleriyle İlişkileri." *Tarih Okulu Dergisi (TOD)* 36 (2018): 104-29.

Güneş, Mehmet. *Osmanlı Devleti'nde Kaymakamlık (1842-1871)*. İstanbul: Kitabevi, 2014.

İnalcık, Halil. "Adâletnâmeler." *Belgeler* 2, no. 3-4 (1965), 2. edition (1993): 49-142.

Karagöz, Rıza. *Canikli Ali Paşa*. Ankara: Türk Tarih Kurumu, 2003.

Mehmed Süreyya. *Sicill-i Osmanî* 2, ed. Nuri Akbayar. İstanbul: Tarih Vakfı Yurt Yayınları, 1996.

Mert, Özcan. *XVIII. ve XIX. Yüzyıllarda Çapanoğulları*. Ankara: Kültür Bakanlığı Yayınları, 1980.

Özcan, Abdülkadir. "Istabl." *DİA* 19 (1999): 203-6.

Özcoşar, İbrahim. "Şehir ve Eşraf: Osmanlı Diyarbekir'inde Eşraf." *Elektronik Sosyal Bilimler Dergisi* 14, no. 53 (2015): 127-44.

Özkaya, Yücel. "Mütesellim." *DİA* 32 (2006): 203-4.

Tızlak, Fahrettin. *Osmanlı Döneminde Keban-Ergani Yöresinde Madencilik (1775-1850)*. Ankara: Türk Tarih Kurumu, 1997.

Türkçe Sözlük. Ankara: Türk Dil Kurumu, 2005.

Yılmazçelik, İbrahim. *XIX. Yüzyılın İlk Yarısında Diyarbakır (1790-1840)*. Ankara: Türk Tarih Kurumu, 1995.

———. "Osmanlı Hakimiyeti Süresince Diyarbakır Eyaleti Valileri (1516-1838)." *Fırat Üniversitesi Sosyal Bilimler Dergisi* 10, no. 1 (2000): 233-87.

———. "Osmanlı Döneminde Diyarbakır'da Yönetim-Halk Münasebetleri." *38. ICANAS-Uluslararası Asya ve Kuzey Afrika Çalışmaları Kongresi (10-15 Eylül 2007)*, Ankara: 3381-96.

CHAPTER ELEVEN

Are we not Ottomans? The Struggle of Shi'a Nureddin and Ibrahim in Returning from Exile

Faruk Yaslıçimen

In June 1894, the *Bâb-ı Âlî* (Sublime Porte) received a petition bearing sixty-eight signatures from the inhabitants of Hilla in Baghdad. This petition told the story of five people from the Jafari community who had been unjustly treated. Upon receiving the petition, the Porte asked the provincial government for an explanation. The details of the petition revealed that certain subjects had complained to the *mutasarrıf* about the maltreatment of Shiites during the Samarra Incident in 1894, an event that had serious international repercussions. In fact, the petitioners first reported the *mufti* of Samarra to the *sancak mutasarrıfı*, due to his insults and provocation against the Shi'a, and they notified the central province of this situation via telegraph. Following this, the governor of Baghdad asked the Hilla administration to investigate the claims. Shortly afterwards, five of the petitioners were called to the government office in Hilla and, according to the claims, they were arrested, insulted, and tortured. Their faces were dabbed with coal dust and mud, they were put on donkeys and, accompanied by two gendarmes on each side, they were paraded in public. Furthermore, the officials stopped in crowded locations to let local people beat and kick them, up until they left Hilla.[1] The peti-

---

1   In the Ottoman society of the early modern period, those who were thought to disturb society's peace were discredited in specific ways, and for the sake of public order, they were banished from the neighborhood, town or city. For example, Haciye Sabah lived in the middle of 16th century, in a period when power struggles between the Ottomans and the Safavids were intensely felt in political and religious domains. An aspect of Haciye Sabah's exile resembles the story of the Nureddin and Ibrahim brothers who lived in the 19th century. of According to the claims, Haciye Sabah was preaching sermons to women promoting the Kızılbaş movement, and men could attend these meetings as well. The court chose to give her a *teşhir* punishment and to sentence her to exile. In the end, the punishment was issued not because of her Kızılbaş propaganda, but because she facilitated the mixing of males and females in the same physical space. However, it

tion that was sent to the Sublime Porte, written in Arabic and bearing sixty-eight signatures, asked for the punishment of the officials responsible for the cruel treatment. The petitioners warned the central government that if the offenders were not punished, similar incidents could occur. They also asked that the *mufti* of Hilla be forced to abandon his offensive attitude towards Shi'ism. The closing remarks of the petition declared the loyalty and obedience of the Shi'a subjects to the state: "Even if the Shi'a are deprived of the civil law here [in Hilla], we still dare ask to be settled anew in an appropriate town under the protection and administration of the Ottoman Empire'.[2]

The Samarra Incident to which the petition referred had taken place at the end of April 1894, i.e. approximately two months before the petition. This incident reflects the polarization between the Sunni and the Shi'a in Iraq, and in historiography, serves as an example of how a minor dispute can quickly snowball into a sectarian conflict.[3] The dispute originated in a credit and debt issue between a student of

---

is not known what kind of *teşhir* punishment Haciye received. Leslie Pierce informs us that while reviewing the contemporaneous legal proceedings to determine Hatice's likely punishment, she came upon a punishment that would have forced Haciye to ride a horse facing backwards and to hold on to the tail of the horse instead of the reins (the punishment given to false witnesses and prostitutes). Another example of *teşhir* punishments is a warning issued in Antep to a woman called Fatma, who claimed that a man had raped her and the claim was found to be baseless. In the court Fatma said: "If I commit such a slander again, you may smear mud on my face in front of the public." The use of public humiliation as punishment from the early modern period to the end of the 19th century is noteworthy, since it points to pattern and continuity regarding the state's preventive measures to ensure public order. It is reasonable to think that the state did not invent new forms of punishment, and instead applied those that already corresponded to the pubic's collective perception of punishment. Leslie Pierce, *Morality Tales: Law and Gender in the Ottoman Court of Aintab* (Berkeley, Los Angeles, London: University of California Press, 2003), 269-75. Among the customary punishments, Fikret Yılmaz also mentions smearing mud on the face for *teşhir*. Fikret Yılmaz, "Zina ve Fuhuş Arasında Kalanlar: Fahişe Subaşı'ya Karşı," *Toplumsal Tarih* 220 (2012): 220.

2   *BOA, BEO* (Bâb-ı Âlî Evrak Odası) 418/31298, 6 *Dhu al-hijjah* 1311 (June 10, 1894). The last sentence in the petition shows that the Shi'a subjects were both part of the lawful order safeguarded by the state, while at the same time experiencing difficulties in adaptation. They were not rebels conditioned against authority. They only expected the state to uphold their rights. Their request to be sent to another region under the administration and protection of the state might be solely rhetorical. It must have been a plea for relief.

3   Gökhan Çetinsaya, *The Ottoman Administration of Iraq, 1890-1908* (London: Routledge, 2006), 113; Meir Litvak, *Shi'i scholars of nineteenth-century Iraq: the ulama of Najaf and Karbala* (Cambridge: Cambridge University Press, 1998), 167.

Mirza Hasan Şirazi[4] one of the most influential Shi'a *mujtahid*s of the time, and a butcher and his brother who was a soldier in the army. However, when the local government failed to prevent the dispute, it got more complicated, and in the end, both the Iranians in town and the students of Mirza Hasan Şirazi, and even the local Sunni community, got involved. Moreover, since there were subjects of other states among the students of Şirazi, the consulates of Britain, Iran and India got involved as well. All in all, the dust of the Samarra Incident would settle only in August, 1894.[5] In other words, at the time of the petition, the sociopolitical and psychological effects of the Samarra incident must have been still going on.

Nine days after the central government requested an explanation, Hasan Refik Paşa, the governor of Baghdad, sent a letter to the Grand Vizierate (Sâdâret), fully denying the allegations. According to him, the contents of the petition were fraudulent, and presented by the criminal judge of Hilla and the head of the Criminal Court who were dissatisfied with the decision to move *mutasarrıflık merkezi* (the seat of government) from Hilla to Divaniye. According to Hasan Paşa, the criminal judge of Hilla, Abdülnâfî Efendi and Emin Efendi, the head of the Criminal Court, enjoyed an income in Hilla they did not wish to abandon. They wanted to prevent the relocation of the seat of government to Divaniye, situated approximately 100 km south of Hilla. At the decisive moment, the Paşa had asked both the Ministry of Justice and the Office of the Şeyhülislâm to transfer the criminal judge and the deputy *qadi* to other locations. Following the governor's request, the Office of the Şeyhülislâm transferred the deputy *qadi* to another location but issued no decision on the criminal judge. In Governor Hasan Refik Paşa's view, the criminal judge and the deputy *qadi* were using the petitions as blackmail propaganda against Mustafa Efendi, the *mufti* of Hilla who had opposed them.

---

4   Mirza Hasan Şirazi's reputation of had grown with his refusal of the gifts sent to him by the ruler of Iran, Nasiruddin Şah, during his visit to Atebat-ı Aliyye in 1870. In the following years he became known as one of the highest ranked *mujtahid*s in both Iraq and Iran. His move to Samarra in 1874 where most of the population was Sunni had surprised many people. Şirazi's activities in Samarra made the Ottoman State anxious. Elie Kedourie, "The Iraqi Shi'is and Their Fate," *Shi'ism, in Resistance, and Revolution*, der. Martin Kramer (Boulder, Colorado: Westview Press, 1987), 138.

5   We must exercise caution when perceiving the Samarra Incident as a small sectarian war between the Shi'a and the Sunni in Iraq and a sign of imminent conflict. The details of the incident show that the opposition was against *foreign* Shi'a residing in especially Samarra, rather than the *local* Shi'a community, and that there were different groups and motives in the background. Faruk Yaslıçimen, "Sunnism versus Shiism? Rise of the Shiite Politics and of the Ottoman Apprehension in Late Nineteenth Century Iraq," PhD dissertation, Bilkent Üniversitesi, 2008, 141-52.

13. Mirjan Mosque, BAGHDAD

FIGURE 11.1 The area surrounding Mercan Mosque in Baghdad at the beginning of the 20th century (Postcard archive of the IBB Atatürk Library).

Fear

Hasan Refik Paşa confirmed that the petitioners had been called to the government office. According to him, even though all the petitioners had been invited to the office, only five of them had arrived. Four of the five admitted that they had signed the petition, but one of them was not even aware that his name and signature were on it. When the investigation determined that these four people willingly took part in the plot, they were warned and sent back, along with official letters transferring their case to the local administration. In effect, the official letters denied that the faces of the Shi'a had been dabbed with coal dust and mud; that they had been made to ride backwards on donkeys and paraded in the bazaars to the sound of drums and trumpets, accompanied by gendarmes. Hasan Refik Paşa argued that this was the essence of the matter, but that after a while, the petitioners had deliberately linked the issue with the Sunni-Shi'a conflict and blown it out of proportion. According to the Paşa, the Iranian Consulate had recently expelled some Iranians who tried to spark social chaos by accentuating sectarian differences. However, people like Nureddin and Ibrahim, two brothers from the locals and the Shi'a of Hilla, whose malicious disposition was already known to the local administration, stayed in Hilla. The month of *Muharram* was approaching and Hasan Paşa feared that conspiracy would seep into traditional Shi'a mourning ceremonies. Aiming to prevent a possible unrest, the Paşa in his petition requested that the brothers Nureddin and Ibrahim should be sent to the Köysancak township in the province of Mosul, if only 'for a little while'.[6]

---

6   *BOA, BEO 420/31450*, 12 *Dhu al-hijja* 1311 (June 16, 1894).

Since the central government wished to avoid any conflict between the Sunni and Shi'a in the province of Baghdad, Hasan Paşa's request was granted. The memory of the Samarra incident was still fresh. After a month, the two brothers (full names stated as Hamza Ağazade Nureddin and Hıllevi Hamzazade İbrahim Hilmi) sent a petition to the Grand Vizierate claiming that they had been exiled from their hometown Hilla to the district of Köysancak in Mosul, without any court decision to that effect. Köysancak was in the Şehrizor *sanjak* of Mosul and 70 km north of Kirkuk. The inhabitants were mostly Sunni Muslim Kurds and, located as it was 500 km to the north of Hilla, we can assume that its climate was different and colder. Therefore, due to health problems, the two brothers requested to be sent to warmer regions. Their petition ended with some touching remarks like those in the aforementioned petition: "If the intention is – God forbid – our death, then, execution is better than torture. For the sake of the Prophet, we seek refuge in Your Majesty's most gracious and merciful benevolence."[7]

Hasan Refik Paşa had not properly described Nureddin and Ibrahim's connection to the allegations. Furthermore, he did not specify to the Vizierate if they signed one of the petitions or not. Neither did he explain their possible connection to the *qadi* of Hilla or the criminal judge, or whether the two brothers were among those who were called to court due to the complaint against the *mufti* filed by the district governor of Hilla. He was content to describe Nureddin and Ibrahim as 'those who disturbed the peace in Hilla and engaged in corruption,' and 'those whose bad reputations were known to the provincial center'.

Although their request to be sent to a warmer region was denied, Nureddin and Ibrahim still succeeded in being transferred to the provincial center of Mosul from the district of Köysancak—where they had resided from March 1894, the beginning of their exile, to July 1895. Their transfer was on the 12th of the month of *Muharram* in the Islamic calendar. However, they still wished to return to a warmer location and specifically to Baghdad, and to this end, they sent petition after petition to the Grand Vizierate. The two brothers' next request, renewed after approximately six months, was once more contravened by the governor of Baghdad, Hasan Paşa. This time Hasan Paşa used a more pointed language and emphasized Nureddin's sect by speaking of him as 'the Shi'a Nureddin'. The governor argued that the two brothers were 'of those factious and misfit groups', and that their provocations and seditions in Hilla continuously caused conflicts between the Sunni and the Shi'a, even disrupting the peace and order of nearby towns. Therefore, Hasan Paşa op-

---

7   *BOA, BEO 418/31298, 6 Dhu al-hijja* 1311 (June 10, 1894).

posed Nureddin and Ibrahim's transfer to Baghdad since their return would be 'neither useful nor politically appropriate', and thus never advisable.[8]

The brothers' petitions gained frequency after January 1895. They must have feared that it would be impossible to return to Baghdad if they ever stopped writing to Istanbul. Nureddin wrote a new petition on January 12, 1895. This petition included more than simply requesting to be transferred to Baghdad. He also gave an account of the hostility between him and the governor Hasan Paşa. Openly stating that he inherited his loyalty and service to the Ottoman state from his fathers and grandfathers, he asserted that his services and contributions to 'the prosperity of the state treasury and important reforms' were known to former governors and *mutasarrıf*s. He added that, influenced by certain malicious people, Hasan Paşa disliked him, and that the Paşa illegally confiscated his property. Nureddin claimed that he brought the issue to the attention of *Şûrây-ı Devlet* (State Council), which, on June 13, 1893, confirmed the legitimacy of his claims. Thus, Nureddin was entitled to compensation. He then prepared a petition on the issue and presented it to the *İstinaf Mahkemesi* (Court of Appeal). However, as the case concerned the governor personally, the court left the case *meskût-u 'anh* (pending), in other words, attempted to sweep it under the rug. As Nureddin was aware of the situation, he did not neglect to repeatedly send telegrams to the State Council and the Grand Vizierate. On December 20, 1893, the Ministry of Justice sent a letter to the İstinâf Mahkemesi Müddeî-i Umûmiyye Müdürlüğü (Directorate of Attorney Generalship of the Court of Appeal) in Baghdad; while the letter was communicated to the deputy public prosecutor of the district of Divaniye, it was allegedly once more glossed over. At this point, Nureddin made a critical move by claiming that Seyyid Süleyman Efendi, the *nakibüleşraf* of Baghdad, confiscated a sizable piece of public land surrounding his own land. Nureddin claimed that the governor Paşa, provoked by this *nakib*, exiled him to Mosul. According to him, the governor did not stop there and had downsized the value of his property, which was worth 5000 liras yet was sold for the very low price of 140.000 *kuruş*.

Additionally, Nureddin requested the sale of 120 *tağar*[9] of grain (96,000 *okka*) from the area harvested in Jazira, a sub-district of Baghdad, and the transfer of the money to the public treasury, yet the governor Hasan Paşa refused to cooperate. According to Nureddin's estimate, at the time 1 *tağar* of land was priced at 600 *kuruş*. However, the provincial assembly of Baghdad sent an order to the sub-district of Jazira to sell, without any appraisal or auction, 1 *tağar* of Nureddin's harvest for

---

8   BOA, BEO 529/39639, 5 *Jumada al-Akhirah* 1312 (December 4, 1894).

9   *Tağar* is a unit of measure for provisions that in the past varied according to the region. 1 *tağar* corresponded to 800 *okka* in Baghdad in that period.

the price of only 80 *kuruş* - a loss of 520 *kuruş* per *tağar*. Nureddin demanded a repayment of 10.000 *kuruş* from the money delivered to the treasury through the transaction,[10] however he never received it. Even though the bail payment was 67.000 *kuruş* in total, the entirety of his property was sold at a loss, and a sum of 140.000 *kuruş* was earned from the sale.[11]

Despair

After describing the financial and legal aspects of his maltreatment in the first part of his petition, Nureddin switches from a formal style to an informal one. He repeats, once again, his loyalty to the state, and declares that he is a 'faithful believer at sixty years of age'. In mentioning his old age, Nureddin must have wanted to underline the fact that he was too old to be involved in dangerous affairs. He emphasized being 'a faithful believer' and omitted the fact that he was one of the Shi'a subjects of the state, both aimed at finding a common religious and political ground with the state officials.

On the one hand, this was a rhetorical strategy, on the other, it pointed to a common reference point. As in previous petitions, towards the end, Nureddin's wording became more sentimental: he claimed that the governor's abuse was one that even surpassed that of Haccac-ı Zâlim (al-Hajjaj the tyrant). Al-Hajjaj ibn Yusuf al-Sakafi was an Umayyad governor known for his despotism and support of the Umayyad Caliphate. He was also known for being reckless enough to besiege Mecca, damage the Ka'ba with catapults, and not caring for the lives of the pilgrims around it. He was responsible for the deaths of thousands of innocent people during the siege of Hejaz.

Nureddin's example was obviously an exaggeration. After all, his main goal, like that of his contemporaries, was not to make a real historical comparison but to underscore and strengthen his position.[12] Nureddin then returned to the legal

---

10   The transaction is defined in the document as "muâmele-i ferâğiyye," a forfeiture procedure. Şemsettin Sami, in his *Kâmûs-ı Türkî* describes this entry as follows: "Arazi-i emiriyye ve musakkafat ve mustagıllât-ı mevkûfenin hakk-ı tasarrufunu eski sahibinin yeni sahibine terkle kat'-ı ta'alluk eylemesi ve buna dair muâmele-i resmîyye ve kalemiyye ki, Defter-i Hâkânî Nezaretince ve taşralarda nezâret-i müşarun-ileyhânın me'mûru ma'rifetiyle icrâ olunur." Şemsettin Sami, *Kâmûs-ı Türkî* (Dersaadet: İkdam Matbaası, 1317), 986. *BOA, BEO* 529/39639, 7 *Jumada al-Akhirah* 1312 (December 6, 1894).

11   *BOA, BEO* 529/39639, 7 *Jumada al-Akhirah* 1312 (December 6, 1894).

12   State officials adopted a similar rhetoric in internal bureaucratic correspondence. For further information see Faruk Yaslıçimen, "Osmanlı Devleti'nin İran Eksenli Irak Siyaseti ve 19. Yüzyılda Bürokratik Bilgi Üretimi," *Bilgi ve Toplum* (İstanbul: İz Yayıncılık, 2013), 321-30.

aspect of the issue. As a Shi'a Ottoman subject, Nureddin, was so self-confident and had such a strong grasp of the principle of the separation of powers that he was able to remind the high-ranking officials of the state that "proceedings such as confiscation and sale are matters of the judiciary, not the provincial assembly". He then reinforced his point, saying: 'If my banishment is due to personal resentment, then the confiscation of my property and goods is unlawful.' Once again, Nureddin wrote in a more personal style and declared that his family of two hundred people was in a desperate situation. After pointing out that he had sent over fifty telegrams, including one from Mosul that contained the Medical Commission's reports on his health, Nureddin declared with regret he did not receive any replies from the government, in whose "affection and mercy" he took refuge. Nureddin stated that if he was a subject entrusted to the Sultan Caliph by God, then he should have been rescued from Hasan Paşa's tyranny. In closing his long petition, Nureddin wrote: "Our generous benefactor the Sultan never consents to such circumstances. If I am not considered a subject of the Sublime State, then I request permission to leave my homeland and relocate to another place to protect my rights against the aforementioned person."[13]

These final sentences are especially interesting. For starters, Nureddin was apparently aware of the concept of *vedîa*, whereby subjects are entrusted to the sultan by God, and he did not refrain from reminding the central administration of this concept. Indeed, Ottoman political thought holds government officials responsible for the protection and care of the subjects and entrusts the safety and welfare of the subjects to them. Just like the land they worked on, the *tebaa* (the subjects) were free yet entrusted by God to the protection and care of the sultan.[14] Halil İnalcık states that the early Ottoman sultans perceived their subjects as *vedîatullâh*, entrusted to them by God. The rulers were responsible for ensuring that the subjects lived in prosperity and justice so that *nizâm* (order) could be maintained.[15] Nureddin must have had a grasp of this aspect of Ottoman political consciousness if only because he shared the same cultural and civilizational crucible. In his correspondence with the state, he directly referred to this concept: "If I am one of the subjects who have

---

13 *BOA, BEO* 529/39639, 7 *Jumada al-Akhirah* 1312 (December 6, 1894).

14 Dick Douwes, *The Ottomans in Syria: A history of Justice and Oppression* (London, New York: I.B. Tauris, 2000), 3.

15 Halil İnalcık, "Osmanlı Padişahı," *Doğu Batı Düşünce Dergisi* 13, no. 54 (2010): 9-20. This article was first published in 1958 in *Ankara Üniversitesi Sosyal Bilimler Fakültesi Dergisi*.

been entrusted to you, the lofty Sultan Caliph..."[16] Taking it a step further, we can assume that he deliberately used this concept when corresponding with the central administration, which he apparently trusted more than the local administration. He believed he could solve his problems with the local administration by petitioning the central administration. Indeed, it was the state council that uncovered the injustice done to Nureddin concerning his finances, and with an order from the center, opened the legal path to his compensation. As for Nureddin's emotional statements at the end of his petition, they reflect the hierarchy between state and society. Nureddin, a subject who expected mercy from above, talks about leaving his homeland and possibly changing his nationality as a last resort. The earlier petition written in Arabic and bearing sixty-eight signatures had concluded with a similar statement. That petition, too, mentions the option of being sent to another location under protection of the state, whereas Nureddin directly speaks of changing his nationality. After affirming his loyalty to the state, it is likely that Nureddin mentioned such a possibility merely to reinforce his argument, and not as a threat to the central government that he might actually seek asylum in Iran or Britain. After repeatedly emphasizing his loyalty to the state and to the caliph, his reference to changing nationality aims at making the petition more poignant.

In fact, Nureddin was not an exception. In both Iran and the Ottoman Empire, the petitions written to the high authorities in the late nineteenth and early twentieth centuries are replete with such rhetoric and exaggerated wording. The petitioners, in their correspondence with the state, made a point of emphasizing their usefulness.[17]

In April 1895, Azer, the governor of Mosul, wrote to the central government about Nureddin's worsening illness and stated that he expected help from the central administration. In June of the same year, Nureddin sent another telegram to the Grand Vizierate and again complained that he never received a reply to his more

---

16 *BOA, BEO* 529/39639, 7 *Jumada al-Akhirah* 1312 (December 6, 1894). It is of course significant that the Ottoman political culture was familiar with this concept and used it consciously. However, what is more interesting is him addressing the Sultan, Abuldahmid II, as *hilafet-penâh* (shelter of the caliphate). The reason for this might be how the petitioner prepared the text as it was sent to the central government as a telegraph. It was customary to add the descriptive *hazret-i hilafet-penâh* (his holiness the shelter of the caliphate) in the bureaucratic correspondence of the Hamidian period. In a similar way, it might also have been necessitated by Nureddin's rhetorical strategy since he hoped to receive a response to his request from the center. Şükrü Hanioğlu, *A Brief History of the Late Ottoman Empire* (Princeton: Princeton University Press, 2008), 128.

17 Serhan Afacan, "Devletle Yazışmak: Türkiye ve İran Sosyal Tarihçiliği'nde Dilekçeler," *Türkiyat Mecmuası* 21 (2011): 14-5.

than fifty telegrams. He had been in exile in Mosul for fifteen months without a court decision, whereas all his family was in Hilla and his property was wasted in the hands of strangers. Yet he had not given up hope: "Not inquiring after a loyal subject who is inoffensive and downtrodden is not in line with the mercy of the splendid Sultan". He finishes this petition with an emotional statement also: "...even angels in the sky are crying from the heart for my sorrow. For the sake of the Prophet and God, may a fair inquiry on my case be ordered! If I deserve to be punished, then I should be ruined; but if not, I would like to be honored with the forgiveness of the Caliph... I plead for a decision allowing my return to Baghdad as soon as possible."[18]

In yet another petition, this one sent in October 1894, Nureddin stated that his illness worsened to such a degree that he was about to give up on life, that he was living in great misery in inns, far away from his homeland, and that, unable to see his family, he was overcome by deep sorrow. Nureddin found it unfair that concerning his petition to the Mosul province, the central government had decided to rely only upon the opinions of the Baghdad provincial administration instead of his. It is quite meaningful that he described himself as "a *muvahhid* (believer in the oneness of God) and among the old and faithful subjects loyal to the state and its people". As witnesses to this fact, Nureddin listed the names of high Ottoman officials of the Imperial Army such as Sırrı Paşa, the governor of Diyarbakır; Celaleddin Paşa, the former *mutasarrıf* of Hilla; and Mahmud Bey, the former governor of Bitlis. He also shared with the central government the information that Celaleddin Paşa was in Istanbul around that time.

That same year, Nureddin sent one more petition before the end of October. The tone of this petition was sterner and more pointed. He rebuked the authorities for not responding to him despite his persistent reports via telegram that explained his deteriorating health. He was unable to pay even the telegram fees. All his goods and property had been confiscated. He did not even have spending money. He was falling into debt and spending his life miserably in inns. He stated that his life was in danger and if he were not shown mercy, he would certainly perish. The medical report on him also demonstrated this. Having reached the end of his patience, he stated that if he did not receive a reply for this telegram either, he would be forced to seek justice by appealing to some unnamed foreign consulates in Iraq. He then added: "Because despair has come to a head". It is worth noting that Nureddin had

---

18   *BOA, BEO* 529/39639, 7 *Jumada al-Akhirah* 1312 (December 6, 1894). Similarly, expressions to move the addressee to action—i.e., "If you do not help us, we will be left all alone"—were used frequently as well. See Afancan, "Devletle Yazışmak," 14-5.

up until then referenced his connections in the government to solve his problems, but now as a last resort, he would be directing his appeal to foreign ambassadors, and he was informing the central government of his plans. Slightly toning down his wording, he requested his return to Baghdad, the central command of the Imperial Army, to at least receive treatment and to see his family once more before his death. He added that even if he was guilty, people in similar situations were forgiven, and that he awaited a reply via telegram.[19]

What did Nureddin mean when he spoke of 'people in similar situations'? In fact, even when more serious and urgent situations arose in Baghdad in the following years, the government was able to act in a more flexible and tolerant way. For example, in 1902 a man called Abdülrezzak had formed a group in Karbala, and along with his partners in crime, had acted almost like a parallel government. To protect their interests, the members of the group used their own courts to judge the Shi'a subjects of the Ottoman Empire and Iran, and collected taxes on their own behalf and even asked for a third of the ransom called blood money. After a while, the members of the group were summoned by the government and exiled to Aleppo when they confessed their crimes during the investigation. Interestingly, the Iranian government interfered in favor of these culprits. As it was the month of Muharram, which meant that Baghdad was swarming with visitors, the central government recommended these men be exiled to the desert areas of the Aleppo province, and specifically to the *sanjak* of Zor. This was to prevent them from instigating any kind of disorder. After Muharram, they could be sent back to Baghdad on the condition that the investigation would resume.[20] Even though Nureddin and Ibrahim's situation was much less serious than that of Abdülrezzak's group, the brothers would have to wait much longer before any obstacles standing in the way of their return were removed.

On the other hand, by sheer misfortune, Sırrı Paşa, one of the people Nureddin cited as reference, was dismissed on the grounds that he was tolerant towards Shi'ism. Sırrı Paşa, who had been under the protection of Gazi Osman Paşa of the Siege of Plevna fame, had served in Anatolian provinces following his posts as *mektupçu* and *mutasarrıf* in the Balkan provinces, and had been appointed as the governor of Baghdad in 1889.[21]

---

19 *BOA, BEO* 492/36893, 11 *Rabi' al-Akhir* 1312 (December 10, 1894).

20 *BOA, DH. MKT* 485/33, 13 *Muharram* 1320 (April 22, 1902).

21 Christoph Herzog, *Osmanische Herrschaft und Modernisierung im Irak: Die Provinz Bagdad, 1817-1917* (Bamberg: University of Bamberg Press, 2012), 155-7. Examples of Sırrı Paşa's inclination and sympathy towards Shi'ism include: preventing approximately 2.000

Sırrı Paşa's misfortune lay in the fact that he began his administrative duties at the same time as "Mad" Nusret Paşa, who constantly stirred trouble in Baghdad, from the time of his appointment until his death in 1896. Nusret Paşa was an old-fashioned Tanzimat man, an opponent of Midhad Paşa, a maverick and a pain in the neck for governors anywhere he went. He was appointed to the post of Honorary Supervisor of the Sixth Army in Baghdad, in part as a measure to remove him from his administrative post. Although Sırrı Paşa had informed the central government in 1891 about the spread of Shi'ism in Iraq with the support of the British, and that this was religiously and politically objectionable, what cost Sırrı Paşa his job would not be Nusret Paşa's accusation but his inability to hinder the rise of Shi'ism and the Iranian influence in the region, thereby losing the trust of Abdülhamid II. Hacı Hasan Refik Paşa, who was known for his pious character, was appointed in his place.[22]

Persistence

Have Nureddin's persistent requests yielded positive results? Not very soon. In every petition to the central administration, Nureddin perceives or introduces himself as a local Shi'a notable and an ordinary subject of the state. He never mentions sectarian issues. When the local government treats him unjustly, he appeals to the central government for justice. He trusts the central authority. However, if Nureddin did not have confidence in the state, he would not have persistently sent petitions to the central government. Nureddin's example also makes us think that the dichotomous relationship and unnatural separation between the center and the periphery is somewhat problematic. In Nureddin's case, the central government seemed closer to the geographically distant subjects than the local government. Ultimately, the 19th century is a period in rural administration where assemblies and

---

Shi'a youth in Kufa and Amara from being drafted (*BOA, Y.PRK. MYD* 9/58, 30 Zilkade 1307 (July 18, 1890); and being accused by Nusret Paşa of acting in unison with the Iranians. (*BOA, Y.PRK.ASK* 73/102, 7 *Dhu al-Hijja* 1308 (July 14, 1891)). According to the claim, the enmity between Sırrı and Nusret Paşas had gone so far that one of the parties appealed to foreign consuls. The Yıldız Palace found the solution in changing the station of duty for either Nusret or Sırrı Paşa. *BOA, İ.HUS* 7666, 9 *Dhu al-Qadah*, 1311 (May 14, 1894). After Baghdad, Sırrı Paşa had been appointed as the governor of Diyarbakır in 1891 and passed away there in 1895.

22 Çetinsaya, *The Ottoman Administration of Iraq*, 52-53 and 106. At this moment, Christoph Herzog shows how the loss of confidence in Sırrı Paşa was not only due to his failure to prevent Shi'ism from spreading, but also to the fraud committed in his administration and his failure to obtain the public's approval. Herzog, *Osmanische Herrschaft und Modernisierung im Irak*, 156.

committees were more common, local voices were heard and represented more, and local agency, like all other developing dynamics, was gaining strength.[23] In desert regions where the state's military authority was weak, the state exerted its political authority through its power to negotiate, while local agency exercised itself within the framework of negotiation.[24]

It is also noteworthy that having not received the response he wanted from the central government for a long time, Nureddin obliquely acknowledged the mediation of other foreign ambassadors and implied that he could change his nationality. In truth, Nureddin's attitude illustrates the search for local agency. When he failed to get responses to his last two petitions in October 1894, he explicitly mentioned the opportunity or possibility of changing his nationality in his December 1894 petition: "Since we are among the subjects of the eternal Ottoman State, we ask for the preservation of our rights. If we are not, that is to say, not considered as subjects of the Sublime State, then I request the appointment of another authority to protect our rights." Unlike in the previous petition, Nureddin did not feel obliged to include in his closing remarks any kind of justification for the urgency and severity of his plea.[25]

It is necessary to pause a bit here to take a closer look at how the central government perceived Nureddin's behavior. First and foremost, the politics of nationality was one of the most important issues in interstate rivalry in the nineteenth and early twentieth centuries. The method for interfering in Ottoman internal affairs was almost always the same: When disorder arose, regardless of whether their own subjects were involved or not, European states could intervene in the process in the name of either their own subjects or their coreligionists.[26] Once the balance of powers

---

23 For the opportunities and dilemmas posed by the assemblies and commissions for the participation of the local community, see Jun Akiba, "The Local Councils as the Origin of the Parliamentary System in the Ottoman Empire," *Development of Parliamentarism in the Modern Islamic World*, ed. S. Tsugitaka (Tokyo, 2009), 176-204. For an efficient comparison between Edirne and Ankara on how the local situation and participation affected the process of reforms, see Yonca Köksal, "Imperial Center and Local Groups: Tanzimat Reforms in the Provinces of Edirne and Ankara," *New Perspectives on Turkey* 27 (2002): 107-138.

24 M. Talha Çiçek, "Negotiating Power and Authority in the Desert: the Arab Bedouin and the Limits of the Ottoman State in Hijaz, 1840-1908," *Middle Eastern Studies* 52, no. 2 (2016): 260-79.

25 *BOA, BEO* 492/36893, 11 Rabi' al-Akhir 1312 (December 10, 1894).

26 Erik Jan Zürcher, *Turkey: A Modern History*, revised edition (London: I.B. Tauris, 2004), 55-6.

were upset, the foreign consulates, originally intended as means of managing and sustaining commercial and political relations, became instruments of pressure and influence for European states. In the nineteenth century, many Ottoman subjects, particularly non-Muslims, tried every means possible to obtain foreign nationality and passports in order to be under the protection of European states. They were willing to pay large sums of money in return for the economic and judicial privileges provided by such protection. Since the reign of Ahmed III, the Ottoman Empire had been working to prevent these practices, but it was never able to stop them.[27]

Nureddin's statements about seeking his rights via the intervention of foreign consulates operating in the empire pointed to this long-standing problem within the central government. The rights of people who obtained passports or secured the patronage of foreign states were protected and defended by the consulates of these states. In Ottoman historiography, there are several instances when subjects moved between states and nationalities.[28] The same was true for the Shi'a subjects of the Ottoman Empire. Carrying a British or Russian passport was advantageous in Ottoman Iraq.

For example, in January 1907, three Shi'a Muslims carrying Russian passports and traveling from Hanaqin, a sub-district on the Iranian-Ottoman border, to Baghdad's provincial center, had an accident and were assaulted. The incident took place two hours away from Baghdad. Two of the men were wounded in the leg, and all of them were robbed. At a late hour, the Russian Consulate in Baghdad informed the governor, who then immediately sent for the commander of the gendarmerie. The commander succeeded in capturing the suspects and forcibly bringing them to Baghdad by the morning. The culprits confessed to their crimes and were transferred to the courthouse. It is clear that the governor continued to follow the case closely. Besides, he must have found the issue important enough to inform the Ottoman central administration of the situation.[29] It would be reasonable to assume that this attention was directly due to their Russian nationality and was unrelated to the victims' denomination.

---

27 İbrahim Serbestoğlu, "Zorunlu Bir Modernleşme Örneği Olarak Osmanlı Tabiiyet Kanunu," *OTAM* 29 (2011): 196-200.

28 James Meyer mentions how Muslim immigrants from Russia emphasized their Russian nationality from time to time, hoping that it would expedite official business when they encountered problems. These immigrants in time obtained a type of dual nationality and used whichever nationality was more useful at different times. According to Meyer, this was a survival strategy. James Meyer, *Turks Across the Empire: Marketing Muslim Identity in the Russian-Ottoman Borderlands* (Oxford: Oxford University Press, 2014), 1-20.

29 *BOA, Y.PRK.UM* 79/47, 10 *Dhu al-Hijja* 1324 (January 25, 1907).

As for Nureddin and Ibrahim, since they had more than two hundred family members and several properties in Baghdad and the State Council at the time had already determined that Nureddin was wronged, the brothers' actual intention might have been to appeal to ambassadors whom they knew to seek their influences rather than to change nationality. Besides, they might have embellished their statements for greater emotional effect, or to highlight the urgency of the situation. Their true intentions remain unknown.

The central government once again considered Nureddin's request and sent a letter about his situation to the province of Baghdad. In reference to a medical committee report that Nureddin had included among his justifications, the letter cited his respiratory illness and the miserable state of his family members as reasons to recommend his return to Baghdad, and it asked the provincial authority for an opinion on the matter.[30] However, the opinion of the provincial authority remained the same. They repeated the serious concern that Nureddin and Ibrahim's return would disturb the public order in Hilla and Baghdad. Trying, on the one hand, to ideologically integrate Shi'a Muslims into the Ottoman caliphate through the politics of Pan-Islamism and, on the other, to popularize the Sunni sect by opening schools and appointing *ulama*, the Ottoman State had been wary of the possibility of a sectarian conflict in the region.[31] Therefore the state approached Nureddin's persistent petitions and even entreaties cautiously, but in the end, decided to trust the word of the governor Paşa.

Hope

The brothers Nureddin and Ibrahim did not despair of receiving the help of God or the state, and sent two more petitions to the Grand Vizierate, one in January and the other in February of 1895. Reiterating Nureddin's claim in an earlier petition, Ibrahim stated that it was Seyyid Süleyman Efendi, the *nakibüleşraf* of Baghdad, who had confiscated public lands, but that Ibrahim's opponents were trying to push the charge on to him to destroy him. He was unable to earn a livelihood and to provide for his family. However, he still retained his belief that "the door of justice was open for everyone." He again cited witnesses for his claims: Mahmud Reşid Paşa and Mahmud Bey, two former governors of Bitlis, and Sırrı Paşa, the ex-governor of Baghdad, all of whom, he said, were aware of his loyalty and service

---

30   *BOA, BEO* 492/36893, 11 *Rabi' al-Akhir* 1312 (December 10, 1894).
31   Faruk Yaslıçimen, "Saving the Minds and Loyalties of Subjects: Ottoman Education Policy against the Spread of Shiism in Iraq during the Time of Abdülhamid II," *DÎVÂN* 21, no. 41 (2016): 65-72.

to the state. If the central government did not believe the brothers, then, the unjust treatment would be uncovered if these witnesses or the *mutasarrıf* of Hilla were questioned. He made two requests from the Grand Vizierate. The first concerned the individuals who caused the brothers' exile from Hilla; he asked the Vizier, 'out of kindness and out of respect for our Prophet, peace be upon him,' to bring those individuals to court and have them both tried in the military and administrative councils. The second was to establish an allowance from the *menfâlar tahsîsâtı* (a special allocation for exiled persons) to provide subsistence for him and his family.[32]

The second petition that Ibrahim sent, also signed by his brother Hamza Ağazade Nureddin, was dated February 16, 1895. This petition recounts in greater detail the injustice done to them. When tax farmers in Hilla, for whom Nureddin and Ibrahim acted as sponsors, went into debt for 67.000 *kuruş*, the local government decided to confiscate the brothers' grain amounting to 300.000 *kiyyes*. Additionally, 10.000 *kuruş* previously delivered by Nureddin and Ibrahim to the state treasury was confiscated. Their property, valued at 5,000 *lira*'s was sold within an hour for 140.000 *kuruş* to someone from Baghdad without a court decision, a report to the bailiffs, or "an official bill of auctions." The issue was brought before the State Council, which confirmed the validity of their appeal, in a decision issued on June 13, 1892. However, as the matter had the potential to affect the provincial governor of Baghdad, the local court of appeal tried to shelve the matter. Hence, the grains, cash and property remained in the hands of the government.[33]

Since the injustice done to Nureddin and Ibrahim dated back to the year 1892, what was their role in or connection to the Shi'a-Sunni conflict in 1894? Nureddin stated that he somehow learned about the outcome of an investigation launched by the field marshal of the Sixth Army concerning the state lands in Hilla, which had been embezzled by Muhammed Şebib, the trustee of the *nakib* of Baghdad. According to Nureddin, the officers in the *Hazîne-i Hâssa* (Privy Purse) were also aware of the situation that was serious enough to warrant the *nakib*'s resignation. In the meantime, however, another event occurred, namely, the Samarra Incident. The five men who filed the complaint against the *mufti* of Hilla were summoned to Baghdad. When the summons reached the district governor of Hilla, especially with the instigation of the *mufti* and the *nakib*'s men, the petitioners were mounted backwards on donkeys, their faces were dabbed with coal dust and mud, and they were showered with insults and sent to Baghdad. Nureddin believed that the abuse

---

32   BOA, BEO 529/39639, 7 *Jumada al-Akhirah* 1312 (December 6, 1894).

33   BOA, BEO 529/39639, 7 *Jumada al-Akhirah* 1312 (December 6, 1894).

these people suffered was nothing more than a display of power by the *mufti*, the *nakib* and the district governor in Hilla, and yet it still betrayed the locals' trust in the government. According to him, the dismissal of the district governor had already been requested, following a complaint to the high levels of government that revealed the corruption of the Hilla governor, *mufti*, and the *nakib*'s trustee. However, as the governor and the *nakib* protected these people, they were not given a hard time. Nureddin stated that the governor Paşa commented on this second issue, and even though the brothers had nothing to do with it, the governor put the blame on them, thus paving the way to their exile to Mosul. For three years since the 1892 injustice, they had been living in difficult conditions, facing financial difficulties and could not receive any responses to their petitions or appeals. Nureddin was now more than 60 years old and requested that the injustice should be righted.[34]

In truth, what Nureddin wrote was not unreasonable. Moreover, this telegram helps us discover how Nureddin's connection to the petition, mentioned at the beginning of our essay, was established or tried to be established. As it turns out, neither Nureddin nor his brother was among the people who claimed they were wronged by the district governor of Hilla. However, Nureddin's position parallels the Arabic petition sent to the central government with sixty-eight signatures, and he narrates the incident in a similar manner. This reinforces the possibility that he had been present while the Arabic petition was composed. Then why did he not share earlier the particulars to which he was privy? Was he afraid that the central administration would sense that he held the same position as the other petitioners? We do not know the answers to these questions, but it is obvious that the hostilities between the governor, the *mufti*, the *nakib* and Nureddin had begun two years before the Samarra Incident of 1894. Moreover, the enquiry of the State Council proved Nureddin was right. However, the governor Paşa knew very well the political meaning of a Shi'a-Sunni conflict and the apprehension it would cause the central government. Consequently, it is probable that he exiled Nureddin on the charges that he instigated sectarian conflict and unrest in society. According to Şemsettin Sami's *Kâmus al-'Alâm*, the population of Hilla, except for a thousand Jews, was almost entirely made up of Muslims: half were Sunni and half Shi'a. In other words, any sectarian conflict could have dire consequences. After all, Hilla in 1894 was one of the six residential centers in Iraq and home to more than a thousand Ottoman soldiers.[35] According to the annals of the Baghdad province,

---

34   BOA, BEO 529/39639, 7 *Jumada al-Akhirah* 1312 (December 6, 1894).

35   Herzog, *Osmanische Herrschaft und Modernisierung im Irak*, 264. According to Herzog, the numbers of soldiers in the aforementioned centers were as follows: Baghdad (4714),

it was classified as a *sanjak* between the years 1874 and 1893 and was made into a *kaza* connected to the *sanjak* of Divaniye only in 1894.[36]

On the other hand, as his persistent appeals yielded no satisfactory results even after the financial wrongdoing he suffered was uncovered, it is also possible that Nureddin had specific political reasons to support the campaign against the *mufti* following the Samarra Incident. The governor never stated that Ibrahim and Nureddin signed any of the petitions he forwarded earlier to the imperial center. Indeed, he linked the two events merely by mentioning them one after the other. None of the correspondence includes any assertion that Nureddin and Ibrahim were involved in the 1894 petition signed by sixty-eight signatories and sent to Istanbul. The only reason to think of a link was that, as mentioned above, Nureddin advanced the same thesis in a similar language in one of his most recent telegrams. It is even more interesting that the central government did not dwell on this connection either.

The efforts of Basra's influential notables to pressure the local government by encouraging the community to write petitions and to send telegrams to the central government had important consequences, and local administrators lost their jobs.[37] Therefore, it is also possible that Nureddin and Ibrahim penned the petition themselves, had it signed by the community, and then sent it to the center. Regardless, the brothers' persistence resulted in hardening the governor's attitude against them. The governor emphasized once again that the brothers belonged to the "notorious and seditious crew" whose provocations in Hilla, he claimed, had given rise to "conflict between the Shi'a and the Sunni and upset civic order". He felt no need to provide further explanations in arguing that they should not be allowed to return to Baghdad.[38] The reason he put forward was apparently important enough in the eyes of the central government.

For quite some time, the brothers did not achieve any results with their petitions, and Hasan Paşa's attitude did not soften either. However, towards the end of 1895, the situation began to change. A correspondence sent from Baghdad to the

---

Mosul (2066), Nasiriyah (1763), Kirkuk (1772) and Hillah (1002).

36   Tahir Sezen, *Osmanlı Yer Adları Sözlüğü* (Ankara: Devlet Arşivleri Genel Müdürlüğü Yayınları, 2017), 350.

37   Burcu Kurt, *Osmanlı Basra'sında Devlet ve Toplum 1908-1914* (İstanbul: Küre Yayınları, 2015), 40-1; Albert Hourani, "Ottoman Reform and the Politics of Notables," in *Beginnings of Modernization in the Middle East*, eds. William R. Polk et al. (Chicago: The University of Chicago Press, 1968), 47-8.

38   *BOA, BEO* 529/39639, 7 *Jumada al-Akhirah* 1312 (December 6, 1894).

Ministry of Interior Affairs does reiterate that Nureddin and Ibrahim had been "of the seditious group" and that they were responsible for the conflict between Hilla's Shi'a and Sunni inhabitants by inciting unrest while being transferred from Hilla to Divaniye. This in fact was the reason behind their exile to Mosul. However, a correspondence sent from Mosul to Baghdad described Nureddin as having "pulled himself together" and sought permission to pardon them and to allow them to return to Baghdad. The governor of Baghdad also reported the situation to the central government. More than a year later, during which Governor Hasan Paşa's attitude somehow softened, he decided to forward Mosul's request directly to the Ministry of Internal Affairs instead of rejecting it. The ministry took up the matter approximately ten days later. As soon as Nureddin learned about the change in the governor's attitude and of his communication with Istanbul that could enable his return to Baghdad, he sent within days another telegram from Mosul to the Grand Vizierate. Nureddin stated that he knew of the letter recently sent from Baghdad about his situation and added that his illness was worsening with each passing day, threatening his life. He did not want to miss the opportunity that took so much effort to bring about. He wrote that it was already October, the weather was getting colder, and that he awaited being pardoned and allowed to hopefully return to his hometown.[39]

Finally, Nureddin and Ibrahim's situation took a turn for the better, when Hasan Paşa's attitude, the greatest obstacle preventing their return to Baghdad, changed. Yet things would not go altogether smoothly. Even though the province of Mosul had requested Nureddin's pardon in writing, the central government was still worried about a possible sectarian conflict, as Hasan Paşa had repeatedly warned them. The Grand Vizierate ordered the Ministry of Internal Affairs to conduct a thorough investigation into whether the brothers' return to Baghdad carried any economic and political risks. The final information we have about this case is in this detailed investigation conducted upon the request of the Grand Vizierate. The investigation also served as a summary of Nureddin's case, which had been going on for some time. The findings fully corroborated Nureddin's account of the unlawful confiscation of his property due to the bail issue, and the antagonism between him and the local administrators of the province of Baghdad. The State Council affirmed Nureddin's claims and reached the conclusion that the actions of the provincial government were unlawful.[40]

---

39   *BOA, BEO* 702/52626, 23 *Jumada al-Awwal* 1313 (November 11, 1895).
40   *BOA, BEO* 702/52626, 23 *Jumada al-Awwal* 1313 (November 11, 1895).

According to the investigation of the Ministry of the Interior, Nureddin's *muqataa* worth 5.000 liras was confiscated and sold as a surety for the 67.000 *kuruş* he owed for sponsoring a *mültezim*. A year's revenue brought by the crops on Nureddin's field that had been confiscated and sold was sufficient to pay off his debt. Besides, the central government determined that, because Nureddin's immovable property was sold in a hurry, there was clearly local corruption involved on the part of the local debt enforcement officers. The government agreed that Hamza Ağazade Nureddin should be given his property and belongings back. At the same time, the government officials worried that this corruption could create an environment of financial insecurity, which, in turn, would adversely affect the property sales of other *mültezim*s as well. The Ministries of Finance and Justice were ordered to take the necessary action. Just when the issue of the lands was resolved, the June 3, 1894 Arabic petition sent from Hilla with sixty-eight signatories, suddenly resurfaced. The officials of the central government, without questioning the contradictions in the statements of the Baghdad Governorate, relayed the situation as it was. According to them, the motive behind the issue of signatures was a scheme devised by Emin Efendi, the head of the Criminal Court, and Abdülnâfî Efendi, the Naib of Hilla, who had real estate in Hilla; the "Sunni-Shi'a" details were included later, in order to exaggerate the issue. Just as Iranians accused of sectarian instigations were banished from the country by the Iranian Consulate, the Baghdad Province declared that people from the 'local Shi'a' such as Nureddin and Ibrahim needed to be banished as well. They were thus transferred to the town of Köysancak in Mosul, then to city of Mosul itself. At every opportunity, the Nureddin and İbrahim brothers kept requesting their return to Baghdad. However, their wishes to return to Baghdad were not accepted. After a period of approximately a year and a half, the Mosul province relayed to the Baghdad province and the latter to Istanbul that the brothers had reformed themselves and should be pardoned.[41] In the end, the likelihood that Nureddin and Ibrahim were pardoned is as high as that of the contrary. It does seem more likely that the brothers' return to Baghdad was made possible thanks to Mosul governor's mediation, and the fact that Baghdad governor's attitude had softened in the year and a half since the Samarra incident.

Instead of a Conclusion

Singular events, although recorded in time and place, are not isolated. They arise in a context and therefore provide information on the context in which they be-

---

41   *BOA, BEO* 702/52626, 23 *Jumada al-Awwal* 1313 (November 11, 1895).

long. In other words, one person's story gives clues as to what kind of stories others might experience since individuals who move in a social space--even if they move according to their interests—need to establish reasonable relationships with other members of society. The goal of this study is to arrive at a conclusion regarding the 'reasonable' or 'probable' relationships that Shi'a citizens might have established with government administrators. Nureddin and Ibrahim, the focus of this study, were two Shi'a subjects of the Ottoman Empire living in Iraq who were rich enough to act both as bailsmen for the tax farmers of state lands as well as being *muqataa* holders themselves.[42] The brothers were informed about the administrative and legal procedures of the Ottoman state and claimed their rights through all official channels available to them. In searching for help in the higher echelons of bureaucracy, they did not refrain from reporting the unlawful acts of the local administration to the central government and pointing to corruption. The two were acquainted with the conventions of communication with government officials and used appropriate manners and etiquette in their correspondence. They were also persistent. They sent telegrams to the central government repeatedly, more than fifty of them. In this regard, Nureddin and Ibrahim's Shi'a affiliations do not seem to have changed anything. Ibrahim and his older brother Nureddin were also aware of the political conflicts in the province they lived in, and they were enterprising and resourceful.

In one of their petitions, Nureddin and Ibrahim also reminded the higher echelons of the government about the differences between the executive and judicial branches of government. It is true that in the Ottoman Empire the principle of the separation of powers between the executive and judicial branches had been put into effect in the 1870s, especially when provincial administration was being formalized. The Constitution of 1876 clearly articulated this separation, and civilian governors were banned from receiving petitions on judicial matters. However, what the two brothers did not know was how, in the times and places where political authority became fragile, the state could turn a blind eye to the violation of the rule of separation of powers so that administrative officials could establish authority.[43]

---

42 The *iltizam* system was repealed with the Tanzimat reforms, however it was reinstated after a short time because of loss of tax revenue. Hanioğlu, *A Brief History of the Late Ottoman Empire*, 88-90. Could Nureddin's situation that seemingly originated due to a financial matter be related to the removal of local *muqata'a* holders? This possibility is not far-fetched, however neither the local nor the central government officials make reference to such.

43 Avi Rubin, *Ottoman Nizamiye Courts: Law and Modernity in the Ottoman Empire* (New York: Palgrave Macmillan, 2011), 38-41.

Another noteworthy detail in the petitions is how Nureddin and Ibrahim identified as reference the high-ranking Ottoman officers with whom they must have worked. They mentioned the names of Sırrı Paşa, the governor of Diyarbekir and senior officer of the Imperial Army, Celaleddin Paşa, the former *mutasarrıf* of Hilla, and Mahmud Reşid Paşa and Mahmud Bey, former governors of Bitlis. However, it is strange that their correspondence contains no information as to whether any of these men were actually consulted in the process.

As governor Hasan Refik Paşa also asserted, framing an issue as a social conflict between the Shi'a and the Sunni in the province of Baghdad in the 1890s could exacerbate it. If Hasan Paşa was telling the truth, the Iranian Consul in Baghdad also worried about the outbreak of a sectarian conflict in Iraq. The case of Nureddin dates back to the beginning of 1892. But the event that caused their banishment to Mosul, or was shown as a justification for it, was an extension of the Samarra Incident of 1894.

Apparently, the effects of this incident had spread to Hilla. The mistreatment of the Shi'a in Samarra disturbed some of the Shi'a inhabitants of Hilla as well. Even though the State Council uncovered the financial wrongdoing that Nureddin suffered, the Ottoman government trusted instead the word of the governor of Baghdad, who did not hesitate to banish Nureddin to Mosul without investigating adequately his relation to the petition with the sixty-eight signatories. This was probably due to the heated atmosphere in Baghdad. However, it is impossible to rule out entirely the possibility that Nureddin was involved in the 1894 petition because the wrongdoing he suffered was not recompensed. Nevertheless, Hasan Paşa, determined to send Nureddin and Ibrahim into exile, neither mentions whether the two brothers had signed the petition nor explains any relation they might have had to the petition. The governor merely states that it had been known for some time that the brothers instigated conflict between Hilla's Shi'a and Sunni inhabitants. This might mean that Nureddin and Ibrahim were exiled unjustly.

In the same vein, using Nureddin's sectarian affiliation as an adjective was a deliberate choice on the part of Hasan Paşa. This is an instance of using labelling for political ends. In the early letters he sent to Istanbul, Hasan Paşa called Nureddin simply by his name. However, after Nureddin's persistent petitions to the central government, the Paşa started identifying him as "Shi'a Nureddin," emphasizing his sectarian identity; the change was also a manifestation of his harsh attitude toward Nureddin. In return, the central government officials possibly adopted the label used by the Baghdad government as an individual identification. As for Nureddin, he never mentioned his sectarian affiliation in his correspondence with the state;

rather he referred to himself as a faithful Muslim. Undoubtedly both preferences were deliberate choices.[44]

A personal enmity between Nureddin and Hacı Hasan Refik Paşa seems unlikely. Based on his own observation, Stephen Longrigg describes Hasan Refik Paşa, who lived between 1834 and 1901, as 'an Istanbulite, portly and an old-school, devout man'.[45] The Paşa was a senior and highly respected person who held prominent posts during the time of Sultan Abdülaziz and who had been given significant duties during the time of Abdülhamid II. His high rank was the most important reason for his influence with the central government. Despite his advanced age, Hasan Refik Paşa was very active as the governor of Baghdad. However, he advocated balance instead of following the principle of "progress" by enacting extensive reforms. During his time in office, Baghdad was regarded as one of the calmest areas among the eastern provinces of the Ottoman Empire.[46] This might have been the reason behind his extremely cautious attitude towards Nureddin. The brothers must have been introduced to him--by someone he trusted--as individuals who had the opportunity and intention to cause a sectarian conflict in Hilla.

From another perspective, the case of "Shi'a Nureddin" is in line with other examples in historiography as well: as long as political order was maintained, Ottoman state officials did not feel the need to emphasize the sectarian differences. However, whenever a problem occurred, especially one of political disobedience, then the administrative style and discourse became sharper and sectarian differences were foregrounded in a negative manner. They became visible and pronounced.[47]

Then again, just as Nureddin and Ibrahim reproachfully pointed out in their petitions, were they not Ottomans? In truth, what colored the discourse of victimhood repeatedly used by these two Iraqi brothers from the local Shi'a community was their agency as much as their passivity and victimization. The fact that they gave various governors as their references and frequently sent telegrams to the

---

44 On the other hand, Nureddin referred to the governor of Baghdad Hasan Refik Paşa as Hasan Paşa in one petition, and as Hacı Hasan Paşa in another.

45 Stephen Hemsley Longrigg, *Four Centuries of Modern Iraq* (Oxford: Clarendon Press, 1925), 301.

46 Herzog, *Osmanische Herrschaft und Modernisierung im Irak*, 157-59.

47 Maurus Reinkowski, "Double Struggle No Income": Ottoman Borderlands in Northern Albania," *International Journal of Turkish Studies* 9 (2003): 239-53; Faruk Yaslıçimen, "Sunnism versus Shiism?," 153-67; Stefan Winter, *The Shiites of Lebanon under Ottoman Rule, 1516-1788* (Cambridge, New York: Cambridge University Press, 2010), 7-29.

central government is one of the indicators. Their persistent requests eventually received a response. They were transferred from Köysancak to Mosul and finally, with the mediation of the provincial officials, were able to see some progress towards receiving pardons. Concerning the financial wrongdoings in Baghdad, the State Council decided in Nureddin's favor. Furthermore, when Nureddin's rights were violated, he referred to involving other consulates in the issue and changing his nationality, which might have carried more than a purely rhetorical meaning. To a certain extent, Nureddin and Ibrahim must have considered all possible means to protect their interests. Of course, one must not forget that Nureddin and Ibrahim made a living by being *muqata*a holders, and that they had developed relationships with high-ranking officials as well. They had no other place to go, yet they trusted the central government more than the local authorities. The perception of central government as being more just, especially in the eyes of subjects living in distant lands, was not uncommon. The center was a reliable authority also due to the development of new communication technologies that broadened the potential of interaction between state and society. Ultimately, if the telegraph lines had not been laid, Nureddin and Ibrahim could not have sent so many telegrams to Istanbul and voiced their concerns and requests, and might not even have had a story like this!

Bibliography

Archive Sources

Başbakanlık Osmanlı Arşivi (BOA)
Bâb-ı Âlî Evrak Odası (BEO)
Dahiliye Nezareti Mektûbî Kalemi (DH.MKT)
Yıldız Perâkende Yaverân ve Maiyyet-i Seniyye Erkân-ı Harbiye Dairesi Evrakı (Y.PRK. MYD)
Yıldız Perâkende Askerî Marûzâtı (Y.PRK.ASK)
İrâde Husûsî (İ.HUS)

Secondery Sources

Afacan, Serhan. "Devletle Yazışmak: Türkiye ve İran Sosyal Tarihçiliğinde Dilekçeler." *Türkiyat Mecmuası* 21 (2011): 1-29.

Akiba, Jun. "The Local Councils as the Origin of the Parliamentary System in the Ottoman Empire." in *Development of Parliamentarism in the Modern Islamic World*, ed. S. Tsugitaka, 176-204 (Tokyo, 2009).

Çetinsaya, Gökhan. *The Ottoman Administration of Iraq, 1890-1908*. London: Routledge, 2006.

Çiçek, M. Talha. "Negotiating Power and Authority in the Desert: the Arab Bedouin and the Limits of the Ottoman State in Hijaz, 1840-1908." *Middle Eastern Studies* 52, no. 2 (2016): 260-279.

Douwes, Dick. *The Ottomans in Syria: A history of Justice and Oppression*. London, New York: I.B. Tauris, 2000.

Hanioğlu, Şükrü. *A Brief History of the Late Ottoman Empire*. Princeton: Princeton University Press, 2008.

Herzog, Christoph. *Osmanische Herrschaft und Modernisierung im Irak: Die Provinz Bagdad, 1817-1917*. Bamberg: University of Bamberg Press, 2012.

Hourani, Albert. "Ottoman Reform and the Politics of Notables." in *Beginnings of Modernization in the Middle East*, eds. William R. Polk and Richard L. Chambers, 41-68. Chicago: The University of Chicago Press, 1968.

İnalcık, Halil. "Osmanlı Padişahı." *Doğu Batı Düşünce Dergisi* 13, no. 54 (2010) (First printed version 1958): 9-20.

Kedourie, Elie. "The Iraqi Shi'is and Their Fate." in *Shi'ism, Resistance and Revolution*, ed. Martin Kramer, 135-57. Boulder, Colorado: Westview Press, 1987.

Köksal, Yonca. "Imperial Center and Local Groups: Tanzimat Reforms in the Provinces of Edirne and Ankara." *New Perspectives on Turkey* 27 (2002): 107-38.

Kurt, Burcu. *Osmanlı Basra'sında Devlet ve Toplum 1908-1914*. İstanbul: Küre Yayınları, 2015.

Litvak, Meir. *Shi'i Scholars of Nineteenth-century Iraq: The Ulama of Najaf and Karbala*. Cambridge: Cambridge University Press, 1998.

Longrigg, Stephen Hemsley. *Four Centuries of Modern Iraq*. Oxford: Clarendon Press, 1925.

Meyer, James. *Turks Across the Empire: Marketting Muslim Identity in the Russian-Ottoman Borderlands*. Oxford: Oxford University Press, 2014.

Pierce, Leslie. *Morality Tales: Law and Gender in the Ottoman Court of Aintab*. Berkeley, Los Angeles, London: University of California Press, 2003.

Reinkowski, Maurus. ""Double Struggle, No Income": Ottoman Borderlands in Northern Albania." *International Journal of Turkish Studies* 9 (2003): 239-53.

Rubin, Avi. *Ottoman Nizamiye Courts: Law and Modernity in the Ottoman Empire*. New York: Palgrave Macmillan, 2011.

Serbestoğlu, İbrahim. "Zorunlu Bir Modernleşme Örneği Olarak Osmanlı Tabiiyet Kanunu." *OTAM* 29 (2011): 193-214.

Sezen, Tahir. *Osmanlı Yer Adları Sözlüğü*. Ankara: Devlet Arşivleri Genel Müdürlüğü Yayınları, 2017.

Şemsettin Sami. *Kâmûs-u Türkî*. Dersaadet: İkdam Matbaası, 1317.

Winter, Stefan. *The Shiites of Lebanon under Ottoman Rule, 1516-1788*. Cambridge, New York: Cambridge University Press, 2010.

Yaslıçimen, Faruk. "Osmanlı Devleti'nin İran Eksenli Irak Siyaseti ve 19. Yüzyılda Bürokratik Bilgi Üretimi." in *Bilgi ve Toplum*, ed. M. Hüseyin Mercan. 301-38. İstanbul: İz Yayıncılık, 2013.

———. "Saving the Minds and Loyalties of Subjects: Ottoman Education Policy against the Spread of Shiism in Iraq during the Time of Abdülhamid II." *DÎVÂN* 21, no. 41 (2016): 63-108.

———. "Sunnism versus Shiism? Rise of the Shiite Politics and of the Ottoman Apprehension in Late Nineteenth Century Iraq." M. A. Thesis, Bilkent Üniversitesi, 2008.

Yılmaz, Fikret. "Zina ve Fuhuş Arasında Kalanlar: Fahişe Subaşı'ya Karşı." *Toplumsal Tarih* 220 (2012): 22-31.

Zürcher, Erik Jan. *Turkey: A Modern History*, revised edition. London: I.B. Tauris, 2004.

CHAPTER TWELVE

Why did Süreyya, Vasfı, Mehmed and İdris become Runaways? Thoughts on the Ottoman Education System by way of a Case of Truancy*

İsmail Yaşayanlar

Introduction

The development of the field of education and its institutionalization in the Ottoman Empire gained momentum during the reign of Mahmud II and continued through the Tanzimat reforms. Education during the Tanzimat period was dominated by modernist principles that triggered a paradigm shift during the reign of Abdülhamid II, when efforts were focused on not what education should be, or how it should be developed, but on what it should not be. The Tanzimat reformers had refrained from creating a synthesis between Islamic teachings and aspects of modernization, lending education a secular character, even if partially so. The positivist mindset adopted by the generations trained with such an educational outlook affected how Ottoman education was to be programmed and reshaped in the time of Abdülhamid II.[1]

In an empire, it was natural that education as an institution aimed to make the individual internalize the relationship between sovereignty-discipline and loyalty to power. As a matter of fact, while education provided children with opportunities

---

*   Bursa, 1901.

1   Selçuk Akşin Somel, *Osmanlı'da Eğitimin Modernleşmesi (1839-1908): İslâmlaşma, Otokrasi ve Disiplin*, translated from the English by Osman Yener (İstanbul: İletişim Yayınları, 2015), 22; Mehmet Ö. Alkan, "İmparatorluk'tan Cumhuriyet'e Modernleşme ve Ulusçuluk Sürecinde Eğitim," *Osmanlı Geçmişi ve Bugünün Türkiye'si*, Kemal Karpat, ed., translated from the English by Sönmez Taner (İstanbul: İstanbul Bilgi Üniversitesi Yayını, 2004), 195.

for socialization at an early age, it also created an environment that ensured they would grow up to be loyal to the empire and in harmony with the other members of the society.[2] Looking at it from this perspective, we might be convinced that it produced a discourse consistent with the Foucauldian approach. Yet in truth, the realities of the period worked in the same way for all multinational structures. Just like all other monarchies, the Ottoman monarchy also utilized education as a tool and tried to create ideal citizens through systematic indoctrination.[3] The ambition to create a 'submissive' citizen had not been a principal objective during the Tanzimat period, but it manifested itself in the Hamidian period, and even became a dominant element in the Ottoman education system.

During the period of Abdülhamid II, obedience legitimized through religion was chief among the constants that the educational curriculum had to incorporate from primary through secondary schooling.[4] Certainly this deep desire "to obey" did not arise randomly. The secessionist movements in the Balkans, together with the first signs of Arab nationalism as well as the presence of the Young Turks, who directly opposed Abdülhamid II, resulted in an autocratic intervention in the Ottoman education system.[5] The reduction in the number of science and history courses at schools affiliated with the Ministry of Education, the concomitant increase in the hours of religion and ethics courses, and even the requirement of some type of worship such as the *salaat* were all new steps taken to create a "pious" generation that was loyal to the sultan and loyal to the country.[6] This educated generation was also expected to produce the obedient officials needed by the state. The creation of a class of government officials who were capable bureaucrats and who believed in the sacredness of service was the most important responsibility of the teachers and the civilian high schools that proliferated in the provinces during the Hamidian period.[7]

---

2   Emine Ö. Evered, *Empire and Education Under the Ottomans. Politics, Reform and Resistance from the Tanzimat to the Young Turks* (New York: I.B. Tauris, 2012), 5-6, 12; Selim Deringil, *İktidarın Sembolleri ve İdeoloji II. Abdülhamid Dönemi (1876-1909)*, 108.

3   Deringil, *İktidarın Sembolleri*, 107

4   Alkan, "İmparatorluk'tan Cumhuriyet'e Modernleşme," 127.

5   Somel, *Osmanlı'da Eğitimin Modernleşmesi*, 24-5; İlhan Tekeli and Selim İlkin, *Osmanlı İmparatorluğu'nda Eğitim ve Bilgi Üretim Sisteminin Oluşumu ve Dönüşümü* (Ankara: Türk Tarih Kurumu Yayını, 1993), 76.

6   Alkan, "İmparatorluk'tan Cumhuriyet'e Modernleşme," 128, 133, 175; Necdet Sakaoğlu, *Osmanlı'dan Günümüze Eğitim Tarihi* (İstanbul: Istanbul Bilgi Üniversitesi Yayını, 2003), 113

7   Deringil, *İktidarın Sembolleri*, 110; Somel, *Osmanlı'da Eğitimin Modernleşmesi*, 154, 160, 227.

The Ministry of Education supervised the expansion of the network of schools, both at the center and in the provinces, that produced the citizens the sultan wished to cast in certain mold as well as the qualified civil service candidates. However, despite its significant charge, the Ministry did not occupy a prioritized status in the bureaucracy. Specifically, the provincial educational organizations were in a state of decay and even, from time to time, despair, while waiting for the funding allocated to them. This hopeless picture in the Ottoman education system did not change significantly throughout Abdülhamid II's reign. Funding allocations for provinces prioritized military and civilian institutions over schools.[8] This order of priorities among institutions or individuals revealed ruptures across the center-province relations, as well as in education. The formal supervisory mechanisms that were created through ordinances mostly remained in theory and non-functional. It was very difficult for the provinces to convey the problems experienced in educational institutions to the center. The offices, from the lowest ranked to the highest, tended to solve problems within their own means, and even to cover up issues and silence the complaining parties.

Starting with some cross-sections of ordinary lives, this study analyzes a rare incident[9] in the history of Ottoman education to provide a general assessment of the manner in which center-periphery relations were administered. The essay describes a chain of events that started with an incident of truancy and developed to reveal conflicts inside a provincial education administration. In between the lines, we will look for the answers to questions such as: How did center-periphery relations work in Ottoman bureaucracy? Did ordinary individuals influence the way history was written? Did the Ottoman Ministry of Education take interest in the corruption affecting the educational institutions under its supervision? Did the

---

8 Benjamin C. Fortna, *Mekteb-i Hümayûn. Osmanlı İmparatorluğu'nun Son Döneminde İslâm, Devlet ve Eğitim* (*Imperial Classroom: Islam, The State, and Education in the Late Ottoman Empire*, Oxford UP, 2002) translated from the English by Pelin Siral (İstanbul: İletişim Yayınları, 2005), 74.

9 Here we are not claiming that incidents that required detailed investigations were rare in Ottoman history. What we mean is the relative rarity of research conducted on such incidents. In this context, we can point to the examples of Benjamin Fortna's research on the profiling of students in Istanbul, the twenty-five high school students in Manastır who complained about their school management with a joint petition, and Eugene Rogan's research on a school administrator at the Mekteb-i Idadi in Damascus who drank alcohol at school and sexually abused the students. See Fortna, *Mekteb-i Hümayûn*, 192-5; Eugene L. Rogan, "The Political Significance of an Ottoman Education: Maktab 'Anbar Revisited," *From the Syrian Land to the States of Syria and Lebanon*, Thomas Phillip and Christopher Schumann, ed.s, (Würzburg: Ergon in Komission, 2004): 77-94.

central state deal with issues in provincial institutions in a solution-oriented way, or was it solely practicing bureaucracy?

How Did This Affair Come About?

On the second Thursday of November, 1901, Süreyya, Vasfi, Mehmed and İdris, four students of the Mekteb-i İdadi-i Mülki (Civilian High School)[10] in the İbrahimpaşa neighborhood of Bursa, were caught by the police right as they arrived in Mudanya to board a ship. They were sent back to Bursa and handed over to their school. While this incident that seemed like an ordinary case of truancy was being investigated, an ongoing problem between the school management and the provincial Directorate of Education surfaced. The reason why the truancy of Süreyya, Vasfi, Mehmed and İdris became the subject of correspondence between the Ministry of Education and the Province of Hudavendigâr was in essence not the act of truancy itself but the tension between Ahmed Muhtar Bey, *müdür-i sânî* (assistant principal) and Hasib Bey, the provincial Director of Education at the time. This tension turned the incident into a problem beyond the school, and investigations led to further investigations. When the Director of Education requested information about the truancy incident, he discovered that the school administration was overseeing the investigation. Hasib Bey doubted the neutrality of the school administration and decided that the truancy should be investigated by an independent entity. When he requested the formation of a new committee the chain of events started.[11]

---

10   The school began instruction in the Akif Paşa mansion in the Veli Şemseddin neighborhood of Bursa, on August 3, 1885 (R. July 22, 1301) under the name Mekteb-i İdadi-i Mülki, and it was one of the educational institutions founded within the framework of the educational reforms of the modernization period. Before moving to its new building in the Ibrahimpaşa neighborhood, the school was providing instruction in four grade levels. Later, with the addition of the *Rüşdiye* with three more grade levels, it moved to instruction in all seven grade levels starting in 1893. Until the years 1910-11, the school provided instruction as an *idadi* (high school). A decision of the Minister of Education at the time, Emrullah Efendi, changed 10 of the 92 high schools in Ottoman lands into "sultani" (imperial high school), at which time the school was given the name Bursa Mekteb-i Sultanisi. The school retained this title until the declaration of the Turkish Republic, and took on the name Bursa High School in 1923-24. Later it was also called Bursa Boys' High School and finally, Bursa Anatolian Boys' High School. *Hudâvendigâr Vilâyeti Sâlnâme-i Resmisi*, Def 'a 34 (Bursa: Matbaa-i Vilâyet, 1325): 329; Kamil Kepecioğlu, *Bursa Kütüğü* 3, Hüseyin Algül, ed. (Bursa: Bursa Büyükşehir Belediyesi Yayını, 2011), 78.

11   The runaway incident that inspired this article appeared in a document in a file of 62 pages on other various subjects on the Bursa Civilian High School at the State Ottoman Archives in the Ministry of Education Scribal Records. Clearly, this case, almost as

The members of the newly formed committee were Mustafa, teacher of *ulûm-ı diniyye* (religious sciences), Mehmed Said, teacher of *hüsn-i hat* (calligraphy) and Tevfik Efendi, teacher of *ulûm-ı riyaziye* (mathematics). Hasib Bey oversaw the committee deliberations. According to Hasib Bey, during Süreyya's interview, Assistant Principal Ahmed Bey entered the room,[12] took the student out of the room and, turning to the committee, said: "This investigation belongs only to the Assistant Principal, that is, to me, and there is no need to form such a committee." He then turned to the Director of Education and shouted: "You do not have the right and authority to intervene in this issue; you have started meddling with everything and have become a despot"[13] Disturbed by the incident, the Director of Education went to the provincial office When he returned a few hours later to check whether the investigation was still going on, no one opened the school gate to let him in. Even though Hasib asked the porter to open the gate, the latter's response was: "By the orders of the Assistant Principal Ahmed Bey, I cannot open the gate to the Director of Education, that is, to you." Hasib returned to the provincial office in a daze, and immediately penned a text addressed to the Ministry of Education, informing them of the incident.[14]

The unfinished testimony of Süreyya indicates that he was a fourteen-year old from Karahisar, and that his father was a doctor at the Gureba Hospital: in other words, Süreyya's family also lived in Bursa while the youngster was a boarder at the Mekteb-i Idadi. During the investigation, Süreyya linked his truancy to the difficulties he was experiencing with Sabri Efendi, first assistant principal. He stated that Sabri Efendi had sent him home at midnight and his father had brought him back to school the next day.[15] A similar complaint came from Vasfi, the second

---

voluminous as a binder, was made up of documents that should be reviewed in detail. This is because the case includes documents on different subjects, even though they all concern the same school. These documents are on the admission of students from Bilecik and Söğüt to the Bursa High School, the appointment of a French teacher to the Bursa High School, the beating of a student by Rıza Bey, one of the Assistant Principals of the Civilian High School, and finally the incident of the runaways and the conflict between the offices as its continuation, making up the most bulky part of the case. Başbakanlık Osmanlı Arşivi (BOA), *Maarif Nezâreti Mektûbî Kalemi Evrâkı (MF.MKT.)*, 596/4; Same document, Leaf 1, 25 Teşrinievvel 1317 (November 7, 1901).

12   Same document, Leaf 2, 25 Teşrinievvel 1317 (November 7, 1901); Same document, Leaf 3, 27 Teşrinievvel 1317 (November 7, 1901). We can see clearly that the interview was interrupted in the record of the interrogation of Süreyya. Same document, Leaf 5.

13   Same document, same leaf.

14   Same document, same leaf.

15   Same document, Leaf 5.

student who was interviewed. He was from Islimiye, eighteen years old at the time, and his father was a bailiff in Bursa. He also pointed to his constant arguments with Sabri Bey as the reason for his truancy. According to Vasfi, Sabri Efendi held him responsible for any and every incident that happened in the classroom. For this reason, he did not even want to remain in school anymore. Indeed, he had requested a release certificate, but when he was turned down because he did not have his father's permission, he resolved to run away.[16] The other members of the group were 15-year-old Mehmed from Bursa and 17-year-old İdris from Simav. Mehmed and İdris skipped school mostly to go along with their friends, and from the statements of both, it was clear that Vasfi and Süreyya were the leaders of the group.

The four boys claimed that they had not decided to skip school on an impulse, and it was clear that they had been considering it. Vasfi and Süreyya had together planned the escape and convinced Mehmed and İdris to join them. From Mehmed and İdris's statements, we understand that Süreyya and Vasfi convinced each separately, telling one, "We will go to Istanbul and work as scribes there", and the other, "We will make a living as apprentices." Yet, in his second interview, Vasfi stated that he ran away to attend the Baytar (veterinary school) or Darüşşafaka (secondary school for orphans) in Istanbul.[17]

After escaping from the bathhouse on Wednesday morning, the four friends decided to walk to Mudanya, even though there was a train that ran between Mudanya and Bursa in this period.[18] If they boarded the train, the gendarme would ask to see their *tezkere-i Osmani,* that is, their identity cards, and once he knew their ages, he would not allow the boys to travel and even might have figured out that they were runaways. The runaways followed the Nilüfer Çayı (creek) and took a rest in the village of Masharahasan.[19] Buying some bread there, they continued their journey, spending the night in the bushes on the outskirts of the village. In the morning, they arrived at the village of Kurşunlu after passing through the villages of Göynüklü and Altıntaş and spent the night there at the coffeehouse of Kostanti.[20]

---

16   Same document, Leaf 7.

17   Same document, Leaf 4.

18   The construction of the Bursa-Mudanya railway began in 1872 yet the line became operational in 1892. Most significantly, the railway afforded a much quicker and more comfortable trip across a distance that could previously be traversed in approximately two hours with horse carriages and landaus. Zeynep Dörtok Abacı, *Modernleşme Sürecinde Bursa Kenti'nin Mekansal ve Sosyal Değişimi (1860-1910)*, PhD dissertation, Uludağ Universitesi, 2005, 18-119.

19   The present-day Çağlayan Village.

20   Same document, Leaf 7.

The fact that the four had gone through Altıntaş to Kurşunlu was quite significant because it showed that Mudanya was not their intended destination at first. Indeed, to go to Mudanya they would have to walk west of Altıntaş and then across the village of Burgaz. That they did the exact opposite and turned towards Kurşunlu, in the direction of Gemlik, was proof that they had planned this route previously. Vasfi's own statements also backed this possibility. Vasfi was interviewed twice possibly because he was the eldest in the group. The interrogation reports that included records of the interviews were not dated; therefore, it is not possible for us to know how frequently they were recorded. Yet when we compare the two interrogation reports, we can see clearly that Vasfi's answers were contradictory at times. In his second interview, Vasfi stated that when they arrived at Kurşunlu, some sailboat owners offered to take them to Istanbul.[21] These were seamen who illegally transported passengers to Istanbul without a permit.[22] The fact that the runaways did not go towards Burgaz makes us think that they already knew of the practice in Kurşunlu and thus moved in the direction of Gemlik.

When asked, "Who would have taken you to Istanbul without a permit?", Vasfi stated that Nuri Bey, a chief in Kurşunlu, had promised to take them to Istanbul for one *mecidiye* per person. This was a significant detail, as it showed the presence of a passenger trafficking industry in the area.[23] Moreover, there are other records that support this information as well.[24] Given the price of one *mecidiye* per person, Vasfi, Süreyya, Mehmed and İdris must have thought better of it, talked among themselves and decided to go to Mudanya.[25] Considering that 1 *mecidiye* equaled 20 *kuruş* and that 1 *okka* of raisins was worth 2,1 *kuruş*, it does not seem possible for a student to readily pay such an amount of money to go to Istanbul.[26] Either

---

21 Same document, Leaf 4.

22 In the Ottoman State, persons who wished to travel to another place other than their birth place had to obtain a travel permit and carry it with them. In the 19th century, domestic travel permits were issued by the city administrators and court officials. The person who wanted to travel would obtain a note from the neighborhood *imam* on where he was headed, and for which purpose he was travelling. He would then present this to the *qadi*, and after paying the cost of the permit his documents would be prepared. Mübahat Kütükoğlu, "Mürur Tezkiresi," *DİA* 32 (2006): 60-1.

23 Same document, same leaf.

24 BOA, *Şûrâ-yı Devlet Evrâkı (ŞD.)*, 6/42, 15 Rebiyülevvel 1308 (October 29, 1890).

25 "...âhîren ba'zı mülâhazaya binâen Mudanya'ya 'azîmet etdik." BOA., *MF.MKT.*, 596/4, Leaf 4.

26 Şevket Pamuk, *Osmanlı İmparatorluğu'nda Paranın Tarihi* (İstanbul: Tarih Vakfı Yurt Yayınları, 1999), 235-6; Şevket Pamuk, *İstanbul ve Diğer Kentlerde 500 Yıllık Fiyatlar*

this or another disagreement must have led them to turn west once again and go to Mudanya via the village of Burgaz.

in his second testimony, Vasfi did not mention his plan to go to Istanbul without a passing permit at all; rather, as if he happened upon Kurşunlu randomly. He explained that he told his friends, "Wherever we go we will be caught; let's go to the village of Burgas from here, and after buying bread from there, let's go to Mudanya."[27] When they set out for Mudanya, the runaways were aware of their helplessness: since they did not have a permit, they could not board a ship. Perhaps because they had no other ideas or because, by then, they wanted to be caught, they decided to go to an inn in Mudanya to spend the night there. However, they needed to show their identity cards. Except for Vasfi, none of the boys was carrying his Ottoman identity card, so the innkeeper turned them away. After they came out of the inn and were walking in the direction of the town hall on the shoreline, they were caught by the gendarme corporal Harun and were taken to the police station. Their arrest by the gendarme was either a coincidence, or the innkeeper might have reported the four boys due to their suspicious behavior. During their statements at the police station, it was revealed that they were runaways and the next day they were sent back to Bursa, escorted by a gendarme supervisor in the same train that they had avoided the day before so as not to be caught.[28]

The events so far present us with two distinct types of relationships. The first is the teacher-pupil relationship, and the second, the supervisor-employee relationship. We have previously described the absolute obedience that was expected from the student in the Hamidian period. The two elements that would ensure such absolute obedience were regulations, and educators. Both elements had been programmed to control the student's life and to prevent any type of indoctrination by dissidents opposed to the sultan and the absolutist state that the sultan represented.[29] The other type of prominent relationship between the supervisor and the employee illustrates the superior-subordinate conflict. The most basic duties of the directors of education appointed to the provinces in the Hamidian period included preventing the distribution and recitation of subversive publications and keeping the Islamic

---

ve Ücretler 1469-1998 (Ankara: Başbakanlık Devlet İstatistik Enstitüsü Yayını, 2000), 172-3.

27   Same document, Leaf 7.

28   Same document, same leaf.

29   Fortna, *Mekteb-i Hümayûn*, 188-9.

schools under close supervision while improving them.[30] These two important duties were enforced through ordinances and gave a wide range of powers to the director of education. This power vested in the director of education must have caused a tension between Hasib Bey, the school administrations, and the teachers in the provincial education system.[31]

The Investigation Continues: Who Corrupted the Students?

While the investigation on the runaway students continued, the focus all of a sudden shifted. The tension between Hasib Bey, the Director of Education, and Ahmed Bey, the Assistant Principal, who crashed into the committee's room and removed Süreyya from the room while he was being questioned, had triggered a larger investigation that would overshadow the truancy of the four students. Hasib Bey, who had gone to the provincial office after Ahmed Bey's insults and was refused entry to the school upon his return two hours later, had penned a letter of complaint on the matter[32] and sent it to the *Meclis-i Kebir-i Maarif* (Great Assembly of Education), which reviewed the letter and decided that an investigation was warranted.[33] In line with this decision, it recommended that the Assistant Principal Ahmed Bey should be questioned.[34] As the new investigation included statements that showed the incident in a new light, the truancy took a backseat. Indeed, Vasfi was permitted to leave and was sent to Pazarköy where his family lived. Süreyya was transferred to a school in Istanbul.[35] As for Mehmed and İdris, they stayed on at the school, and were even consulted for their statements as witnesses in the investigation.

In his deposition dated January 19, 1902, Hasib Bey stated that the school principal Hamid Bey was on leave in Istanbul, and although he was required to leave the Assistant Principal as his deputy, he left Ahmed Efendi, the school's purchasing officer, in his stead. Hasib Bey also stated that Ahmed Efendi did not report the truancy incident to the Directorate of Education and appealed directly to the police administration, and that he learned of this incident from Assistant Principal Sabri Bey when he stopped by the school, just like he did every day. He added that

---

30   Bayram Kodaman, *Abdülhamid Devri Eğitim Sistemi* (İstanbul: Ötüken Neşriyat, 1980), 81; Somel, *Osmanlı'da Eğitimin Modernleşmesi*, 144.

31   Somel, *Osmanlı'da Eğitimin Modernleşmesi*, 28-9.

32   Same document, Leaf 3, 27 Teşrinievvel 1317 (November 9, 1901).

33   Same document, the copy of the decision on the other side of the same leaf, 17 Teşrinisani 1317 (November 30, 1901).

34   Same document, Leaf 6, 11 Kânunuevvel 1317 (December 24, 1901).

35   Same document, Leaf 59, 13 Kânunusani 1317 (January 26, 1902).

he immediately created a committee under the leadership of the Deputy Principal there. He requested the committee to investigate the issue after he heard from the runaway students that the reason for their truancy was the oppressive conduct of Second Principal Ahmed Bey and Assistant Principal Sabri Bey. This was also why he did not include anyone from the school administration in the committee. Hasib Bey then described how Ahmet Bey interrupted the committee meeting, shouting, "This is my duty, I got permission from the governor," and then insulting Hasib Bey. However, from this point on in his deposition, some of Hasib Bey's claims did not match the testimony of other parties and witnesses. Indeed, not a single witness could be found to corroborate Hasib Bey's claim that, when he returned from the governor's office and was refused entry to school, approximately fifteen students whistled and jeered at him, instigated by Ahmed Bey.[36]

It was also clear from some of his statements during the investigation that Hasib Bey had personal problems with the Assistant Principal Ahmed Bey. Tension between the two were indicated by his statements that "he had not even seen him pray," that "Ahmet Bey was strolling outside the mosque even during Ramadan prayers," and that "it was absurd for Ahmet Bey to be teaching students history and ethics when he was so morally weak himself".[37] The Director's allegations were not surprising, because the notion of obedience at the core of the Hamidian educational philosophy required piety and good morals. The students would be pious and of good morals, that is, obedient, only if the teachers served as role models for their pupils by being "pious and of good morals" themselves.[38] Hasib Bey was trying to prove that Ahmed Bey was not a pious person. He went even further and asked some of Ahmet Bey's subordinates to confirm that "Ahmed Bey shouted at him" and that "the students jeered at him." Naturally, the dynamics of the supervisor-employee relationship cast a shadow over the truthfulness of these statements. Indeed, the subordinates either resorted to equivocations or stated that they did not witness any type of incident.[39]

---

36   Same document, Leaf 52, 6 Kânunusani 1317 (January 19, 1902).

37   Same document, Leaf 53, 7 Kânunusani 1317 (January 20, 1902).

38   Somel, *Osmanlı'da Eğitimin Modernleşmesi*, 231.

39   Same document, same leaf, the statements of the accounting official Mehmed Şükrü of the Directorate of Education in the Hudavendigâr Province and Hasan Bey, the correspondence officer, 7 Kânunusani 1317 (January 20, 1902). Same document, Leaf 54, the statement of the correspondence officer Hüseyin Hasan Bey in the Directorate of Education in the Hudavendigâr Province, 8 Kânunusani 1317 (January 21, 1902).

FIGURE 12.1 Bursa Mekteb-i Idadi-i Mülki (Abdul-Hamid II collection of photographs of the Ottoman Empire, Library of Congress Archives).

When we consider Ahmed Bey's account of the events, a completely different picture emerges, and one that several witnesses supported. After the truant students were delivered to the school, Ahmed Bey claimed that the Deputy Principal Ahmed Efendi asked him to conduct the investigation, and that when he started questioning the students, Hasib Bey crashed into the Principal's office, and humiliated him saying, "You cannot handle this job!" and "This is not your job!"- statements that the students could also hear. Several other teachers who were in the other room overheard Hasib Bey as well. Then Ahmed Bey left the room and went to the provincial administration and was verbally ordered by the governor to personally conduct the investigation. Upon his return to school, he learned that Hasib Bey had created a new committee, saying, "I talked to the governor; this is my duty, who is this committee made up of and why are they interfering with my job?" As Hasib Bey was leaving the school to speak to the governor, he told the porter: "The school gate will not be opened even to the Director of Education until the school principal arrives".[40]

40 Same document, Leaf 55, 10 Kânunusani 1317 (January 23, 1902). Same document, Leaf 56, 10 Kânunusani 1317 (January 23, 1902).

Although the sequence of events in Ahmet Bey's version overlaps with the one Hasib Bey described, the slanderous party in the incident turns out to Hasib Bey. Several witnesses corroborated Ahmet Bey's version: members of the investigating committee made up of Hasib Bey; Mehmed and İdris, the runaway students; the porter Salih; the scribe and administrative officer; and assistant principals Ali Rıza, Ziya and Sabri.[41] No one had witnessed Ahmed Bey insulting Hasib Bey or students booing the Director of Education, instigated by Ahmed Bey. Both the students and the porter confirmed that when Hasib Bey was refused entry, no one had seen or heard any students showing disrespect toward the Director of Education.[42]

The employees in the Department of Education as well as the school staff and teachers challenged Hasib Bey's claims, and this, in a way, indicated their courage. The Director of Education had the authority to dismiss all personnel working under his supervision; furthermore, if he suspected in the least that a teacher was engaged in political activities, he could dismiss the teacher as well.[43] This much authority created a culture of fear in both the school and the organization at large. And yet both the personnel and the teachers took a common stance against their supervisor, which can be seen as an indirect indicator of the problem experienced in the province.

Ahmed Bey mounted a counterattack against Hasib Bey's accusations during the proceedings, and his information was corroborated by other deputy principles on duty at the school as well. We learn from these statements that Hasib Bey was involved in a few other incidents at this school. In the first incident, he requested exam questions from some teachers and held "special" examinations for some students

---

41 Same document, Leaf 57, The statement of Ahmed Efendi, clerk and administrative official, 12 Kânunusani 1317 (January 25, 1902). Same document, Leaf 57, The statement of Assistant Principal Ali Rıza Efendi, 12 Kânunusani 1317 (January 25, 1902). Same document, Leaf 58, the statement of Assistant Director Ziya Efendi, 12 Kânunusani 1317 (January 25, 1902). Same document, Leaf 59, the statement of Assistant Principal Sabri Efendi, 13 Kânunusani 1317 (January 26, 1902). Same document, same leaf, the statement of the runaway student Mehmed Efendi, 13 Kânunusani 1317 (January 26, 1902). Same document, leaf 60, the statement of the runaway student İdris, 13 Kânunusani 1317 (January 26, 1902). Same document, same leaf, the statement of the custodian, Salih Ağa, 13 Kânunusani 1317 (January 26, 1902).

42 Same document, same leaf, the statements of the runaway student Mehmed Efendi, 13 Kânunusani 1317 (January 26, 1902). Same document, Leaf 60, the statement of the runaway student İdris, 13 Kânunusani 1317 (January 26, 1902). Same document, same leaf, the statement of the custodian Salih Ağa, 13 Kânunusani 1317 (January 26, 1902).

43 Somel, *Osmanlı'da Eğitimin Modernleşmesi*, 30; Kodaman, *Abdülhamid Devri Eğitim Sistemi*, 80.

without the knowledge of the teachers or the school administration, and thanks to these exams, the students were able to graduate. When the administration objected to the exams, Hasib Bey did not refrain from deflecting the issue by saying "These students are my such-and-such relatives." His conduct earned him a warning from the Minister of Education.[44] In the second incident, Hasib Bey used the school budget set aside for repairs to get his own house repaired and a large birdcage installed in his garden. This occurred at a time when the stairs and floors at the school needed repair—the floor of one of the classrooms had completely rotted away—and the staff had requested funds from the provincial Directorate of Education. Although Hasib Bey had promised to send an inspector, this official never showed up. Later the school received some lumber of dubious quality that turned out to have been stored wet for a long time. Ahmed Bey and Assistant Principal Ziya Efendi claimed that the lumber was purchased at a much higher price than its worth from a store owned by Hasib Bey's father-in-law.[45]

The Investigation Pivots: What was the main issue?

With new claims emerging, the investigation changed its course completely, and this time a new committee was formed to investigate the issues between Ahmed Bey and Hasib Bey. This committee included the then-mayor of Bursa Ahmed Bey, the provincial accountant for pietistic foundations, Mahmud Efendi, one member of the provincial administrative assembly, and, the assembly scribe Cemil Bey.[46] The investigation began in mid-July, 1902, and since it targeted the Director of Education, the first interview was conducted with Ahmed Bey, who had brought forth the claims about Hasib Bey.[47] Ahmed Bey's answers were similar to his previous statement, and even included more detailed information from time to time. For example, he gave the names and ID numbers of the students who took Hasib Bey's exams (Mustafa Efendi, no. 731 and Rauf Efendi, no. 231), and added that the exams were administered "at night". Even though these exams were invalidated by

---

44 Same document, Leaf 56, the statement of the Second Principal Ahmed Bey, 10 Kânunusani 1317 (January 23, 1902). Same document, Leaf 57, the statement of Assistant Principal Ali Rıza Efendi, 12 Kânunusani 1317 (January 25, 1902). Same document, Leaf 58, the statement of Assistant Director Ziya Efendi.

45 Same document, Leaf 56, the statement of the Second Principal Ahmed Bey, 10 Kânunusani 1317 (January 23, 1902). Same document, Leaf 58, the statement of Assistant Director Ziya Efendi.

46 Same document, Leaf 10, 30 Nisan 1318 (May 13, 1902).

47 Same document, Leaf 24, 18 Haziran 1318 (July 1, 1902).

the school administration, the Director of Education, Ahmet Bey claimed, ensured that both students graduated and received their diplomas.[48]

In the interview with Hasib Bey, who was now the main subject of the investigation, he was asked about the construction of the "bird cage," described at length in the investigation records. Other questions inquired about his purchase of lumber from his father-in-law. His responses to these questions and the witness testimonies he brought forward revealed that this matter was not as serious as claimed by Ahmed Bey.[49] However, his response concerning his administration of independent exams to students was not deemed satisfactory. Hasib Bey had said, "This matter has been resolved in correspondence with the Ministry of Education; if you would like, I can present a copy of each communication."[50] The committee then considered the communications concerning the exam and found that there was indeed a problem. Although the facts were somewhat different from those provided by Ahmet Bey, Hasib Bey's attitude towards the issue was problematic.

Before Mustafa and Rauf could graduate, they still had to take three exams that were scheduled for August 2, 1901. On that same day, the students had to take the placement exam for the Mekteb-i Mülkiye-i Şahane in Istanbul; therefore, the Ministry of Education recommended that, as a favor to these students, makeup graduation exams should be given to them a day earlier. This solution was communicated in a letter sent to the Hudavendigâr Directorate of Education, but Hasib Bey decided to solve the matter on his own and administered the exams himself. However, in the correspondence that the Ministry of Education received, the situation was presented differently. Hasib Bey stated that, consistent with regulations, he had informed the school administration about the exam, but there was no written communication to that effect. Moreover, on that same day, he had sent one of the teachers who was supposed to proctor the makeup exams to serve as examiner at another school. At the same time, he communicated with the Ministry that the students had been notified, but when the teachers did not arrive to give the exam on the day and time specified, he had administered the exam himself so that the students would not be disadvantaged.[51]

---

48 Same document, Leaf 28, 30 Haziran 1318 (July 13, 1902).

49 Same document, Leaf 30, 2 Temmuz 1318 (July 15, 1902). Same document, Leaf 31, the statement of Mustafa Efendi who worked in fiduciary service in the construction of the High School, 2 Temmuz 1318 (July 15, 1902).

50 Same document, Leaf 30, 2 Temmuz 1318 (July 15, 1902).

51 Same document, Leaf 34, the report of the investigation committee, 9 Temmuz 1318 (July 22, 1902).

This unconventional exam administered by Hasib Bey even became a news item in *Servet,* one of the newspapers of the period. A piece published in the issue no. 1156 dated August 14, 1901, described that the "honorable Hasib Efendi" administered the make-up exam at a time when the actual examiner had to be present at another school, and made sure to secure the Minister of Education's certification of the exam results so as to prevent procedural irregularities.[52]

The fact that a provincial Director of Education acted in such an independent way, and even made up some correspondence, is extremely significant for it shows the functional weaknesses of the education system. Indeed, in Ottoman education, the matter of inspections had been pushed to the background.[53] The director at the head of the provincial education system was also the inspector for the educational institutions under his supervision. When we consider the problems between the head of the organization and the lower ranks, it is apparent that this situation presented a serious challenge.[54] The absence of inspectors who would travel from the center to the provinces at regular intervals paved the way to arbitrary implementations in the provinces, conflicts between offices, and perhaps most importantly, disruptions in teaching and learning. As inspectors, the directors of education were chiefly responsible for taking preventive measures against politically divisive materials and unethical behavior in schools.[55] "Inspection" was understood as forestalling negative attitudes towards the state and the Sultan who represented it. This obsessive mindset is indicative of the state's effort to control institutions rather than ensuring their proper operation and improving them through a centralized organization. The Hamidian concern that the Tanzimat education system had created a disobedient and disloyal generation appears to have persisted into the first years of the 20th century.[56]

When the investigators realized that there was indeed corruption, they conveyed the situation to the Ministry of Education with a report.[57] In the meantime, Hasib Bey sent a letter to Mahmud Efendi, one of the committee members conducting their final interviews. In this letter, he denied the allegations against him, describing himself as an extremely hardworking employee who especially prioritized religious

---

52 *Servet,* no. 1156, 1 Ağustos 1317 (August 14, 1901), 3.

53 Kodaman, *Abdülhamid Devri Eğitim Sistemi,* 97; Somel, *Osmanlı'da Eğitimin Modernleşmesi,* 142.

54 Kodaman, *Abdülhamid Devri Eğitim Sistemi,* 99.

55 Fortna, *Mekteb-i Hümayûn,* 127-8.

56 Alkan, "İmparatorluk'tan Cumhuriyet'e Modernleşme," 195.

57 Same document, Leaf 36, 27 Temmuz 1318 (August 9, 1902).

and moral education, and stating that all of the administrators and teachers in the Mekteb-i İdadi were against him and therefore slandered his name.[58] Contrary to his claims, Head Assistant Principal Ali Rıza and the other assistants, Ziya and Sabri, accused Hasib Bey when questioned by the committee, and complained of being treated as liars.[59] During this time the Hudavendigâr province received a letter from the Ministry of Education that had reviewed the report of the committee. The letter stated that the exam administered by Hasib Bey was illegal and ordered all exams henceforth to be administered under the supervision of the teacher who taught the particular subject.[60]

While the investigation was nearing its end, three students from the Mekteb-i İdadi penned a letter on behalf of the 3rd, 4th and 5th graders and sent it to the Ministry of Education. This shed further light on the situation. According to the letter, their peer who last year took, the entrance exam for the Mekteb-i Mülkiye-i Şahane in Istanbul had ranked in first place; their peer who took the same exam this year ranked in second place; and those taking the exam next year would, in the best scenario, rank third or fourth, since the quality of education at the school had deteriorated significantly. The students pointed to the ongoing tension between the Director of Education and the school administration in the past year as the main cause of this deterioration. The teachers could no longer pay attention to their courses or their students because they spent most of their time discussing how to respond to the investigation concerning the Director of Education. Since they worked together, none dared filing a report against another. The students had registered their complaints to the administration via their parents, but the Director of Education, knowing that the weakness in administration resulted from his own incompetence and unauthorized practices, turned a deaf ear. For both the Director of Education and the school administration, the only issue that mattered was proving that they were right. Therefore, the main focus of education, the "students," was ignored while the administrators and teachers had turned their respective positions into areas of conflict.[61]

Ali, Ahmed and Mehmed, expressed their feelings, their experience and their concerns for the future, and their only wish was to see "their school reach the previous rating, their honor and good name preserved, and their curriculum deliv-

---

58   Same document, Leaf 38, 29 Ağustos 1318 (September 11, 1902).

59   Same document, Leaf 40, 30 Ağustos 1318 (September 12, 1902); Same document, Leaf 41, 10 Eylül 1318 (September 23, 1902).

60   Same document, Leaf 43, 10 Eylül 1318 (September 23, 1902).

61   Same document, Leaf 48-49, 15 Eylül 1318 (September 28, 1902).

ered properly."[62] We do not know if this candid letter, written in an extremely eloquent and candid style, made a difference. However, a month after its composition, the Minister of Education, who understood that the issue would not be resolved through local committees, sent an inspector from Istanbul to Bursa to investigate the incident.[63] Halid Bey, Inspector for Non-Muslim and Foreign Schools, arrived in Bursa in November 1902,[64] and conducted another investigation. Unfortunately, we have not been able to find the details of this investigation, but we do know its conclusions. It recommended to the *Meclis-i Kebir-i Maarif* (Great Assembly of Education) that the Hasib Bey should be demoted and appointed as education director to

FIGURE 12.2 Students of the Bursa Mekteb-i İdadi-i Mülki (Abdul-Hamid II collection of photographs of the Ottoman Empire, Library of Congress Archives).

another province. The decision made by the Great Assembly included information on other complaints about Hasib Bey during his previous appointment at the province of *Cezayir-i Bahr-i Sefid* (the Islands of the Mediterranean Sea). He caused disturbances there as well, and especially in the Island of Lesbos, where reports were filed both by the employees of the school and by the community, claiming that he intervened in the administration of the Mekteb-i İdadi, and engaged in inappropriate and loose behavior with the students.[65] The text penned by the Great Assembly issued a decision concerning Assistant Principal Ahmed (Muhtar) Bey as well. Ahmed Bey had done his job well until then and acted to protect the interests of the school. However, it was decided that he would receive an admonition so

---

62 Same document, Leaf 50, 15 Eylül 1318 (September 28, 1902).

63 Same document, Leaf 62, 10 Teşrinievvel 1318 (October 23, 1902).

64 *BOA., MF.MKT.*, 671/23, 14 Teşrinievvel 1318 (October 27, 1902).

65 *BOA., MF.MKT.*, 678/49, 31 Kânunuevvel 1318 (January 13, 1903).

that he would not engage again in negative behavior such as refusing entry to a Director of Education.[66]

Instead of a Conclusion: What became of them?

The incident we described above, fit for a short film or story, enables us to evaluate the Ottoman education system and its intra-organizational connections at the beginning of the 20th century in the context of center-province relations. In provincial cities, intra-organizational and inter-organizational relations usually proceeded with an eye to keeping the superior-subordinate ranks in place. Unless there was an issue that necessitated appeals, the central administration did not learn about misconduct or injustices. Ordinary individuals, unless their names were recorded in historical sources, did not have any influence in the chronicling of institutional history. The central administration only took an interest when it became aware of the corruption in educational institutions. In other words, there needed to be a concrete problem that the administration faced. Despite the formation of supervisorships to promulgate the control mechanism, usually it was problems that inspired the development of solutions, and this mechanism did not have a practical function. Lastly, if there was a "problem," the state acted in a solution-oriented way, and in other cases did little more than following due bureaucratic process.

The chain of events that started with runaways Süreyya, Vasfi, Mehmed and İdris—the most innocent actors in the incident—diverged from the students themselves and became a conflict between superiors and subordinates. Süreyya was sent to a school in Istanbul,[67] Vasfi left school by obtaining his certificate[68], and Mehmed and İdris remained at the school.[69] Ahmed Bey was "congratulated" in the manner of a hero for his struggle but was also "admonished" because he showed disrespect towards the Director of Education.

There is only one person whose fate we have not mentioned and that is Hasib Bey, who had been appointed to the Directorate of Education a year before the investigation started.[70] His demotion and reappointment must have been deemed insufficient punishments since, after a short while, Hasib Bey received news of his

---

66   Same document.

67   The Archive of the Bursa Boys' High School, *Burûsa Mekteb-i İdâdî-i Mülkîsi Talebe Künye Defteri* 1306- 1318, 264.

68   Same register, 292.

69   Same register, 150, 273.

70   *BOA., İrâde Maarif (İ.MF.)*, 6/5, Lef 12, 1 Mayıs 1316 (May 14, 1900).

dismissal.[71] Meanwhile, he had even taken time off to perform the *hajj*.[72] While objecting to the accusations directed at him or accusing the other party, Hasib Bey constantly fell back on "religion and disbelief" and "morality and immorality." The fact that he was dismissed due to corruption was certainly an ironic outcome. However, this dismissal did not mean that he was completely removed from the education system. Indeed, two years and two months after his dismissal, he was appointed as the director of the İzmid High School and resumed duty.[73] All told, the state's philosophy in center-province relations had manifested itself once again: intervene in the case of a problem, remain indifferent in the absence of one.

Kaynakça

Archival Resources

Başbakanlık Osmanlı Arşivi (BOA), *Maarif Nezâreti Mektûbî Kalemi Evrâkı (MF.MKT.)*, 596.

BOA., *Bâbıâlî Evrâk Odası Evrâkı (BEO)*, 20171/151274.

BOA., *İrâde Maarif (İ.MF)*, 6/5, Lef 12, 1 May 1316.

Bursa Erkek Lisesi Arşivi, *Burûsa Mekteb-i İdâdî-i Mülkîsi Talebe Künye Defteri*, 1306-1318.

Secondary Sources

Alkan, Mehmet Ö. "İmparatorluk'tan Cumhuriyet'e Modernleşme ve Ulusçuluk Sürecinde Eğitim." in *Osmanlı Geçmişi ve Bugünün Türkiye'si*, ed. Kemal Karpat, translated from the English by Sönmez Taner, 73-242. İstanbul: İstanbul Bilgi Üniversitesi Yayınları, 2004.

Deringil, Selim, *İktidarın Sembolleri ve İdeoloji. II. Abdülhamid Dönemi (1876-1909)*, translated from the English by Gül Çağalı Güven. İstanbul: Doğan Kitap, 2014.

Dörtok Abacı, Zeynep. 2005. *Modernleşme Sürecinde Bursa Kenti'nin Mekansal ve Sosyal Değişimi (1860-1910)*. Ph.D dissertation, Uludağ Üniversitesi.

Evered, Emine Ö. *Empire and Education Under the Ottomans. Politics, Reform and Resistance from the Tanzimat to the young Turks*. New York: I.B. Tauris, 2012.

Fortna, Benjamin C. *Mekteb-i Hümayûn. Osmanlı İmparatorluğu'nun Son Döneminde İslâm, Devlet ve Eğitim*, translated from the English by Pelin Siral. İstanbul: İletişim Yayınları, 2005.

Hudâvendigâr Vilâyeti Sâlnâme-i Resmîsi, Def'a 34, Bursa: Matbaa-i Vilâyet, 1325.

---

71 *BOA., Bâbıâlî Evrâk Odası Evrâkı (BEO.)*, 20171/151274, 23 Şubat 1318 (March 8, 1903).

72 *BOA., MF.MKT.*, 679/70, 10 Şevval 1320 (January 10, 1903).

73 *BOA.*, MF.MKT., 857/29, 19 Rebiyülevvel 1323 (May 24, 1905).

Kepecioğlu, Kamil. *Bursa Kütüğü* 3, eds. Hüseyin Algül et al. Bursa: Bursa Büyükşehir Belediyesi Yayını, 2011.

Kodaman, Bayram. *Abdülhamid Devri Eğitim Sistemi*. İstanbul: Ötüken Neşriyat, 1980.

Kütükoğlu, Mübahat. "Mürur Tezkiresi." *DİA* 32 (2006): 60-61.

Pamuk, Şevket. *Osmanlı İmparatorluğu'nda Paranın Tarihi*. İstanbul: Tarih Vakfı Yurt Yayınları, 1999.

———. *İstanbul ve Diğer Kentlerde 500 Yıllık Fiyatlar ve Ücretler 1469-1998*. Ankara: Başbakanlık Devlet İstatistik Enstitüsü Yayını, 2000.

Rogan, Eugene L. "The Political Significance of an Ottoman Education: Maktab 'Anbar Revisited'." In *From the Syrian Land to the States of Syria and Lebanon* eds. Thomas Phillip, Christopher Schumann. Würzburg: Ergon in Komission, 2004, 77-94.

Sakaoğlu, Necdet. *Osmanlı'dan Günümüze Eğitim Tarihi*. İstanbul: İstanbul Bilgi Üniversitesi Yayınları, 2003.

Somel, Selçuk Akşin. *Osmanlı'da Eğitimin Modernleşmesi (1839-1908) İslâmlaşma, Otokrasi ve Disiplin*, translated from the English by Osman Yener. İstanbul: İletişim Yayınları, 2015.

Tekeli, İlhan and İlkin, Selim. *Osmanlı İmparatorluğu'nda Eğitim ve Bilgi Üretim Sisteminin Oluşumu ve Dönüşümü*. Ankara: Türk Tarih Kurumu Yayını, 1993.

SECTION THREE

Out of Category: The Adventures of a Dubious Broker

CHAPTER THIRTEEN

Nicolò Algarotti: A Life Shaped on the Border of Conversion*

Buket Kalaycı

The Mediterranean and its ports in the early modern period have remained among the primary subjects for many researchers, especially those interested in financial structures and developments. In this context, studies of networks operating in the world of a merchant have only recently, and only partially, found their way into the field. The subject of our research is the fraudulent conduct of a Venetian broker called Nicolò Algarotti who we come across in documents produced between 1604 and 1608. His conduct led to a lengthy correspondence between the Venetian *bailo* and the Ottoman *kazasker* in Egypt and Alexandria. Algarotti did not conform to either the "time-honored laws" or the rules articulated in treaties, and consequently became the subject of complaints filed with the Venetian *bailo*. As for his relations with the Ottoman state, one could say they required maintaining a delicate balance.

In early modern Venice, commercial activity was run by merchants and intermediary brokers who built networks across the Adriatic. Nicolò Algarotti was one of those who engaged in commerce between Venice and Alexandria, together with his friend Andrea Guadagnico, also a merchant. Algarotti was a broker who ensured that the goods travelled from Venice, and Guadagnico sold these goods to the local buyers. The trade system depended on Venice preserving good relations with its eastern neighbors, ever since the Ottomans' expansionist dominance over the eastern trade routes.[1] Algarotti was among the interesting characters involved in this reciprocal trade adventure. He was probably not the first of his family to come to Alexandria or to Egypt. Either his

---

* The beginning of 17th century, between Alexandria and Egypt.

1 Christer Jörgensen, Michael Pavkovic, Rob Rice, Frederick Schneid, Chris Scott, Erken Modern Çağ Dünya Savaş Tarihi (1500-1763) 2 (Fighting Techniques of the Early Modern World: Equipment, Combat Skills, and Tactics, Thomas Dunne Books, 2006), translated from the English by Özgür Kolçak (İstanbul: Timaş Yayınları, 2011), 219. Venice always fell into the dilemma of avoiding any situation that would interrupt its commercial activities while trying to avert new Turkish conquests at the same time.

father, paternal uncle, maternal uncle, or some of his distant relatives must have established ties between Western merchants and Eastern markets. Brokerage was an occupation that he had been familiar with since childhood. He obtained the right to trade on Ottoman lands, but because he did not have a residence permit, he had to build a network of trust to ensure that goods would flow be-

FIGURE 13.1 Venetian merchants. Francisco Apellániz, "Venetian trading networks in the medieval Mediterranean," *Journal of Interdisciplinary History* 44/2 (2013).

tween Alexandria and Venice. He also shipped finished goods sold by Western merchants into Middle Eastern markets, making a fortune. He was constantly aware that he engaged in risky business. It had been a long time since he left Venice. Who knew if he could go back one day, or even if he did, that he would find those he left behind? Although the Venetians were more advanced in marine transportation than their contemporaries, hurricanes, riptides, and other inclement weather conditions could change their reality in an instant. Even if they were not harmed by natural disasters, they faced the possibility of being captured by notorious pirates. Trading meant courage. One had to risk everything. In an instant, it was possible for a wealthy merchant to turn into a slave awaiting a buyer in a market. For this reason, engaging in trade, at least in the 16th and 17th century, necessitated strength, courage, and a sharp wit.

Nicolò Algarotti, with his unusual commercial activities, was beyond the ordinary. His rush from pillar to post between Alexandria and Egypt, the network of trust he developed with Venetian merchants, and his illegal acts had occupied the agenda of the Venetian *bailo* in Alexandria for a very long time. The *bailo* could not compete with the wily, swindling broker of the state that he represented. Even the regional *qadi* failed to stop him when Algarotti, by leaving his crimes and the people he swindled behind, became a convert and vanished without a trace.

In this article, we will focus on the life of a merchant in an Ottoman city at the beginning of the 17th century, to investigate how a network of trust was built with commercial connections, why one would engage in activities antithetical to commerce, and the role of trickery, swindling and a damaged reputation in commercial life.

Istanbul in the Shadow of Commerce

The Ottoman domination of world trade routes[2] had forced the Republic of Venice into heightened contact with the Mediterranean. many Venetian merchants operated in the Mediterranean, and Venice acted as a commercial intermediary between East and West. The relations between the two states had started in the first half of the 14th century and continued until the dissolution of the Venetian state in 1797. Until the last quarter of the 16th century Venice boasted the largest trade volume with the Ottoman state and dominated almost all the commerce that occurred via Egypt and Syria. The Venetian merchants usually carried goods such as woolen cloth, embroidered velvet, glassware and paper to the Ottoman ports, and brought back spices, silk, wool, cotton yarn, leather and chemicals with them.[3]

The trade that seasoned Venetian merchants conducted for years at the ports and commercial centers of the Mediterranean was shaped through the consulates and trade networks they established, and to the extent allowed by the Ottoman State. Mercantile activities were regulated through agreements between the two states. The oldest examples of the treaties that the Ottomans signed with foreign states and those that spelled out the process in the Mediterranean were, without a doubt, the ones signed with Venice.[4] Each text would have two copies, one duly sworn by the Sultan, and the other by the "Doge of Venice".[5] A unilateral order[6]

---

2   The first of the trade routes where the Venetian-Ottoman trade intensified passed through Central Asia, Iran, north of the Caspian sea, the Caucasus, the Black Sea and the Balkans, and the other through Iran, Syria and Anatolia, and yet another through the Indian Ocean, the Persian Gulf, and the road to Alexandria via the Red Sea. For more detailed information see Şevket Pamuk, *100 Soruda Osmanlı-Türkiye İktisadi Tarihi (1500-1914)* (İstanbul: Gerçek Yayınevi, 1990), 68-9; Ahmet Tabakoğlu, *İktisat Tarihi Toplu Makaleler* (İstanbul: Kitabevi Yayınları, 2005), 237.

3   Tabakoğlu, *İktisat Tarihi*, 248.

4   İdris Bostan, "Osmanlılarda Deniz Sınırı ve Karasuları Meselesi," in *Türkler ve Deniz*, Özlem Kumrular, ed., (İstanbul: Kitap Yayınevi, 2007), 34.

5   Maria Pia Pedeni, "Venedik," *DİA* 43, (2013): 44. Doge, originated from "dux". Later, the words "duke" or "doge" derived from this word. It is the title given to the rulers of the State of Venice. Maria Pia Pedani, *Doğu'nun Kapısı Venedik*, translated from the Italian by Gökçen Karaca Şahin (İstanbul: Küre Yayınları, 2015), 11.

6   Treaties were documents issued following the *fatwa* of the *sheikhulislam*, while also taking the principles of Islamic law into consideration. According to Islamic law, the countries of the world are divided into two: *Darü'l-harb*, the lands falling outside of Islamic rule, and

signed by the Sultan gave permission to the merchants of a country to arrive at the Ottoman ports with their ships and engage in imports and exports.[7] In Venice, a type of trade center named "Fondaco dei Turchi"[8] had been reserved for Turkish merchants who lodged, shopped, and safely stored their goods there.

We note the existence of a *bailo*, a title frequently mentioned by the Ottoman state, already in 13th century in Constantinople. In Eastern Rome, the *bailos*[9] had the status of permanent delegates, or consuls, who were responsible for the safety of the life and property of Venetian citizens who lived in Constantinople.[10] After the conquest of Constantinople in 1453, the Ottomans granted the same privilege to the Venetians and allowed the *bailo* to maintain his position as an envoy on Ottoman land.[11]

The *bailo* was aided by an advisory council of twelve people called Consilium Majus,[12] and tasked with implementing the orders coming from the homeland and solving conflicts that could arise between their own citizens. Additionally, the *bailo* would petition the Sultan to provide solutions to the problems he encountered among his own subjects and would consult the *qadi* in disputes between the Venetians

---

Darü'l-İslam, the lands under Islamic rule. In order for the Dar'ül-harb to be protected under Islamic law and to be issued treaties, they would have to ask for protection. The protection would be ensured with a contract, and the document prepared would be called a treaty, with its articles called *uhud* or *şurut*. The treaty would be prepared in the form of a certificate. Mübahat Kütükoğlu, "Ahidnâme," *DİA* 1 (1988): 536; Halil İnalcık, "İmtiyâzât," *Encyclopedia of Islam* 3 (1971): 1179.

7 Bülent Arı, "Akdeniz'de Korsanlık ve Osmanlı Deniz Hukuku," in *Türkler ve Deniz*, Özlem Kumrular, ed., (İstanbul: Kitap Yayınevi, 2007), 288.

8 Şerafettin Turan, "Venedik'te Türk Ticaret Merkezi," *Belleten* 32 (1968): 247. From the second half of the 15th century onwards, Ottoman merchants and ships traveled to Venice in order to engage in commerce. Usually, the Fondaco dei Turchi would house seventy merchants who would arrive in spring and stay until fall, and arrive in the fall and stay until spring. Its normal capacity was approximately 300 people. See Pedani, "Venedik," 45-6.

9 The term Bailo derives from the Latin *bailus* and means "carrier." This concept emerged at the end of 12th century as a result of Arabic documents being translated into Latin, and it has been used to describe the state officials of the Ayyubids. Pedani, *Doğunun Kapısı Venedik*, 89.

10 Cavit Baysun, "Balyos," *İA* 1 (1970): 291-5.

11 Sevil Doğaner, *Denizle Nikah Tazeleyen Kent Venedik* (İstanbul: Medical Yayıncılık, 2006), 32.

12 Geoffrey Parker, *Sovereign City: The City-State Through History* (England: Reaction Books, 2005), 89.

FIGURE 13.2 Fishermen in Venice (Postcard Archive, IBB Atatürk Library).

and the Ottomans.[13] Beyond all these, as a representative with great sensitivity, he would aim at developing and stabilizing social, cultural, and political relations between Venice and the Ottoman State.[14]

The *bailos* would be chosen by the Maggior Consiglio[15] and sent to Istanbul. The senate would determine their salaries and expenses. When travelling to Ottoman lands, they would not neglect to bring presents for the Sultan and the paşas.[16] In the city of Istanbul, the Venetian delegates treated Galata and its environs where non-Muslim subjects lived as an obligatory area of settlement, and they resided on a hill to the north of Galata called Vigne di Pera[17] (Beyoğlu). Starting in the second half of the 16th century, Vigne de Pera became the location of the embassy of the Republic of Venice and the official residence of *bailos* and their families. Due to its proximity to the Port of Galata and as the residence of other foreign merchants,

---

13 Serap Mumcu, *Venedik Balyosu'nun Defterleri* (1589-1684) (Venice: Hilâl Studi Turchi e Ottomani 4, 2015), 19.

14 Eric R. Dursteler, *Venetians in Constantinople: Nation, Identity and Coexistence in the Early Modern Mediterranean* (Baltimore: The Johns Hopkins University Press, 2006), 122.

15 Donald E. Queller and Francis R. Swietek. *Two Studies on Venetian Government* (Cenevre: Librairie Droz, 1977), 63.

16 Mahmut Şakiroğlu, "Balyos," *DİA* 5 (1992): 44.

17 Dursteler, *The Venetian Nation in Constantinople*, 25-6. Pera had the qualities of a center of commerce, owing to the character of the topography of Galata and the opportunities it provided for commerce (there were famous brokers around the Tower). See Robert Mantran, *17. Yüzyılın İkinci Yarısında İstanbul* (Ankara: Türk Tarih Kurumu, 1986), 80.

Pera gained reputation in a short time and became an attractive and very valuable location for the Venetian community.[18] The *bailos* also acted as a type of intermediary, relaying information on the Ottoman State to the Christian lands. For this reason, they were an important reference point in diplomatic correspondence all throughout the Mediterranean basin.[19] The presence of Venetians in Istanbul also contributed to the balance between the two states. In the 1600's, Venetians made up the largest merchant population in the city.[20] As the Venetian merchants were highly renowned and had established themselves, they lived comfortably with the privileges granted to them.

From Serenissima to the Port of Alexandria

The word "Serenissima" means 'The most serene Republic,' and has been used to describe Venice. Pedani calls Venice, 'Gate to the East.' Nicolò Algarotti was born in this sea state founded on lagoons, and like all Venetians, inevitably got into commerce. The documents we have do not give any information on Algarotti's birth year; however, like all young people in his country, he must have ventured into trade with the East at an early age. At the beginning of the 1600s when he actively engaged in maritime commerce and when his activities were reflected in the documents, he appears as a well-seasoned broker who had already established his networks along eastern trade routes. He carried out his activities in the port of Alexandria,[21] the hub of local and global trade routes of for Mediterranean trade with the Ottomans.[22]

The Egyptian cities of Alexandria and Cairo were hubs of commerce on the spice routes.[23] Alexandria was the most popular port in the Mediterranean and Africa. With its status as a commerce and transportation hub and due to its location at the intersection of the roads connecting Asia, Africa and Europe,[24] it attracted Venetian

---

18   Dursteler, *Venetians in Costantinople*, 25-7.

19   Stefan Hanss, "Baili e ambasciatori," in *Il Palazzo di Venezia a Istanbul e i suoi antichi abitanti*, ed. Maria Pia Pedani, (Venice: Hilâl, Studi Turchi e Ottomani 3, 2013), 35.

20   Dursteler, *Venetians in Costantinople: Nation*, 26-7.

21   Michael J. Reimer, "Ottoman Alexandria: The Paradox of Decline and the Reconfiguration of Power in Eighteenth-Century Arab Provinces," *Journal of the Economic and Social History of the Orient* 37 (1994): 107.

22   Mumcu, *Venedik Balyosunun Defteri*, Clause 130, 88.

23   Suraiya Faroqhi, "Krizler ve Değişim 1590-1699," in *Osmanlı İmparatorluğu'nun Ekonomik ve Sosyal Hayatı*, (*An Economic and Social History of the Ottoman Empire*, Cambridge UP, 1997), translated from the English by Ayşe Berktay (İstanbul: Eren Yayıncılık, 2000), 611.

24   Reimer, "Ottoman Alexandria," 107.

merchants. Its location at a crossroads provided extraordinary opportunities for buyers and sellers. The most important advantage a merchant could gain to reduce his costs was being able to easily sell his merchandise at his port of arrival, and to load new merchandise onto his ship and return to his country. Especially with their command of the spice trade in the Mediterranean, Venetians would arrive at Egyptian ports, load spices and other Eastern merchandise onto their ships, and would distribute these through the Mediterranean.[25]

As an ordinary merchant highly knowledgeable about the advantages of the port of Alexandria, Algarotti had caused a minor crisis. Taking the conditions of the period into consideration, we can describe Nicolò as a bold *müstemin*.[26] Indeed, engaging in commerce in a region far from one's homeland, and in a different cultural environment, and building networks by promoting trade relations required a fearless, entrepreneurial and enterprising mindset, and even a bold, and perhaps adventurous disposition. Algarotti's family and relatives must have been living in Venice; as his ability to travel frequently can be explained by the existence of individuals who could take care of what he left behind. In this sense, sailing away to distant seas required some sacrifices. Moreover, international waters did not provide unconditional guarantees regarding trust. There was always the possibility of being cheated, swindled, and taken captive or robbed in areas far away from one's homeland.

If Algarotti sailed out against all the odds to the Mediterranean, he probably had savings that would be sufficient to cover his expenses. He had most likely inherited a fortune from his family. When we take the conditions of the time into account, it is possible to stipulate that commerce was a family business. Another strong possibility is that he was using *barcos* (ships) that belonged to wealthy families from Venice. In such a situation, mutual trust must be established and both parties need to profit from it.

A decree during the reign of Ahmed I[27] mentions a petition that the *bailo* at the time, Ottaviano Bon, presented to the "exalted throne." The document claimed that Algarotti was a swindler and included the complaints of the people he tricked, presumably to save the merchandise of those for whom he worked as an intermediary. The petition reads "From the merchants in Venice, those Venetians named Valentin Cesare and Giacomo Narcisi, Gottardo Lonsello, Simon Grisoztomo, Izeppo Volta,

---

25   Faroqhi, 611.

26   Mübahat Kütükoğlu, "Avrupa Tüccarı," *DİA* 4 (1991): 160.

27   Mumcu, *Venedik Balyosunun Defteri*, Madde 130, 88.

Domenico Formenti, Nicolò Polverin, Francesco Pavanello, Andrea Alessi and Alessandro Singritico who traded at Alexandria with the Venetian *barcos* La Reatta, Ruba and Berton Venier (Galeon Venier) and sent thirty bales of broadcloth, ninety five bales of paper, one chest of hardware, six chests of glass beads and a few Venetian piasters to Nicolò Algarotti and Andrea Guadagnico, merchants from Venice."[28] The fact that the names of ten merchants were mentioned indicates that they were part of an established and organized network. Loading three Venetian ships with Venetian goods and sending them to Alexandria would have been possible only with the co-operation of different parties. Algarotti had to have established relations with these people who wanted to trade without leaving Venice and win their trust in the name of safe trade. However, in their petition to the *bailo*, the merchants accused Algarotti and his friend of cheating, and this makes us think that their business partnership was formed not as the result of direct meetings but through intermediaries. For the merchant in Venice, sending his representative to the Ottoman state was a very risky practice. The trustworthiness of these representatives was the major problem.[29]

Inevitably, the merchants who heard that Algarotti was a cheater and a swindler feared that their goods would be lost, and therefore tried to take precautions. Their goods were of considerable value in the context of international trade, and the loss of these goods meant the loss of earnings. For the first quarter of the 17th century, the material value of the goods loaded onto the *barcos* from Venice was extremely high. The most important products exported to the Ottoman lands by Venetian merchants were broadcloth, fabrics, silk textile and glass.[30] They also sold the wines of the Aegean islands to several buyers.[31] As for the goods they imported, they were raw materials to be used in the textile and glassware industries. Fabric dyes, cotton, cotton yarn, alum, Indian spices, silk, fruits and vegetables and other products from the East made up the main items imported from the Ottoman lands.[32] Among the commodities that arrived at the port of Alexandria from other Ottoman ports were carob, olive oil, clarified butter, cheese, raisins, walnuts, hazelnuts, tobacco, millstone, licorice, dried apricots, goat millet, sieves, horse hair, Arab rugs, fleece wool, rings, togas, belts, broadcloth, satin, moiré cloth, *hatayi*, strings, Persian tur-

---

28   Mumcu, *Venedik Balyosunun Defteri*, Madde 130, 88.

29   Metin Ziya Köse, *Osmanlı-Venedik Ticareti (1600-1630)* (İstanbul: Marmara Üniversitesi Türkiyat Araştırmaları Enstitüsü, 2005), 93-5.

30   Benjamin Arbel, *Trading Nations Jews and Venetians in the Early Eastern Mediterranean* (Leiden: Brill, 1995), 16.

31   Köse, *Osmanlı-Venedik Ticareti*, 149-50.

32   Turan, "Venedik'te Türk Ticaret Merkezi," 254.

bans and brimstone.[33] Among the commodities coming from Europe to the port of Alexandria were plums, almonds, yellow tin, white tin, paper, beads, types of broadcloth, cochineal, varieties of processed coral, knives and needles.[34]

I am a Venetian Broker: My Name is Nicolò Algarotti

A "swindler" in the early modern period was not different from our contemporary perception of it, nor was the form of deception he used.[35] In the context of international law, the prevalence of swindling or cheating in trade has to do with the skills of merchants and brokers. In Ottoman jurisprudence, the term is "*tağrîr*"[36] and means deliberately deceiving a party through onerous contracts such as selling and leasing by someone or a third party related to them, through words or deeds. Nicolò was mentioned as a cheater in the Venetian sources because he deceived the people he traded with. Indeed, by claiming others' property as his own, he engaged in inappropriate behavior, and as a result, victimizing both the people he traded with in Alexandria and his partners in Venice.

Ten merchants who entered partnership with Algarotti in Venice[37] appealed to the *bailo*, describing their situation and victimization, in hopes of recovering their goods. Going even further, they granted the Venetian *bailo*[38] who was in Egypt[39]

---

33 İdris Bostan, "Doğu Akdeniz'de Bir Osmanlı Üssü: XVIII. Yüzyılda Mısır İskenderiyesi," *International Conference of Egypt During the Ottoman Era* (November 26-30, 2007): 5.

34 Bostan, "Mısır İskenderiyesi," 5.

35 Cheating, the dictionary definition of which is "solution, skill, cunning," in the legal jargon expresses the act of misleading someone by giving them a false idea or ensuring that a misguided opinion perseveres, in order to manipulate them into expressing a declaration of will in the desired direction. For more information, see Saffet Köse, "Hile," *DİA* 18 (1998): 28.

36 Hacı Mehmet Günay, "Tağrîr," *DİA* 39 (2010): 375-6. In the literature of the jurisprudence, words such as "hılâbe, gış, tedlîs, hıyânet, hud'a/hıdâ" are also used for this act. The equivalent of Tağrir in Turkish legal jargon is "hile" (trickery).

37 Valentin Cesare and Giacomo Narcisi, Gottardo Lonsello, Simon Grisoztomo, Izeppo Volta, Domenico Formenti, Nicolò Polverin, Francesco Pavanello, Andrea Alessi and Alessandro Singritico, see Mumcu, *Venedik Balyosunun Defteri*, Madde 130, 88.

38 According to the Treaty of 1604, the following are the regions in which Venetian merchants were permitted to engage in activities: Anatolia, Arabia, Albania, Beirut, Bosnia, Bursa, Galata, Gallipoli, Lepanto, Alexandria of Egypt, İstanbul, Tinos, Corfu, Maghrib, Morea, Methone, Parga, Preveza, Rumelia, Damascus, Tripoli, Tarablus, Ionia and Zakynthos. *BOA*, Düvel-i Ecnebiye Defteri, 13, 7.

39 Venetian consulates would be established in cities, counties and provinces where Venetian merchants had settled or would engage in commerce without taking up residency, or where the products that Venice needed were sold, i.e. in places that were in line with

at the time, the power of attorney so that he can confiscate the goods, sell them, and deliver the profits to them.

In resolving disputes concerning both states, the Ottoman state was always careful not to harm the ongoing alliance with Venice and not to contravene the imperial pacts. The *bailo*, in his appeal to the palace, referenced the pacts and tried to prevent any potential harm to the Venetian merchants who were in the position of plaintiffs. As for the verdict, it clearly revealed the terms of the imperial pact between the states.

The merchants in Venice had told Andrea Guadagnico and Nicolò Algarotti, who were in Alexandria, to purchase various goods such as spices and send them to Venice. Additionally, the merchants had sent Nicolò several chests of goods. This makes us think that the Venetian merchants who had loaded their merchandise onto the ship had also conveyed their wishes to Algarotti. In his turn, Algarotti bought the requested goods from Muslim merchants in Egypt and had them loaded onto a Venetian *barco* in Alexandria.[40] The merchants in Venice then sent a few bales of goods such as broadcloth, paper, fabric...etc. to Alexandria. However, as we learn from the documents, the merchants in Venice eventually learned that their partners in Alexandria were swindlers. And that's the extent of information we gather from the documents. We do not know how the merchants in Venice, in the middle of an ongoing business partnership, discover the true character of their partners. The situation makes us think that the partnership must have been the first contract signed between the parties. If this was not the case and they had done business earlier, they would have known what kind of a man Nicolò was. Or perhaps this was not their first transaction, yet the original terms and conditions were changed. Regardless, we have no information about the circumstances on the Algarotti front, except that he engaged in commerce in Alexandria, and that he took loans from Jewish and Muslim merchants.[41] As a merchant who needed to pay off his debts, he might have resorted to such a scheme.

Venice's interests. By the 1600s, Venetian consulates in several centers of commerce in the Ottoman Empire had been established. Venetian merchants were attached to the consulates of Damascus and Aleppo. The center of the consulates in Alexandria, Egypt, was moved to Cairo in 1555. A Venetian consul continued to hold office in Alexandria. Venice also had emissaries in the cities of Eğriboz, Damascus, Trabzon and Sur, and the bailo in Istanbul held the most authority. See Köse, *Osmanlı-Venedik Ticareti*, 52; Şakiroğlu, "Balyos," 44.

40 Serap Mumcu, *Balyos Defteri*, Clause 157, 100.

41 Mumcu, *Balyos Defteri*, Clause 130-57, 88-100.

The *bailo*, who was granted power of attorney, succeeded in recovering the goods and secured them in a storehouse to proceed with the sale as instructed by the aggrieved merchants.[42] Around the same time, Nicolò Algarotti banded with his Muslim, Nazarite and Jewish creditors and went to the Venetian *bailo* in Aleppo to declare that the goods were sent to him. He requested that the merchandise should be returned to him. He also reached an agreement with some of his men in Egypt and had the merchandise registered under his name.[43]

It is noteworthy that, of the two partners in Alexandria, Andrea's name gets less frequent mention. He might not have been a party to Nicolò's debt. Andrea also had a residential permit. It is more likely that the only party who was indebted to Egyptian merchants and acted inappropriately was Nicolò. As he did not have a personal debt, Andrea must have adopted a passive attitude. However, the documents frequently mention Nicolò's men. That Algarotti formed multiple partnerships in the years he engaged in trade is to be expected. He also had an influence on merchants who qualified to be his men. The fact that these men fought for Algarotti in Egypt could be explained by the increased profit they made, the friendships they formed, and the commerce network they joined, all thanks to him.

The tensions between the Venetian merchants, their intermediaries in Egypt, and the local merchants that agreed to trade with the intermediaries increased. While the parties fought to claim their rights, all of a sudden, Nicolò Algarotti decided to convert. It is known that conversion would elevate him to the rank of a *mühtedi*.[44] Conversion was a normal practice in the early modern Mediterranean world. The conversion from Christianity to Islam[45] was triggered by cultural interactions and concerns related to commerce. By choosing Islam, Algarotti seems to have traversed beyond the boundaries separating religious communities. When a Jewish or Christian subject converted to Islam, any form of segregation would disappear. Algarotti, like all other *mühtedi*s, was now dignified with the honorable

---

42   Mumcu, *Balyos Defteri*, Clause 158-63, 101-3.

43   Mumcu, *Balyos Defteri*, Clause 130-57, 88-100.

44   Ihtida (conversion) has a dictionary meaning of reaching truth and finding the right path. As a term, it denotes the adoption of the Islamic religion by either a disbeliever or someone who was the follower or a different faith. The person who would convert in this way would be called *mühtedi*. For more information see Ali Köse, "İhtidâ," *DİA* 21 (2000): 554-8.

45   For examples of Muslims converting to Christianity, see E. Natalie Rothman, *İmparatorluk Simsarları Venedik-İstanbul Arasında Mekik Dokuyanlar* (İstanbul: Koç Üniversitesi Yayınları, 2016), 115-7.

religion of Islam,[46] and gained an even more esteemed rank. In the early modern world, it is difficult to determine the reason for conversion since distinctions such as spiritual or sincere motives versus the promise of material benefits were not altogether clear.

Algarotti, who was perceived by Venetian merchants as a swindler, did not inspire much trust in his Muslim friends either. To pay off his debt, he needed the merchandise originally sent from Venice. His share from the sale must have been sufficient to clear his debt. However, both the reciprocal agreements and the official verdicts ruled that the *bailo* could not be held responsible for the debts of any Venetian merchant on Ottoman lands.[47] Algarotti's conversion to another religion, which must have been a commercial maneuver, did not provide him with the anticipated privilege. He passed away shortly after choosing Islam. Following his death, his men initiated a lawsuit, claiming that they were the rightful owners of the goods that had been previously loaded onto the Venetian *barco* to be sent to Venice.[48] The lawsuit determined that Alfarotti's men would have to wait for the ruling from Istanbul. As for the merchandise, it was delivered to the *bailo*, on the orders of the *beylerbeyi*. As required by the imperial pact, a verdict was issued by imperial order. The verdict dated August 20, 1607 ruled that the merchandise would be confiscated and sent to the merchants in Venice.[49] The order also decreed that no one should engage in abuse or harassment based on the decision.

Instead of a Conclusion

By converting, Nicolò Algarotti widened his range of activities; he was no longer an expatriate in the Ottoman lands. By changing his religion, he acquired legal rights equal to those of Muslims and obtained the same benefits as they did. His conversion can also be seen as evidence that the status of individuals within the social hierarchy could change.

The case of Algarotti marks an attempt at change in the nature of commercial practices. The broker, whose life details we cannot fully know, chose to deceive both his counterparts in Venice and the Ottoman legal system. In this instance, the

---

46 In order to become a *mühtedi* (convert), Algarotti must have appealed to the Ottoman *shari'a* court and recited the *shahadah* (bearing witness to faith). In this way, he would achieve the grace of Islam, and begin his new life purified and devoid of sin. This provided a certain amount of exoneration regarding his former acts.

47 Mumcu, *Balyos Defteri*, Clause 130, 88.

48 Mumcu, *Balyos Defteri*, Clause 157, 100.

49 Mumcu, *Balyos Defteri*, Clause 157, 101.

treaties played a decisive role in protecting mutual interests. In the court records, we find several examples of individuals who convert to extricate themselves from an unresolvable situation. Without a doubt, Algarotti was aware of which legal obligations he would be freed of through conversion and tried to turn the situation into an advantage. This change, which might have potentially solved his problem at least in the short term, came to an abrupt end with his unexpected death.

The presence of the Republic of Venice and the Ottoman Empire in Mediterranean commerce made the Mediterranean a cultural transit zone. The trade and trust networks, while facilitating cultural exchange, also led to assimilation. With all his connections, Algarotti was someone who possessed networks, trust and partners, as his Mediterranean merchant identity necessitated. Yet he began to lose all this when his business started to deteriorate, he had to borrow money from his clients, and as a result of his scheme to pay off his debt, he lost the trust of his Venetian partners. Commercial life in the early modern period was shaped around a theme of cautious trust. As our example shows, reciprocal treatises strived to protect such trust and counteract the challenges of overseas trade, especially through intermediaries. The requests, complaints and warrants conveyed to the *bailo* were addressed as a result of such treatises. The existence of the *bailo* in the Ottoman lands was significant in terms of protecting the interests of his subjects, regulating relationships among them and remaining in close contact with the Ottoman bureaucracy, all of which also ensured the continuity of trade relations.

Bibliography

Archival Sources
BOA, *Düvel-i Ecnebiye Defteri*, 13.

Secondary Sources
Arbel, Benjamin. *Trading Nations Jews and Venetians in the Early Eastern Mediterranean.* Leiden: Brill, 1995.

Arı, Bülent. "Akdeniz'de Korsanlık ve Osmanlı Deniz Hukuku." in *Türkler ve Deniz*, ed. Özlem Kumrular, 265-318. İstanbul: Kitap Yayınevi, 2007.

Baysun, Cavit. "Balyos." *DİA* 1 (1970): 291-5.

Bostan, İdris. "Osmanlılarda Deniz Sınırı ve Karasuları Meselesi." in *Türkler ve Deniz*, ed. Özlem Kumrular, 297-316. İstanbul: Kitap Yayınevi, 2007.

———. "Doğu Akdeniz'de Bir Osmanlı Üssü: XVIII. Yüzyılda Mısır İskenderiyesi." *International Conference of Egypt During the Ottoman Era.* Cairo, 26-30 November 2007.

Concina, Ennio. *II Doge e Sultano Mercarura, arte e relazioni nel primo' 500- Doç ve Sultan 16. Yüzyıl Başlarında Ticaret, Sanat ve İlişkiler.* Rome: Logert Press, 1995.

Doğaner, Sevil. *Denizle Nikah Tazeleyen Kent Venedik.* İstanbul: Medekal Yayınları, 2006.

Dursteler, Eric R. *Venetians in Costantinople: Nation, Identity and Coexistence in the Early Modern Mediterranean.* Baltimore: The Johns Hopkins University Press, 2006.

Faroqhi, Suraiyya. "Krizler ve Değişim 1590-1699." in *Osmanlı İmparatorluğu'nun Ekonomik ve Sosyal Hayatı* II, tr. by Ayşe Berktay. İstanbul: Eren Yayıncılık, 2000.

Günay, Hacı Mehmet. "Tağrir." *DİA* 18 (1998): 375-6.

Hanss, Stefan. "Baili e ambasciatori-Balyoslar ve Büyükelçiler." *II Palazzo di Venezia a Istanbul e i suoi antichi abitanti-İstanbul'daki Venedik Sarayı ve Eski Yaşayanları.* Venezia: *Hilâl*, Studi Turchi e Ottomani 3, 2013.

İnalcık, Halil. "İmtiyâzât." *Encyclopedia of Islam* III (1971): 245-52.

Jörgensen, Christer, Michael Pavkovic, Rob Rice, Frederick Schneid and Chris Scott. *Erken Modern Çağ Dünya Savaş Tarihi (1500-1763)*, eds. Adem Koçal and Özgür Kolçak, vol. 2. İstanbul: Timaş Yayınları, 2011.

Köse, Ali. "İhtidâ." *DİA* 21 (2000): 554-8.

Köse, Metin Ziya. 2005. "Osmanlı-Venedik Ticareti (1600-1630)." Ph.D dissertation, Marmara Üniversitesi.

Köse, Saffet. "Hile." *DİA* 39 (2010): 28-9.

Kütükoğlu, Mübahat. "Ahidname." *DİA* 1 (1988): 536-40.

———. "Yabancı Tüccar." *DİA* 4 (1991): 160-3.

Mantran, Robert. *17. Yüzyılın İkinci Yarısında İstanbul.* Ankara: V Yayınları, 1986.

Mumcu, Serap. *Venedik Balyosu'nun Defterleri (1589-1684).* Venice: Edizioni Ca' Foscari-Digital Publishing, 2015.

Pamuk, Şevket. *100 Soruda Osmanlı-Türkiye İktisadi Tarihi (1500-1914).* İstanbul: Gerçek Yayınevi, 1990.

Parker, Geoffrey. *Sovereign City: The City-State Through History,* England: Reaction Books, 2005.

Pedani, Maria Pia. "Venedik." *DİA* 43 (2013): 44-6.

———. *Venezia e Islam: Venezia tra Mori,* Vicenza: Turchi e Persiani, 2005.

———. *Doğu'nun Kapısı Venedik.* translated form Italian by Gökçen Karaca Şahin, İstanbul: Küre Yayınları, 2015.

Queller, Donald E. and Francis R. Swietek. *Two Studies on Venetian Government.* Genève: Librairie Droz, 1977

Reimer, Michael J. "Ottoman Alexandria: The Paradox of Decline and the Reconfiguration of Power in Eighteenth-Century Arab Provinces." *Journal of the Economic and Social History of the Orient* 37, no. 2 (1994): 107-46.

Rothman, E. Natalie. *İmparatorluk Simsarları Venedik-İstanbul Arasında Mekik Dokuyanlar.* İstanbul: Koç Üniversitesi Yayınları, 2016.

Şakiroğlu, Mahmut. "Balyos." *DİA* 5 (1992): 43-7.

Tabakoğlu, Ahmet. *İktisat Tarihi Toplu Makaleler.* İstanbul: Kitabevi Yayınları, 2005.

Turan, Şerafettin. "Venedik'te Türk Ticaret Merkezi." *Belleten* 32 (1968): 247-83.

Contributors

Nurcan Abacı works at the Faculty of Arts and Sciences at Uludağ University. He received his B.A. in 1991 from the History Department at the Faculty of Arts and Sciences in Middle East Technical University. His PhD dissertation is an analysis of the implementation of 17th century Ottoman law via the case of Bursa. As the recipient of TÜBA and Alexander von Humboldt scholarships, he has conducted research in several countries. Recently he has been working on the lives of taxpayers in Ottoman society, and in order to reach a larger audience with his short essays and open them up to common use, has been sharing them at his personal website (http://www.abacinurcan.com).

Özlem Başarır is a faculty member of the History Department in the Faculty of Arts and Sciences at İnönü University. She received her B.A. between the years 1996 and 2000 from the History Department in the Faculty of Languages and History-Geography at Ankara University, and completed her M.A. at the History Department (Modern) in the Social Sciences Institute of the same university between the years 2000 and 2003, with the thesis titled "A contribution to Ottoman Social History in the 18th century: The analysis of Konya Court Record no. 60 No and an Attempt at a Method related to its use as a Source of Historical Information". She completed her Ph.D. between the years 2003 and 2009 at the same university by preparing a dissertation titled "Estate Practices in the 18th Century and the Voivodship of Diyarbekir". Her research focuses on Ottoman social and economic history.

Yasemin Beyazıt is a faculty member at Pamukkale University. She published her Ph.D. dissertation completed at Ankara University in 2009 with the title *Osmanlı İlmiye Mesleğinde İstihdam XVI. Yüzyıl* (Türk Tarih Kurumu, 2014), and completed her post-doctoral work at the Center for Middle Eastern Studies (CMES) at Harvard University in the academic year 2010-11. Her research mostly focuses on the Ottoman *ilmiye* class and its organization. She has also contributed to publications (*Denizli Dediği Tekkesi*, 2014) (*Denizli Teslim Baba Tekkesi*, 2016) on the history and the convents of the Bektaşi in Western Anatolia as a co-author. She was awarded the Halil Inalcık Special Award as part of the 2019 TÜBA TESEP Scientific Authored Book Awards.

Cemal Çetin is a faculty member at the History Department of Selçuk University. He completed his Ph.D. dissertation titled *"Menzilhanes in Operation in Anatolia (1690-1750)"* in 2009 at Selçuk University, and in addition to the book titled *Ulak Yol Durak, Anadolu Yollarında Padişah Postaları (Menzilhaneler) (1690-1750)* published through expanding on his dissertation, has done research on several issues related to transportation and communication in the Ottoman Empire, social history and control mechanisms. His most recent book is an analysis of the captivity conditions of prisoners of war, titled *Sultan'ın Esirleri, İstanbul'da Bir Esir Kampı (1715)*.

Emine Dingeç is a faculty member of the History Department at Dumlupınar University. She completed her Ph.D. dissertation titled "Gypsies in the Service Organization in Rumelia (16th century)" in 2004. Dingeç is continuing to do research on the Roma in Ottoman society and has articles in several journals and books on this subject. Some of these are "XVI. Yüzyılda Osmanlı Ordusunda Çingeneler" (2009), "Kocaeli Sancağı'nda Çingeneler ve Cizye Meselesi" (2015), "About Gypsy Perception in the Ottoman Empire" (2016), "Gypsies in the Ottoman Empire and Hassa Services" (2017), "Osmanlı Devleti ve Eflak ve Bogdan'da Köleleşen Romanlar" (2017), and "Kıbrıs'a Kıptiyanların Gelişleri" (2017).

Zeynep Dörtok Abacı is a Faculty Member at the History Department in the Faculty of Arts and Sciences at Uludağ University. She completed her Ph.D. Dissertation titled "The Spatial and Social Transformation of Bursa in the Modernization Process" in 2005 at the Department of Public Administration. After her doctorate, her research has focused on Ottoman social history, *qadi* registers, social network analysis (SNA) and subjects called "inauspicious" such as cursing, violence and suicide.

Suraiya Faroqhi is the Professor of History at Istanbul Bilgi and Ibn Haldun Universities. She has taught at Minneapolis/St Paul Minnesota University, Middle East Technical University and Ludwig Maximilians Universität in Munich. Among her published work are *Osmanlı Zanaatkârları: İmparatorluk Döneminde Zanaatlar ve Loncalar*, translated by Zülal Kılıç (İstanbul: Alfa, 2017), *Osmanlı İmparatorluğu ve Etrafındaki Dünya*, translated by Ayşe Berktay (İstanbul: Alfa, 2017) and *Sultan'ın Kulları*. She is the editor of *Türkiye Tarihi, 1603-1839: Geç Osmanlı İmparatorluğu*, translated by Fethi Aytuna (İstanbul: Kitap, 2011) and has co-edited the second volume of the same series with Kate Fleet. She continues to do research on Ottoman social history.

Zübeyde Güneş Yağcı is a faculty member in the History Department at Balıkesir University. She completed her Ph.D. dissertation titled "The Wardenship of Ferah

Ali Paşa in Soğucak (1781-1785)" in 1998. Her post-doctoral work has focused on slavery in the Ottoman Empire and she has published several articles on the subject. The book she has co-edited with Fırat Yaşa titled *Osmanlı Devleti'nde Kölelik: Ticaret, Esaret, Yaşam* was published in 2017. She continues to do research on Ottoman social history, slavery and the slave trade.

Z. Buket Kalaycı is a research assistant in the Department of History at Bozok University. She is currently writing her dissertation on the Ottoman palace cuisine of the 18th century. In the context of culinary habits in the early modern period, her research focuses on the cuisines of elites, the influences of trade networks and commodities in cuisines, bookkeeping in the kitchen, and legalization of society through food and beverage.

Saadet Maydaer is a faculty member in the Faculty of Theology at Uludağ University. She has published her Ph.D. dissertation completed in 2008 with the title *Osmanlı Klasik Döneminde Bursa'da Bir Semt: Hisar*, and has published the books titled *XVI. Yüzyılda Bursa Kadınları* and *XVI. Yüzyılda Bursa'da Asayiş*. She has published several articles on Ottoman social history in the classical period and is continuing her research in the same area.

Faruk Yaslıçimen is a faculty member in the History Department at Ibn Haldun University. He received his B.A. in History and International relations from Istanbul Bilgi University in 2004. He completed his M.A. degree in 2008 at the History Department in Bilkent University with his thesis titled "Sunnism versus Shiism? Rise of the Shiite Politics and of the Ottoman Apprehension in Late Nineteenth Century Iraq". He received his Ph.D. in 2016 with the dissertation he wrote at Ludwig Maximilians Universität in Munich, titled "Ottoman Empire and its Shiite Subjects: State-Society Relations in the Late Nineteenth and Early Twentieth Centuries". Among his areas of research are modernization and reforms in 19th century Ottoman Empire, religion, state and society in the Ottoman Empire, social history and cultural policies in Turkey.

Fırat Yaşa is a faculty member at the History Department of Duzce University, Turkey. He received his Ph.D. in Ottoman History from the University of Sakarya (2017). His dissertation is a micro history of Bahçesaray between the years 1650 and 1675, in which he looks at the lives, ideas, and expectations of urban and rural people, their attitudes towards law, and their roles in the social and economic life of the 17th century. His research areas include asymmetrical social dependency, slaving practices, slavery laws, captives, discourses about social dependency, and manumission in the early modern Ottoman Empire and the Crimean Khanate (1500-1700).

Much of his subsequent academic works deal with ordinary subjects of the sultan. He has recently published an edited volume: Other faces of the empire: ordinary lives against social order and hierarchy (Istanbul: Koç University Press, 2020). For his other works, see https://duzce.academia.edu/FıratYaşa.

Filiz Yaşar is a faculty member in the Faculty of Arts and Sciences at Mersin University. She completed her Ph.D. in 2013 in the Department of History at Hacettepe University, with the dissertation titled "Bir Osmanlı Adasında Toplum ve Ekonomi (XVI. Yüzyıldan XVIII. Yüzyıla Sakız)". She completed her post-doctoral work at the Department of History of the University of California Berkeley in the academic year 2016-17. She has received scholarships from several institutions to receive her education and continue her research in Greece. Her research focuses on Ottoman socioeconomic history, and specifically on Greeks in the Ottoman era.

İsmail Yaşayanlar is a faculty member in the History Department of the Faculty of Arts and Sciences in Düzce University. He received his B.A. in 2010 from the History Department in the Faculty of Arts and Sciences at Uludağ University. He completed his M.A. in 2012 in the Department of History (Modern) at the Social Sciences Institute at the same university with the thesis titled "The Socioeconomic State of the Kirmasti (Mustafakemalpaşa) Township in the 19th century". He completed his Ph.D. in 2015 with his dissertation titled "Cholera Outbreaks in Sinop, Samsun and Trabzon'da Kolera, Organization of Quarantine and Public Health Services (1876-1914)". His research focuses mostly on Ottoman socioeconomic history in contemporary times, and urban history.

Index